Difficult Reading

NEW WORLD STUDIES
Marlene L. Daut, Editor

Difficult Reading

FRUSTRATION AND FORM IN ANGLOPHONE CARIBBEAN FICTION

Jason R. Marley

University of Virginia Press
Charlottesville and London

University of Virginia Press
© 2023 by the Rector and Visitors of the University of Virginia
All rights reserved
Printed in the United States of America on acid-free paper

First published 2023

9 8 7 6 5 4 3 2 1

Library of Congress Cataloging-in-Publication Data
Names: Marley, Jason R., author.
Title: Difficult reading : frustration and form in anglophone Caribbean fiction / Jason R. Marley.
Description: Charlottesville : University of Virginia Press, 2023. | Series: New World studies | Includes bibliographical references and index.
Identifiers: LCCN 2023012232 (print) | LCCN 2023012233 (ebook) | ISBN 9780813950136 (hardcover ; acid-free paper) | ISBN 9780813950143 (paperback ; acid-free paper) | ISBN 9780813950150 (ebook)
Subjects: LCSH: Caribbean fiction (English)—History and criticism. | Caribbean fiction—20th century—Political aspects. | National characteristics, Caribbean, in literature. | Frustration in literature. | LCGFT: Literary criticism.
Classification: LCC PR9205.4 .M37 2023 (print) | LCC PR9205.4 (ebook) | DDC 813/.5099729—dc23/eng/20230531
LC record available at https://lccn.loc.gov/2023012232
LC ebook record available at https://lccn.loc.gov/2023012233

Cover art: Another Call From Africa, Turgo Bastien, 2009

Contents

Acknowledgments — vii

Introduction: The Aesthetics of Inscrutability in Caribbean Fiction — 1

1. The Politics of Interruption: Metafictive Critique and Historical Aporia in the Midcentury Jamaican Novel — 37

2. To Become So Very Welsh: Denis Williams's *The Third Temptation* and the Effacement of Afro-Caribbean Identity — 81

3. Language as Animosity: Pejorative Speech and National Identity — 107

4. "The Menace from the Bush": Abstraction and Indigenous Violence in the Work of Wilson Harris and Denis Williams — 149

5. Rhysian Disgust and the Politics of Complacency — 198

Coda: Inscrutable Pasts, Inscrutable Futures — 229

Notes — 237

Bibliography — 255

Index — 269

Acknowledgments

I SHOULD begin by acknowledging that this book—a work that, at its core, is a study of difficulty and making sense of that which cannot be easily made sense of—was, through an unfortunate coincidence, completed at a time when nothing made sense, and the coronavirus pandemic made every day uncertain, uneasy, and often inscrutable. Among the uncertainty and isolation, this book would not exist without Gina Lachacz, whose love, advice, and encouragement has inspired this book at every turn. Words can never express my gratitude and gratefulness.

I am particularly thankful for the support of Eric Brandt and Marlene Daut and the University of Virginia Press, whose enthusiasm for the book has never wavered (even in its early stages) and whose guidance and clarity has been a model of professionalism.

I am also indebted to the three anonymous readers who reviewed this book and its initial proposal. This book has evolved enormously as a result of their careful and courteous feedback, which was continuously thorough, supportive, and critical when it needed to be. I am a better scholar because of their feedback—and this book bears their mark and influence in innumerable ways. Academic labor is often a thankless task and, for those readers who may now be reading this book, please know that I am eternally grateful for your time and energy. It will not be forgotten.

A version of chapter 2, "To Become So Very Welsh: Denis Williams's *The Third Temptation* and the Effacement of Afro-Caribbean Identity" was originally published in *ariel: A Review of International English Literature* in 2018 (49, no. 2) and is republished here in revised form courtesy of Johns Hopkins University Press and the journal. Thank you for the opportunity to reprint this material.

This book was aided by the generous financial support of Francis Marion University, including several summer research grants that aided its completion, as well as sizable funding to attend conferences and present many generative versions of the ideas that are presented in this book. I am immensely thankful for this support of my work. I also want to give a special thank-you to the English department, and my colleagues at Francis Marion as a whole, who have provided continued encouragement of my research. In particular, Chris Washington, Benjamin Hilb, and Dillon Tatum have offered innumerable insights and advice in completing the book. Thank you!

I would also like to thank Damien Keane, Christina Milletti, and Bill Solomon at the University of Buffalo for their mentorship. Their scholarship has influenced me in ways that I could never properly articulate here. Though the years fade and memory grows feeble, please know I remain entirely thankful for your guidance and for believing in my work.

Difficult Reading

Introduction

The Aesthetics of Inscrutability in Caribbean Fiction

IN 1932, frustrated by submissions to their short story contest, the editors of Trinidad's experimental literary and political journal *Beacon* published a bitter, antagonistic invective that was directed, surprisingly, at their own audience. The somewhat infamous editorial, released after the group failed to receive what they perceived to be any worthwhile submissions for the contest, boldly asserted that their readers were incapable of creating confident, valuable art. It should be noted that the *Beacon*'s castigation of their audience in the article was not subtle, and that they attributed the failure of their contest to a wider sense of Caribbean self-loathing and complacency, arguing that "the average Trinidad writer regards his fellow-countrymen as his inferiors, an uninteresting people who are not worth his while. He genuinely feels (and by this, of course, asserts his own feeling of inferiority) that with his people as characters his stories would be worth nothing" ("Local Fiction" 1). As the group saw it, Caribbean writing of the 1930s was mired in a state of stagnancy, and the failure of the short story contest was indicative of a larger aesthetic crisis in the region that suggested Caribbean authors were hesitant to write about the experiences and struggles of their own people. The *Beacon* group thus responded with anger and, as they would do time and time again, sought to enact, via a violent, aggressive jostle, the creation of a more innovative and political literary aesthetic in the Caribbean.

Repeatedly, the *Beacon* group viewed themselves as guardians of an emerging aesthetic that repudiated colonial literary influence, and they tirelessly chastised aspiring and established authors for relying too heavily on British aesthetic forms. Despite their harsh rhetoric, the group's ethos was rooted in guidance and instruction—and, above all, in its literature and political writings, the *Beacon* sought to provide a model of literary development in the Caribbean. As Albert Mendes, editor of *Trinidad* and a key member of the *Beacon* group, affirmed, "[The group] established the norms—dialect, way of life, racial types, barrack-yards, West Indian character and poverty—and these were postulates that bought a West Indian literature into being" (75). As Mendes's statement reveals, he, along with figures like editor Albert Gomes, viewed the *Beacon* as the forebearer of a burgeoning literary tradition—and, indeed, it is not entirely misplaced to suggest that the group was in part responsible for establishing a number of key themes and tropes that would pervade Caribbean literature throughout the twentieth century.[1] Much like George Lamming's antagonistic, seminal essay, "An Occasion for Speaking," the group's editorials are often anthologized today as a call to arms, or as a moment of artistic awakening that ushers in the emergence of a Caribbean literary aesthetic. Viewed this way, the *Beacon* group's confrontation with Trinidad's literary scene in the 1930s is revolutionary in its antagonistic aims, and the group's overt anger, juxtaposed against texts like Roger Mais's incendiary anticolonial manifesto "Now We Know" (1944) and Lamming's seething disgust directed at the Caribbean middle classes in *The Pleasures of Exile* (1960), capture an overarching sense of unyielding disgust and confrontational resentment toward both the colonial authority and the placated Caribbean masses. For Mendes and Gomes, the *Beacon* was less a magazine than a societal model of aesthetic and political resistance.

Although the *Beacon* published a considerable number of important, inventive literary works, the fact remains that the group struggled to dictate the prerequisites of a successful Caribbean aesthetic to its audience—in part because the model they provided was often deeply contradictory. The group's often explicit resentment for their audience is thus more complicated than it first appears, particularly because their middle-class authors were fairly disconnected from the peasant and lower-class Trinidadians that they often wrote about. In this regard, the group's emphasis on rupture, revolution, and anticolonial aesthetics is not, as Leah Rosenberg has convincingly pointed out, as innovative as it seems, as the *Beacon*'s middle-class politics were at odds with the revolutionary nature of their literary efforts. As Rosenberg has observed in *Nationalism and the Formation of Caribbean Literature,* "While scholars are correct in claiming that the *Beacon* established a new and powerful national aesthetics, they are mistaken in viewing the aesthetics as reflecting a radical new politics that would empower the working class. With respect to key political issues, the *Beacon* was significantly more conservative than contemporary black middle-class and Indi-Trinidadian organizations" (126). More troublingly, however, was the fact that, juxtaposed against an antagonistic petition to produce a new Caribbean aesthetic that eschewed the British tradition—an aesthetic largely focused on narratives depicting the lives of Trinidad's lower classes—its pages also contained an excoriation of the Black working class, a thoroughly racist teardown of the value of African art and culture, and a rejection of universal suffrage (Rosenberg 126).[2] In this way, the group expressed and championed, to some degree, principles of colonial ideology that explicitly undermined the agency and humanity of colonized peoples, while nevertheless publishing literature that vehemently argued against the perpetuation of such rhetoric. The group wrestled, in other words, with its own intentionality; many of its literary aspirations and public decrees were rooted in a demand for a pro-Caribbean and anti-British aesthetic, but the articles and guidelines published in the *Beacon*'s pages provided little in the way of a sustainable or consistent ideological or literary model.[3]

Nevertheless, throughout its duration, the editors of the *Beacon* continued to express significant consternation that their audience was not following their instruction, when, in fact, their instruction was seldom as clear, convincing, or consistent, as they believed.[4] In any case, it is clear that the group's aesthetic aims, which privileged a focus on the experiences of the Trinidadian lower classes, could not be properly articulated in a way that would result in a body of work that mirrored the kind of literature they desired and expected from their audience. What I find interesting here is that the group's resentment for the masses indicates, first and foremost, a crisis of instruction and understanding. Far from revealing a cohesive Caribbean aesthetic, the *Beacon* articulated a muddled discourse of anticolonial resentment that required persistent clarification and a repeated acknowledgment that the aesthetic the group sought to create was failing to emerge. The group's aesthetic guidelines could thus be neither clearly articulated nor understood.

In highlighting this example, my goal is not to emphasize the fact that the *Beacon*'s message was hypocritical—though it was, to be sure—or to suggest that the group's contributions should be viewed as a failure. Rather, I begin with this example because the complex interplay of misunderstanding and confusion that emerges as the group struggles to define a Caribbean aesthetic says more about the difficulty of articulating anticolonial resistance than a properly anticolonial, didactic literature ever could. Indeed, the group's prevailing sense of frustration, confusion, and genuine bewilderment that their audience could not implement their intended strategies does much to elucidate the challenges and occlusions that threaten the emergence of effective resistance. In this sense, I am compelled by the group's push for an antagonistic rupture that they cannot initiate, a rupture that becomes inscrutable—a call for a radical break that ultimately cannot be properly or consistently articulated. Reflecting back on the group's work today, one of the most significant aspects of the *Beacon* is not its precursory yard fiction or its emphasis on a peasant aesthetic, as critics have tended to focus on, but in its tense, difficult relationship with its audience: a point that raises larger questions about reception, form, clarity, and resistance, and the very potentiality that literature may serve as a means to enact social change. In short, I am interested in the relationship between the attempt to create new anticolonial aesthetic forms and the feelings of failure—and, more importantly, frustration—that emerge in trying to articulate those very forms. What can such moments of failure and frustration tell us about colonialism, trauma, and the very nature of Caribbean literary aesthetics?

Difficult Reading, simply put, is a book about frustration. At its core, I contend that rethinking the role of frustration in terms of its effects on the audience may deliver newfound insights into Caribbean literary aesthetics. As such, my goal is relatively straightforward, in that I seek to highlight a unique body of experimental Caribbean anglophone literature that foregrounds questions of reception and difficulty to argue that inscrutability can function as a productive strategy to confront the legacy of colonial trauma. In the texts I address, the struggle to articulate the nature of colonial oppression—and to connect to the audience—captures the inherent trauma of Caribbean identity in a way that demands readers take an active role in dismantling the often disorienting, obfuscated reality of colonial violence. In other words, the questions and issues inadvertently raised by the *Beacon* group, particularly those concerning reception and scrutability, became an increasingly important problem within the field of Caribbean twentieth-century literature, particularly in the mid-twentieth century, as writers wrestled not simply with how to incorporate national and anticolonial themes of resistance into their writing, but with the central question of whether or not these themes could be clearly articulated at all. *Difficult Reading,* therefore, pinpoints an alternative current of experimental Caribbean literature by writers such as Denis Williams, Eric Walrond, and Vera Bell, as well as by more canonical Caribbean experimental writers, that demonstrates how an inability to process, understand, and enunciate the stakes of colonial oppression can itself function as a decolonial aesthetic. I view such works as invested in a search for expression or method outside the colonial purview in a way that continuously urges readers to evaluate and question both the clarity and meaning of what they read. More importantly, such works encourage, and in many ways force, the reader to acknowledge that the trauma of colonial ideology cannot simply be articulated as such, but must be actively unraveled if it is to be properly confronted and potentially understood.

Central to the theory of inscrutability I outline in this book is a rethinking of the role of reception in terms of Caribbean aesthetics. The struggle to represent (or even imagine) a worldview or narrative landscape free from the reverberations of colonial violence fosters a narrative space that is disorienting, confusing, and, above all, inscrutable. In the works I discuss, the seeming inescapability of colonial modes of thought and the frustrating struggle to escape and imagine new forms thus demands a uniquely Caribbean form of readerly engagement that compels the reader to confront the aporias wrought by the colonial project. Thus, the diverse subset of anglophone experimental Caribbean texts I address build off the central problematics of reception, innovation, and form ushered in by the *Beacon* group. They privilege inscrutability to capture the frustration and disorientation that emerges from not simply resisting or creating anticolonial forms, but acknowledging that these forms and these alternatives are inherently difficult to be "made sense" of or reconciled concretely or logically. The reader must thereby engage forms of colonial violence in new ways, as such works effectively narrate and reveal a desperate attempt on the part of the text to divest and divert itself from colonial doctrine, but often struggle and fail to do so, resulting in narrative forms that engender an experience of immense frustration. This book rethinks the relationship between formal experimentation, reception, and colonial trauma and examines how such texts—texts of immense difficulty and frustration—might be productively read. In so doing, I hope to articulate a uniquely Caribbean theory of aesthetic innovation that may allow us to rethink the implications of difficulty and frustration in ways that provide a new methodology for examining not only experimental Caribbean fiction but also the nature of colonial oppression itself.

Inscrutable Histories

The historical focus of this book is rooted in an examination of experimental mid-twentieth-century Caribbean fiction, focusing specifically on the fifty-year period between the late 1920s to the early 1970s. While the anglophone emphasis of this study may on the surface appear exclusionary, my emphasis on midcentury anglophone Caribbean texts—many of which have received little critical attention, fallen out of favor, or been ignored altogether—follows David Scott's *Conscripts of Modernity*, Alison Donnell's *Twentieth-Century Caribbean Literature*, and J. Dillon Brown and Leah Reade Rosenberg's *Beyond Windrush* in suggesting that we need new models for thinking beyond stale narrative frames of anticolonialism, Windrush exile, and peasant experience in Caribbean literature. The mid-twentieth-century anglophone Caribbean canon remains in need of rethinking, as many Caribbean authors and texts—such as that of Denis Williams, Vera Bell, and Lindsay Barrett, among others—remain largely ignored and understudied, and criticism on more canonical writers like Roger Mais has become stagnant. There is, in much the same way, greater attention needed for the often unacknowledged formal intricacy of the period—especially in terms of the novel. This is, of course, not to say that questions of form and difficulty are in any way exclusive to the anglophone Caribbean, as francophone Caribbean literature is rooted in surrealism and the baroque and also addresses key issues of formal frustration, but, rather, that critics of the mid-twentieth-century anglophone Caribbean canon in particular have yet to fully explore the implications of inscrutability as a decolonial aesthetic.

A key claim of this book, as such, is that an emphasis on the receptive implications of inscrutability pervades midcentury Caribbean fiction, and that critical inattention to the receptive strategies of Caribbean inscrutability has often left many vital Caribbean authors unacknowledged, while more canonical writers are read in predictable and sometimes prescriptive ways. An analysis of Caribbean literature through the receptive implications of inscrutability thus allows us to establish compelling links across the mid-twentieth century that reveal thematic trends that have gone largely unnoticed and unexplored. Indeed, Caribbean authors have long wrestled with inscrutability and the implications of reception. As I see it, a Caribbean emphasis on difficulty and inscrutability begins in the late 1920s with work of Eric Walrond, C. L. R. James, and Jean Rhys and peaks in the late 1960s and early 1970s with the publication of Orlando Patterson's radically experimental text *An Absence of Ruins* and the later inscrutable fictions of Denis Williams. In highlighting this trajectory of experimental Caribbean literature—and rethinking definitions of what is typically perceived as midcentury Caribbean literature—I thus seek to embolden new critical trajectories that put a seemingly disparate group of Caribbean writers, such as those of the *Beacon* group, Roger Mais, and Wilson Harris, in conversation with one another by analyzing the receptive implications of inscrutability and the frustration such writers' works produce.

In this regard, though the history of Caribbean criticism and, more generally, definitions of periodization in Caribbean literature have evolved considerably over the past three decades, my usage of the term "midcentury" in this book no doubt requires some clarification, especially given its associations with the Windrush period and with the 1950s "boom" of largely male Caribbean writers such as George Lamming and Samuel Selvon. Definitions of "midcentury," furthermore, generally do not extend from the late 1920s to the early 1970s. Accordingly, in working to reconceive how the concept of midcentury literature is typically deployed in Caribbean studies, I am particularly indebted to Alison Donnell's work, which has long sought to establish a critical methodology that would help to redefine the often prescriptive and constraining nature of midcentury Caribbean literature. As Donnell argues, the frequently rigid emphasis on the midcentury—or, more specifically, the year 1950—as a watershed moment of Caribbean literary expression, and its thematic focus on masculine exile, has in many ways stifled critical analysis of lesser-known texts. As she notes, "Some texts from the pre-1950 period have been brought into view but because the claims and narratives that have persistently kept the majority of works out of sight and marginal to configurations of the canon have not been self-reflective about their own exclusions, new conditions for their critical visibility have not yet been established" (11). Indeed, rigid definitions of the midcentury boom often led to the exclusion of earlier and later texts, especially those that were not easily categorized, from critical conversations. Until recently, this was the case with works such as Eric Walrond's 1926 collection *Tropic Death*, which had been largely omitted from discussions of similarly daring Caribbean experiments with form and reception. Confronting restrictive critical perceptions of midcentury Caribbean literature is an ongoing project, as recent works like Cambridge's massive three-volume set *Caribbean Literature in Transition* (2020)—which seeks to reimagine the historical and critical purview of Caribbean literature—and Brown and Rosenberg's *Beyond Windrush: Rethinking Postwar Anglophone Caribbean Literature* attest.[5] My usage and redefinition of the term "midcentury" in this book, therefore, is in many ways intended to continue the work of unshackling twentieth-century readings of Caribbean literature from stubborn critical vantage points that often overlook the connections and resemblances between formally innovative works.

Of course, it must be noted that the struggle of articulation and frustration I examine in this book is in many ways reflected in the political and cultural unrest that dominated much of the Caribbean in the midcentury.

The hope that the widespread labor revolts of the 1930s that spread across the Caribbean would engender new social and cultural reforms that resulted in more opportunity and equity was largely stifled by the onset of World War II. The British, who responded to the unrest by forming a commission to investigate what had taken place, ultimately failed to put in place the reforms demanded by workers and instead focused on the war effort and, in so doing, once again intimated the potential of coming reforms only to not enact them.[6] In much the same way, the promise of the West Indian Federation collapsed into despair and a newfound sense of resentment and competition between Caribbean nations and not the brighter future that the federation promised. We can thus turn back to the literature of the midcentury and reorient our gaze toward the overwhelming and explicit frustration of the moment. Artistically, this same sense of genuine uncertainty and disorientation lingers throughout the period that, today, does not reveal the emergence of an effective literary counterculture or a weaponized social realist aesthetic that sparked, as the *Beacon* group hoped—a new aesthetic that challenged the foothold of colonial oppression to confront the drastic and overbearing consequences of the plantation system—but, rather, a pervasive struggle to reconcile conflicting ideologies of resistance into artistic form.[7] This sense of artistic uncertainty, combined with the fear that independence, once achieved, would fail to create the kind of sustained social change and emancipation that it both promised and yearned for, reveals mid-twentieth-century Caribbean literature entrapped in a moment of impasse, in which a struggle to imagine a coherent or truly emancipated space fosters aesthetic interventions that are unable to represent a worldview that is scrutable, logical, or sensible.

This is not to say that formal experimentation in the Caribbean can be reduced to an allegory of national identity, but that the sense of frustration and longing that emerges along with civil unrest, labor revolts, and larger schemas of resistance against colonial authority helps to contextualize the sense of confusion, uncertainty, and disorientation that is undeniably present in Caribbean literature throughout the period. An emphasis, then, on what was possible and what could be achieved—both aesthetically and politically—remained, throughout the midcentury and throughout the works I discuss, thoroughly tentative and uncertain. Formal experimentation and semantic resistance, as well as the larger questioning of narrative forms and the very idea that a narrative had, as it were, a clear ending or outcome, thus reflect the larger sociopolitical Caribbean struggle to invent, or imagine, a new reality.

My aim in this book, however, is less about how experimental forms can be used as a means of negotiating burgeoning and conflicting ideologies of nationalism and resistance throughout the Caribbean, but more about how the understudied proliferation of experimental and receptive techniques that emerged in the region across the midcentury draw the reader into moments of crisis and confusion. My emphasis is on receptive engagement—that is, it is not on how the Caribbean texts I discuss *depict* the frustration of both legacies of colonial trauma and the uncertainty and confusion of the historical moment, but how they seek to *produce it* by instigating, through formal techniques, an emotive response on the part of the reader. My contention is that the difficulty of imagining seemingly impossible futures bred, throughout the mid-twentieth century, a myriad of experimental forms that placed often understudied and ignored demands on readers in ways that sought to replicate and enact the experiences of frustration, uncertainty, and aporia that were pervasive across the Caribbean.

Before continuing, it must be acknowledged that many of the texts I address are often—rightly or wrongly—perceived and labeled as exceedingly difficult. To be clear, my argument here is not that such texts are simply ignored, and that we should, accordingly, appreciate them, nor is my goal to render the inscrutable scrutable. Instead, I want to suggest that the kind of formal difficulty such texts engage in, which produce mechanisms of frustration and disorientation and embrace a kind of overt opaqueness, posit decoding as a decolonial, and some ways anticolonial, method that can generate new ways of understanding Caribbean aesthetics, as well as methodologies of colonial resistance as a whole. These works suggest that articulating the reverberations and repercussions of colonial dominance demand serious and invested effort and labor. Labor in this regard, however, should not be perceived as a path to total understanding or enlightenment, as such works also imply that no amount of labor can fully encapsulate or capture the entrenched nature of colonial violence. The overwhelming sense of confusion and disorientation these texts implement thereby highlights Caribbean experience as a tireless process of decoding, and a continuous, sometimes exhausting, struggle to put practices of oppression and exploitation into words.

Thus, all of the works I examine in this book employ acts of disorientation, frustration, and confusion to render historical moments, in part, inscrutable. In so doing, they argue that framing cultural and historical acts through the lens of abstraction and difficulty does not further obfuscate them, but encourages readers to engage in the necessary struggle to make sense of them. This book, then, is rooted in how inscrutability forces critical reflection on the part of the reader and, as such, addresses several key historical and cultural moments in the anglophone Caribbean, all of which are rendered inscrutable through narrative forms that coerce readers to adopt strategies of decoding and unraveling that acknowledges that reverberations of colonial violence cannot be easily expressed or understood. Accordingly, the scenes and sites of colonial violence I discuss are varied and widespread: they include the continued suppression and disenfranchisement of indigenous peoples in Guyana, the rise of Rastafarianism in Jamaica, Jim Crow labor laws and the construction of the Panama Canal, the Mau Mau rebellion, and the history of Afro-Caribbean erasure in Wales, among others. In searching for new ways to make sense of—and represent—these events and historical moments, these works repeatedly question whether it is at all possible to articulate a convincing vision of what an emancipated future might look like. They capture, in other words, the perpetual difficulty to narrativize the reverberations of colonial violence in literary form by frustrating the clarity and precision of their prose in a way that demands self-reflection, while acknowledging that the complexity of these events remain buried and suppressed. The experience, for example, of confronting the violent segregation of the Canal Zone as described by Eric Walrond through immensely difficult experiments with vernacular forces the reader to negotiate how language and race was used as a means of dehumanization in immediate, performative terms. I am interested in acknowledging the possibility that the effects of confusion and frustration on the reader—if the goal is to influence one's views and interpretation of colonial violence—might, in fact, reveal and capture aspects of the trauma of colonialism that a realist (or scrutable) text cannot.

My argument thus responds to David Scott's call to develop new problem spaces through which to analyze Caribbean and postcolonial literature by rethinking the nature of formal ingenuity in the Caribbean vis-à-vis its receptive strategies. I am drawn to Scott's assertion, in *Conscripts of Modernity*, that the methodologies for which we confront anticolonial aesthetics have become both stale and ineffectual in light of the tragic failure of independence movements to create equitable spaces and overturn entrenched systems of oppression.[8] Given the continued perpetuation of colonial forms of oppression, Scott thus questions the romantic nature of postcolonialism's often idealistic framing of anticolonial resistance. As he writes, anticolonialism has been written in the narrative mode of Romance, and consequently, has projected a distinctive image of the past (one cast in terms of what colonial power has denied or negated) and a distinctive story about the relation between that past and the hoped-for future (one emplotted as a narrative of revolutionary overcoming). But. . . after the end of anticolonialism's promise, our sense of time and possibility have altered so significantly that it is hard to continue to live in the present as though it were merely a transitionary moment in an assured momentum from a wounded past to a future salvation.[9] (209–10)

Scott's point has important implications for this project, in that the works I address are not antiquated or utopic in their representation of anticolonial resistance; rather, they are unable to articulate a clear vision, or to imagine an emancipated present, with a coherent narrative form. They are undoubtedly anticolonial works, but they are above all unable to reconcile or fathom not only a sustained, active form of colonial resistance but also a discernible future. It is for this reason that the sense of impasse in these works that I have previously discussed is so important. It is not that impasse here represents a kind of stasis, but that it captures a perpetual longing for a mode of understanding with the capacity to be espoused in a form that will enact social and cultural transformation. A theory of textual inscrutability builds off of Scott's rethinking of anticolonial romance in embracing the rejection of romantic linear resistance: none of the texts I am concerned with can muster a sense of an anticolonial future. My project, however, diverges from Scott's in that it emphasizes that reconciling the atrocity of colonial oppression is itself immensely difficult to express; in drawing the reader into such problems of articulation, the texts I address struggle and fail to imagine a decolonized existence and, in so doing, capture the sense of bewilderment and hopelessness that is inextricably etched into Caribbean existence.

Form and Difficulty in Caribbean Fiction

This book, at its core, seeks to examine how textual mechanisms of inscrutability can generate new understandings of colonial trauma by drawing the reader into processes of frustration and disorientation. The midcentury works I discuss urge a new understanding of difficulty by suggesting that linear or didactic expressions of colonial violence often cannot properly convey experiences of loss and trauma in a way that effectively resonates with the potential reader. In contrast, the feelings of bewilderment, puzzlement, and disenchantment that authors like Denis Williams and Lindsey Barrett work to instill better capture, for the reader, a sense of the fracture and loss that is an integral aspect of colonial oppression. As such, the frustrated reader, whether or not they complete the text—or become too frustrated to continue—nevertheless engages in an attempt at decoding and unraveling and is forced, as it were, to think about how language and suffering is (and can be) articulated in the Caribbean. My approach in this book resists the pejorative connotations of difficulty and argues that the readerly act of negotiating a difficult text can reveal insights into Caribbean experience that are not otherwise visible. In this sense, my work builds off Édouard Glissant's seminal theory of opacity, which calls for the radical embrace of difficulty as an integral aspect of Caribbean identity.

Any discussion of difficulty and inscrutability in the Caribbean must begin with the work of Glissant. Of course, Glissant's theory of opacity remains, today, the most essential theorization of intelligibility and its implications. Glissant argues that opacity, in the Caribbean, is both a right and a form of resistance. In *Caribbean Discourse,* he petitions for what he calls a need for "stubborn shadows" that enact a "perpetual concealment, which is our form of resistance" (4). In a refusal to adhere to Western demands for transparency, Glissant's work instead turns toward the refusal to answer or reveal oneself and in so doing rejects the very idea that Caribbean identity and experience can be articulated in terms of clarity, precision, or completeness. As Glissant warns, the presumption that a lack of cohesiveness suggests a moral or cultural failing is thus ideologically dangerous, in that it grafts a Western vision of culture and history onto Caribbean experience in a way that insists the Caribbean's fractured colonial history is indicative only of its own inferiority and not a result of the centuries of colonial violence that dominated its history. As Glissant writes, "The attempt to approach reality so often hidden from view cannot be organized in terms of a series of clarifications. We demand the right to obscurity. Through which our anxiety to have a full existence becomes part of the universal drama of cultural transformation: the creativity of marginalized peoples, who today confront the ideal of transparent universality, imposed by the West, with secretive and multiple manifestations of Diversity" (2). In other words, Caribbean and creole experience, because it has been shattered into vast shards of multifaceted trauma and violence engendered by the slave trade, the plantation system, and the legacy of colonialism, occludes the potential of narrativizing history in a discernibly linear fashion.

My argument resituates Glissant's work on opacity in terms of readerly reception, emphasizing how textual inscrutability forces readers to perceive the trauma of colonial violence in the Caribbean in more complex, visceral ways. After all, texts that privilege a sense of radical opacity—such as Orlando Patterson's 1967 novel *An Absence of Ruins* or the work of Wilson Harris—suggest that it is only by lessening a reliance on clarity or simplicity that we can develop new reading practices that begin to confront the nuances of Caribbean experience. Such works expound on Glissant's notion of shock and interruption as a means to access and understand fractured memory. As Glissant argues,

> Many of us have never fully understood our historical times; we have simply experienced them. That is the case of Caribbean communities which only today have access to a collective memory. Our quest for the dimension of time will therefore be neither harmonious nor linear. Its advance will be marked by a polyphony of dramatic shocks, at the level of conscious as well as the unconscious, between incongruous phenomena or "episodes" so disparate that no link can be discerned. Majestic harmony does not prevail here, but . . . an anxious and chaotic quest. . . . An exploration of the chaos of memory (obscured, alienated, or reduced to a range of natural references) cannot be done in the "clarity" of linear narrative. (107)

Opaque works thus replicate the fits, snaps, and shocks that reflect the nature of historical and collective memory in a way that negotiates conscious and unconscious experience. Yet, as I see it, the goal of reevaluating mid-twentieth-century Caribbean texts in terms of their inscrutability should not be to emphasize and expose, as it were, the "chaos of memory," but to examine the extent to which such chaos can be represented in narrative form. What interests me here is not the idea that the opaque text reflects a successful depiction of the fracture of collective memory, but that it cannot—or that it fails to do so—in a way that draws the reader into larger struggles of articulation and an acknowledgment that experiences of historical and colonial trauma are resoundingly difficult to express.

Accordingly, the theory of reading I outline in this book is influenced by Elleke Boehmer's study of reception and readerly engagement as described in *Postcolonial Poetics: Twenty-First-Century Critical Readings*. Echoing Glissant's examination about the potentially recuperative effects of difficulty, Boehmer's rethinking of reader response theory is particularly relevant for elucidating the role of reception and inscrutability in Caribbean studies; her work reveals how formal devices can initiate new levels of immersion that engender a deeper readerly engagement with mechanisms of oppression. *Postcolonial Poetics* considers the extent to which experimentation with narrative form in the postcolonial novel might allow readers to foster new forms of insight and cultural understanding that are otherwise inexpressible. As Boehmer writes,

> Reading involves negotiation, in the first place between the reader or interpreter and the text, but also between readers and the different cultural and political worlds that the text may open up for them, and with which, through their reading, they may to some degree, if in different measures, come to identify. This is perhaps the more so in writing that consciously uses juxtaposition and nonsynchrony, impelling the reader to double back, follow fresh lines of implication, and broach hitherto unasked questions. The back-and-forth processes of conjecture and speculation that juxtaposition encourages also allow hidden and as-yet-unsayable meanings to be suggested, in ways that are at once powerful and oblique, especially for those who are forbidden or excluded in some way. (52–53)

The concept of readerly identification Boehmer describes contends that narrative devices such as juxtaposition and nonsynchrony—two narrative techniques common to the experimental Caribbean texts discussed in the book—generate a more engaging practice of reading that encourages the reader to rethink both what they have read and what it may mean. Boehmer's theory of reading therefore suggests that the historical legacy of colonial violence cannot be easily articulated or expressed by traditional narrative forms, and, what's more, that postcolonial writers, if they are to better reveal the nuances of colonial oppression, must seek to engage the reader to confront that very difficulty of articulation through narrative techniques that initiate readerly sentiments of "conjecture and speculation" (53).[10]

Boehmer's text therefore helps to elucidate the ways in which experiences of readerly frustration can be seen as a means to better expose the complexities of Caribbean oppression in literary form. Indeed, for Boehmer, reading experimental postcolonial texts becomes an act of encoding and decoding that manifests experiences of discontinuity. The reader is forced to negotiate the gaps and fissures of the textual landscape in a way that encourages an active search for meaning. Boehmer asserts that "intercalated modes of writing (layering, cross-cutting, bricolage, intertextuality), are made possible by the cultural code concatenations of postcolonial experience, and offer a way of encoding, interpreting, and even vicariously experiencing something of that variety and discontinuity. . . . Especially where our attention is directed at one and the same time to different contiguous items (images, themes, figures), *and* to their interstices between them or the spaces through which they relate, we are invited to work *between* and *across,* and to read in differential ways" (53). An analysis of the processes of reception that emphasize acts of encoding and decoding are in many ways integral and inherent in Caribbean literary analysis. After all, Stuart Hall's seminal essay on "Encoding and Decoding" sought to examine misunderstandings—or what he referred to as "distortions"—between text and audience.[11] As Boehmer suggests, the juxtaposition of seemingly oppositional textual forms and narrative strategies emphasizes a struggle to make sense of, and not dismiss or ignore, aporia. Disconnect and misunderstanding, then, function as a productive force, compelling the reader to actively acknowledge the gaps that occlude cultural and historical acts of oppression. Through the formal ingenuities Boehmer describes, reading becomes speculative—a process of tense uncertainty that must be actively unraveled.

This theory of reader reception, in privileging active engagement, no doubt brings to mind Roland Barthes's concept of the "writerly" text. For Barthes, the writerly functions as an innovative form of writing that forces the reader to become more inquisitive and invested in the text. It should be noted that Barthes's conception of the writerly text—the text that makes "the reader no longer a consumer, but a producer of the text"—was instrumental in crafting the central claim of this book: the very idea that an aesthetics of inscrutability engenders a sense of productive frustration on the part of the reader in such a way that reflects the inherent trauma of colonial violence and oppression and, in so doing, reveals a uniquely Caribbean aesthetic (4). Barthes's work privileges texts that generate a sense of activity and engagement. His critique of what he calls the "readerly" text is rooted in the fact that it is largely sterile: readerly texts do not demand a sense of reflexivity but are instead simply rejected or accepted; consequently, they leave the reader trapped in a sense of what he calls "idleness" (4).[12] This book examines the extent to which the reader can be drawn into processes of colonial trauma through the implementation of frustration and confusion as formal devices and suggests that the acts of colonial decoding such works initiate is a process that demands heightened activity and concentration on the part of the reader. The formal devices common to the works I discuss may enable readers alternate pathways of thinking through and confronting forms of oppression, and these pathways are in many ways rooted in experiences of reading that are synonymous with that which Barthes labels writerly experience, in initiating a process of active engagement that is achieved through the negotiation of textual complexity.

Building off Glissant's, Bohemer's, and Barthes's examination of the engaging potential of experimental forms, my analysis provides a counterargument to Neil Lazarus's critique of formalism in his seminal *The Postcolonial Unconscious,* in which he derisively labels experimental postcolonial works as "pomo-postcolonialism" (25). Far from appropriating Western forms, as Lazarus argues, Caribbean experiments with form engender new, unforeseen methods of understanding colonial violence. *Difficult Reading* rejects notions that formal experimentation is ahistorical or apolitical; it contends instead that challenging readerly sensibilities through difficulty and abstraction provides an alternate pathway of understanding how colonialist and imperialist tendencies dominate and disenfranchise. This is not to suggest that there is no value in a realist aesthetic that shines a legible light on atrocity and oppression, but that the nuances of inscrutability and frustration, as a Caribbean aesthetic, constitutes a uniquely Caribbean mode of writing that needs, as I show throughout this book, further attention.[13]

Such a reading of the performative demands of inscrutability emphasizes the ways in which readers can be made to more deeply engage with processes of historical obliteration and the legacy of colonial violence and trauma in the Caribbean. Such is the case in Wilson Harris's 1971 collection, *The Age of the Rainmakers:* a text in which Harris attempts to create a mythology of fables and stories centered around the history and achievements of indigenous Guyanese peoples. Yet much of the book narrativizes this history through the lens of immense difficulty, as the narrator engages in an almost metafictional search to make sense of the tattered fragments of Arawak civilization. Thus, in stories like "Arawak Horizon," readers confront abstract numerology, astrological forms, and thoroughly alien experiences and information that no historical research or contemporary knowledge can properly elucidate. Furthermore, the stylized glyphs and numbers that function as part of the story's Arawak mythology are typeset on the page in a way that cannot be properly cited or quoted without distorting the style and precision of its original form. Hence, to discuss—or even cite—the text is immensely difficult. There is, in short, no simple methodology for reading it that will make it clear or easier to understand; readers are thereby forced to adopt and devise alternate strategies of understanding. As such, *Age*'s struggle to imagine and narrate the buried, destroyed history of the Arawaks in Guyana emphasizes the very idea that cohesion and completeness is a fantasy of the West, and that mythmaking and meaning-making in the Caribbean must interweave historical and imaginative sources in a way that embraces the absence of cohesion and linear history. And while I will explore the relationship between inscrutability, difficulty, and indigenous erasure in depth later in this book, for now it will suffice to simply state that Harris's text reminds us, through its perpetual experimentation with linguistic and narrative forms, that what we know and how we know it is often irrefutably concealed from us, and that history, as such, cannot be retrieved but must repeatedly confront its own erasure. Harris's work indicates the potentiality of a theory of literary inscrutability, in that it suggests new aesthetic and ideological pathways that emerge thorough a rethinking of how we frame and negotiate issues of clarity through a distinctly Caribbean lens. At the same time, Harris also leaves the reader with a perpetual sense of unease and frustration by creating narratives in which the central message or ideology cannot be properly verbalized or understood. In "Arawak Horizon," no amount of reading or understanding can provide the cohesive picture of Arawak mythology and culture that the reader perhaps expects and demands. Indigenous trauma remains, in all of Harris's novels, a struggle of articulation.

The works I discuss in this book therefore provide new insights into how Caribbean forms of trauma can be expressed. In this regard, it is worth pausing here to acknowledge how my argument builds off contemporary notions of trauma. On the one hand, this connection may seem obvious; after all, the very nature of trauma—and trauma studies—is often explicitly linked to questions of articulation and unintelligibility, or what Irene Visser calls the "ultimately unknowable and inexpressible nature of traumatic wounding" (11). Trauma theorists since Cathy Caruth have long argued that trauma "resists simple comprehension" (6), and that "the most direct seeing of a violent event may occur as an absolute inability to know it" (91–92). My usage of the term "trauma" here thus echoes the history of its inextricable relationship to both unintelligibility and articulation. While there has been much recent debate concerning the Eurocentric nature of trauma studies, I find Boehmer's contention that postcolonial trauma writing can more deeply draw the reader into writerly processes of engagement particularly important for a reading of Caribbean inscrutability.[14] As Boehmer contends, postcolonial trauma narrative "draws upon the complex resources of literary language to express and reflect upon a particular collective experience of crisis, pain, distress, or shock. Its poetics is marked by hesitations, breaks, and repetitions, not only compelling the reader to relive the traumatic experience along with the speaker or writer, but also drawing them into the difficulty of its articulation" (88). Taken this way, the opacity of Caribbean trauma may serve as a form of textual engagement in which the struggle to express historical acts of violence becomes a collaborative act.

Of course, the readerly challenges such works provide, particularly concerning questions of intelligibility and historical trauma, no doubt brings to mind the issue of accessibility, and a question could be raised whether or not the effort and frustration such texts demand and enact risks disengaging the reader from the larger issues of colonial violence they seek to confront. Of this question of difficulty, effort, and audience, Glissant has much to say, as he details in *Caribbean Discourse*. In the passage below, Glissant wrestles with notions of audience and distance, arguing that the opaque work's goal is not to produce a sense of familiarity or comfort, but to reveal how systems of inequity might be dismantled. For Glissant, this sense of dismantling produces, not surprisingly, a sense of discomfort that raises a number of questions:

> Now this raises the question of *the one whom the work is written*. A generous tendency in our works tempts us to place ourselves from the outset "within reach" of those who suffer social or cultural alienation. A justifiable tendency insofar as we have a concrete effect on the symptoms of this alienation. But an almost elementary statement of our needs, if it is valuable in our daily struggle, can also prevent us from seeing the deeper structures of oppression which much nevertheless be brought to light.... Western thought has led us to believe that a work must always put itself constantly at our *disposal*.... It can happen that a work is not written *for someone,* but to dismantle the complex mechanism of frustration and the infinite forms of oppression. (107)

At stake is the importance of what the opaque work achieves, and Glissant argues here that we must think beyond the question of whom the work is written for in favor of an analysis of how the text may work to destabilize entrenched forms of oppression. Glissant's reorientation of the mechanisms of what he calls "disposal" thus opposes the idea that the work's use is less in meeting an intended or speculative reader's needs or expectations, and more in exposing the methods and means of exploitation and structures of systemic violence in the Caribbean. In contrast to Glissant, however, I want to suggest that the works I discuss in this book do not effectively dismantle the mechanisms of frustration and oppression, but rather struggle to crystalize and emphasize them, and that this sense of desperate futility, in which the mechanisms of oppression cannot be expressed or effectively overthrown in a way that is coherent or logical, captures instead their overbearing presence in Caribbean life. It might be said that an aesthetics of inscrutability is rooted in its attempt to highlight, confront, and potentially overturn forms of oppression only insomuch as it fails to do so, but that that very failure, in its propagation of readerly frustration, instigates an attempt to make sense of and decode the reverberations of colonial horror that are inherent and imbricated within Caribbean experience.

This book, however, is not simply about overtly experimental texts like Harris's that provide immediate and undeniable difficulty; it provides a wider analysis of innovative narrative devices and strategies that entrap the reader within a sense of frustration that engenders new forms of reflection. To be sure, mechanisms of difficulty and inscrutability are employed in a myriad of forms in Caribbean anglophone fiction. In some instances, a hesitation to embrace opacity has led to critical tendencies that often obscure the larger questions of inscrutability that permeate key Caribbean works. Victor Stafford Reid's 1958 novel about the Mau Mau rebellion, *The Leopard*, for example, has traditionally been read as a realist text. On the surface, the novel seems didactic, and its message is clear, with the 1952 uprising serving as a potential model for future acts of Caribbean resistance. Yet the novel, as I discuss in chapter 1, is so rife with attempted clarifications and qualifications, most of which are set in italics, that it functions less as a narrative of the Mau Mau than a desperate attempt to imagine and express a convincing ideology of resistance. A close reading of the novel lays bare a sea of contradictions and impasses that reveal a lack of textual sense and logic and produce a profound sense of readerly confusion. The text therefore functions as a work of frustration and failure that cannot be easily be negotiated, reminding us that the linkages between Kenyan resistance during "The Emergency" and contemporary Jamaican politics and anticolonial movements cannot and should not be framed as interchangeable. Reid's narrative approach, then—in privileging how occlusion, difficulty, and failure can foster insights into how we both perceive and express the nature of resistance—suggests that historical crisis and acts of protest are far too often reduced to simplistic models of resistance, and that, as such, a newfound attention to inscrutability may open up more nuanced vantage points for reconciling and understanding anticolonial narratives.

Toward an Aesthetics of Inscrutability

Typically, discussions of experimental mid-twentieth-century Caribbean texts have been rooted in a rethinking—and resituating—of Caribbean works through the lens of literary modernism. In addition to Simon

Gikandi's seminal *Writing in Limbo: Modernism and Caribbean Literature*, a number of recent monographs have addressed the relationship between modernist forms and Caribbean aesthetics. For example, in *Migrant Modernism: Postwar London and the West Indian Novel*, J. Dillon Brown suggests that "modernism's self-reflexive, counterdiscursive impulses migrated into the very foundations of Anglophone Caribbean fiction"; Brown thus labels the "migrant" Caribbean texts he discusses as an "alternative strain" of modernism (5).[15] In much the same way, Mary Lou Emery's *Modernism, the Visual, and Caribbean Literature* explores the extent to which Caribbean writers, such as Wilson Harris and Jean Rhys, "engage the dynamic of vision as a transforming element in the process of cultural decolonization and, through it, claim the authority of their own perceptions" (2). Situating her argument within the schema of literary modernism, Emery argues that this newfound authority of vision is both enabled and made possible by burgeoning early and mid-twentieth-century independence movements (2). Similarly, Charles W. Pollard, in *New World Modernisms: T. S. Eliot, Derek Walcott, and Kamau Brathwaite*, contends that the relationship between Caribbean literature and modernism is less antagonistic than theorists like Gikandi suggest, and that the work of Brathwaite and Walcott, in particular, "creates a modernist poetics that diverges from European modernism because it responds to the Caribbean/ New World cultural situation" (19).[16]

The writings of Brown, Pollard, and Emery, among others, have been enormously valuable in thinking through the relationship between experimental Caribbean aesthetics and modernist practice. My approach in this book builds off these analyses by taking as a point of fact that twentieth-century Caribbean literature is deeply invested in both a rethinking and sometimes repudiation of modernist forms. That said, while these studies offer considerable insight into the relationship between form and modernist practice, I have no stake in categorizing the works I discuss as modernist, not modernist, or anti-modernist, as these ongoing debates continue to be discussed as the field of global modernism ever widens. Nevertheless, despite excellent criticism by Donnell, Brown, and Rosenberg, anglophone Caribbean studies can sometimes seem caught in a stranglehold between Windrush and modernist aesthetics. My goal in this book is less about situating the works I discuss in terms of existing categories and more about thinking through the formal and aesthetic tendencies of how inscrutability can engage readers in a uniquely Caribbean decolonial aesthetic that generates productive reflection and insight into the means and mechanisms of oppression.

In other words, the aesthetics of inscrutability I develop in this book is not rooted in a rethinking of modernism, but in Caribbean theories of frustration and difficulty. While recent and historical studies that address questions of difficulty and frustration provide the vital groundwork for this study, they have not fully examined the potentiality of inscrutability as a decolonial aesthetic. Jean Bernabé, Patrick Chamoiseau, and Raphaël Confiant's seminal but controversial *In Praise of Creoleness,* for example, reimagines creole identity vis-à-vis Glissant's conception of opacity and thus links a theory of hybridity with the expression of aesthetic forms. As they contend, "Creoleness is the annihilation of false universality, of monolingualism, and of purity" that tends toward "chaos and our mangrove of virtualities" (90). Arguing for a renewed emphasis on complexity, which they argue "is the very principle of our identity" (90), the group champions what they call "the richness of the unknown." (91). For the authors, the path forward is an aesthetics of difficulty that they hope will place their "writing within the progressive forces working at . . . liberation" (103). They contend, therefore, that "it is already clear we have to write the difficult way, to express ourselves against the current of usuries, clichés, and deformations, and that it is only through the difficult way that we might trail deeply our authenticity" (104). For the Créolistes, creole forms of difficulty are an innately Caribbean aesthetic that bear almost utopic designs in providing a counterdiscourse to forms of colonial oppression.

Yet, as Shalini Puri, in *The Caribbean Postcolonial: Social Equality, Post-Nationalism, and Cultural Hybridity,* convincingly argues, the Créolistes often fall back on the concept of authenticity in a way that undermines the transgressive nature of their call for difficulty. "In their desire to revalue creole culture," Puri writes, "the Créolistes understate the ways in which it is scarred by colonial history. In the contradiction between their recognizing that there is no physical 'outside' to which one can retreat to mount an attack and their claiming an intact Creole culture, we see a familiar move by which hybridity discourse often smuggles back the concept of value and authenticity" (33). The end result is that the text does not reveal "the full consequences of the fact that popular culture is itself infiltrated, compromised, and responsive to changing political pressures" (33). Puri is skeptical, in other words, of the potential of creoleness (as defined) to function as an emancipative discourse of hybridity given that it is postulated as an alternative mode of being that resists colonial oppression—in part because the Créolistes do not fully consider the extent to which creole identity is already enmeshed in the mechanisms of power it seeks to resist. For the purpose of my argument, my view here mirrors

Puri's criticism of the Créolistes in that they overlook the very fact that there exists no anticolonial "outside" per se to foist a critique; thus, the works I address do not reveal success or authenticity, but a failure to escape—and articulate—a counterdiscourse. This point, as I've been arguing, is brought to the forefront by an aesthetics of inscrutability.

More recently, two contemporary monographs address the concept of difficulty through new vantage points. First, Sheri-Marie Harrison's book *Jamaica's Difficult Subjects: Negotiating Sovereignty in Anglophone Caribbean Literature and Criticism* argues that "patterns of illegibility, perplexity, and challenge in contemporary Caribbean literature mark the emergence of a new wave of writing that deploys confusion or dissonance in relation to the traditional politics of Caribbean literature as a key formal strategy" (5). As such, Harrison turns attention to "moments of difficulty or incomprehensibility across the Caribbean literary landscape" (5). Yet, while Harrison's study persuasively articulates a model for rethinking the notion of "difficulty," her approach is less an examination of experimental forms and more of an analysis of what she labels the "difficult subject." In examining the difficult subject, she elucidates, "the terms within which particular subjects remain at the margins are rendered unknowable, even in their capacities as major agents in texts that are definitive of significant moments in the development of the region's literary tradition" (5). In highlighting the ostracized or difficult subject, Harrison "focuses on the politics which at each historical juncture render difficult" (15). Therefore, while Harrison's study makes an important intervention into the rhetorical and structural implications of difficulty in the Caribbean, it does not consider a wider purview of the receptive implications of experimental aesthetics that I seek to address.

Second, of all recent criticism on the implications of difficulty in terms of a Caribbean aesthetic, J. Dillon Brown's "Engaging the Reader: The Difficulties of George Lamming," from his book *Migrant Modernism*, stands out most explicitly for its careful attention to reception and readership. Brown's goal is to situate Lamming's notorious difficulty and density in terms of its effects on readings practices, arguing that his texts demand a kind of slowness and careful attention that seek "to transform the uncritical, passively receptive readers into skeptical, suspicious ones, alert to cultural, ideological, and political frames which all narrative is produced and received" (74). Situating Lamming's strategies of difficulty in terms of modernist aesthetics—and building off Leonard Diepeveen's and Frederic Jameson's theorizations of difficulty—Brown argues that readers participate in the "mutual creation of meaning" that embraces an engaging sense of interactivity (102). Negotiating such difficulty "has unmistakable utility in the Caribbean context as a foundational step in the process of what Lamming sees as mental decolonization by questioning and undermining the easy certainties inherited from colonial rule" (101). Though my book focuses more on the implications of inarticulation and the readerly struggle to reconcile inscrutability, Brown's examination of how opacity can forge new methods of connection that reveal a "Caribbean worldview" offers a compelling analysis of the interactive potential of difficulty.

While the above overview reveals a continued, but tepid, critical engagement of the importance of difficulty in Caribbean literature, considerably less attention has been paid to the potential of frustration as a rhetorical and aesthetic device. For the purpose of this study, then, I want to return to Kamau Brathwaite's infrequently discussed and mostly forgotten examination of frustration in his 1967 essay, "West Indian Prose Fiction in the Sixties: A Survey," which bears an enormous influence on the theory of Caribbean inscrutability that I outline in this book. Simply put, Brathwaite's goal is to examine what he sees as a shift in late 1950s and 1960s Caribbean fiction, which he calls a "kind of pessimism . . . which reflects the continuing West Indian sense of political and cultural rootlessness and failure" (11). It is, of course, not difficult to understand Brathwaite's interest in the period, given the failure of resistance movements to enact their anticolonial potential. Brathwaite thus explores what he perceives to be several emergent forms of Caribbean fiction, the most important of which, significantly, he calls "novels of frustration."[17]

While Brathwaite's discussion of frustration is brief and undeveloped in the original version of his text, his 1970 revision of the essay further elaborates on the concept through an analysis of the work of little-known Caribbean novelist Lindsay Barrett.[18] Barrett, a Jamaican-born poet, teacher, journalist, and broadcaster, migrated between the Caribbean, Europe, and Africa throughout his life, and his first novel, *Song for Mumu,* was written during the 1960s and finally published in 1967. Today, his work remains long out of print and, more generally, has received no recent critical attention. Initially, Brathwaite heaps praise on Barrett's text, highlighting how its disparate narrative threads "glitter and echo" (12) a complex tableau of Caribbean forms that reveal Barrett's unique stylistic and experimental ingenuity. He writes: "In terms of the categories being used in this study, this is a novel of frustration if ever there was one: poverty, insanity, failure, murder, death. But out of it, Barrett sings and swings. Folksong, folktale, blues shout, sankey, jazz, pocomania hymn; Africa, black America,

Jamaica, all come together in splendid undisciplined harmony; celebration of the ex-slave's dreams and oral tradition. Lamming, Harris, Mais, Reid, Selvon, Ellison (of *Invisible Man*), Baldwin (of *Go, Tell it on the Mountain*) and Joyce, all glitter and echo together with Barrett's own muse, out of these imagist pages" (12). As should be immediately clear, Brathwaite's analysis of Barrett's novel is incredibly important, as it lays the groundwork for linking both Caribbean societal and aesthetic frustration within a larger tradition of literary experimentation. But, surprisingly, Brathwaite soon pivots to a bitter critique of Barrett's work, suggesting that *Song for Mumu*'s competing vision of experimental and conventional forms ultimately reveal what he calls a "a failure of vision" (13). The crux, he argues, is that Barrett, by frequently reverting to clichéd, almost romantic, narrative devices, belies his vision of a discordant Caribbean landscape mired in frustration, and ultimately the novel's experiments in form are pulled into the mire of the narrative's refusal to see its vision through. As Brathwaite writes, "The problem here is that the headlong fantasy has, from time to time, to be abruptly halted . . . for the demands of conventional narrative or explanation. . . . This kind of sentimental realism, repeated so often in the novel, involves a sacrifice of metaphor which is the poet's only beacon" (13). The tension between the novel's immense difficulty and moments of what might be called "conventional prose" results in Braithwaite's conclusion that the text "becomes a private, wilful and erotic indulgence; an aesthetic escape out of a hopeless landscape" (14). The novel, it seems, cannot fulfill its thematic focus on frustration, in that its momentary lapses of clarity sever its aesthetic achievements. Thus, while Brathwaite's study suggests the potential emergence of a new form of Caribbean literature that blends experimental aesthetics with experiences or sensations of frustration, he quickly abandons the concept in favor of a stylistic critique of Barrett, whose writing he finds distasteful.

Brathwaite's citation and subsequent dismissal of Barrett's work, however, has significant implications for this study, as the novel speaks to important questions of frustration and form that Brathwaite quickly glosses over. Barrett's *Song for Mumu* is not a stylistically flawed novel, but, rather, a model text that reveals how an aesthetics of inscrutability can foster newfound methods of readerly engagement. Thus, while Brathwaite's essay opens up an important discussion of the mechanics of the novel, we might reevaluate his assertion that Barrett's text "fails . . . not in its details of energy, or in intention, but on the question of the content of its narrative line" (14). How might we reconcile aesthetic and artistic failure, however, in a text that is quite literally *about* failure and escape? In the novel, Mumu, the central character, becomes repeatedly entrapped in abusive relationships, and, as she struggles to understand how or why these relationships fail, the coherence of the narrative itself collapses. The juxtaposition of experimental and conventional forms therefore reveal the text as a locus of instability that repeatedly cancels itself out. Mumu can never find a way out of her suffering, and thus the disorienting shifts of narrative perspective function as hypothetical methods of escape that always fail in tone and consistency. The degree to which Barrett's novel tries and does not succeed in initiating a consistent narrative tone is strangely viewed by Brathwaite as a failure rather than an aesthetic site of crisis that represents a struggle to express a coherent narrative vision of Caribbean experience that will engender physical and psychological emancipation. Barrett's novel resists adopting a monolithic narrative approach and instead demonstrates how a multitude of approaches fail. It taunts the reader with moments in which the scrutability of its narrative promises moments of sense, logic, clarity—and even hope—only to strip those moments away.

Thus far, critics have not yet seriously considered the aesthetics of difficulty and the struggle for meaning in Barrett's text in terms of its receptive implications, nor have they considered how the novel's difficulty embroils the reader in an endless search for consistency and clarity in a way that mirrors the central quest of its protagonist. We should not, then, read the text's interruptive punctures of clarity as an artistic failing, but we should examine the implications of these interruptions on the act of reading itself. In my view, textual moments of clarity are both deeply antagonistic and performative: they cajole the reader to remember that simple affirmations and easy, uncomplicated answers belie the complexity of forms of oppression. In the text, clarity always unravels and spirals back into inscrutability. In this way, the novel forces readers to examine how we might break cycles of abuse that have been engendered by centuries of colonial violence.

In fact, *Song for Mumu* juxtaposes passages of steam of consciousness, poetic language, verse, abstraction, and puerile comedy together in an assemblage of horror in which the central character tries but always fails to escape. In short, the novel is centered around Mumu's entanglement in a series of abusive relationships that, predictably, end in death and tragedy. Yet the nature of these relationships—and the way Mumu talks about and remembers them—is seldom easy to understand or process. The violent cycle of abuse repeats, and, in the scene below, the thoughts of Mumu's violent lover, Poet, dominate the scene in a long scatological passage that is both confusing and uncertain, until the style and clarity of the passage suddenly shifts. Here, impressionistic abstraction and an explicit depiction of violence clash together uncomfortably on the page:

> The beginning is not the beginning, he said, and the end we never know and before all this is the middle, the centre, the continuation of the finality is always the middle, meddlesome meat and bite, how is it to be a porkchop . . . or an egg . . . but if the fart should be squeezed in E flat it would break the mouse's ear . . . ho ho is a word I've always loved and hated . . . heh heh, a plea, but the leaf of the shit tree disappears ain the great wind from the arsehole of the cloud . . . ho ho. He leaps from the bed throwing the covers away in a storm of white and blue and senselessly slams her senseless against the wall and begins to drive home harsh soundless heavy blows to the soft flesh of her belly and she bears the pain in silence, having learnt never to scream or cry for such signs of weakness only angers his demon. (132; ellipses in original)

It could be said that the literal explanation of the abstract struggle with Poet's demons that occurs at the end of the passage undermines the complexity of his struggle and the horrifying violence that results. But I do not believe that the shift from abstract to precise language is indicative of Barrett's artistic uncertainty—nor do the novel's moments of clarity counteract its investment in abstraction. Long sections of the text unravel without any explanation of what or who is speaking, and the text seldom provides the reader with the larger context of the experimental vignettes it describes. The novel's pace, style, and tone differs radically, as temporary moments of clarity erode into impressionistic scenes of abstraction. The key point here is that the novel isn't just a work that thematically reveals frustration but, rather, one that *produces* it: Barrett's text, which blends allegorical language, stream of consciousness narration, surrealism, and experiments with poetic form, smashes against moments of clear narration, providing a reading experience that propagates a sense of pronounced unease. What makes Barrett's forgotten text so important is that its narrative and formal ebbs and flows create a readerly experience that is perpetually jarring, where the text forces the reader to constantly adjust the strategies they use to confront it. Violence, as the text shows, always demands an active understanding that is not static or predicable: to represent it in a singular or uniform fashion denies the complexity and pervasiveness to which it appears and to which it can be confronted.

The novel continuously challenges how readers understand the nature of violence by frustrating its clarity and precision. Early in the novel, we meet the spectral River women of what is referred to only as the Green: a fictional, countryside landscape that exists buttressed against an unnamed

Caribbean city. The existence of the Green is threatened by the power and wealth of "the Rich Man," who predictably and tirelessly exploits the people's labor and resources. In a key scene, the River Women, who speak only in verse, enact their revenge on their oppressor: they systematically eviscerate the Rich Man—quite literally tearing him apart, ripping his flesh from his bones and brutally severing his genitals. It is one of—at least on the surface—few moments in the text in which oppressed peoples enact any form of sustainable revenge. Yet the scene is considerably more complex than it initially appears:

> *River Women:* Money bought.
> *Rich Man:* Bought what?
> *River Women:* Everything.
> *Rich Man:* It did? Yes? No closer. Don't come closer . . . hey hey, what is this . . . I never did . . .
> *River Women:* Yes, yes is all is yes, yes you did
> *Old River Women:* Never know when you going to die.
> *Rich Man:* What is this? Help! Oooh I'm blinded blinded, bring back my eyes . . . my eyes.
> *River Women:* Money bought you limbs too . . .
> *Rich Man:* Aieee my arms my arms, bring back my arms. (49–50)

On the face of it, this scene between the River Women and the Rich Man is fairly straightforward, and it echoes the fictive strategies of a literature of "moral degeneracy" that Rosenberg discusses in *Nationalism and the Formation of Caribbean Literature.*[19] It is clear, certainly, that a key goal of the scene is to reveal the depravity of the white capitalist class. The literal punishment of the white colonist—who is a persistent force of terror in the novel and who is, in some ways, comically evil (in addition to exploiting the populace, he frequently engages in bestiality) depicts an overt, if not fantastical, moment of revenge against the peoples' oppressor.

What is interesting, though, is that the River Women scene, when viewed more closely, appears to be less an effective act of revenge against colonial power than an examination of intelligibility and misunderstanding. The novel questions how we narrate stories of resistance, as Barrett quickly undermines the River Women scene by suggesting it may not have happened the way it is described in the narrative. Though the people in the novel revere the River Women, they cannot, in actuality, truly understand them or make sense of their actions. When the River Women speak, the Green's people hear only an incomprehensible chanting. As the text later describes, "River Women's voices rise now and a scream not joined by sound or texture to their choral chant shatters the bright curtain of light and silence in the villagers' heads and on the far side of the river we can see The Farmers running down slopes from the Rich Man's farm to watch the water" (51). The retributive violence of the killing of the Rich Man occurs, therefore, through the haze of unreality and spectral abstraction. Though this is a celebratory moment in the text, it is also one mired in obfuscation, and its veracity is undercut by the River Women's uncertain ontological status and vague, seemingly untranslatable, speech. Notice, too, that the scene in which the Rich Man is murdered lacks descriptive markers, and we are never entirely certain of how, exactly, the River Women maim the Rich Man. So, while we may read this scene as a rather uncomplicated anticolonial narrative of revenge, the text suggests something else altogether, and, if we read closely, we can observe what Barrett is doing here, in revealing that moments of clarity may not, in fact, be as clear as we imagine; in this way, the novel repeatedly undermines its own clarity and didacticism. What is initially assumed to be a powerful act of colonial resistance is in fact only a hypothetical act—a confusing, misunderstood fantasy that the people of the Green, and the readers themselves, can never fully process or understand. Such scenes, in other words, cannot be convincingly reconciled: they do not fit together neatly, and the picture of violence and abuse Barrett creates is not so much a narrative that fails to articulate a vision, but one that argues that we must challenge and confront the very nature of how we depict and understand acts of violence and resistance.

What makes Barrett's text inventive and powerful are the ways in which the interplay of its inscrutable and conventional narrative structure interact and thus create a frustrating reading experience that reflects the unease, despair, and confusion of a newly independent Jamaica. The aesthetics described is continuously disorientating and demands considerable readerly attention, as clarity flickers in and out, and perspectives and styles rapidly shift. Such an uncomfortable blend of narrative styles and forms asks if there is any appropriate ideal or rational narrative method that will aid in understanding the nuances of colonial violence. We are left to make sense of an underlying current of systemic disenfranchisement that simply cannot be rectified, as the novel creates a sense of unease that reminds us the colonial reverberations that dominate the novel's characters are no longer always articulatable. Far from being a stylistic failure, then, Barrett's novel eschews a spiraling sense of despair that seeks to reproduce in its readers the frustrating, bewildering sensations and experiences that accompany Caribbean decolonization. It is my hope that this book can build off the analyses of difficulty and frustration espoused by Harrison, Brown, the Créolistes, and Brathwaite, to demonstrate how an examination of the receptive strategies of inscrutability allows us to better examine the reverberations and nuances of colonial trauma in texts such as Barrett's.

Blockages, Occlusion, and Reception

The texts I address in this book are all invested in the idea that readerly activity must be a demanding, interactive process that privileges a textual confrontation with obstacles and impasses. This sense of impasse—one that produces frustration and confusion in a way that demands self-reflection—is evident and pervasive throughout mid-twentieth-century anglophone Caribbean fiction. A key contention of this book is that blockage and impasse in the works I address functions not as an obstacle, but as a formal strategy that opens up new spaces of debate and exploration. In this regard, critics such as Simon Gikandi have previously explored the significance of blockage in the Caribbean in seminal works such as *Writing in Limbo: Modernism and Caribbean Literature*, noting that "when Caribbean novelists tried to use their narratives to activate the past, or to recenter the marginalized, they were confronted by a historical paradigm informed by both blockage and possibility" (68). In particular, Gikandi views this emphasis on impasse as both a dominating tendency of Lamming's work as well as a wider thematic tendency in the midcentury, arguing that Selvon's work is too representative of "a blockage of desires . . . manifested in the colonial subject's inability to be gratified its traditional culture or the colonial realm" (115). My interpretation of blockage, however, expands on Gikandi's thematic reading to examine the way impasse opens up to better define how Caribbean literature generates a unique receptive space that engages the reader to confront experiences of impasse and occlusion—for how the reader responds to such narrative devices is, of course, at the core of the Caribbean aesthetic I examine in this book.

As will be made apparent, in the works I address blockage becomes not solely a textual theme, but a larger readerly crisis. In Denis Williams's *The Third Temptation*, for example, the historical erasure of Afro-Caribbean identity in Wales leads to a narrative that is ultimately unable to adopt a cohesive or even scrutable narrative voice, leaving the novel (as I explore in chapter 2) to be literally submerged in a chorus of white voices that makes its Afro-Caribbean presence almost invisible, and that prevents the vocalization of Afro-Caribbean perspectives in the text. Yet *The Third Temptation* only makes sense if the reader, as Williams's text carefully invites, begins to observe the voices bubbling below the surface of the novel's white landscape—voices that are pleading to be heard. In much the same way, such an aesthetic tendency of submersion—in that it leads toward not just a thematic fascination with occluded desires, but textual disorientation and confusion that demands readerly reflection—is a frequent formal tendency employed by Jean Rhys. A theory of inscrutability that generates readerly frustration to threaten intelligibility and challenge historical modes of oppression is well suited to Rhys's early work, particularly *Voyage in the Dark* and *Good Morning, Midnight*, which smash the protagonists' inability to express themselves against the mark of formal absence on the page: the ellipsis. Throughout Rhys's works, the ellipsis reminds readers that something is missing—that the nature of oppression is never truly articulatable. The abuse and oppression the protagonists describe can never be expressed in a manner that leaves the reader comfortable or at ease with the knowledge that their understanding is complete; that is, readers are constantly reminded that they can never fully grasp the nature of the protagonists' suffering. The frustration that such blockages initiate enact a response in which the reader is forced to decode the text's meaning in a way that questions the very foundation of how language and knowledge is disseminated in the Caribbean. Blockages and impasses in these works, in the Barthesian sense, therefore occlude the potentiality of a predetermined reading and thus demand critical reflexivity and a writerly sense of active engagement that potentially entraps the reader within experiences of dislocation intrinsic to colonial trauma.[20]

Of course, one may rightly ask if the difficulty of such novels is worth the necessary investment. Indeed, some critics have cautioned against the implementation of difficulty as a narrative device. For example, in discussing Brathwaite's radically experimental Sycorax video style—in which computer-generated images and fonts smash together uncomfortably on the page and that cannot properly be cited given its unique formal principles—Pollard argues that there is "too much interpretive work necessary in reading Sycorax video-style to assert such immediacy between this new style and either a collective sense of identity or a free expression of nation language" (129). The style, he continues, "stretches the conventions of intelligibility and undermines the claim for nation language as a common speech" (129). Though my concern in this study is with prose, I would counter that such works' generation of textual frustration and general confusion place demands on the reader that acknowledges the ability to reconcile and formulate neat or coherent narratives of enslavement, oppression, and resistance are ultimately (and this is a point Scott, in *Conscripts of Modernity,* has made clear) both utopic and romantic. The failure of emancipative national, social, and cultural structures to stifle the perpetuation of colonial oppression allows us, in many ways, to reevaluate the frustrating difficulty of midcentury texts with new eyes. Their narratives might be said to be anti-romantic not because they do not yearn for an anticolonial overturning of forms of oppression, but because they acknowledge that the language used to initiate, or even begin to enunciate, a method of colonial resistance is buried and submerged under a historical onus of failure that cannot be easily expressed. Inscrutability captures the nature of this process.

Nevertheless, it is important to acknowledge questions of access and audience. The historical dismissal of writers such as Williams and Barrett might suggest that readers are not up to the task of confronting the challenges their works demand. While I am sensitive to these concerns, an overemphasis on highlighting didactic, realist Caribbean aesthetics, particularly concerning midcentury fiction, often distracts us from thinking through the compelling implications of inscrutability as an aesthetic device in the Caribbean. The issue at stake is not, then, whether or not the works in question champion or refute the potential of literature to engender a sense of social resistance or create an ethical anticolonial aesthetic, but rather that they help us confront the obstacles and misunderstandings at play when we attempt to challenge and engage forms of colonial authority. The works I examine thus urge a rethinking of reading practices that enable audiences to experience and think through the mechanisms of oppression in the Caribbean, and, in that sense, their contributions should not be readily dismissed. This book, in turn, provides a model for a more productive theory of literary inscrutability in the Caribbean.

Taken together, throughout this book I examine how formal difficulty presents readers with an inventive array of receptive challenges that instigate uniquely Caribbean forms of readerly engagement. The receptive implications of inscrutability and frustration, however, do not function as a monolith in midcentury Caribbean literature. All of the chapters thus present a reading of different formal narrative strategies, and the way such texts confront a struggle to understand and make sense of forms of oppression is unique and diverse. The works I address struggle to articulate the narrative and events they seek to describe and embrace opacity as a literary device to generate a more immersive and engaging reading experience. As Boehmer's work has helped to show, such experimental narrative techniques work to "recast critique as an involvement or engagement with a text, an experience that encompasses both immersion and detachment, or, indeed an oscillation between the two" (184). In the five chapters of this book, I explore experimental narrative devices that seek to enact a sense of productive readerly frustration that more deeply reveals the nuances of colonial violence and trauma. Each chapter demonstrates how the narrative strategies at play frustrate and challenge readers to perceive the nature of Caribbean oppression in new and particularly immersive ways.

Accordingly, chapter 1, "The Politics of Interruption: Metafictive Critique and Historical Aporia in the Midcentury Jamaican Novel," examines how metafictional interruption serves as a means to prompt readerly self-reflexive analysis into the nature of colonial resistance. Highlighting a number of underexplored experimental Jamaican novels by Victor Stafford Reid, Vera Bell, and Orlando Patterson, I analyze how the novels in question both confront and manifest the gaps and impasses that stifle resistance movements and anticolonial action by presenting narratives that struggle to maintain verisimilitude and believability. In so doing, they prompt the reader to evaluate not only what they read but also what they know. In examining the struggle in these texts to posit a convincing theory of resistance, in part because of formal elements that threaten intelligibility, I thus demonstrate how textual inscrutability may engender deeper insights into the nuances of Caribbean resistance. As such, the chapter surveys an overview of largely ignored Jamaican Caribbean metafiction that focuses on protests and uprisings through a metafictive lens. Focusing what I call their "interruptive elements"—a narrative device in which the text repeatedly turns in on itself, ultimately threatening linearity and thereby creating a new kind of generative space—I suggest such works perform interminable cycles of colonial grief, in which the story is less important than the narrator's inability to tell it.

In other words, these works are locked in a dialectical process of imprisonment and emancipation, in which the fictive space they create and the resistance movements they confront are repeatedly shattered by a metafictive return to the hopelessness of the present moment. I begin with an exploration of Victor Stafford Reid's metafictional retelling of the Mau Mau rebellion in his novel *The Leopard* (1958) and then shift to an analysis of largely forgotten Jamaican novelist and poet Vera Bell. Focusing on Bell's 1971 prose-poem novel *Ogog*, I demonstrate how the novel's use of textual negation reveals the difficulties of imagining a decolonized future by urging the reader to think through the holes in its own plot. I then turn to Orlando Patterson's immensely difficult and experimental 1967 novel, *An Absence of Ruins,* underlining the extent to which Patterson's formal innovations expose the dangers of how intellectual and philosophical stagnancy in the Caribbean obviate societal progress. In rethinking the ingenuity of these works, I show how the metafictional poetics of struggle and failure they enact produce a reading experience that captures the trauma and desperation that comes with trying to imagine a history and origin free from the unbearable, overwhelming mark of colonial violence.

Chapter 2, "To Become So Very Welsh: Denis Williams's *The Third Temptation* and the Effacement of Afro-Caribbean Identity," examines how the radical difficulty of Denis Williams's underexplored second novel, *The Third Temptation,* both veils—and urges readers to see through—historical processes of Afro-Caribbean erasure. Published in 1968, Williams's novel is a highly experimental musing on identity that shares much in common with, strangely, the Nouveau Roman movement. The novel, told from multiple perspectives, embraces an experimental aesthetic rooted in repetition and confusion. Characters and events collapse into one another, and the novel provides an immensely challenging reading experience that, I argue, has distracted critics from its focus on racial oppression. As I note, since its release, the novel has been met with critical silence and is seldom addressed in terms of postcolonial or Caribbean literature, in part because of its difficulty, but also because its major characters are white Europeans, and because the novel is set in Wales. I argue that that the novel's absence of Black identity functions as a critique of Welsh colonialism, evidenced in the text both by Williams's personal experiences in Wales, and repeated, veiled images of Welsh missionary William Hughes, who worked exhaustively to convert African children into Welsh Christians. I suggest that the experimental collapse of subjectivity in the novel is designed to mirror the process by which Hughes attempted to efface African identity. Turning to a history of Hughes's Congo Institute—as well as Williams's own struggle to reconcile his role as a European artist with his Afro-Caribbean roots—I demonstrate how the novel's experimentation with perspective is enacted to examine Wales's often-overlooked involvement in colonial oppression. I thus reveal the means through which Williams's novel coerces readers to consider how legacies of colonial violence are often veiled and obfuscated.

Chapter 3, "Language as Animosity: Pejorative Language and National Identity," examines the distancing and alienating effects of vernacular language when it is rendered inscrutable. The chapter focuses on works that present difficult and abstract representations of Caribbean speech that are frequently used, within the narratives of the fictions I discuss, to other and dehumanize impoverished and disenfranchised peoples. In focusing on the pejorative language of the narrators in the works of Roger Mais and Eric Walrond, I show how linguistic difference can often function as a tool of abstraction that obscures the nature of poverty and systems of colonial oppression, and I thus consider the receptive implications of the narrators' disparaging speech on readers of the novel.

In so doing, I argue that Mais's and Walrond's notoriously difficult linguistic experiments with vernacular demonstrate a pronounced skepticism toward what I call "linguistic essentialism"—a simplistic and reductive monolithic snapshot of the poor enforced through vernacular and communal speech that is often employed by the colonial order. As I show, both writers' employment of experimental vernacular language forces readers to consider how linguistic uniformity threatens cultural plurality. I therefore examine the extent to which Mais and Walrond employ pejorative vernacular to estrange and alienate, and not to foster a greater sense of communal or national understanding. In creating difficult, contradictory, and antagonizing linguistic patterns, the two writers raise profound questions about the relationship between language and national identity that fundamentally challenge whether or not a monolithic language of the folk can or should be convincingly articulated as a national ethos. First, through a close reading of Mais's *Brother Man*, I argue that questions of monolingualism and abstraction at play in his work urge readers to evaluate the dangers of essentializing marginalized peoples under a single voice. Next, I turn to a reading of Eric Walrond's *Tropic Death*, arguing that the narrator's racist vernacular is used as a form of readerly distraction to distance readers from practices of exploitative colonial labor. Emphasizing both texts' receptive strategies, the chapter offers a new method of viewing linguistic representation in Caribbean fiction by demonstrating how Walrond's and Mais's fictions experiment with vernacular to expose the pitfalls of uncritical representations of communal speech.

Chapter 4, "'The Menace from the Bush': Abstraction and Indigenous Violence in the work of Wilson Harris and Denis Williams," examines the relationship between abstraction, difficulty, and the narrativization of indigenous struggle. Rooted in an analysis of literary representations of Guyana's indigenous populations, I focus on two writers, Wilson Harris and Denis Williams, whose work foregrounds formal innovations as a means to expose both ideological and physical violence directed at indigenous populations. I suggest that the experimental structure of their work encourages readers to adopt new methods of understanding indigeneity in Guyana by effectively unsettling, and undermining, conventional reading practices that demand new ways of seeing. I explore how such works enact a process of readerly unsettlement—a term that signals both the physical displacement of indigenous populations as well as the practice of disrupting conventional manners of reading and understanding narratives of indigenous struggle. Foundational to my argument is a rethinking of Denis Williams's concept of cultural catalysis—a theory of fractured Guyanese identity that handcuffs the Guyanese subject in a permanent state of becoming—to theorize the narrative ingenuity of Wilson Harris's early work. I then turn to an analysis of intercultural tension in Harris's Amerindian fables and Williams's own *The Sperm of God* by examining the way such works frame creole and indigenous identity in oppositional terms. Building off of Melanie J. Newton's and Shona Jackson's work on indigeneity, the chapter elucidates the degree to which the inherent formal difficulty and disorientation of such texts reveal powerful insights into the role of indigenous identity in the Caribbean

In Chapter 5, "Rhysian Disgust and the Politics of Complacency," I argue that Rhys's work struggles to render entrenched forms of oppression visible by instigating the reader to acknowledge their own complacency (and sometimes complicity) within forms of oppression. I examine how Rhys's work suggests that though the mechanisms of oppression can be discussed, they often remain inscrutable until they are felt. As such, I show how Rhys's early work aims to produce feelings of readerly disgust, guilt, and shame that make the inscrutable more explicit and present. Typically, Rhys embraces expressions of social disgust and disenchantment—expressions that are often directed at social institutions and those that would deny women and the poor agency: men, employers, the wealthy, and those that have social capital. Yet, frequently, Rhys's protagonists direct that ire at that reader, who it is assumed cannot—or will not—understand their suffering. Texts like "Hunger" and *Voyage in the Dark* implicate the reader in processes of social disenfranchisement. This rhetorical device, I argue, demands an act of reading based on self-reflexivity, in which the reader must actively negotiate the implications of their own potential investment in acts of oppression—an investment that is not always visible or evident. In unraveling this process, I show how Rhys's prose seeks to challenge complacency by demanding the reader to confront it: by making them themselves the oppressor (through the use of narrative techniques), or by cajoling the reader to see through the haze of oppressive discourse by implementing formal techniques that undermine the veracity of the narrative. In so doing, I situate Rhys's early work within a larger tradition of Caribbean writing (such as that of George Lamming and the *Beacon* group) that attempts to jostle the reader out of a sense of middle-class complacency by making visible underlying processes of disenfranchisement and oppression and inducing feelings of readerly disgust and guilt.

In addressing how such texts' formal strategies produce a receptive space that compels readers to think through the implications of colonial trauma, *Difficult Reading* points toward a new interpretation of inscrutability in Caribbean literature. By bringing to light forgotten anglophone Caribbean texts—while rethinking other key canonical works—the book demonstrates how midcentury Caribbean fiction embraces a uniquely engaging, interactive aesthetic. Thus, I acknowledge that this book is only a starting point, and it is my hope that the examination of inscrutability I discuss will open up new spaces for exploring a broader geography of inscrutable literature throughout the Caribbean.

1 The Politics of Interruption
Metafictive Critique and Historical Aporia in the Midcentury Jamaican Novel

IN AN early scene in Victor Stafford Reid's *The Leopard*—a novel that recounts the brief, fictional life of Nebu, a wounded Mau Mau warrior who is stalked, interminably, by a bush leopard that views his withered body as prey—readers are met with a single word, italicized on the page, that has a curious effect on the act of reading. The word, "*panga*," sits oddly on the page: we know not its origin, nor its etymology, only that it means, as we are told, a "long, sharp knife" (12). Readers of *The Leopard* thus confront a Swahili word, in a Jamaican novel written in English, that is marked as alien. It is a word that must be translated, and, more importantly, a word that is assumed the reader does not understand. The novel, set in Kenya in the midst of the Mau Mau rebellion, makes it clear that the setting, language, and people it represents are distant and unknown to its audience—a point that the novel reminds us of again and again. For the "*panga*" interruption is the first of many, a narrative intrusion that, no doubt, serves as an instructive moment that acknowledges the book's intended audience: the reader unfamiliar with African culture and language, and, perhaps more significantly, unfamiliar with the Mau Mau rebellion. Published just six years after the Emergency was declared, Reid, angry over representations of the rebellion in "the foreign press," composed the novel, as he argues, for largely didactic aims ("Writer and His Work" 6). Yet *The Leopard*'s setting, the East African bush, proves to be a significant obstacle, as the novel is rife with moments of metafictional interruption that struggle to translate the culture and landscape of Kenya to a contemporary Caribbean audience.

Such problems of realism, accessibility, and authenticity are pervasive in Reid's work. Almost all of his novels seek to establish linkages between historical resistance movements and life in the colonial Caribbean, as his writing highlights unforeseen corollaries and connections between marginalized peoples across the globe. Reid's novels are thus didactic and deeply invested in theories of reception. Some are written for children, while others are difficult, experimental musings on the nature of violence. All, however, are rooted in Jamaican history and acts of resistance. *New Day* (1949) and *Sixty-five* (1960) are based on the 1865 Morant Bay rebellion; *Peter of Mount Ephraim* (1971) concerns the Christmas Rebellion of 1932; and *The Jamaicans* (1976) is centered on the life of seventeenth-century Maroon chief Juan de Bolas. Yet, more so than any of Reid's other works, *The Leopard,* with its transnational focus on the Mau Mau uprising, reveals an uneasy connection between African and Caribbean resistance movements. The novel is punctuated with interruptions, asides, and explanations that repeatedly attempt to clarify and explain the African landscape in which the novel is set. Even though Reid's work is didactic, in seeking to narrate a real, concurrent event to forge a connection that is relatable to its audience, *The Leopard* is unique in toiling to maintain both its realism and authenticity, as it repeatedly severs readerly immersion by acknowledging, via textual interruption, its own fictionality. To read *The Leopard* is to be constantly confronted by a political and cultural moment that cannot easily be reconciled or understood, as textual interruptions continuously undermine the connections that the novel is attempting to make.

As I will argue in this chapter, the ingenuity of texts such as Reid's—and the narrative devices that guide them—is not rooted in their effectiveness to engender political or cultural change, or even commiseration, but, rather, in their very failure to do so. In other words, such metafictive works establish a constructive investigation into the failings of emancipatory ideologies and forces readers to evaluate—and reevaluate—the impasses and obstacles that obviate social and cultural progress and historical acts of resistance. In these texts, the reader is drawn into and implicated in the central crises of the plot. In *The Leopard,* for example, the act of reading becomes an experience of perpetual unease and distraction; as metafictive interruptions threaten immersion, the reader is constantly reminded of their own perceived ignorance of the setting and people on which the narrative is focused, and, as such, the novel's struggle to reconcile Caribbean and African resistance movements demonstrates the seeming impossibility of establishing convincing cultural connections.

Formal narrative devices, in these works, challenge the ways in which we process and understand Caribbean trauma and colonial oppression by highlighting the difficulty, and potential impossibility, of articulating an anticolonial aesthetic in linear or realist terms. Metafictive interruption thus functions in the Caribbean novel as a poetics of struggle and articulation. Accordingly, the narratives I address in this chapter produce frustrating reading experiences that capture the challenges of imagining a world free from colonial influence. Rather than viewing metafiction as an outmoded formal tendency, I argue that the metafictive techniques these novels embrace capture the nuances of midcentury Caribbean trauma in ways that are not only compelling, but also have frequently been overlooked in their ingenuity. This chapter therefore investigates the degree through which Caribbean writers employ metafictive interruption as a struggle to articulate experiences of trauma and ideologies of resistance. I begin with an examination of the interruptive strategies of Reid's *The Leopard* and then move to the work of the almost entirely forgotten Jamaican poet and fiction writer Vera Bell, whose 1971 poetic novel *Ogog* endeavors to imagine a concept of human civilization free from imperialism. I conclude by turning to an analysis of Orlando Patterson's experimental 1967 novel, *An Absence of Ruins*, a text of absolute pessimism that attempts to reconcile the hope and subsequent failure of contemporary resistance movements. Set against the backdrop of a newly independent Jamaica, Patterson's novel, through a dizzying array of formal experiments, wrestles with the very idea that both the nation and the educated middle class have failed to meet the needs of their people. In all of these works, interruptions engage the reader in an uncomfortable dialogue that forces self-reflexive critique, and this critique, enacted through frustration and severed immersion, engenders a deeper confrontation with the historical aporias that dominate Caribbean diasporic identity.

Victor Stafford Reid's Inscrutable Africa

Written four years prior to Jamaican independence, *The Leopard* is set against the backdrop of an increasingly evident global animosity toward colonial occupation. The novel encapsulates a larger discussion of competing ideologies of emancipation, particularly concerning the nature of political and physical forms of resistance. Published the same year that inaugurated the West Indies Federation, Reid's text captures the federation's complicated, mixed legacy, which, on the one hand, anticipates the hope of colonial emancipation, but, on the other, portends an ominous future of continued inequity—particularly for Jamaican citizens, many of whom felt that the federation's parliament did not fairly represent Jamaica's interest. Indeed, skepticism that the federation would lead to independence fostered a sense of both ambivalence and anger, and Jamaica's decision to leave it in 1961 ultimately led to its dissolution. While Reid's novel could not have anticipated the collapse of the federation and the larger sense of disenchantment that came along with yet another failed attempt at emancipation, his fictions reflect a sense of growing, overwhelming despair that political and legislative action will not usher in independence.

At first glance, Reid's novel appears to confront such a moment of historical uncertainty with a clear solution; thus *The Leopard* suggests that a historical understanding of other cultures, combined with a deeper knowledge of transnational strategies of rebellion, may serve as a future model of global resistance against colonial tyranny. On the surface, the novel appears to have been written to serve as a guidebook for future Jamaican resistance movements and to trace connections between oppressed peoples across the globe.[1] As Alison Donnel remarks, in "The African Presence in Caribbean Literature' Revisited: Recovering the Politics of Imagined National Co-Belonging 1930–2005," "Reid's novel is an attempt to extend an understanding of a brutal and brutalizing assault on Africa—not as a gesture of co-belonging to the ancestral homeland but as a gesture of co-belonging to the condition of unfreedom" (46). At a moment in which the federation plots a speculative, gradual method of decolonization and self-governance, Reid views the Kikuyu's violent uprising as a more effective model of resistance. The novel thus seeks to a foster a deeper understanding of colonial oppression and resistance by examining the nature of a contemporary moment of rebellion that may prove instructive to Jamaicans and those across the Caribbean fighting for their own independence. As Reid himself bluntly states, his novel aims to set the record straight and to inform his audience of the true nature of the uprising. As he argues, "Along came the Mau-Mau uprisings, rebellions, what you will, and along came the foreign press in their usual way of deciding who are the good guys and the bad guys, and making out the Mau-Mau to be the bad guys. And along came me, being very angry about all this also: how dared these fellows talk about my ancestral people like that?" ("Writer and His Work" 6). Reid's anger stems from how the press depicts the resistance movement, as the Mau Mau are typically not represented as heroic, anticolonial revolutionaries, but as immoral thugs who embrace violence for violence's sake. Essentially, Reid's stated goal is the establishment of a counternarrative, as his novel aims to sabotage colonial propaganda that obscures the atrocities carried out by the British. *The Leopard* seeks to expose the abominable violence of the colonial order—and, in so doing, frames the Mau Mau as virtuous freedom fighters that, Reid suggests, can serve as a model of resistance in the Caribbean.

The plot of *The Leopard* focuses on Nebu, a Kikuyu resistance fighter who wanders away from his party to give chase to a white colonizer who has escaped a Kikuyu raid. In the midst of his hunt, Nebu begins to notice that he is being stalked by a hungry leopard, which tracks him throughout the novel. As he traverses the bush, he begins to reflect on his former enslavement by Bwana Gibson, whose wife Nebu previously had an affair with and who has since given birth to his illegitimate child. Surprisingly, when Nebu eventually catches the fleeing colonizer, it is revealed to be none other than Gibson himself. The shock of seeing Gibson again stuns Nebu into inaction, and, in the ensuing struggle, Nebu is shot, and Gibson is killed. Before he dies, however, Gibson tells Nebu that his son is here with him in the bush, and that his life's work has been to turn Nebu's son against him. Moments before his death, he boasts to Nebu that "I have made [your son] hate you so much that he would rather die than see you live" (40). The relationship between Nebu and his son serves as a key site of tension in the novel, and, as the story continues, Nebu, who is severely wounded, travels through the bush with his son in a desperate effort to return him home to his village. Yet his son, as Gibson has warned, despises him and repeatedly sabotages their progress. All the while, the presence of the leopard grows increasingly more ominous, stalking both father and son as they move closer to their destination. Toward the end of the text, Nebu's wound begins to fester, and the coherency of the narrative quickly unravels as Nebu's hallucinations become increasingly disorienting. Eventually the leopard and British soldiers converge on Nebu and his son, killing them both—though the certainty of what has happened, or if the leopard is even real, lingers after the novel's conclusion. The implication, however, is that, despite Nebu's death, his sprit of resistance lives on, as his final act is to embrace the call of continued resistance. "Great one . . . give us long knives," he affirms, and thus he dies, but not before the novel ends with the dawning of a new day and the suggestion that his story is just the beginning of a larger fight (159).

However, this simple plot summary belies the fact that the novel is much more complex than it initially appears. After all, this is a book about inscrutability, and the frustration and obstacles that manifest when trying to articulate transgressive and anticolonial expression. Despite the relatively straightforward plot and Reid's original intent for writing the text, the novel is less a handbook for colonial rebellion than it is a complicated analysis of the difficulties that arise when attempting to establish cross-cultural networks of resistance. In this sense, what makes *The Leopard* fascinating lies not in its plot or inspirational narrative of resistance, but in its metafictional undertaking to create for its audience an accurate rendering of the Mau Mau, as its narrative tirelessly second-guesses and undermines itself through a disorienting array of formal devices. It is therefore misplaced to read the novel as a realist text—as it has typically been read—because the novel's formal strategy fundamentally questions the efficacy of realism and historical connection as a means of confronting colonial violence and resistance. *The Leopard,* to be sure, is a book about the problems and the questions that arise when negotiating between facticity, knowledge, and imagination. In other words, though Reid tended to frame the novel in interviews as a realist tale of resistance, the novel is in actuality a compelling experiment with reception and articulation that raises deeper questions about how resistance narratives can connect with their audiences. Reid's text exposes the way a realist aesthetic often collapses into misunderstanding and misrepresentation, as the narrator and narrative structure perpetually undermine the accuracy and veracity of the African landscape in which the novel is set.[2]

In fact, the novel never renders the landscape and narrative it describes as coherent or scrutable. Persistent interruptions seek to clarify the landscape for readers, but, in so doing, repeatedly fractures its realist veneer by exposing the fraught, fragile connections between Africa and the Caribbean. It is little surprise, however, that the italicized language of the text—and other sections that attempt to explain Africa—appear as moments of metafictive crisis. As Glissant has long argued, a theory of cross-cultural relation must embrace the opacity of the Other, not foster superficial connections that emphasize an articulable or reducible similarity. As he insists, writers must be wary of trivializing the potentiality of cross-cultural forms of interaction. Glissant thus argues that it could not

> be asserted that each particular culture is plainly knowable in its particularity, since its proper limit is not discernable in relation. Each particular culture is impelled by the knowledge of its particularity, but this knowledge is boundless. By the same token, one cannot break each particular culture down into prime elements, since its limit is not defined and since Relation functions both in this internal relationship (that of each culture to its components) and, at the same time, in an external relationship (that of this culture to others that affect it). Definition of the internal relationship is never-ending, in other words unrecognizable in turn, because the components of a culture, even when located, cannot be reduced to the indivisibility of prime elements. (169)

Taken this way, the aforementioned subtle intrusion of Swahili words like *boma* and *morani* that occur throughout *The Leopard* do not provide the reader with a deeper or more complex understanding of the Kikuyu, but instead call into question the idea that a few translated words or objects can foster acts of cultural understanding.[3] The novel functions as a larger analysis of cross-cultural understanding, in that it repeatedly forces readers to question what they know—and what they think they know—about other cultures and peoples. *The Leopard*'s attempt to create a convincing cross-cultural model of resistance is shown to be unyieldingly difficult, as repeated interruptions, clarifications, uncertainties, and contradictions blow holes in the text's narrative. In this way, Reid's text carefully warns readers against adopting naive theories of cultural exchange and transnational communicability.

The very potentiality of "knowing" or "understanding" Africa serves as a key point of tension in the early narrative, as the reader is reminded that they have not experienced the landscape in which the novel is set and are largely ignorant of its cultural and linguistic heritage. Thus, the novel's constant interruptions seek to explain and justify the narrative's representation through the use of italicized asides and intrusive translations. Reid's incorporation of metafictive interruption, however, is multifaceted; it does not rely simply on acts of linguistic translation. Early on in the text, for example, readers are met with a new kind of interruption, in which the second-person perspective intrudes and informs the reader of what they would have seen, had they been in Nairobi: "You would have noticed how the unshod black feet fell absolutely only upon those parts of the trail that were hard as stone after the long drought. And how the men ran with their elbows devotedly glued to their ribs" (11). On the one hand, the use of the second person is peculiar here, as it is used sparingly in the text. But its usage is made all the more important by its placement: it appears at the start of the narrative and effectively draws the reader into the scene by positing—and assuming—the reader's viewpoint. The second person tells us, as readers, what to notice, what to think, and what to feel, but, in so doing, suggests that there is a singular (or preferable) lens through which we can and should view the novel's African landscape. Such moments of interruption thereby instigate a sense of textual tension between narrator and reader, for the narrator is less concerned with giving readers the details of the landscape than explaining how they should interpret it. In other words, the interruption serves to metafictively frame the scene in terms of what is important, rather than let it speak on its own. While such scenes may seem fairly innocuous, these interruptions reveal a larger thematic focus on articulation in the novel, as the narrator constantly worries that the reader cannot visualize the Africa that it intends them to see. The constant slippages into the second person establish an uneasy relationship between the narrator and the reader, reminding readers that the narrator has failed to create a landscape that is legible without constant clarification.

In this regard, the implications of interruption in the novel grow increasingly complex, as Reid's work continuously exacerbates the textual tension between narrator and reader. Indeed, careful attention to the novel reveals that the narrator's attempt to clarify and help us understand the Kikuyu and landscape of Africa is itself a practice of abstraction and Othering. The implication that what we are seeing is what *you* would see or notice, had you been there, is made all the more problematic in chapter 2, when the narrator focuses its gaze—a gaze in which the reader is already implicated—on a "stubborn black servant" (12). The servant's refusal to work does not appear heroic, but is implied to be boorish and inappropriate; here, the novel, which seemingly champions resistance movements, turns its critique not toward the economic and colonial system that exploits the servant, but toward the servant himself, who refuses to work quietly and happily. In a similar vein, moments later, the narrative is interrupted by a brief geography lesson, as the narrator reveals that the story is set on "a mountain called Kenya (which has given the name to all the land) to the mountain called Ngong, and beyond it, is Kikuyu land. It is a land of immense folds and rolling parks. . . . The wind is hot and dry when it enters the continent . . . and they say it is like summer in Kent. . . . There are buffaloes and lions and rhinos and leopards and antelopes in the forests" (15). The tone of this passage, it should be noted, resembles a children's encyclopedia, conjuring the presence of an array of exotic animals frolicking through the wilderness in a deliberately exoticized fashion. From its start, then, the narrative appears to be framed from the vantage point of the colonizer, who, here, knows nothing of the landscape, language, or geography, and who can only reconcile the landscape in terms of being on holiday or safari. It is this colonial vantage point, which begins the novel, that the reader is drawn into. Thus, the narrator's use of the second person perspective and the incorporation of encyclopedic intrusions, combined with the frequent interruptions of vocabulary that puncture the narrative, repeatedly reminds the reader that what they are reading is alien and Other (12–13). The interruptions do not provide a clarification of African culture, but instead abstract both the Mau Mau and the nature of the conflict even further.

In fact, once readers begin to see through the narrator's colonial vantage point, they will no doubt notice that there is no attempt in his narration to clarify and articulate the human cost of colonial violence, and almost no attention is given to the question of land rights, or the suffering and starvation that accompanied the dispossession. Instead, the narrator frames the Mau Mau primarily in terms of their physicality and strange spectral unity—and it is this point, he argues, that is most important. Thus, despite Reid's initial claim that the novel is a simple attempt to set the record straight and reveal the truth of the uprising, *The Leopard* reveals a considerably more complex representation of colonial rhetoric and violence by embedding the reader within a colonial perspective and urging them to see through it. Indeed, the narrative opens with an extraordinarily reductive view of the Mau Mau and, what's more, suggests that this view is, too, the reader's view. Such a scene is therefore indicative of the larger sense of tension that seeps from *The Leopard*'s narrative structure, in which the narrator repeatedly embraces a dehumanizing view of the Mau Mau, but nevertheless affirms its observations by insisting that the reader, should they find themselves in its position, would draw the same conclusions.

In attempting to understand and provide an accurate view of the conflict, the novel challenges readers to rethink the nature of historical truth and knowledge by filtering that knowledge through a racist, distorted lens under the guise that it is an enlightened cultural perspective. Understanding and clarity, here, take on a dangerous meaning, as the narrator's emphatic but fragile and unconvincing interruptions and asides actively seek to coerce the reader to adopt troubling and reductive views of Africa and the Mau Mau. The novel, in this way, works to examine the reverberations of what happens when cultural representation is forced through a lens of scrutability and simplification. As Glissant reminds us, "Understanding cultures . . . become more gratifying than discovering new lands. Western ethnography was structured on the basis of this need. But we shall perhaps see that the verb *to understand* in the sense of 'to grasp'. . . has a fearsome repressive meaning" (27). The ingenuity of Reid's text is evident in the very idea that, in reducing the landscape to an encyclopedic description, and evaluating and insisting that the reader cannot understand Africa unless they are told how to interpret it, we can observe the novel not as a detailed articulation of a resistance movement, but as a crisis of representation, and an analysis of the way hasty and uncritical cultural comparison fails.

Shifting Perspectives and Narrative Instability

The novel's colonial narrator, however, is not a permanent fixture in the text, and *The Leopard*'s representation of the uprising becomes more complicated in lieu of its narrative's frequently shifting vantage points, which moves from the position of a colonialist narrator to that of its main protagonist, the Mau Mau warrior Nebu. Under such narrative shifts, the novel labors to maintain its inchoate vision of Africa, collapsing, via interruption, into contrasting viewpoints that constantly cancel each other out. To read *The Leopard* is to confront its tense instability, in which the competing perspectives of Nebu and the colonialist narrator clash together—often multiple times on a single page—as the text's narrative voice is seemingly unable to maintain a singular viewpoint. Moments after establishing textual norms in which the narrator's colonial perspective tirelessly intrudes upon the story to translate African culture, Nebu's consciousness begins to puncture the narrator's vantage point, destabilizing the coherence of the narrative voice and repositioning who or what the "you" described in the novel's opening moments is aimed at. The narrative, which begins by describing the Kenyan landscape (a landscape currently in the midst of genocide) through the eyes of a British tourist, quickly moves to a snapshot of colonial resistance, in which the narrator slips into the position of the Kikuyu revolutionary. The scene morphs in tone and perspective, moving from a pastoral image of a British, exoticized Africa to an act of violent revenge, shifting to a vantage point that champions the literal execution of those that hold colonialist beliefs. As the narrator describes, "If you got up close to [the pink cheeked soldiers], then it could be the duty of your knife. Some Kikuyus who had done this splendid thing spoke of how beautiful the white men became when the saw the *panga,* the long sharp knife, purse its mouth to kiss their throats. But it was only at a great sacrifice that you could get up close" (12). The rapid alternation of narrative perspectives, depicted here without any textual referent or marker, is indicative of the aesthetics of interruption in Reid's text, in which the narrative vantage point oscillates wildly within a single passage. Here, the second person at the start of the passage is not indicative of the British tourist who, ignorant of both the landscape and the conflict, imagines sunning himself on an African beach that resembles Kent, but shifts to the consciousness of the Mau Mau, who execute their oppressors unapologetically—whose very duty is to eradicate the colonizer from the landscape that they stole.

Throughout the novel, textual vantage points rapidly shift from the colonizer to the colonized, flickering in and out as well as blending together. What emerges is a disorienting process of negation in which the narrative's perspective is remarkably tenuous. Nebu's story is always subject to interruption, as the British vantage point continuously inserts itself into the narration. In the following scene, readers are briefly granted deeper access into Nebu's consciousness, as he remembers a moment of intimacy, until the scene is abruptly interrupted: "And right now he remembered the rough thrusts of the msabu's hips when she fought for him to fill her, using the rich language of her body to talk away his fears. And the unfumble of her fingers opening the blouse to offer and offer. Planting, blooming, and bursting while the rain lashed in at the window. Meanwhile, in Mombassa, in the narrow cobbled streets built by the early Arab conquerors, the Negro policemen began evacuating the children of the English soldiers from a flooded schoolroom" (23). What is striking in this passage is the degree to which a moment of sexual gratification, described vividly and from Nebu's perspective, fluctuates, within the span of a sentence, to the plight of English schoolchildren, which concludes the chapter. These rapid shifts in perspective are not isolated to Nebu's interior monologues. What we observe are conflicting intentionalities throughout the text in which the position of the colonizer vies uncomfortably with that of Nebu. This process repeatedly implicates the reader to question the veracity of what they read, as they are torn between the perspectives of the Kikuyu resistance fighters and the British colonizers. This push and pull, where the reader is literally told how they feel and what they stand for by an array of conflicting narrators and perspectives, makes *The Leopard* a text of perpetual unease and discomfort that forces readers to question their own knowledge and ethics concerning the very nature of their ability to process and understand colonial violence.

Reid's novel asks to what extent we can properly represent or access a convincing representation of a Mau Mau freedom fighter that does not essentialize or trivialize the complexity of the movement. This question becomes more important when we focus on the nature of the two previously cited examples, which focus on violence and sexuality and, in this case, seem to adhere to a narrow and simplistic snapshot of Mau Mau and African identity that filters the protagonist through the lens of sensational racist, Western stereotypes of Black bodies. Yet Reid's novel warns us that we should be suspect of its assessments by undermining the believability of its narrative voice. Early on in the text, the veracity of Nebu's narrative is put in question when it becomes clear that the text we are reading is, for all intents and purposes, an impossible narrative, as we learn that Nebu cannot speak English but nevertheless narrates his sections of the story in fluent English. The narrator's assertion that "Nebu had been (only once) to an Adult Education class at Kiambu and had seen some tribal elders stuttering over the words in the white man's book" vies uncomfortably with the fact that Nebu—and, indeed, every character in the text—speaks convincing English (31). In the scene immediately following, for example, Nebu's consciousness thinks in English: "Who saw the land in the morning, from Kilindini to where the snow flies?" (31). We know, then, that what we are reading is not the story as it appears; thus, the tension between the translated Kikuyu words in the novel and the English of the narrative makes little contextual sense, given that, here, it is revealed that Nebu knows but a few English words. This linguistic aporia forces readers to question and speculate on the accuracy of everything Nebu speaks and thinks, and the novel's definitional interruptions take on new meaning, in revealing to us that what we are reading must be, somehow, a translation, for Nebu cannot speak English, but speaks it anyway. Therefore, someone has translated the text that we are reading. Passages such as these, which remind us of Nebu's linguistic prowess, throws the believability of the narrative into question, intimating that what we are in fact reading may be a mistranslation—that there is a process of translation not marked in italics, that what we are reading is indeed a loose interpretation of Nebu's thoughts and words. This point deserves emphasis, as there is, beyond the definitional interruptions, no attention given to translation in the text, nor is there any acknowledgment of the fact that Nebu's thoughts and words are not his own.[4] The passage reveals a snapshot, buried below the textual surface of Reid's prose, of a character whose speech and language has been remade and redeployed without his consent, which furthers the tragedy of the novel. The representation of the Mau Mau the novel depicts, if we read closely, is revealed as both a textual fabrication and Western fantasy that readers are urged to see through if they are to begin to better understand the nuances of the Mau Mau. Reid's intervention, therefore, works to reveal processes of cultural misunderstanding and misrepresentation that trivialize and undermine acts of resistance.

Hallucination and the Poetics of Interruption

The poetics of interruption that dominates Reid's text forces readers to confront the obstacles that obviate forms of cross-cultural connection and commiseration by suggesting that we think more deeply about how practices of resistance and representation are framed. As such, I've worked to highlight how the novel raises larger questions about misunderstanding by constantly undermining its didactic façade. The careful tension between author and reader that the text enables through its interplay of shifting and contradictory vantage points compels readers to consider new pathways and methodologies of establishing cultural and historical connections. Such a process of rerouting and remapping is an integral component of what Antonio Benítez-Rojo, in *The Repeating Island,* has suggested is an essential aspect of Caribbean aesthetics. Yet, as Benítez-Rojo emphasizes, such acts of rerouting have larger extratextual implications. As he writes, "The Caribbean text, to transcend its own cloister, must avail itself in search of routes that might lead, at least symbolically, to an extratextual point of social nonviolence and psychic reconstitution of the Self. The routes, iridescent and transitory as a rainbow, cross at all points the network of binary dynamics extended by the West. The result is a text that speaks of a critical coexistence of rhythms, a polyrhythmic ensemble whose central binary rhythm is decentered when the performer (writer/reader) and the text try to escape" (28). While I am less interested here in Benítez-Rojo idea of psychic reconstitution, his approach, in emphasizing a polyrhythmic decentering that is made possible by the collaborative interaction between author, reader, and text, is useful here, given the novel's examination of perspective and intelligibility, which persistently asks readers to question available methods of cultural representation. Indeed, what makes *The Leopard* significant today, in my view, is its attention to the ways subaltern perspectives are interminably misrepresented, and its suggestion that there does not exist an easy way out from schemas of misunderstanding and misinformation. In this sense, Benítez-Rojo's assertion that the Caribbean text embraces the carnivalesque by engaging in "the most daring improvisations to keep from being trapped within its own textuality" echoes the novel's rethinking of representation and its metafictional attempt to sabotage its own veracity (29).

Building off of Benítez-Rojo's work, it is clear that the text's struggle with representation, textual self-sabotage, and rerouting grows more complex as the novel nears its conclusion. This struggle is complicated by the plot of the narrative itself, in which Nebu's gunshot wound drives him to hallucination, confusion, and an inability to determine where, or who, he is. Whereas the use of the second person and the novel's interruptive structure undermine readers' ability to make sense of the narrative, a third textual element, that of the hallucination, engenders an even greater sense of readerly unease. Interruptions, under the guise of hallucinations, become more frequent, and the crisis of representation becomes more overt and disorienting. As Nebu's body quite literally begins rot from the inside out, he starts to hallucinate in a fever-induced delirium. The plot of *The Leopard,* in which the leopard hunts the wounded Nebu and his son, is rooted in the very fact that, as the story progresses, Nebu, like the reader, cannot be certain of what he sees or experiences. The breakdown of form that propels the narrative to its conclusion, then, ultimately abandons the textual strategies that it establishes in its first one hundred pages. Increasing hallucinations instigate the possibility that *everything* we are reading is not simply misunderstood or misrepresented, but potentially false, as hallucinations dominate the text; we can never know exactly what has actually been said or thought. As the text concludes, the potential of misinterpretation at the hands of the narrator who represents the values and ethics of the colonizer is replaced with a larger schema of disorientation, and, in many ways, the narrative moves from a sense of implicit misunderstandings and misrepresentations to an overt, explicit erosion of time and linear space that cannot be reconciled.

In fact, the presence of hallucinations in the text obfuscates its actual conclusion, leaving us uncertain as to what has actually happened. At least initially, unclear or irrational passages are revealed and labeled in the text for what they are: hallucinations. In an early hallucination scene, for example, in which the narrator's estranged son expresses a rare moment of kindness, readers are quickly told that what they have just read is incorrect and misleading, and that Nebu had not been talking to his son at all. As the narrator informs us, "The black had been talking to a tree" (123). As the novel concludes, however, we can no longer distinguish a hallucination from an actual occurrence. In the final scene, as Nebu, trapped in a cave, seemingly confronts the leopard, jabbing his spear at it, he asks, "Whose arm are you?" of his limb, which now seems detached and alien (152). We do not know, in other words, if Nebu is actually fighting the leopard, or if the leopard is even present. In the midst of this conflict, time and space collapse, as Nebu is transported to another place, remarking how, "We burnt the papers to obtain our salt, and drank the blood of our cattle from the jugular. Our women fed on the milk of goats and bore children more numerous than the nuggets mined by the Great One in the evening sky" (153). Yet, as the leopard seemingly kills him and his son, the kill scene is replaced with an image of a British jeep firing into the cave (158). When the scene resumes, Nebu and his son are dead, and the British fill in the story that Nebu must have been "one of the loyal bucks" (159) attempting to save a white child. The battle between Nebu and the leopard—a battle that has intensified throughout the novel—thus sputters into uncertainty, hallucination, and confusion, making Nebu's act of resistance inscrutable.

At least temporarily. For it is important not to gloss over the British soldier's musing that Nebu must have been "one of the loyal bucks" (159). As the novel concludes, the soldier provides a new narrative—a new story—that effectively interrupts and replaces the narrative we have just read. As the center of authority in the text, his official report, should he make one, will no doubt articulate his perceived truth: Nebu is not a resistance fighter, but a loyal servant who died for Queen and country. He is not a Mau Mau at all. Indeed, the soldier's assessment that Nebu's quest was to save a white child from the Mau Mau returns us, momentarily, to the beginning of the text, in which the narrator asserts that the Kikuyu's stolen land is significant not because it is a site of colonial struggle, but because of its similarity to a sunny, seaside British vacation home in Kent. Meaning, once again, is evacuated, and the story as we read it is effectively canceled out, with readers witnessing the effacement of Nebu's struggle in a way that enforces the overriding, inextinguishable hand of colonialism that dominates the African landscape. By the end of the novel, Nebu's narrative is essentially absconded by the colonial order, as his consciousness, and the very story we have read, is forcibly wrested from him.

Thus, the novel, which repeatedly forces readers to question if Nebu's positions and thoughts are really his own, or whether the colonizer is speaking on his behalf, ends by further obfuscating the nature of Nebu's resistance. Despite the officer's articulation of the "real" story, Nebu, now dead, continues to assert his presence in the text's final moments, as he continues to sing, chanting "give us long knives" (159). Even in its final moments, the narrative continues to be interrupted, as the specter of the colonial subject interrupts the colonial narrative that has suppressed, and will continue to suppress, his struggle. The novel thereby ends with an overwhelming sense of disorientation and confusion as to what happened, and whether or not the narrative is accurate, as we can never be sure if the thoughts Nebu expressed throughout the novel were his own, or the extent to which they have been altered or erased. In a narrative of resistance in which the protagonist's resistance is repeatedly undermined, the novel concludes by emphasizing the degree and perversity to which the quest—and indeed, all forms of resistance—are interminably, and inevitably, misappropriated and misunderstood.

Vera Bell and the (Alternate) Historical Novel

The investigation of realism and resistance in metafictional Caribbean works such as *The Leopard*—and the kind of epistemological questions they raise—in many ways parallels a theory of postcolonial fiction explored by Hamish Dalley, in *The Postcolonial Historical Novel: Realism, Allegory, and the Representation of Contested Pasts*, that Dalley labels "allegorical realism." As Dalley writes, allegorical realism is "the manner in which interpretations of the past are produced via an oscillating process of signification in which fictional elements shuttle between abstract and singular referents. This movement links historical interpretations in ways that invite intertextual dialogue but are also ambivalent, multivalent, and disjunctive" in a way that reveals "fissured temporalities" (11). Dalley envisions a new interpretation of realism that is not realism per se, but that instead exposes disjunctions and fissures in interpretations of recorded history. Dalley's conception of a new realism insists on what he suggests is an epistemological seriousness: a plausible, serious investigation of history that may be fractured or incomplete, but is not entirely fantastic. In other words, he is critical of novels and critics that embrace the kind of anti-realist aesthetic present in such works as Salman Rushdie's *Midnight's Children* (10), in that they disengage with the larger questions of historical gaps and aporia that dominate postcolonial studies. As he states, "The contested nature of postcolonial pasts prompts novelists to frame their work vis-à-vis norms of plausibility, verifiability, and the dialogue with archives and alternative accounts" which "produces a realism rooted neither in conventional (nineteenth-century) tropes, nor in faith in the transparency of language, but in the requirement that each novel be read as a provisional interpretation of historical evidence, complete *only* in its constitutive intertextuality" (9). Under these conditions, *The Leopard*'s struggle and failure to maintain verisimilitude meets Dalley's criteria, in that the novel engages, but does not overthrow, the relationship between occluded and recorded history.

But the process of applying Dalley's theory of allegorical realism, and his new conception of a historical postcolonial novel that privileges epistemological investigation over ontological concerns, to metafictional Caribbean literature is no doubt complicated by the late work of Vera Bell. Bell's 1971 experimental prose-poem novel *Ogog* provides a history of the world through a primitive tribe whose story is an impossible historical hybridization of human development that seemingly attempts to imagine an alternate history of humankind by suggesting, and bolstering, the linguistic and cultural advancements of people deemed primitive or uncivilized. For Bell, it is a question of ontology—the very potentiality of creating a world, or any physical space, free from colonial ideology—that is, as I will discuss, the central crisis of her work. Whereas Reid's work attempts to articulate a model of resistance based on a historical event whose veracity has been obfuscated by the colonizer to the point that it has become inscrutable, Bell's aim, in *Ogog,* is to eschew history and reimagine a human civilization free from colonial domination. The novel displaces and rejects the problematics of historical fissure and speculates, instead, on what an alternative Caribbean reality might look like once the colonizer is stripped of their power. As I will show, however, the novel, which attempts to obliterate the effects of a historical reality rooted in centuries of colonial oppression, labors to imagine and create a world absent its influence, as the specter of colonial atrocity repeatedly punctures the fictional veneer of the novel's setting.

The work of Vera Bell requires some introduction. It would be unfair to say, as is the case with Reid, that Bell's work has fallen out of favor, simply because Bell's work has been ignored for her entire career. Born in 1904 in Jamaica, Bell wrote plays, poems, short stories, and one novel, but she has been almost entirely forgotten, and her works remain out of print. She is best known for her 1948 poem "Ancestor on the Auction Block," which Jahan Ramazani, in *The Cambridge Companion to Postcolonial Poetry*, argues is an "imperfect but undoubtedly electrifying poem. . . in which the modern West Indian struggles to first meet the gaze of the slave ancestor, and then to come to terms with that exchange" (20). Her short stories and poetry also appeared in *Public Opinion*, including "Sky Pilots," "My Son," and "The Bamboo Pipe" (1940), and some of her work was also included in Victor Stafford Reid's 1950 collection, *14 Jamaican Short Stories*. A brief discussion of her short story "Joshua" appeared on the *First Person Feminine* program on WOI-FM Radio in Ames, Iowa, in 1981, but, like nearly all of her writing, both the story and the discussion remain out of print. Recently, Bell's work was mentioned in the volume *Beyond Windrush*, but it was not discussed in any depth.[5]

It is *Ogog*, however, that remains Bell's most innovative work. The novel describes a confrontation between a decimated tribe and their struggle against the "roundheaded men" (7), narrated from the position of its central character, Ogog, who, as the text progresses, develops weapons, language, and communal relations that enable his rise to power. In this regard, the events of the plot are fairly straightforward. As the novel opens, Ogog tells us that his tribe has been almost entirely eliminated. The roundheaded men, who are presumably colonizers, have killed all of his people except his family, and considerable tension exists between Ogog and his brother, who has taken command of what remains of the tribe. Eventually, the tribe—who must keep moving to avoid the roundheaded men—comes upon another village, and the two tribes band together to survive "The Great Cold" (17). As the novel progresses, Ogog, who is initially physically weaker and subservient to his brother, begins to grow more powerful, and, at the end of the novel, he overthrows the Old Women who lead the tribe and becomes chief. Told in verse form and occasionally punctuated with diagrams and drawings, the novel attempts to create a universe that bears much in common to our own, but explicitly counters narratives and ideologies of Western superiority by undermining the extent to which the modern world is a product of Western culture. In other words, while the novel's historical intervention embraces what Dalley might call "anti-realism," it does so to posit a serious critique of the dissemination of history. *Ogog* imagines a reality in which peoples deemed primitive or uncivilized by Western culture are quite literally responsible for the creation of the modern world. It is Ogog and his tribe, and not the roundheaded men, who invent hunting methods, philosophy, and sign language, and, in this universe, the colonizer, seemingly, does not win. To be sure, a rethinking of the perceptions of native cultures—or cultures perceived primitive or uncivilized—is a repeated theme in Bell's writing. As George Lamming has argued, Bell's work exists "squarely at a liminal moment in the process of establishing contact with a previously objectified or fetishized Other" (quoted in Breiner 163). To expand on Lamming's point, Bell's novel is compelling in that it fosters a continuous sense of disorientation and is rooted in the reader's knowledge that the version of history depicted in the novel is incorrect—that what it describes did not happen the way it occurs in the text. Thus, *Ogog* relies on historical perceptions of indigenous peoples, and cultures deemed primitive, and repeatedly attempts to overturn them.

The text asks its readers a troubling question: How do we create a universe unaffected by the hand of imperialist practice? The narrative struggles throughout to create an alternative history not dominated by colonial power. In so doing, Bell's work depicts a frantic attempt to escape from the reality of centuries of colonial domination by establishing alternate histories and geographies outside of the historical or geographical context in which the text itself is produced. Yet the novel, as I see it, can never disentangle itself from the historical reality that produced it and, thus, its experimental elements—metafictional interruptions that comment or reveal the text as a work of fiction—highlight the seeming impossibility of creating a fictional landscape (and in some ways a literary history) outside the purview of colonial order. In what follows, I investigate Bell's struggle to articulate an imagined history free from colonial influence by highlighting how the novel repeatedly undermines the coherence of its own narrative. Certainly, the use of textual interruption in Bell's novel is considerably less overt than in works such as Reid's.

Interruption functions in *Ogog* through a series of subtle reminders that the text being told is inaccurate, or that the events of the narrative did not happen in the same way they are presented. As such, the novel's attempt to think beyond colonial domination is repeatedly called into question. Readers are forced to confront the fictionality—and, in some ways, impossibility—of alternate histories or ideologies. Therefore, the novel, as I want to argue here, both rejects centuries of colonial domination but also enforces it.

Impossible Futures and Perpetual Negation

In no uncertain terms, what makes *Ogog* fascinating is its metafictional struggle to unshackle itself from a European conception of the founding of the modern world. Though the novel attempts to imagine a world in which the colonizer has no power, its reliance on European forms of communication results in a jarring reading experience. Its fictional landscape unstable and always posed to collapse, it stands torn between an imaginative and ideally emancipating revisioning of the birth of modern civilization and a more realistic—but decidedly more bleak—reminder that the ineffable mark of colonial violence cannot be readily cast off. *Ogog*'s experimental aesthetic is thus one of perpetual negation: to read it initiates a constant reminder that the world it posits cannot and does not exist, as the novel continuously announces and affirms its own impossibility. In this way, *Ogog* begins by acknowledging that the tribe's mode of communication exists outside of a system we can perceive. It cannot be adequately represented on the page, for, as the text repeatedly reminds us, the novel, told in English, is composed through a series of thoughts and gestures that do not resemble any modern form of language, writing, or communication. This point is made evident early in the novel, in a scene in which Ogog and his men strategize making peace with a rival tribe by offering them a deer. The meeting is a tense one, as the rival tribe has fire, and Ogog fears that his peace offering will be rejected. He prepares to offer up the deer carcass, but preps his tribe for battle, should his negotiation tactics not succeed.

> there is a freshly killed deer
>   and during the night
> we collect two of the best axes
>   and two spears each
>   they have fire (11)

On the one hand, it is easy to see Bell's intent in this passage: the first real representation of the tribe captures them in a moment of careful negotiation and respect for their rivals. Violence, which Ogog and his tribe repudiate, is not the goal here; thus, we begin to see the guiding principles of the alternate universe Bell is creating, in which peoples deemed primitive show a sense of careful sophistication that suggests the world would be a better place if it was they that inherited it.

Or so it seems. Moments after this scene, we are told that the exchange we just read did not happen the way we read it: the text reveals that Ogog explained to the rival tribe that "the deer is for them" by "signs" (12). Suddenly, the strangeness of the passage becomes evident as we are informed that Ogog and his people do not have a common language, and that they lack any unified form of communication. Yet the passage we have just read is written in English verse, and it is clear that the planning the text describes does not occur the way it is represented. While the action of the novel is framed in terms of linguistic communication, in actuality it occurs through a complicated system of signs and gestures that is not English but nevertheless can only be described in English. Less than a page after a passage in which Bell frames Ogog's tribe as the virtuous bearers of a world that rejects the cruelty of its modern counterpart, the novel forces readers to confront their unreality—reminding us that this is a work of fiction, that the deeds just described are impossible—and that the narrative we are reading must be told in English, because there is no other way to tell it. Distinctions between the past and present collapse as the novel becomes less about the struggle of Ogog's tribe than about a metafictional crisis as to how to best represent them. Shortly after the scene, Ogog himself questions the usefulness of verbal communication, asking, "what are the use of words . . . you cannot use them when you are on a hunt . . . and yet could I say what I am thinking in sign language" (14). The novel, then, begins by emphasizing the impossibility of its task by problematizing the ability to read and understand the very people that are its focus while at the same time insisting that the cycle of colonial violence is unending and inevitable, as any attempt to imagine a world free from colonial oppression must rely on the language of the colonizer it seeks to critique.

Bell therefore constantly reminds readers that there may be a form of communication that exists outside of colonial history, but that imagining and articulating what that form of communication looks like is impossible. In this way, legacies of historical trauma handcuff imagination. Bell tells readers about an alternative form of communication, but can never *show* it. As such, *Ogog* is a compelling examination of the aesthetics of inscrutability. Ogog's tribe communicates primarily through gesture—and these gestures are never revealed or explained in the text in any depth. We know that they serve as the primary means of communication, but as readers we are always occluded from understanding them. While there is some unspecified verbal communication in the novel, it is secondary to sign language and gesture. Moreover, the narrator does not distinguish between verbal communication and other forms of expression. To that end, following a scene in which Ogog tells the tribe they should not try to hunt or capture a group of small animals, he remarks: "I try to tell them it is foolish" (15). Yet we know that what is happening in the text is not what actually occurred, as there is no linguistic or verbal system present in the text that can capture the communicative methods of Ogog's tribe—that is, we cannot know how exactly Ogog expresses the "foolishness" of the task. While Reid's novel urges readers to confront the fractures and fissures that emerge in simplistic acts of cultural comparison by forcing the reader to question the veracity of what they see and hear, Bell's text constantly reminds us that what we are reading is a historical and linguistic impossibility. Textual interruptions posit that the contents of the narrative cannot be effectively translated or understood, and, therefore, that our knowledge of the story will always be an incomplete approximation. As the novel proceeds, the narrative focus shifts from its attempt to create an alternative history of human civilization void of colonial violence to the more pressing concern of cultural and linguistic inscrutability.

To be sure, the inscrutability of the tribe, of which we are constantly reminded, exists outside any articulable reality. But this obfuscation and inscrutability vies uncomfortably with the stark, ever-present reality of English identity, which intrudes upon the text in an aesthetic and metafictional sense by reminding us that the alternate history the novel describes is inevitably rooted in the values and beliefs of the colonizer—values that Ogog himself gradually begins to adopt. *Ogog* is a work of overwhelming pessimism, for it reminds us that the history (or even potentiality) of forgotten peoples is doomed to misunderstanding, and, more significantly, that no worlds exist outside of the purview of British identity. Characters speak English before the advent of verbal or written communication. Worse, as the novel proceeds, Ogog himself begins to inscribe the values of a colonial authority that does not yet exist, as he grows obsessed with not simply achieving power, but manipulating and subverting the will of his fellow tribesman. He becomes increasingly selfish and egotistical, distorting the already-in-doubt sequence of his narrative for his own benefit and misrepresenting his experiences to bolster his own semblance of power. The conclusion of the novel, in which Ogog muses "PERHAPS I AM A GOD"—after he is told by his fellow hunter Gerd that "everything comes from . . . gods"—is significant in that Ogog's rise to power is based on stolen and absconded labor (65). Repeatedly, his success comes from accidents or happenstance, not from strength or cunning. Although many of the animals he kills are largely due to luck or accident, Ogog frames himself as a hero and distorts the nature of his struggle for personal gain, acknowledging at one point that "it is a good thing my dog cannot talk" because he knows that his reputation is built on lies (32). When another tribesman teaches him how to bake bread, he boasts, "I have found it all out for myself," and then forces the women to gather the supplies and carry out the process of making it, noting, "all of it work the women must do" (61). His strength, then, is exploiting his peers' labor. Toward the end of the novel, he acknowledges: "I know these things but I must make others do them / like I make the young men do the running in the hunt" (65). The novel, then, is less about the humanization of a people and tribes perceived as primitive, and more about the gradual evolution of communal peoples into schemas of colonial and imperialistic ideology.

While, on the surface, the text humanizes the tribe and provides an alternate history of the world, the novel is not a narrative of empowerment. In this sense, the utter lack of critical attention directed at Bell's work, troublingly, leaves its dust jacket as one of the scant commentaries available on the text that, it is worth noting, argues that the novel is a narrative of ancestral empowerment and inspiration. Bell's book, it asserts, "tells us of the birth of civilization—or perhaps it is only a rebirth of civilization. . . . In each of us, born among ancient traditions and tabus, is the necessity of fighting free of the past into a future that we may make ourselves." The actual future depicted in the novel, however, is not one of rebirth or hope, but of grim potentiality, as Ogog's achievement is, essentially, to learn how to exploit and abuse his own people. The narrative we are told is not so much an alternate history of empowerment, but an alternate history of enslavement, in which empowerment and enlightenment quickly collapse into disenfranchisement.

In a text rife with moments of uncertainty and contradiction—and passages that defy logic or clarity—by the end of the novel Ogog's development is unmistakably clear, placing him in a position of unmitigated power and superiority in which he privileges the individual over the communal and, further still, deifies himself as a "GOD" to whom all are subordinate. The novel ends on a bleak note, with Ogog's rise to power leaving him corrupted, deluded, and dangerous. As the text concludes, Ogog, convinced that he can predict the future, believes that he has seemingly supernatural powers, and it is all but certain that his rule over the tribe will be tyrannical. Indeed, by its conclusion, the hope of a counternarrative of colonial resistance has vanished, as Ogog submits to the seemingly inevitable, inescapable lure of power and exploitation. Such an observation no doubt reminds us of Frantz Fanon's contention that colonial authority is rooted in the embrace of an individualism that denies the efficacy—or very notion—of collective action and resistance as, unavoidably, Bell's novel ends with a familiar refrain: domination at the hands of an individual pursuit of power.[6] Despite the dust jacket's assertion that "Vera Bell, steeped in the lore of archeology, sees glory in man's destiny. There is no excuse, *Ogog* demonstrates, for the human race to be condemned to slavery to old fear and limitations"; the novel fails to provide a sustainable alternative to colonial rule, ultimately creating a reality not unlike the history it seeks to challenge. The text reveals the extent to which representations of the subaltern collapse into familiar stories, with its inability to imagine a narrative that does not end in the explicit, unrelenting oppression of native peoples.

Ogog depicts a fascinating tension between history, realism, and imagination, as Bell's novel continuously fails to create a landscape free from the lingering, perpetual effects of colonial horror. Its ingenuity is not found in its attempt to create a believable alternative history extricated from colonial rule, but in its struggle and subsequent failure to rupture entrenched colonial narratives in productive ways. The tribe exists only in a sea of contradictions and negations, their unique presence flickering in and out, threatened by a series of textual interruptions that undermine their reality and believability. Seemingly, the only feasible end is one that has already been written, in which native peoples surrender and are forced to accept colonial values; in this regard, the novel reveals the ease with which colonial ideology destabilizes and infects indigenous and native populations. *Ogog* thereby challenges Dalley's notion that the historical novel may reshape "contested pasts," particularly because what makes Bell's novel such a compelling site of tension and anxiety is its inability to contest the past at all: indeed, an alternative conception of the past, it seems, leads always to the same present.

As should be clear from this discussion of Reid's and Bell's work, the landscape of metafictional interruption at play in late 1960s and early 1970s Jamaican fiction is resoundingly bleak. As the hope of the West Indies Federation quickly died—and independence was achieved, but as a commonwealth nation—texts like Bell's and Reid's acknowledge the fact that newly independent Jamaica failed to create a more equal society excised from British influence and domination. Building off Brathwaite's concept of frustration in Jamaican fiction, in "Radical Skepticisms: Literatures of the Long Jamaican 1960s" Donette Francis argues: "Jamaican fiction published in the 1960s was fundamentally pessimistic but nuanced in its discrepant varieties. . . . the heterogeneous nature of the decade's literary pessimisms to argue for a sensibility of radical skepticisms that utilized critical distance *to cast doubt on the past, the present, and the very idea of single-island sovereign futures*. Radical skepticisms reveal that there was not a uniform nationalist romance about what independence signified. Instead, diverse writers entered the 1960s at a critical juncture, with frustration, reservation, and doubt as a foundational core" (48; emphasis added). Hence we might say that Bell's and Reid's sense of frustration and pessimism is a temporal crisis, one that cannot convincingly imagine a past, or an alternate future, free from colonial oppression. In Reid's novel, the overwhelming, frantic struggle to connect Caribbean oppression to Mau Mau resistance falls into misinterpretation and misunderstanding; the novel does not embrace the virtue of cross-cultural connection as a form of shared resistance but emphasizes instead the many ways in which it fails. Similarly, *Ogog* presents an alternate universe entirely unable to free itself of the violence of imperialism: by the end of the novel, the only certainty is that Ogog will brutalize and exploit his fellow man. His evolution, if it could be called an evolution at all, is one of immense violence: he has learned to lie, cheat, manipulate, and deceive.

Both novels, then, point to what Francis might call a vision of an "impossible future" in the face of an independence movement that, seemingly, did not emancipate. As Francis writes, "Jamaican writers did not have a homogeneous idea of, or desire for, 'the nation-state'; and in fact, with hopes of federation fading, many questioned the very project of independent state sovereignty and offered differing responses about what was on the horizon. For some, the demise of federation meant impossible futures for developing third world economies; for others, it was the internal and intimate racial, ethnic, and class hierarchies within national, communal, and diasporic formations that proved the impasse" (48–49). This notion of impasse and missed opportunity guides the aesthetic of interruption that dominates both texts, serving as a constant reminder that, somehow, there must be a way out or a path forward. Yet the failures of the past hang over the present, intruding upon it and occluding the potentiality of a future not dominated by oppression and disenfranchisement. It is this very notion of crisis and indecision that emerges toward the end of *Ogog*, as he, confronting other hunters for the first time, imagines another way and senses a bifurcated path. Drawing a line in the sand with a stick, he has a sudden epiphany: his path is not set. He can go one way, or the other. As he ponders,

> if I can tell them things with my hand
> > why cannot I with marks on the ground
>
> if I put a stick to point the way I have gone
> > no
> I could have gone that way or the other way
> > ah (47)

Ogog's choice, however, matters little—even in an alternate universe, his fate will be the same—and, indeed, by the end of the novel, he is an unrelenting tyrant who exploits and oppresses his own people without remorse. The overwhelming pessimism of this scene, in which Ogog imagines an alternate pathway, one that might lead not to inevitable suffering and exploitation and that, of course, can never be fulfilled, provides a particularly bitter commentary on the state of modern Jamaica. The bleakness of the contemporary moment in which the text was written most assuredly did not escape Bell. Set against the historical backdrop of a newly independent nation struggling to rectify problems of social and racial inequity, readers are forced to watch as Ogog embraces a path of imperialist violence that seems unavoidable, as the hope of an alternative future meets the same fate that it desperately sought to avoid.

Rethinking Metafiction in Caribbean Fiction

In many ways, the texts discussed in this chapter compel us to think more deeply about the relationship between metafiction and colonial—and postcolonial—identity in the Caribbean. Attention to Caribbean metafiction, especially in the mid-twentieth century, has waned, but a theory of inscrutability allows us to revisit its broader implications for a Caribbean aesthetic. I want to argue here that the kind of metafiction we see in Reid's and Bell's works is distinct, structured through a kind of subtle interruption that makes it significantly different in scope from what Linda Hutcheon has called "historiographic metafiction."[7] As Hutcheon writes, "Historiographic metafiction . . . keeps distinct its formal auto-representation and its historical context, and in so doing problematizes the very possibility of historical knowledge, because there is no reconciliation, no dialectic here—just unresolved contradiction" (107). In referencing Hutcheon's work, my point here is not to recycle the now-tired debate between postmodernism and postcolonialism—a topic that has been long debated and explored.[8] Rather, I want to emphasize the extent to which the Caribbean metafiction explored in this chapter diverts from common analyses of postcolonialism and experimental form.

Far be it from problematizing the possibility of "historical knowledge," what is interesting about texts such as Reid's and Bell's is the degree to which colonial rhetoric sabotages any articulation of an alternative history of subaltern struggle. There emerges, in such works, no sustainable counternarrative. We can observe this point in *The Leopard,* which fails to provide a cogent narrative of Mau Mau resistance and leads, instead, only to frayed endings and potential interpretations that further exacerbate aporia. Bell's work is similarly unable to imagine a historical reality free from the crippling effects of imperial ideology. Indeed, both texts depict a historical reality that can be neither escaped from nor resisted. As Hutcheon has argued, historiographic metafictional novels "openly assert that there are only *truths* in the plural, and never one Truth; and there is rarely falseness *per se,* just others' truths" (109). Such texts, she argues, captures the "failures of recorded history" (114). But the metafictive interruptions of *Ogog* and *The Leopard* do not ultimately challenge recorded history so much as reveal the extent to which colonial forces dictate that very history; these texts do not struggle to "assimilate" historical "data" (4) but reveal the unavoidable conclusion that the truth we receive is always filtered through the lens of the oppressor.[9] In the case of *The Leopard,* the British soldier's interpretation of Nebu's quest is, of course, a grotesque distortion of the facts; nevertheless, the soldier's version will become the official version of the narrative's events. There is no means to challenge or overturn that telling.

History, then, in such novels, is firmly established and is, in many ways, a burden that is impossible to overturn. In this regard, historiographic metafiction of the kind Hutcheon describes provides a considerably more overt, explicit challenge to history, whereas Bell's and Reid's works yearn but fail to muster a counternarrative against a reality of oppression that is firmly entrenched. In addition, the experimental elements of both novels are considerably less explicit than other works of historiographic metafiction, such as Rushdie's *Midnight's Children* or G. V. Desani's *All About H. Hatterr.* What I want to suggest is that the historical confrontation evident in Caribbean metafiction operates on a decidedly more minimalist scale—a pinprick as opposed to a rupture. Acts of interruption signal a brief, momentary site of resistance and retelling that is almost immediately swallowed back into the larger narrative. Interruption reveals flickers of momentary resistance that do not so much overtly confront the nature of history but instead highlights how colonial history always overshadows the visibility of its alternatives. Such texts capture a distinctly Caribbean form of resistance, in that they cannot muster the kind of sweeping historical critique Hutcheon associates with historiographic metafiction.

In much the same way, these texts are not recuperative or restorative; they are not a branch of metafiction that Ahmed Gamal, in his essay "Rewriting Strategies in Tariq Ali's Postcolonial Metafiction," calls "postcolonial metafiction." As Gamal defines it, "Postcolonial metafiction is that type of self-reflexive fiction that fundamentally espouses non-mimetic narrative strategies usually embraced by indigenous literary texts to engage with the problematics of writing about Third-World postcolonial history. Postcolonial metafiction could be said to have two major characteristics: 1) the deconstructive interrogation of the factuality of colonial history, document, and otherness; and 2) the reconstructive mode of recuperation of native language" (6). In contrast, Reid's and Bell's works *attempt* to challenge the factuality "of colonial history," but instead end up highlighting the interminable difficulty of creating worlds outside of the vantage point of colonial history; they do not muster a recuperation of what has been lost. In *The Leopard,* Kikuyu speech is pedantic and definitional; it reveals nothing of the nuances of language it seeks to represent. The Kikuyu in the text does not restore or recuperate a suppressed language: it marks the impossibility of its own authenticity once embedded in a colonial context. The form of Caribbean metafictional interruption at play here is one that functions quite differently than that described by Gamal and Hutcheon, in both scope and strategy. Mid-twentieth-century Caribbean metafiction's approach to history is not restorative; rather, it reveals the degree to which sustained resistance seems impossible and collapses under the weight of entrenched forms of colonial oppression.

Orlando Patterson and the Interruptive Fiction of Despair

In the face of an aesthetic that privileges interruption and negation to expose the despair and frustration that accompanies failed acts of resistance, it seems appropriate to conclude this chapter with an analysis of perhaps the most nihilistic Caribbean novel of the twentieth century: Orlando Patterson's *An Absence of Ruins.* Patterson's second novel, published in 1967, is a scathing, intellectual takedown of the bastions of twentieth-century Caribbean literature and philosophy filtered through a disorienting, experimental lens. Before examining the methods through which Patterson's use of experimental forms confronts the bleakness of a newly independent nation, it is useful to consider the ways Patterson's fictions have—and have not—been previously addressed. Perhaps more than the work of any other author addressed in this book, Patterson's criticism requires little introduction; his 1982 text, *Slavery and Social Death: A Comparative Study*, remains a monumental achievement in illuminating the psychology and practices of enslavement. Yet Patterson's work as a cultural theorist at Harvard has largely overshadowed his fiction, which has been mostly forgotten. While Patterson's critical work is not without controversy and debate, his novels—*The Children of Sisyphus* (1965), *An Absence of Ruins* (1967), and *Die the Long Day* (1972)—also generated considerable controversy on release, a point that is most evident in the bitter public dispute between Patterson and fellow Jamaican novelist John Hearne, who was so incensed by Patterson's writing that he accused him of being "an intruder" in the Caribbean literary scene and not a real novelist. Hearne's unwavering anger toward Patterson emerged predominantly over a question of form and style, as Hearne argued that Patterson's emphasis on sociology led to the emergence of an aesthetically irresponsible, "corrupt," anti-realist "sociological" fiction (70).[10]

My point is not simply to regurgitate Hearne's critique of Patterson, nor is it to debate the place of sociology in Patterson's work (a topic recently explored by George Steinmetz's "Sociology and Sisyphus: Postcolonialism, Anti-Positivism, and Modernist Narrative in Patterson's Oeuvre") but to examine the nuances of experimental form and inscrutability in his complex and understudied novel *An Absence of Ruins*.[11] Taking Hearne's observation that Patterson's novels contain an "extraneous" element that undermines their realism, I contend that Patterson's second novel deliberately eschews questions of realism in an effort to undermine the very kind of narrative form that Hearne champions (78).[12] More specifically, I read Patterson's use of metafictional interruption in *An Absence of Ruins* as an experimental attempt to critique Caribbean philosophical and intellectual communities, in that the novel repeatedly exposes the inefficacy of these communities to enact lasting social change. Thus, while Reid's and Bell's works attempt to negotiate the historical effects of cross-cultural colonial trauma in terms of both historical and imaginary acts of resistance, Patterson's work confronts the present directly, by dismantling the perceived shortsightedness of burgeoning ideological forms of resistance throughout the Caribbean. The novel aims to uncover intellectual modes of emancipation that Patterson finds ineffective by metafictively sabotaging their clarity and convincingness through a narrative strategy that embraces interruption and, in doing so, encourages the reader to evaluate both the sustainability and viability of contemporary forms of resistance.

Exhaustingly, Patterson's novel regurgitates Caribbean ideologies of resistance and emancipation—and also explicitly references seminal Caribbean literary texts—but, in nearly every instance, does so solely to mock and repudiate them. Patterson's novel, sometimes compared to *Ulysses* due to its intertextual structure (Poynting 6), creates a venerable roadmap of Caribbean art and literature in the twentieth century, but is rooted in an aggressively experimental metafictional structure that undermines the truthfulness and realism of the world it creates. *An Absence of Ruins* is rife with intertextual references; the novel makes frequent allusions to George Lamming—particularly *The Pleasures of Exile*—Roger Mais, John Hearne, Frantz Fanon, and Aimé Cesaire, among many others.[13] And, as Jeremy Poynting points out, the novel has frequently been misread, in part because of its parodic, intertextual composition. As Poynting notes, "The parody is done so faithfully and exactly that contemporary reviewers missed it" (8). Concerning its plot, the novel is difficult to summarize: characters and vignettes often contradict each other, the perspective shifts from the third to first person, and much of what we read is seemingly from the main character's metafictional diary or novel. In short, the novel focuses mostly on the plight of ex-academic Alexander Blackman (sometimes referred to as "Richard"), who has recently returned home to Jamaica from London, where he held a teaching position. Early in the novel, Blackman pays a visit to his former friends and colleagues, a cabal of socialists and intellectuals, but the meeting with the group leaves him feeling surprisingly "cold" and disenchanted (65). Blackman, severely depressed and now uncertain of what he believes, drifts aimlessly throughout the novel's Jamaican landscape, writing in his diary and trying to make sense of the world. Unable to find a purpose, he eventually decides to fake his own death. However, it is not the depressing plot that makes the novel marvelously strange and compelling, but, rather, its experiments with metafiction and interruption and its intertextual critique of Caribbean literature and theory. Significantly, reviewers and many critics have missed not only the subtlety of the novel's parody of Caribbean works but also the nuances of its "metafictional strategies" (8).[14] In this regard, it is not surprising that Patterson's novel, published just a year before Denis Williams's *The Third Temptation*, is perhaps one of the most overtly experimental Caribbean texts of the twentieth century, and, like Williams's novel, it, too, has largely been ignored or misread.

While the novel most assuredly *has* been misread, it is not simply because of the complexity of Patterson's references, but due to the disorienting array of interruptions that not only sever linearity, but also mock the very potentiality of any form of effective social or ideological resistance. The text is thus a confrontation with cohesion that leads, ultimately, to readerly frustration. It narrates a consistent struggle to simply tell a story and maintain a consistent ideological position. In other words, both plot and characters in Patterson's novel collapse into uncertainty and contradiction. Readers are met with three major obstacles early on. First, Patterson's text embraces overt metafictional interruption—interruption that is much more explicit and unavoidable than was the case in Reid's and Bell's work. The narrative frequently stops and starts; scenes are abruptly canceled out, become "diary" entries or dreams, or begin in medias res and left largely unclear. It is therefore difficult for the reader to situate where they are in the narrative, or even what is happening. Second, the protagonist, Alexander Blackman, is less a character than a sketch of conflicting behaviors and ideologies. At various points, Blackman is a well-regarded intellectual that, in some ways, resembles Patterson himself, but, at other points, he is an infantilized, babbling buffoon. In these scenes, his behavior, thoughts, and speech express explicit comic naivete to the point of absurdity. The protagonist is a constant source of annoyance, never becoming a developed character and existing solely as a bizarre series of contradictions. The novel's frequent interruptions, combined with its wildly inconsistent protagonist, fosters a sense of continuous distraction that produces a notable sense of readerly frustration. Third, the narrator's intended audience frequently changes (as Patterson's experimental novel does not maintain a singular or clear audience), and the focus of the narrator's ire frequently changes and is often inconsistent. On the one hand, the novel seems to be written for an educated, middle-class Caribbean audience, but, on the other, Patterson's text assumes that the reader is ignorant, unaware, and in some ways distrustful of the references it makes. Thus, whereas Reid's and Bell's work seems to confront the general reader, Caribbean or otherwise, in an attempt to urge a deeper reflection on the nature and mechanics of colonial oppression, Patterson's text confronts—and often antagonizes—multiple audiences. Taken together, it is not difficult to imagine why the novel has been mostly ignored: its difficulty and uncertain audience, combined with its antagonistic metafictional interruptions, produce a frustrating experience for the reader.

The sense of frustration and interruption that guides the novel, however, is ultimately a confrontation of what I want to argue is a desperate attempt to narrativize any meaningful ideology or narrative of effective resistance, as well as to express a deeper skepticism with the idea that contemporary Caribbean literary and intellectual communities are posing an effective threat against the colonial order. Patterson's novel coerces readers into feeling this skepticism and frustration. Hence, readers confront an interminable series of failures: nothing maintains its consistency or effectiveness. Patterson's citation of Caribbean literature, and the collapse, as we will see, of almost every narrative vignette into an unbelievable series of contradictions, creates an overbearing sense of frustration and failure that parallels Patterson's larger critique in the novel: that the burgeoning Caribbean canon of literature and theory has failed to hold any resonance or enact any permanent sense of social change. Consequently, the novel presents an overwhelming discourse of failure: failed resistance, failed unification, and extant, fleeting theories of emancipation that can never maintain or establish any effective form of social efficacy. Patterson weaponizes his frustration with Caribbean literature and theory and turns it onto the reader, forcing them to confront what he views as a broken trajectory of crumbled forms of resistance. The text asks readers to confront the implications of their own annoyance and, what is more, prompts critical reflection on the state of Caribbean aesthetics. It asks us, in its serious but mocking tone, to evaluate the convincingness of Caribbean aesthetics and philosophy—but, more importantly, it pushes readers to question whether or not such theories of resistance are ultimately effective in confronting and overturning forms of colonial power.

The Politics of Emotional Interruption

The opening scenes of Patterson's *An Absence of Ruins* firmly—and boldly—establish the textual prerequisites that will guide its narrative—namely, that every moment and action in the text is subject to ridicule, erasure, and interruption, and that no story or ideology is free from critique and censure. Indeed, censure and skepticism is the novel's guiding axiom. The early moments of *An Absence of Ruins* present a narrative that ridicules readerly expectation by first establishing and then undermining a moment of emotional crisis; the first chapter of the text affirms that we cannot take what we see or read at face value. The text begins in medias res, starting with an ellipsis in which the narrator "stands with his forehead pressing on [his] arm which was creased against the mango tree," deeply entrenched in an existential crisis (37). Parodying Sartre's *La Nausée*, the narrator articulates a feeling of crushing isolation and loneliness, noting that he can feel nothing and is "lost in the oblivion of [his] being" (38). He continues, "I was simply there. A crude animal thing, outside of time, outside of history, outside of the consciousness of other beings. I was just there" (38). The text, then, starts akin to many other postcolonial and Caribbean novels: with a moment of suffering in a world out of joint. Expectations are thus firmly set. The narrative will reveal the cause of the protagonist's trauma and surely confront the nature of life in Jamaica and the circumstances that enable his suffering.

Yet Patterson's novel reveals none of those things. The protagonist's suffering does not become a central plot point of the novel, but an object of derision. He is quickly revealed as a fool: his pain, far from an authentic snapshot of human suffering, is absurd and stupidly mollified. He needs only a swig of beer to fill the void in his soul: "As I walked I kept remembering all the advertisements for Red Stripe beer. I believed it all now. Anything that would fill, if even momentarily, the vacancy within me; anything that would end the crippling sense of indecision that was becoming increasingly unbearable. And why not a Red Stripe beer? They said on the radio that it was a man's drink. I knew at least that I was a man—so there, it was something meant for me. . . . I would be satisfied at least" (39). While the beginning of the novel sets up an explicit psychological and interpersonal crisis, this crisis quickly collapses into parody, as what the narrator experiences is not a feeling of societal disenfranchisement—or even depression—but thirst, and he is satiated, at least briefly, by a beer that will fill him and "make him a man" (39). He is only briefly appeased, however: immediately after taking his fourth sip of beer, he spits it in "revulsion" and disgust onto the barmaid, who responds with violence. The stupidity of the scene—the existential crisis solved by, or presumed to be solved by, a beer advertisement—is heightened by the thoroughly unsympathetic narrator, who, as the chapter proceeds, continuously boasts about his intellectual superiority. He ridicules the masses for all wearing "the same mask" and dancing with "meaningless contortions of abandonment," while he himself lacks the insight to see through a vapid beer advertisement (41). The next scene is equally frustrating, as the narrator attempts to bed a prostitute, but cannot perform. He harshly critiques her appearance, forcing himself to try "to believe, to understand—a woman, a whore, a beast with two legs, to arms, two breasts" (45). Predictably, the narrator blames his impotency on the prostitute and not on himself; thus, the image we see, at the end of the chapter, is that of a character who is bitterly critical of the world around him, but comically blind to and ignorant of his own faults. By the end of this opening vignette, we observe a character who is self-assured but, above all, annoying and contradictory. He, and the existential crisis he is enveloped in, is a farce.

The opening scenes of the novel are the first of many scenes that cite aesthetic and philosophical theories only to quickly demolish them. Here, Patterson situates Sartre as a central figure to analyze disenfranchisement in the Caribbean; indeed, we can imagine a narrative that interweaves Sartrean existentialism within crises of colonialism. In this way, the novel begins by using La *Nausée* as an interpretive lens, but discards the motif early on, as it proves an ineffectual method to explore Caribbean identity. Thus, Patterson's novel expands—and, in many ways, explodes—the central premise of Reid's *The Leopard* by not simply confronting one potential method of colonial resistance, but many. Whereas Reid explores the potentiality of cultural commiseration in terms of forms of resistance, Patterson confronts a seemingly endless array of philosophical and literary principles that are furiously incorporated and discarded. Effectively, this makes the novel less a narrative than an experiment, one that tirelessly confronts methodologies to disarm colonial ideology.

Yet the novel's use of parody, effacement, and ridicule is furthered by its primary formal device: metafictional interruption. In terms of its plot, *An Absence of Ruins* is skeptical of ideological theories of emancipation and deliberately attacks and ridicules them, creating a sense of continuous textual unease. These attacks are complicated by interruptions that challenge the narrative veracity of what occurs in the novel. At the end of the first chapter, for example, the protagonist's first-person narration suddenly ends and is replaced by a new, third-person narrative that reveals that everything we have been reading did not actually occur, but was the diary—or dream—of another character, whom we have not yet met. In this scene, the first-person narrator, interrupted by his mother, suddenly snatches "himself out of bed," and the narrative position quickly shifts to the third-person perspective:

> Suddenly I felt sick. I snatched myself out of the bed and . . .
> "Richard!" he heard his mother calling.
> "Yes!" he answered impatiently.
> "Darling, it is time for you to get some sleep."

> He looked round and saw her standing at the door. She was a tall, stout, dark-brown woman with short hair who looked remarkably like Bessie Smith. Her expression was kind, concerned and slightly curious as she looked at him.
> "I'll soon turn in, Mam; honestly, I just want to finish this thing . . ."
> "Is it your diary?"
> "Yes."
> "Seems more like a book you're writing." (45)

This shift, from the first person to the third, is the first of many such shifts in the text, and Patterson's experiments with form consistently unsettle readerly expectations by sabotaging the veracity of the present moment, frequently changing the point of view or narrative perspective in an abrupt, jarring fashion. In this sense, this textual shift in perspective further problematizes the mock existential crisis that it interrupts. What we have previously read is not the "real story" per se, but a potential memory of "Richard," who, here, chastised by his mother, seems infantile and immature, but in a considerably less confident manner than the protagonist that emerged at the beginning of the text. Therefore, the existential crisis, along with its subsequent mockery and erasure, is itself canceled out by the interruption, suggesting that we should not take what we have previously read seriously.

Further, Richard's mother's assertion that what he is writing does not seem like a diary at all but "more like a book" metafictively complicates the nature of the text, in that we are unsure if what she is referring to is actually her son's diary or the very book we are reading. The lines between fiction and reality are continuously blurred, and Richard's mother soon begins to merge with an image of Bessie Smith, to whom he compares her, and whose song "Young Woman Blues" is quoted as an epigraph at the start of the novel. As Avis G. McDonald argues, in "The Crisis of the Absurd in Orlando Patterson's *An Absence of Ruins*," "The liberally sprinkled epigraphs and allusions through *An Absence of Ruins* encourage a hunt for sources and parallels" (94). While it is clear, then, that the text is built upon the citation and repudiation of literature and theory, it continuously disrupts the consistency of its own form, thereby creating a self-reflexive structure that is hesitant to adopt any fixed or permanent position.

I do not mean to suggest, however, that Patterson's novel is politically unengaged, or that it champions a kind of postmodern chaos, nor does it approach the kind of destructive anti-realist aesthetic that Lazurus, in *The Postcolonial Unconscious Novel*, disparagingly labels "pomo-postcolonialism" (34). As Lazurus argues in an interview with Sorcha

Gunne, "The 'pomo-postcolonialist' tendency has led to a hypostatisation of certain formal aspects in literary works (self-consciousness, contingency, a stress on incommensurability and the failures of language to signify, etc.)" (5). Yet, far from a typical reliance on self-consciousness and incommensurability, Patterson's novel encourages, and in some ways demands, that readers think through the fault lines of Caribbean aesthetic development. By forcing the protagonist to endlessly adopt and regurgitate a myriad of different Caribbean ideologies, theories, and aesthetics, *An Absence of Ruins* functions as less of a novel than as a series of counterarguments against stale theories of emancipation. In sum, the novel proposes an ever-active, evolving method of resistance that highlights the danger of intellectual stagnancy.

Frustration as Intellectual Crisis

The novel's interruptive strategy—which persistently undermines the consistency and believability of its highly educated protagonist by forcing him to revert to puerile behavior and actions—is indicative of what Patterson views as an intellectual crisis in the Caribbean. Opposing ideologies of resistance do not simply paralyze but ensnare him in a perpetual state of adolescent becoming that engenders only disorientation, confusion, and anger. As McDonald argues, the protagonist's "crisis is riddled with paradox and contradiction. In his primal experience of the Absurd, at Green Bay, he feels trapped by the sea and sky—the least confining elements in nature. He experiences a loss of connection between desire and fulfillment, yet still has a desire for desire and for fulfillment. He lacks commitment, yet cannot achieve a detached life. He desperately searches for a sense of purpose, but convinces himself that there can be no purpose" (93). I want to further consider the intellectual implications of the inability of the protagonist—who, it should be noted, is a respected academic—to articulate a consistent ethos or worldview, torn as he is between ideological positions that never fit or remain stable. The degree to which he is locked in a kind of adolescent stasis, from which he can break free momentarily, only to revert back to juvenilia, is evident from the start of the novel. His ontology proves inconsistent and uncertain, and his behavior is frequently erratic and contradictory, at times cartoonishly juvenile, submissive, or even infantile. For example, the novel's first metafictive interruption, in which the narrator is woken by his mother, ends with a wet dream in which he stares "in disbelief" at his "pool of semen" covering the sheets (49). The juxtaposition in this chapter—which begins with a Sartrean existential crisis in which the narrator struggles to find philosophical meaning in the world and ends with a character surreptitiously masturbating while his mother prays in the "other room"—oscillates wildly between a narrative of mock existential torment and one of teenage sexual awakening (49). The start of the narrative, which begins with an investigation of psychological and emotional trauma is not simply canceled out, as previously discussed, but becomes little more than an adolescent masturbatory fantasy.[15]

We can trace this pattern—in which the lure of serious philosophical and academic investigation always collapses as the novel reverts to scenes of juvenile frustration or resentment—throughout the novel. Early on, the focus on existentialism is discarded to focus on beer and sex. Later, the diary Blackman writes evaporates as he ejaculates, and, embarrassingly, he is left to confront the shame of staining his mother's sheets. In a key scene toward the end of the novel, Blackman fakes his own death in a comic act of stupidity, and the fake suicide attempt leads to the tragic, inadvertent death of his mother. The scene is made stranger, however, by Blackman's bizarre fear of his uncle, who lurks over him like a disappointed father figure and infantilizes him with his criticism (133–36). Yet, as we learn from the obituary published after his fake suicide, Blackman has his doctorate, is a university professor, and is esteemed by his colleagues both in Jamaica and abroad—a point, of course, that makes his current and past behavior all the more unlikely. As the obituary reveals, "Mr. Alexander Blackman" completed a doctoral dissertation at Oxford on "The Contribution of the Negro to Western Civilisation," and he taught in both England and at the University of the West Indies (129). While the obituary curiously remarks that Blackman has recently become "disillusioned" with "the human condition," this disillusionment seems far different than the kind of baffling incompetence and idiocy of Blackman, who, following his mother's death, is terrified by the ire of his authoritarian uncle to the extent that he seems more an adolescent boy than a prestigious academic (129). In other words, readers confront a series of unlikable, largely selfish versions of the same protagonist who are constantly revised and rewritten, who lack a clear history or consistent identity, and who are in a constant state of infantile regression that is itself frustratingly unclear and, moreover, vies with the protagonist's stature as a public intellectual.

The extensive revision and inconsistencies of the protagonist in the novel signal Patterson's displeasure with the failure of academic and intellectual communities to serve as a means of positive social change.

Accordingly, Blackman's unlikely but explicit regression from an intellectual to a petulant child echoes a larger discussion of the role of academics in a free Jamaica taking place at the time Patterson was writing the novel. As Donette Francis has pointed out, Patterson's early novels pre-date, and in some ways anticipate, the crises of anti-intellectualism in late 1960s Jamaica, especially concerning the Walter Rodney riots of 1968. Such tensions between academics, the middle class, and the Jamaican government lurk behind both *The Children of Sisyphus* and *An Absence of Ruins*. As Francis notes in "'Transcendental Cosmopolitanism': Orlando Patterson and the Novel Jamaican 1960s," *The Children of Sisyphus* "was published in 1965, on the eve of Patterson's return to Jamaica to teach Sociology at the University of the West Indies. The Walter Rodney October 1968 crisis, which led to the University Professor being expelled and prohibited from returning to the island, crystallized the draconian tactics of the governing Jamaican Labor Party, and changed Patterson's own desire to stay in the newly sovereign island nation." Echoing Francis's point, Patterson himself, in an interview called "The Paradox of Freedom," argues that *An Absence of Ruins* is a particularly bleak novel. As he reveals, following independence, he found himself with an overbearing sense of loneliness and isolation—feelings exacerbated by his migration from the Caribbean to England. The novel, as he puts it, was

> written while I was still in the Caribbean, and the final half was written in my first year in Britain. By the time *An Absence of Ruins* came along, I was in Britain and I really was in the midst of contemplating [my situation]. It was this transition I mentioned, whether basically I was going to live in Britain and abandon the whole Caribbean thing. . . . It was the most negative period of that process of thinking through the destructivist view of the past, and one in which you could interpret what came out of that chaos in more positive terms. But it was the climax of the most negative, destructive period, and written at a time when I was seriously thinking of not going back. (168)

An Absence of Ruins thus captures Patterson confronting an overwhelming sense of disillusion and hopelessness, of feeling out of place and unwelcome. As the Walter Rodney riots would make explicit, the tension between an academic progressive Left, the very kind that Patterson represents, and the Jamaican government—as well as the public's response—revealed a deep-seated distrust of academics. And it also revealed a threat: that the kind of political inquiry Blackman and his friends undertake in the novel would be met in a free Jamaica with ideological and physical violence. This sense of all-consuming despair appears overtly in *An Absence* of *Ruins* as, troublingly, Blackman's selfish, juvenile behavior represents a more acceptable ethos than that of his academic identity.

Read this way, Blackman's shifting, unstable identity that is constantly interrupted and canceled out both captures Patterson's uncertainty of his role in Jamaica and posits a serious critique of Jamaican resentment toward intellectual communities. As Francis argues in "Radical Skepticism,"

> After his academic training abroad, the protagonist's central conundrum is his inability to resettle into the nation or commit to the socialist agenda of his intellectual peers, which results in his exodus from Jamaica back to England. *An Absence of Ruins* captures a mounting sense of disillusion and detachment well before the 1968 expulsion of Walter Rodney, which is often credited as being the catalyst for intellectual flight from the island. Critiquing a brand of intellectual activism that mobilized around race and an uncomplicated championing of the folk, this campus novel demonstrates that intellectuals cannot be homogeneously categorized as nationalist, and that, in fact, they did not achieve any sense of a nationalist hegemony over the people. (53)

Blackman's radically unstable identity thus mirrors, for Patterson, the coherence and efficacy of postindependence political ideologies, which have seemingly failed to chart a way forward. The rejection of intellectual nationalist politics in the novel is evident in Blackman's attempt not to take a side when, midway through the novel, he argues that he is tired of being made an ineffectual abstraction: "I don't want to spend my life *being* a Negro or being a Jamaican or being a socialist or being a capitalist or what you like. . . . I'm bored, absolutely bored with being things, with being abstractions" (65). There is, then, no ideology that is effectively transgressive or empowering. This point becomes even more bleak when we consider the almost optimistic creation of Blackman's university in the novel, as the university that his obituary implies he worked at did not actually exist at the time Patterson was writing—at least not in the form in which it is described. In "Sociology and Sisyphus: Postcolonialism, Anti-Positivism, and Modernist Narrative in Patterson's Oeuvre," George Springer notes that "these biographical details are, in a literal sense, impossible, since there was no social sciences degree at Mona in 1953 and since this was still a University College, not a University, at the time. These are not the only instances where the text introduces slight, sometimes uncanny differences between Blackman's and Patterson's biographies" (18). Patterson's novel points toward a moment of hope and burgeoning intellectualism by imagining a university space that does yet exist, while at the same time implicates the creation of this hypothetical university's inevitable failure—a point, horrifyingly, that is played out in the coming Walter Rodney scandal.

Counterarchival Resistance and Alternative Futures

Not surprisingly, the tension between the pull of adolescent disinterest and mature political engagement serves as a point of crisis in the novel that, I argue, is designed to engender a distinct sense of readerly frustration. The reader confronts—and perhaps fosters anger at—a character who is largely antagonistic because he lacks a consistent identity and past, and who seems to be shifting rapidly between stages of intellectual development without any clear spatial or temporal textual markers. This performativity of annoyance signals a sense of overwhelming but productive frustration, where the reader must confront a character without a determinate arc or sense of development, forcing them to question the demands and social expectations placed on postcolonial subjects.

Indeed, we cannot say by the end of the novel that Blackman has progressed in any consistent or identifiable way. But it is this very sentiment—the notion that the main character must "behave," evolve, or remain consistent—that is ridiculed at the novel's conclusion. The ending, citing and referencing Fyodor Dostoevsky's *Notes from Underground*, is punctuated with a mocking air of a faux apology, in which the narrator antagonistically confronts what he perceives to be the reader's annoyance with his narrative. Blurring the line between a fictional interlocutor and the reader, Blackman cites and responds to a confrontation on the street, where he is asked, "You have the appearance of the savage, yet you would pretend to be exactly like us. . . . Where do you come from? What of your past? Who are your ancestors? Are you savaged or civilised? Identify yourself, sir!" (145). The implication made in this scene is a damning one, in which the protagonist, now in London, implies that the audience's anger is rooted in the societal rejection of colonial subjects' lack of a discernable cohesiveness and ancestry. Significantly, the narrative ends by effectively weaponizing readerly guilt, implying that annoyance is a discriminatory practice at the hands of those, unlike himself, who in fact have a historical and personal foundation to stand on. In other words, Blackman intimates that the reader, as the bystander, devalues and dehumanizes him because they cannot view someone without a past as human. He thus implies that the anger the reader experiences is engendered not by the text's hostile metafictional structure, but by his status as Caribbean Other. The novel ends with the narrator walking out, so to speak, of the story he is telling, noting, "I am busy going nowhere, but I must keep up the appearance of going in order to forget that I am not. So if you'll excuse me, I will be on my way" (146).

The absence of a past or historical foundation that guides the novel, combined with the collapse of a cohesive identity, is, of course, inextricable from larger questions of diaspora, as metafictional interruptions that struggle to reconcile the loss of an ancestral legacy permeate the text. At times, Blackman is obsessed with finding a "true" or lost identity, and the narrative frequently stops to confront the psychological effects of a history dictated by colonization. As he muses,

> There is a past here. There must be a past here. My city goes back a thousand years. If you dig deep you will find the relics of even more ancient times. They tell me that all I would find are the twisted bones of crippled, mutilated black slaves, or, if I dig deeper, the decapitated bodies of Arawak Indians. . . . But they are all lies, lies. I will not believe them. . . . They are all vile, treacherous, scheming propagandists, brainwasher, inventors of fables designed to make me feel inferior, to deprive me of the knowledge of my glorious heritage, which must be there, hidden somewhere. (104)

Convinced that history, as it were, is a lie, Blackman seeks to unearth what he cannot fathom as truth: that his ancestral heritage is one only of suffering and enslavement. Blackman concludes that he must "destroy those evil institutions"—that is, museums, archives, and public records offices. Clearly, Blackman's desire to overturn history is rooted in the obliteration of narratives of oppression with new, more empowering ancestral narratives, though, it is worth noting, he never articulates, or can even fathom, what those new narratives might look like (104). We can read this passage, then, against the scene at the end of the novel, in which Blackman is forced to account for a past that does not exist. Here, the source of the trauma is not simply that the past does not exist, but that its very nonexistence is, for Blackman, impossible to reconcile or accept. Throughout the novel, Patterson asks readers to negotiate ideologies of recuperation against those of total destruction, as the novel yearns for the creation of a new interpretation of history that will topple legacies of historical oppression.

Blackman's refusal to accept the history of Caribbean atrocity—and his rejection of institutional knowledge and the archives of history—echoes what Deborah A. Thomas, in "Caribbean Studies, Archive Building, and the Problem of Violence," labels a "counterarchive," which would begin to establish "the significance of the [the Caribbean] to the global processes that have shaped it over the past five centuries" (27) As Thomas writes, "These acts of reconstruction are oriented toward the creation of an historical consciousness, one that often stands in opposition to forms of state memory, and this is why they constitute a counterarchive, or what Anthony Bogues calls a 'dread history'" (28). In *An Absence of Ruins*, Blackman is not so much interested in discovering what has been hidden—or searching for an alternate telling of history—but destroying the archives before a counterarchive can be built. If the consecration of a new history begins by "generating evidence that could both counter the old, racist epistemologies and serve as the foundations for new, more liberatory claims" in a way that "dismantl[es] enduring tropes," Blackman at no point searches for the evidence; indeed, he has no idea how he would begin searching for it, and the hope of a counterarchive quickly evaporates in the novel (38).

Interestingly, the questions Patterson raises in *An Absence of Ruins*, while appearing to reject the state of Caribbean literature and theory, parallel and anticipate questions of history, paradox, and historical legacy that, in the years following the novel's release, became increasingly urgent for Caribbean writers and thinkers—among them Walcott and Brathwaite, who engaged in similarly confrontational investigations with the Caribbean's relationship to history. That Patterson was exploring many of the same themes as Walcott is, of course, hardly surprising, given that the novel begins with an epigraph from (and indeed references in its title) Walcott's 1962 poem, "The Royal Palms . . . An Absence of Ruins." So, it should be noted that, despite its overwhelming pessimism and disdain for its contemporaries, Patterson's novel can in many ways be seen to both contribute and engage with the larger philosophical reevaluation of history by Caribbean theorists that took place throughout the 1960s and 1970s. As Edward Baugh argued in his seminal 1977 essay "The West Indian Writer and His Quarrel with History," works by Walcott and Brathwaite do not assert simply that "history is irrelevant in the Caribbean," but rather work to find their "way round the bogeyman that history . . . has become . . . by denying its importance" (61). Walcott, argues Baugh, embraces a "'loss of history,' as a positive, creative condition of Caribbean man, and the supremacy, for Caribbean man, of imagination over history, this is his way of arguing for the Caribbean potential for cultural identity and achievement" (61). Baugh thus shows how Walcott's poem "The Almond Trees" claims "freedom from bondage to the idea of having some glorious past to worship (or, conversely, some sorrowful past to lament)" (70). Despite these similarities—and, indeed, the questions Walcott were raising at the time do resonate strikingly with the novel—*An Absence of Ruins* remains hesitant of kinship with its contemporaries.

The novel, mournful over the suppressed and shattered cultural history of the Caribbean, painfully laments that loss, but nevertheless viciously—and somewhat paradoxically—dismantles the foundations of Caribbean art and culture while explicitly rejecting the value of many current Caribbean theorists. *An Absence of Ruins* is entranced in a state of yearning—yearning to reestablish a stolen history, but vehemently opposed to the aesthetic and intellectual foundation established in the twentieth century. The novel views contemporary theories of colonial resistance with ambivalence and, in some cases, disgust; they do not serve as a means to erect a counterarchive so much as they engender a sense of intellectual sterility. In this regard, Lamming's *The Pleasures of Exile* suffers a particularly harsh critique, evident in a key scene midway through the novel, in which his musings on colonial indoctrination serve as a point of ridicule in the text. The scene, simply put, focuses on Blackman's childhood, as he recalls how the heroes of the novels of his youth were all British, and how, subsequently, he spent a large segment of his childhood sending letters to those same fictional characters. He recounts having his mother compose notes to his favorite "hero of the books I used to read," a British figure named only "William" (108). The scene, however, literalizes Lamming's theory of the insidious nature of colonial influence on the Caribbean psyche by transforming it from a concept into a person. Here, its traction in the narrative is rooted in its absurdity: the influence of the British on the Caribbean child is not psychological, but physical, as the scene becomes heavy handed and clichéd. The narrator reads the books and thinks they are real characters; he writes to them and emulates them, making the scene a farce and bitter parody of Lamming's work. It is, of course, worth noting that Patterson's critique is a decidedly ungenerous reading of Lamming's work—especially given that Lamming explores a complex and nuanced examination of historical legacy and influence in *The Castle of My Skin*—and also through his concept of the backward glance, which wrestles with ambivalence and one's relationship to the past.[16] But the point remains that, in the novel, Patterson remains thoroughly unsatisfied with any of his contemporaries' theorizations of history and Caribbean identity and insists that they are outmoded. The recycling of such theories of emancipation have now, the novel argues, become banal, and Lamming's notion of colonial influence is recontextualized as a tired myth that is unable to enact any effective sense of colonial resistance or cultural enlightenment.

One might be tempted to read such moments of critique, which metafictively confront what Blackman no doubt believes to be an ineffectual cultural foundation, as pointing to an alternative path forward. Blackman's narrative thus undermines Caribbean art and culture to point toward something new. It is in new, experimental aesthetic forms, as the text intimates, that emancipation lies, and the novel proposes a thorough rejection of art and philosophy that Patterson perceives as stale. Taken this way, we can read the text's metafictional interruptions as a metaphor for sabotaging or undermining the trajectory of contemporary Caribbean aesthetics. Under this pretense, the real narrative of *An Absence of Ruins* can be found in its desperate effort to break free from stale tradition, as well as in its tireless search for a new theoretical and literary means of resistance.

However, as I have previously noted in my discussion of Caribbean metafiction, the works in this study always fail to muster resistance against entrenched ideologies. Patterson's interruptive strategy consistently denies readers the comfort of a simple answer or solution. Not unexpectedly, Blackman's momentary yearning for a counterarchive is not simply rejected, but reversed—an unsurprising point, given that no ethical or ideological positions in the text remain stable. Shortly after he expresses his need to overturn history, he realizes that his musings are idiotic, excuses that only point to the absence of an answer or solution. Seemingly revising his call for the violent destruction of a history, he writes, "No, there is no longer any excuse, any reason, any explanation to be found outside myself. I come before history, I come before race, I come before culture, I come before parents, I come before God. At this point the very effort of finding such excuses has become mockingly self-defeating. . . . There are no excuses to be found. There are no explanations" (117). Here, Blackman's anger—and, more importantly, his refusal to accept the horror of the past—is negated as foolish. The counterarchive is a form of hypothetical resistance that, once pondered more deeply, is too prone to failure. On the surface, this scene mirrors Patterson's claim in "The Paradox of Freedom" that the novel ponders "the possibility of starting from scratch and creating a world for yourself" (169). But even this realization proves fleeting. The scene ends in an interruption that essentially cancels out the narrator's moment of enlightenment: with an abrupt cut, as we learn that what we are reading is yet another diary entry, and not the "real story." We are informed: "Suddenly he could write no more. He flung his diary from him in disgust and got up" (117). The epiphany of the potential counterarchive and, with it, the second epiphany that a counterarchive is doomed to fail are both canceled out, dismissed as philosophical speculations, as mere jottings in a notebook; they are not, Blackman determines, worthwhile valid positions or beliefs. As the narrator argues, "It would be taking self-mockery too far to make another entry in this diary.... I can never take such probing seriously" (140). What readers are left with is not the absence of a solution, but a snapshot of the fragility of those very solutions that, here, always crumble under the weight of the text's experimental, interruptive narrative structure.

In sum, the aesthetics of Caribbean metafiction that I have worked to highlight in this chapter ponders the potentiality of effective methods of resistance by acknowledging, through interruption, the challenges and seemingly insurmountable obstacles of overturning colonial ideology. In the novels that I have addressed, all forms of resistance and emancipation are false starts: they collapse in on themselves, creating an endless vortex of recirculated indecision and failure. Such works urge the reader to reconsider their own assumptions and knowledge of Caribbean life and culture by metafictively exposing the obstacles and impasses that engender misunderstanding and misrepresentation. The aesthetic at play is one that demands an active evaluation of impasse and failure by forcing the reader to evaluate practices of meaning making by bringing to light surreptitious fissures and instabilities in colonial ideology. The metafictional works of Bell, Reid, and Patterson thus work to provide a deeper understanding of the means through which experimental aesthetics can foster new insights into the mechanisms of colonial power and, in so doing, reveal a theory of Caribbean literature that demands a self-reflexive, actively engaged reader to decode and confront systems of oppression.

2 To Become So Very Welsh
Denis Williams's *The Third Temptation* and the Effacement of Afro-Caribbean Identity

EXCEPT FOR a few publications, there has been almost no critical attention directed at the work of Denis Williams—an underappreciated and largely forgotten Guyanese painter, archaeologist, and writer. This point is especially true in regard to his two innovative novels, the semiautobiographical *Other Leopards* (1963) and the overtly experimental *The Third Temptation* (1968). Like his fiction, the trajectory of Williams's career is multifaceted and disorienting, and it resists easy classification. Born in Georgetown, Williams studied painting in London in the 1950s as a protégé of Wyndham Lewis and achieved acclaim for his experimentation with modernist forms and racial identity, most notably for his *Human World* series. Williams, however, resented being labeled and marketed as a "Negro artist" and, in 1957, left Europe to live in Africa, where he taught art courses in Sudan, Nigeria, and Uganda (Cambridge 115). There, he developed an interest in archaeology, to which he devoted his career; shortly thereafter, in 1967, he returned to Georgetown. While Williams is most known and respected for his painting and archaeological work, his fiction has mostly faded into obscurity.

Williams's interdisciplinary background and disparate interests led him to fuse, rethink, and sometimes appropriate cross-cultural literary forms in decidedly innovative ways. Like the fiction of his countryman Wilson Harris, Williams's writing is explicitly—some might say aggressively—experimental. His second novel, *The Third Temptation,* is a dense examination of narrative perspective that, surprisingly, takes its influence from Alain Robbe-Grillet and the French Nouveau Roman movement. The novel is rife with repetitions and extended, hyperdetailed descriptions of inanimate objects. It lacks a single narrator, and the vantage point shifts, frequently and exhaustingly, between minor and major characters: a constable, a pregnant woman, a dead man, and an accident victim, among others, all of whom exchange narrative responsibility. The novel's plot, however, is relatively simple. Set in Wales and centered on an affair between a wealthy businessman and his employee's wife, the novel's main character is a middle-aged white European named Joss Banks. Joss is an unapologetic misogynist struggling with the effects of aging on his virility and status: he has recently retired from his printing press, and his wife, Bid, has just left him. The central motif of the novel is largely a question of domestic trauma. Bid has left Joss because she is unable to cope with the death of her ex-husband—Joss's former employee—who took his life as a result of her affair with Joss. The suicide, depicted in the opening scene, festers like an open wound, and much of the action revolves around it: the plot focuses largely on Joss and his friend Sean's conversations about their failing relationships and Bid's ex-husband's suicide. However, a plot summary reflects almost nothing of the novel's ingenuity, which lies in the way the story is told and retold from multiple angles and perspectives. Key scenes in the novel appear again and again, and constantly shifting narrative perspectives repeatedly undermine everything that is said, making the exact sequence of events, and even the identity of who is speaking, frequently impossible to discern. Hyperattentive descriptions describe multiple vantage points and angles of Joss and Sean's conversations, as narratorial interruptions sever linearity to muse on the efficacy and ethics of power and violence.

What is perhaps most striking about the novel, however, is its whiteness. Set in a fictional version of the Welsh seaside town Llandudno, all of the main characters are white Europeans. Furthermore, the Afro-Caribbean autobiographical elements common to Williams's work are seemingly absent, and the novel appears, at least on the surface, unconcerned with race, politics, or colonialism altogether. As such, it is a radical departure from his first novel, *Other Leopards,* in which the Guyanese protagonist struggles to reconcile himself to his African heritage. Whereas *Other Leopards* was fairly well received, *The Third Temptation*—perhaps due to its difficult prose and Welsh setting—has garnered almost no critical attention. Even Williams's daughters, who have published extensively on their father's legacy, largely omit *The Third Temptation* from their analysis. And, despite Peepal Tree Press's reissue of the novel in 2010, it has still remained a footnote to the corpus of Caribbean literature, with some critics refusing to consider it a Caribbean novel at all (Ramraj 16). In any case, Williams's dense prose, combined with the novel's apparent absence of interest in race, politics, or the Caribbean, makes it, perhaps, one of the strangest and least discussed works in all of Caribbean literature.

As I will argue in this chapter, *The Third Temptation*'s abstract, dense prose subtly, surreptitiously intimates the racial oppression and exploitation buried below the surface of the largely white textual landscape. Thus far, the scant criticism on the novel has focused almost exclusively on its strange connection to the French Nouveau Roman movement, while ignoring the larger questions of racial identity that surround the novel. Victor J. Ramraj argues, for example, that the novel "has little or nothing to do with Africa or racial identity. Williams, in fact, is concerned less with themes than with formal and technical experimentation, based on the theories of the Nouveau Roman school, particularly as advocated by its chief exponent, Alain Robbe-Grillet. . . The novel is a difficult one, and it makes demands on the reader for which he may or may not feel amply compensated" (488).[1] Questions of racial politics are not explicit in the text, and the Welsh landscape Williams portrays is one almost exclusively white, in which only two black characters emerge, briefly, as sexual objects. It is misplaced, however, to suggest that the novel does not confront larger questions of racial and colonial identity. *The Third Temptation*'s experiments with perspective function not as a loving ode to the Nouveau Roman, but as a means to acknowledge a history of racial violence that is deeply embedded into Welsh society.[2] As I will show, the novel is ripe for rediscovery, in part because in many ways it not only precedes a current trend in thinking about Wales in a postcolonial context, but also speaks to larger questions of how formal experimentation may reveal new methods of expressing Caribbean trauma.[3]

This chapter argues that close analysis of the novel reveals the Wales of the 1960s to be a complicated, conflicted intersection of colonial resistance and imperialist tendencies. To do so, I resituate *The Third Temptation* within its biographical and historical context and, in so doing, demonstrate how the novel's use of abstraction functions as a way of examining the entrenched nature of colonial oppression. Taking Charlotte Williams's memoir *Sugar and Slate* (in which her father, Denis Williams, plays a central role) as a critical starting point, I show how Williams's personal trauma provides key context for understanding Wales as a site of racial and psychological tension in the novel, in which Afro-Caribbean identity and European art and culture clash uncomfortably. Williams's personal crises—his struggles to "shrug off the influences of the West"— emerge against a veiled, yet resoundingly important, historical investigation of Welsh colonialism, as the novel confronts the imperialistic pursuit of the Welsh missionary William Hughes, whose "Congo Institute" in the early twentieth century aimed to convert transform Africans into Welsh

Christians (C. Williams, *Sugar and Slate* 190). Accordingly, the novel's depiction of Wales as a symbol of overbearing European influence and colonial domination manifests as an ontological crisis in the narrative, in which identity exists only in flux and crisis. Every major character possesses an identity that is unfixed and unstable. Characters are frequently swallowed up by one another; indeed, the primary trauma of the text is the fear of erasure: the very notion that European identity will overwrite and stifle Black individuality. As such, I read the novel's aesthetic ingenuities not as ahistorical or apolitical experiments, but as ways of unveiling acts of racial and colonial oppression. Williams incorporates experimental narrative techniques that repeatedly undermine the stability and fixity of identity, thereby suggesting that the effacement of Afro-Caribbean identity is both inevitable and integral to the landscape of twentieth-century Wales.

As I will show, Williams's novel demonstrates how entrenched forms of colonial violence splinter and sever identities in ways that cannot be easily described—that confronting the sometimes inscrutable psychological repercussions of legacies of colonial trauma is an experience that remains an ever-present struggle of articulation. The novel asks readers not to dismiss radically experimental forms as art for art's sake, but to consider how the nature of colonial violence is itself difficult to express, in threatening the perceived wholeness or clarity of the subject's perceptions. Readers confront an array of fractured narrators and events that must be actively unraveled and made sense of, for beyond *The Third Temptation*'s embrace of obfuscation and abstraction, lies a scathing condemnation of how European legacies of colonial violence are often suppressed and ignored. The novel, in this way, serves as a profound experiment with readerly perception, in challenging readers to confront and evaluate what may lurk beyond obfuscation.

Wales and the Aesthetics of Hostile Space

The fact that Williams's novel is a complex analysis of race and oppression may not be immediately evident upon a cursory reading of the text. After all, the entirety of *The Third Temptation* is set in Wales—a point that may be surprising, given Williams's devotion to African and Guyanese culture. The setting of the novel, however, is not arbitrary. Wales was essential to his artistic development: the site of a momentous aesthetic crisis in which he faced a seemingly irreconcilable conflict between embracing a theory of Western art and culture and embracing a new anticolonial artistry. This crisis began in London, where, in the late 1950s, while working on his first novel, Williams reached a sudden breaking point in his life and work and began to repudiate the mark of white European influence on his increasingly Afro-Caribbean aesthetic. Long frustrated with the exoticization of his art and "patronizing overtones" toward his work, he abruptly left Europe in 1957 and settled in Khartoum, where he took on a lecturer position in the School of Fine Art (E. Williams, *Art of Denis Williams* 31).[4] Yet Williams's familial obligations meant that he was unable to leave his European life entirely behind. His wife, Katherine Alice, was Welsh, and they had several young children to care for. Although his family joined him in Africa for a short time, Katherine was unhappy there and soon left with the children to settle in Llandudno, which becomes the setting of *The Third Temptation* (fictionalized in the novel as the town Caedmon). Williams's need to escape Europe to hone his artistic sensibilities was met with the realization that he could not divorce himself from his familial obligations in Wales, and he began migrating back and forth between Khartoum and Llandudno. This sense of tension, of being caught between two places and two identities, became central to his career.

Wales was thus Williams's central site of personal and colonial trauma, where he could neither escape his previous life nor fully embrace a new identity that rejected the oppressive ideology of the West. As Charlotte Williams argues, "[My father] spent his life trying to shrug off the influences of the West; everything he did was a rejection of European domination" (*Sugar and Slate* 190). Williams's view of Wales was not simply engendered by familial resentment, but by a need to escape the growing realization that he was losing his heritage and becoming, essentially, a European artist. Frequent migrations between Wales and Africa exacerbated Williams's aesthetic crisis. Throughout the late 1950s and 1960s, while working on *The Third Temptation,* he traveled so frequently between Africa and Wales that Charlotte Williams refers to these years as the start of her family's "to-ing and fro-ing" or perpetual state of being "somewhere and elsewhere," in which the family moved repeatedly between Africa and Wales (5). Whereas Africa existed as a space that gave Williams a newfound sense of power and artistic sensibility, Wales was a place of obligation and European influence. He wrote to his wife, Katherine, "[In Africa] I feel much more confident in my own power. . . . I feel I'm worth much more to myself and to everyone as what I am—an artist, and must try to work up to the brim of my own possibilities" (4). For Williams, the rapid movement between two spaces—one in which he felt aesthetically emancipated, and one in which he felt aesthetically imprisoned—shape the central exploration of space in the novel.

The predominantly white Wales of *The Third Temptation* thus functions as a hostile space that strips the Black artist of their creative autonomy, as Williams imagines it in the novel as a landscape in which European influence has effaced the Black artist's presence, both literally and figuratively. The novel reveals from the outset Williams's conflicted emotions about Wales and its effect on his art, and it functions as an examination of the psychological trauma that emerges when Black artists are forced to create art in predominantly white, European spaces. Wales, in *The Third Temptation,* becomes both a prison and a symbol of colonial disempowerment. Though there are no major Black characters, there remains in *The Third Temptation* the pervading sense of wanting to be *elsewhere* and an underlying desire to escape the European landscape of the novel. In the text, the trauma of physical displacement and racial isolation is a veiled but omnipresent horror that can never be fully articulated and nevertheless permeates every facet of existence.

Therefore, while the action of the novel takes place in Wales, Williams investigates larger questions of diaspora, and images of dislocation emerge as a central theme in the very first scene. The novel begins with an examination of physical and psychological trauma, opening with a suicide that disturbs and disorients geographical space. Lawrence Henry Owen, or "Lho," a commercial artist, hangs himself in the forest just outside the fictional Welsh town of Caedmon. Traumatized by his wife's infidelity and the realization that the child she is carrying is not his but his employer's, Joss Banks, Lho takes his own life. The suicide, however, is not simply a death, but an act of dislocation. As Lho swings, dying, from the tree, he oscillates in and out of ontological spaces, as the temporal boundaries between here and there, then and now, is and is not, collapse into a grotesque amalgamation of fear and sadness.

In Lho's death throes, time and space break down as he experiences a "darkness. . . a circumambience that might possess being but no centre, a function of space and yet not space" (23). At this moment, he is both living and dead, husband and ex-husband, Welsh and not Welsh. He is, the narrator tells us, there and not there: "Without effort he could distinguish this previous state from the suspended nothing which dwelled in him, there and not there . . . an unseen and terrible space whose quivering cavities relayed echoes to further terribly trembling spaces there and not there" (23). This notion—the impossible space between here and there—becomes a thematic principle of the novel; in fact, the first chapter, immediately following Lho's suicide, goes on to depict a constable who, like Lho, is trapped between two spaces. The constable, it seems, is both "on his island jeweled in the morning sun" and "not on his island" at the same time (26). It is this push and pull, and the feeling of psychological and physical displacement that emerges with it, that the novel's opening scenes immediately foreground. The fact that these scenes mirror Charlotte William's descriptions of her father's visits, in which she repeatedly describes him as being "somewhere and elsewhere," firmly plants Williams's crisis of identity, as well as his larger exploration of the ways in which European space stifles Afro-Caribbean identity, as a profound influence on the ideological and narrative strategies of the novel.

While Williams's own identity crisis is a key element of the text, careful readers will also discover how the novel reveals considerably wider implications for the way detachment and isolation dominate Caribbean experience. In this sense, themes of dislocation frequently center on the novel's Welsh setting, as images of Afro-Caribbean art and culture repeatedly puncture the white, European landscape of the novel. The word "Guyana" is scattered throughout, reminding us that, in this story, the Caribbean is more real than the European landscape in which the novel is set. In an early scene, we see a spinning globe that repeatedly reminds readers of life outside of Wales: "How masterful to rotate the earth with one's fingertips—50° . . . 60° . . . longitude east . . . 80° . . . 90° . . . 100° to Gilbert Island 180°; then back to 170° . . . 160° . . . 130° longitude west . . . 120° . . . 110° . . . . 100°, Galapagos Islands 60° . . . the Amazon 40° . . . the Equator . . . Torrid zone . . . Alto Trombetas . . . the virgin forests of Guyana" (28; second ellipsis added). This scene is particularly important, as none of the characters have any relationship to Guyana at all, yet Guyana appears again and again, anchoring the discord of the novel. The frequent signposts toward Caribbean identity intimate the mark of something lost—or overwritten—by the overbearing whiteness of the text, as the presence of the Caribbean repeatedly punctures the textual veneer that would lead readers to believe the novel is a European one. As Vibert C. Cambridge suggests, *The Third Temptation* embeds "numerous clues" in its many "micro-stories" that signal "West Indian/ Guyanese geography and cultural life" (120). Cambridge notes the novel's references to Guyanese games such as "Duck and Drake" and "Riddle Me, Riddle Me," which appear out of context and alien, given the Welsh setting (120). The near-invisibility of these images is telling: readers will note that the novel alternately signals and suppresses Afro-Caribbean identity, but is unable to erase its presence from the textual landscape entirely. Thus the Wales of the novel is a hostile space in which flickers of a subverted culture, place, and people repeatedly threaten to emerge, but always ultimately recede into the background. While Cambridge's essay is an ideal starting point to examine the novel's Caribbean elements, there has been no in-depth analysis of the implications of the novel's obfuscated allusions to Caribbean life and its larger poetics of abstraction.

In the novel, as in Williams's life, the tenuous boundaries and demarcations between geographical space—and the sense of disorienting abstraction that accompanies them—almost always intimate the presence of racial trauma. It is this push and pull, evident in Lho's death, that bears the novel's first mark of colonialism. Lho's death, a hanging, is synonymous with colonial violence and evokes the image of a lynching, in which readers watch his corpse swing from the tree. The scene is immediately followed by an image of power and authority: the constable. Indeed, the sole authority figure in the text, the constable is referenced almost exclusively in terms of his "island": the traffic police stand from which he observes the town. Yet it is worth noting here that the word "island" and many of the other subtle references to the Caribbean in the text, such as the woodlands surrounding Caedmon that resemble the forests of Guyana, are almost always punctuated by images of domination, most notably in the form of the constable, as well as Joss Banks, who appears in the text during Lho's death throes. And, although the word "colonialism" is never uttered, the novel repeatedly pairs images of colonial landscapes with explorations of violence, authority, and oppression. The in-between space and the fluctuating ontological status Lho experiences during his death is described as a loss of autonomy. The narrator remarks that "he could not use his mind; he had lost that power" (24). These allusions to oppression, power, and displacement firmly solidify the key themes of the novel as colonial in nature, a colonialism enforced by the absence of Black identity in the text. Resoundingly, all of the characters that possess authority are European—and power, in *The Third Temptation,* is an entirely white phenomenon.

The relationship between oppression and geographical disorientation is essential to understanding the novel, and *The Third Temptations*'s narrative abstractions push readers to think more deeply about the implications of dislocation and racial violence. The move from Africa, where Williams felt empowered and invigorated, to Wales, where he felt isolated psychologically and racially, guides the depiction of Welsh life in the novel. While Charlotte Williams in *Sugar and Slate* acknowledges that, in part, her father "loved Wales although it had something of a fairytale quality to him" (53), the prejudice he felt and the racial climate complicated

Williams's love of Wales, where he frequently felt ostracized. As Charlotte Williams argues, "He was the outsider, he needed us to mediate this alien environment.... He never belonged. He never could" (52–53). His blackness, she reveals, made him a spectacle: "We were a traveling show... a curiosity that people came out of their houses to see. Black people and countryside don't go together in white people's thinking" (53). Williams's skin, considerably darker than that of his children, combined with his marriage to Katie Alice, marked him as a racial threat in the predominantly white Welsh countryside. Accordingly, the text tries to capture the trauma of such feelings of social, cultural, and racial exclusion while acknowledging that that trauma cannot be easily expressed.

For Caribbean émigrés, Wales, the text suggests, was a place of radical alienation and understated, but ubiquitous, oppression. Indeed, Welsh life for Williams was a constant negotiation of racial and geographical tension, rapidly fluctuating between moments of inclusion and exclusion. This sense of constant tension emerges most explicitly in Williams's reflections on Wales in 1958, one year after his relocation to Africa. His retrospective accounts in several interviews speak of a defining moment when he catches sight of a photo of himself in the window of the family home in Wales. This image of himself is so wholly alien that he begins screaming and tearing off his clothes. As he explains: "I was ranting, tearing ... something had gone wrong. That's not me. What is this about? ... And I think from the moment I began to reverse from that image" (C. Williams, "Young Man with a Hope" 95).[5] This sense of detachment from oneself—Williams, as a modernist Black Guyanese artist living in Africa but unable to sever his connections to Wales—became a source of pronounced horror. As he gazes at the photo, he realizes he cannot shed his associations with his European life and feels trapped in a warped "fairy tale" from which he cannot escape.[6] For Williams, Wales threatens to efface and suppress his newfound African identity—to stamp it out entirely.

This trauma of recognition, or the fact that Wales exists as a site of perpetual estrangement that brings a sense of overt panic and terror to the extent that one can no longer recognize oneself, is essential to understanding the novel's experimentation with perspective. At the same time, the novel makes clear that the psychological trauma Williams himself experiences in Wales—and the sense of racial isolation he struggles to negotiate—is both commonplace and pervasive. Such a trauma, the text suggests, can best be revealed through experimental forms. The novel tirelessly undermines the very notion of identity, which, for all of the characters, is never stable or fixed. The narrative shifts from perspective to perspective and eschews a single dominant narrative point of view, so that characters are unable to maintain their individualities. The novel often blurs subjectivities, making it difficult for the reader determine who is talking, or to what or whom a character refers. For example, early on, Joss Banks and his friend Sean discuss Lho's death in graphic detail, but constant interruptions make it impossible to determine who is speaking. Images of advertisements, postcards, and letters briefly intrude on the narrative. In one case, we see a violent pornographic postcard intersected with snippets of a love letter detailing the end of Sean's relationship, as Joss, Sean, the letter, and the postcard merge together uncomfortably (52–53). These exchanges occur throughout the passage until the collision of identities and narratorial responsibilities culminates in a literal wreck: a car accident in which a blue Ford slams into a minivan suddenly interrupts the scene. Mangled bodies and onlookers become one; the narrator notes a crowd gathered around the scene as "people have accumulated [into] . . . blobs, masses" (53–54), violently stripped of any discernable identity. Overwhelmed by the confusion, a narrator suddenly interrupts the narrative to voice his frustration: "Even though monochromatic and attenuated the movement was a movement of men. There was at last a He, a They. They swam before him, uncertain vestments, grey intensities of unstable mass and contour hovering on the visual threshold so that it was impossible to establish for certain that these were not mere spots dancing and swimming there . . . [in] continual flux, endless interpretation" (56). Speech and thoughts blend together, sometimes exhaustingly, throughout the novel. Identity, as such is always under duress, as seemingly every major character in the text is afflicted by Williams's own crisis of recognition, struggling, like him, to negotiate the trauma of multiple, conflicting identities. Yet it is perhaps the scene's emphasis on color that is most telling: despite the comingling and distortion of bodies that dominates the accident scene, the image remains, for the narrator, in black and white. While we might struggle to negotiate the seeming inscrutability of the image, the monochromatic scene nevertheless reminds us of the presence of racial hierarchy that remains despite the seemingly impenetrable moment of collision and "flux." That race remains ever present, even in a moment where interpretation and what we see is entirely uncertain, undercuts the scene and emphasizes, for the reader, the very fact that systems of inequity are not only etched into the fabric and landscape of European space but also that they cannot, even in moments of crisis of confusion, be readily destabilized or disarmed.

The Corruptive Force of the Martyr

The novel's reminder of the presence of racial hierarchies—and the very idea that, in Wales, there remains always a black and a white, and that these distinctions are not easily obscured—grows increasingly important in the novel. In this regard, while the presence of Afro-Caribbean identity emerges only fleetingly, a tribute to power, oppression, and disenfranchisement appears as a distinct monument—one that readers may be prone to miss, but that the novel urges us not to overlook. Standing tall in the center of the city is a physical embodiment of colonialism: a statue of a "Welsh Martyr" who left Wales to plant Christianity in "Darkest Africa" (54). Looming over the horizon, its bronze image gazes down upon citizens of Caedmon. Impossible to ignore, its presence infects the everyday speech of the town's inhabitants, who are inexplicably drawn to it. The statue seemingly celebrates the power of European civilization. Lho muses that it functions as a reminder of European superiority: "[For] us Europeans . . . life's never lost, sort of, we keep inheriting like, from the dead, inheriting it, so it goes on . . . indestructability of spirit you know, stuff this Welsh Martyr brought back from Africa" (78). The statue of the martyr that adorns the novelistic landscape thus serves as a visual reminder for the characters that power is never equally distributed. In this way, the novelistic focus on effacement, conversion, and the fragility of identity is set against the specter of colonial trauma, as embodied in the statue's reminder of Europe's power over Africa. Simply put (and as Lho's quote implies), the statue of the Welsh Martyr is enormously important both within the landscape of Caedmon and for rethinking *The Third Temptation* in terms of colonial violence.

Indeed, the image of the statue brackets the novel: it is the first and last image readers see. Its initial appearance is juxtaposed with the figure of the constable, the novel's lone authority figure who endlessly patrols the city but never comments or intervenes. He gazes into "the bronze eyes of the statue placed there by an African government, weathered, bleached on brows, cheeks, shoulders, its protuberances etched like highlights against the grey rockface, against the patina of the figure itself" (27). Here, the statue is not a Welsh landmark per se, but a pact with Africa—a kind of vague, uniform representation of Africa that lacks all specificity. No one can tell, really, where and how the statue emerged into being. It simply exists, worn and partially indecipherable. As a relic, to gaze upon it is to see only obscurity; neither the man nor his mission or his history, is evident. The statue marks merely a severed connection to Africa, now lost.

What is more, its image is set against a commodified vision of wild Africa: an image or advertisement of a zebra, which is first visible in the window display of a butcher shop. The statue firmly etches the image of Africa's supposed inferiority into Caedmon's consciousness.

But the statue's origins can, in fact, be traced. Though Caedmon is a fictional version of Llandudno, the martyr—not the statue—is entirely real. One of the most widely ignored aspects of the novel is its historical confrontation with Wales's troubling history of Christian missionary work in Africa throughout the nineteenth and early twentieth centuries. The Welsh Martyr, identifiable by his birth and death dates (1856 and 1924), noted in the statue's third appearance in the novel, as well as repeated textual references to "Dark Africa," is none other than Reverend William Hughes, a figure who, today, seemingly holds little historical or cultural relevance in Wales. Nevertheless, Williams's fictional town of Caedmon is built around Hughes's life and work. To be sure, there is no statue of Hughes in modern Llandudno: his missionary work has never been monumentalized, nor is it imbricated in the public consciousness as it is in the text. Given Williams's struggle with Afro Caribbean identity during the writing of the novel, Hughes's project, which was quite simply to use Wales as a site to convert and remake African savages in Europe's image, no doubt mirrors Williams's own concerns over the danger of European influence and racial effacement. In his introduction, Ramraj remarks on the connection between Hughes and the novel and contends that the "presence of the statue hints at. . . imperial resonance," but that Williams "considers it out of place in [the] novel, though he could not omit it altogether" (12). Hughes's statue, however, is much more significant than Ramraj suggests; in fact, its history and symbolism firmly establishes Wales as a site of colonial violence in the novel.

In 1892, Hughes opened his Congo Institute—sometimes referred to as the African Training Institute, or simply the Congo House—at Colwyn Bay. Hughes's methodology is outlined in *Dark Africa and the Way Out, or A Scheme for Civilizing and Evangelizing the Dark Continent,* a book *The Third Temptation* frequently references and that was originally published in 1892 by Sampson Low and later reprinted in 1960 by Negro Universities Press. Hughes's goal was not simple missionary work; he aimed to bring "uncivilized" African children to Wales to educate them using Western principles in the hope that, once converted, they would be returned to Africa to spread Christianity. Hughes's project was one of unapologetic conversion: his goal was, foremost, to strip his students of their identities and their African-ness. In *Dark Africa,* for example, Hughes contends that Africans must be segregated from the negative influences of their own people; his African students must be "kept away from the surrounding superstitions and evil influences of their people" (2). Hughes's project, then, attempts to erase and suppress cultural identity, which spreads like cancer. As he argues, "It avails little to scatter a dim light in the midst of dense darkness, or to train a few of the natives, as some missionaries do, and let them return too soon to their own people, whose bad customs destroy the good that has been done, the powers of evil being too great for the few young native converts to overcome" (6). Here, Hughes, in no uncertain terms, marks the African as not simply savage, but resoundingly evil—a malicious force that acts not out of ignorance but out of spite and hate that tempts and ruins (20).[7] The project of every good Christian Welshman is thus to aid in the effacement of African identity.

This explains in part the rapid collapse of individuality that pervades the novel. The martyr's project is one of rapid change, as Hughes's success depends on the speed and effectiveness at which he can convert the largest number of African students. Conversion, in Hughes's ideal world, happens quickly and repeatedly. In *Dark Africa and the Way Out,* he remarks on the rapidity with which he can train an African to read the New Testament, noting that he taught the entire book of Revelation to a student in nine days: "Someone may say: 'Is this possible?' It is possible, even to an African" (113). This very notion, in which Hughes celebrates the quickness through which one's identify can stripped from them, is also evident in *The Third Temptation;* in one scene, a narrator is momentarily taken aback by the ease in which agency is stripped from the subject, noting that "it is surprising too how rapidly a body surrenders its identity, merging into the general ambience—three or fourscore yards, no more, beyond which it becomes impossible to recognize even intimate relations, wives or lovers. Surprising, alarming even, when the mind thus perceives the visual constriction within which human personality manages to operate, and even to flourish" (108). Hughes's ideology of rapid conversion thus becomes a textual norm. The quickness with which one's identity is blurred and subverted is startling, as every character in the text is subject to conversion; as I've mentioned, their identities always exist under duress, subject to rapid erasure and immediate replacement.

While none of the characters fully understand the significance of the statue, it is hard to overstate its significance in the text. Williams's fictional Wales, its greatest achievement—in fact, its only monument—is the carrying out of Hughes's project. The text, then, depicts the effacement of African identity as integral to Welsh national identity. Hughes saw his missionary work as a decidedly global project, from which Wales was the starting point. In *Dark Africa and the Way Out*, he argues that Wales must be the center of African repurposing project: "We appeal. . . to the whole English-speaking nations, which happily includes America. . . . We regard this scheme as too great for little Wales to have the honour of carrying it to completion" (105). Hughes viewed his project as inextricable from Welsh nationalism, which would initiate a process of global conversion affecting all nations and peoples; his Welsh missionary work would provide a model for the world. In this sense, the Congo Institute represented not only a symbol of national pride but also the incipient emergence of a global coalition—an international network, led by Wales, whose mission was the eradication of African identity. The project of conversion was thus essential to Welsh national identity and the future of Wales's development as a nation, and this project lurks below the surface of the novel.

Although Hughes viewed his Congo Institute as the start of a larger global coalition of missionary work, he was emphatic that such a coalition must not impinge upon Welsh linguistic and cultural identity. Indeed, in the passage quoted, Hughes makes a subtle distinction between English and Welsh-speaking nations, which makes sense given Hughes's criticism of Britain's suppression of the Welsh language. In this regard, his interpretation of nationalism is considerably more complicated and contradictory than it first appears. While Hughes's institute aimed to sever Africa from the African, it was nevertheless an outspoken critic against legislation that devalued the Welsh language and sought to champion forgotten and disenfranchised Welsh art and culture. Ironically, Hughes critiques colonial practices that devalue a nation's linguistic identity:

> It is wrong and a blunder to appoint Englishmen as judges, preachers, and magistrates over the people of Wales. . . . They are ignorant of the Welsh language, unacquainted with the affairs of the Welsh people, their poverty, history, wrongs; they cannot sympathize with the sentiments, hopes, and aspirations of a conquered people like their own flesh and blood. It is an injustice that suitors and persons charged with offences cannot give in their own language, unless they employ an interpreter. The English church has failed in Wales because it came here with an unnatural way, preaching in another tongue to people who spoke Welsh.[8] (50)

Williams's allusion to Hughes's project opens the space to discuss the most overt connection that *The Third Temptation* shares with recent scholarship on colonialism and Wales: mainly, the fight for, and historic suppression of, Welsh linguistic rights. Simply put, for Hughes, a Welsh national identity is one in which Wales speaks Welsh, and the formation of a global coalition can and should only be achieved provided Wales is able to maintain its linguistic and cultural autonomy.

Predictably, though, Hughes critiques colonial practices that suppress Welsh art, language, and culture, but sees no contradiction in his own quest to stifle African art and culture, which he views as inferior. Despite his grotesque devaluing of African cultures, Hughes frequently championed festivals of Welsh art and literature and advocated for a rediscovery and embracement of Welsh identity, even though, during the late nineteenth and early twentieth centuries, Welsh was banned in schools, and students speaking it were reprimanded and punished (C. Williams, *Sugar and Slate* 30). His institute thus both participates in and repudiates imperialism concurrently. Hughes, like other missionaries, insisted that he operated on moralistic grounds, and he defended his work from critique by foregrounding England's injustices against Wales.

For Hughes, Wales is a different kind of colonizer, one that attempts to correct—or set right—the sins of Mother England. As Jane Aaron explains in "Slaughter and Salvation: Welsh Missionary Activity and British Imperialism," Welsh missionaries, especially in the nineteenth century, were often viewed distinctly different from their English counterparts. As Aaron puts it, the Welsh missionary's reputation "arises from [a] redemptive role as a savior not only of the natives but also Welsh pride in the face of the by now much-documented historical humiliations of the century" and represents a "better mode of relating to the world at large than that of the English imperial officer" (58). According to Aaron, while Welsh missionaries appropriated (and were only possible) through England's colonial model, they nevertheless saw themselves as resisting colonial power rather than embracing it (58). This contradictory logic emerges overtly in Hughes's writing and at the same time explains the historical precedent for Hughes's view that his missionary work is an anticolonialist gesture. Undoubtedly, for Hughes, the African conversion movement functions as a form of warped colonial resistance. Given *The Third Temptation*'s focus on erasure and replacement, it is significant that the central figure of racial exploitation and horror in the novel was an advocate of a Welsh language movement that foregrounded Welshness at the expense of African identity. Throughout the novel, the implication that Blackness matters *less* than Welsh identity constantly lurks below its racial subtext.

In this regard, what is both evident and striking about Hughes's project is how the effacement of African identity is in many ways designed to engender a sense of nationalistic pride. Converting Africans to Welsh

Christians provides both a repudiation of a British dominance and also a means by which to strengthen Welsh nationality. In *Sugar and Slate*, Charlotte Williams extensively addresses Hughes's nationalist project, arguing that

> [Welsh missionaries] had to tell about their work in a way that condemned exploitation and plunder and disassociated itself from the forces of colonialism. . . . They managed to be both saviours of the natives and at the same time bolster a sense of Welsh pride and self-identity that had been so cruelly robbed and pillaged by the same English colonisation. . . . "Little Wales" would have a finer, spiritual glory untainted by the savagery of and slaughter of the English at whose hands Wales itself had suffered centuries before. So the African and the Welshman were linked in a spiritual haven from the encroachments of the English. (34)

The contradiction Williams outlines is essential in perceiving the complexities of postcolonial Wales. In much the same way, Kirsti Bohata draws attention to Wales's double role as the oppressor and the oppressed. Arguing against writers like Ned Thomas, who suggest that imperialist Welsh behavior was enacted and essentially inscribed into the fabric of the Welsh society by the colonizer, Bohata insists that we not ignore "Welsh involvement in imperial missionary work throughout the Empire . . . as well as Welsh colonization of Patagonia, not to mention North America, Australia, and so on. It is neither helpful nor acceptable to divide desirable and undesirable attitudes to imperialism into Welsh and British (read English) perspectives" (5). It is, Bohata contends, not accurate to think of Wales and England in terms of colonizer or colonized, but instead preferable to "reveal the ways in which the Welsh have been subjected to a form of imperialism over a long period of time, while also acknowledging the way the Welsh have been complicit in their subjugation and in the colonization of others" (5).

While Williams was no doubt interested in Hughes's hypocrisy, it is worth pausing here to acknowledge that there is no Welsh in *The Third Temptation*. It is not certain how well Williams himself could speak Welsh, or whether he was invested or interested in Welsh linguistic rights. Charlotte Williams notes that their family spoke a hybridized language that teetered between English and Welsh—a language that resembled both "Llandudno Welsh" and "Llandudno English" (52). And though Williams notes that Welsh vernacular influenced her father's speech long after he left Wales, it is clear that his knowledge of Welsh was sparse at best.[9] Indeed, she recalls that the family would speak mostly English when Williams returned. In any case, it is unclear how supportive Williams was of Welsh linguistic rights, especially given the representation of the Welsh language—and Welshness as a whole—in the novel (53). See, for example, a key scene in which Lho, tired, frustrated, and experiencing, like Williams, a moment of domestic trauma, seeks to ease his pain by "becoming Welsh": he secludes himself in a "hut" in the Welsh countryside to reclaim his lost ancestry and language, trying on a new Welsh identity as a coping mechanism. However, Lho's quest for identity and language results only in failure and incomprehension: "How did he come by this hut in the woods? By walking a bit farther than usual one Sunday morning.... Up at the farm to which it belonged he drank skim milk with a couple of the seventeenth century, felt very Welsh with them, their furniture, their bric-a-brac, their language.... He became so very Welsh, incomprehensible consequently to his countrymen" (65–66). This is not the only time in the text that Welsh is associated with incomprehension and inscrutability as, later, Lho's ability to speak Welsh, and his quest to become more Welsh, is described as an "affront" that makes him unapproachable (66). It is interesting that Lho's linguistic mastery does not result in a sense of satisfaction, but leads only to further resentment. Lho's Welsh is never accepted (and significantly is never heard in the novel), and a return to a Welsh "way of life," both linguistically and culturally, is seen as a comic gesture of futility. Lho cannot find solace in the language of the past, and the novel, as a whole, seems critical of the value of Welsh linguistic emancipation.

More importantly, while Cambridge suggests that the struggle for Welsh linguistic rights is implied in the text, the martyr in *The Third Temptation* carries only the image of his missionary work.[10] The Hughes of the novel does not sustain Welsh art and culture, nor does he have any interest in linguistic rights: he is committed only to oppression. It would, of course, be easy to assume that *The Third Temptation*'s examination of violent temporal disorientation is set in Wales not solely because of personal trauma, but because of Wales's unique double role as the colonizer and colonized—that is, the Welsh are at the same time victims of colonial oppression and perpetrators of it. The notions of belonging and exclusion, victim and oppressor, and the space between "here and there," in some ways speaks to the colonial history of Wales as well as Williams's own sense of being caught between European and Afro-Caribbean aesthetic and cultural values. Yet the landscape of the novel focuses only on Wales as a site of oppression, and, while Williams's biography reveals a conflicted sense of belonging to Welsh culture, the fictional world depicted in *The Third Temptation* focuses almost exclusively on Wales as the oppressor.

The Wales of the novel is not under duress, nor is it oppressed; it is instead a resoundingly dangerous place for Black men and women—a place that signals only fear, hostility, and confusion.

The martyr of the novel is referenced, repeatedly, only in reference to "Dark Africa." What overwrites the historical image of a Wales struggling for linguistic emancipation while committing its own imperialism is the undeniable nature of violence Hughes carried out. In this regard, as the text concludes, the statue begins to signal more and more overt images of violence: "Pivoting, the eyes of the constable light on the bronze figure of the Welsh Martyr rising you might say from an ocean of blood, its undiscriminating gaze fixed on the restless tides of Sweeley Street, a gaze whose objectivity the constable might well envy, persons and objects being so uniformly unemotive from this godlike view. . . . beyond which a body surrenders its identity and merges into the general ambience" (131). The penultimate image of the martyr, then, is inextricable from violence. The statue of Hughes possesses what neither the constable nor the narrators can possess: a limitless gaze that, from its vantage point, sees and affects all, that cannot be restrained or suppressed. The fixed, all-consuming totality of the statue, overlooking the port (indeed, Hughes viewed Colwyn Bay's proximity to a port as integral to the success of the Institute) stands in stark contrast to the characters' inability to maintain their individual identities. In this passage, submission to the statue is enviable; pleasure and comfort exist not in resistance but in surrender. Williams articulates how much colonial power strips individuality from the subject, noting that "you can't be a man if your head has been cut off by colonialism. How can you speak, act, create anything if your every thought has been shaped for you by Europeans? If you can't think of a thought that hasn't already been cast with meaning by the coloniser" (C. Williams, *Sugar and Slate* 53). Here, Williams argues that resistance itself, under the guises of colonial power, collapses: colonization always limits the subject's ability to express individual thought. This articulation of colonial suppression bears much in common with the novel, in which no character is able to fully resist because their ideological positions are never stable and exist under duress. It is the statue's attempt to mollify, to normalize ideological surrender and to suppress the clamor of resistance, that marks it as a threat. There is no linguistic or cultural empowerment in submitting to the statue in the text. For Williams, Hughes and the statue represent only corruption, violence, and surrender.

It bears repeating that readers should not be expected to intensively investigate the historical implications of Hughes's statue. The novel's disorienting narrative structure, as previously stated, engenders a sense of confusion and frustration that captures sensations of both racial trauma and geographical dislocation to the extent that the statue may be overlooked. Yet its repeated presence in the novel is difficult to ignore, and Williams's larger goal in the novel is to emphasize how forms of oppression are frequently abstracted from clear view and often societally and culturally obfuscated in particularly complex ways. The statue's presence—which even critics and reviewers have missed—thus speaks to the difficulty of both observing and understanding the historical trajectory of colonial and racial oppression.

Miscegenation and the Legacy of the Martyr

The institutionalized reverence of the martyr and the unmistakable physical presence of his colonial ideals normalize and ingrain the inferiority of Blackness—specifically Black men—in Caedmon. Given the centrality of the martyr in Williams's novel, it is important to consider the most significant element of the text: the troubling representation of its Black characters. Simply put, the overbearing, undeniable image of the martyr, who is worshipped and venerated, means that Black identity in the text is mostly invisible—or, worse, exists only in terms of racial stereotypes. As such, the only Blackness in *The Third Temptation* is Blackness that affirms the martyr's stereotypes of uncivilized, savage Black men. Fears that Black men will corrupt white women pervade the narrative; in this regard, the novel is rife with intimations of miscegenation and violence. If the meaning of the statue remains opaque throughout the text, the novel's experimental examination of the pervasiveness of Black stereotypes is a considerably more overt motif.

Repeatedly, the novel represents Blackness as a corruptive force and a threat to white women. Even before we see any Black characters, Blackness is paired with an explicit depiction of sexuality, and, what is more, infects the white European masses with its destructiveness. For example, early on, a pregnant white European woman wearing a pink and white smock suddenly transforms into a lurid, pornographic blonde, with legs spread "over her head, in dozens of postures, a blond figure appears, now in mink, now in mist, now in a foamy bath, now reflected in a million mirrors, now nude among floating bubbles, now her hair, her eyes, now bare legs, pelvis bare, augmented breasts" (32). This transformation occurs only as the woman stares at a phallic, burning image of kaleidoscopic "blackness"; indeed, it is the exposure to Blackness that transforms her from a chaste white woman waiting for her husband to an aroused seductress. In sum, Blackness functions as a signifier for sexual deviance that will consume the virtue of white women: it engenders heightened sexual arousal and unnatural poses, gestures, and behaviors. The scene again evokes Hughes by mirroring the martyr's insistence that Blackness needs to be civilized if it is to function in Welsh society. It is significant that the Blackness described in the passage is not a human being, but a concept: an amorphous blob of destruction lingering over the white populace, begging for someone to contain it. Such scenes seemingly provide a moral justification for Hughes's project to civilize African men by repeating the racist trope that Black bodies need to be pacified before they can be integrated. In the novel, however, these scenes do not endorse stereotypes of Black sexuality, but critique Welsh society's views on race, as citizens of Caedmon cannot conceive of a Black populace beyond sensational depictions of jungle savagery.

The novel introduces only two Black characters—both men—who embody racial hysteria. They exist only through their relationships to "the blonde": Chloë, the *Chronicle* girl, a beautiful white woman who is a constant source of desire. They are both her lovers: her ex-boyfriend, Gent, a rail worker and most likely a Caribbean immigrant; and the man without a nose, a savage caricature of sexual violence and desire who preys on unsuspecting white women, including Chloë. During an awkward, failed sexual encounter with Joss Banks in a historic church, Chloë details a need to be violated as she narrates an animalistic sexual encounter by the man with no nose, a hysterical depiction of a Black savage possessing "just two black holes in the middle of his face" (104). Yet the man with no nose represents the height of Chloë's sexual desire, so much so that she is unable to tell the story without becoming excited, stopping twice, shouting, "It was the best ever, ever, Oh God!" (104) and "God, how he made love to me! It was like I'd never done it before the way he made love to me" (105). Indeed, Chloë frequently waits by the window hoping the man with no nose will return and ravish her. Just as the amorphous "blackness" morphs the pregnant woman in the pink smock into an object of sexual desire, Chloë cannot resist the lure of the sexual violence of the Black savage. This hypersexualization of race in the text depicts a Welsh landscape that, long after Hughes's martyrdom, remains a hostile space unable to free itself from its dehumanization of Black men.

In this sense, it is likely that the martyr's role in *The Third Temptation* functions as a means through which to examine Welsh and European perceptions of miscegenation, a topic that increasingly interested Williams.[11]

Following his move to Africa, Williams argued that miscegenation must be an aspect of all his future creative work (E. Williams 104). Miscegenation, he contended, is "the first reality of Guyanese being" and must be confronted if the arts are to achieve "autonomy and authority" (quoted in E. Williams 104). Williams's newfound obsession with the aesthetic implications of miscegenation—and his increasing emphasis on the work of Frantz Fanon—in many ways explains *The Third Temptation*'s close attention to the topic. His racial depictions of Black men and white women were likely influenced by Fanon, whose analysis of violence and the power dynamics of gender in *Black Skin, White Masks* has much in common with the racialized, sensational images of Black men in the novel. For Fanon, Blackness always functions as a sexual threat—associated with fantasy and pain—to white women. In an oft-quoted passage, Fanon analyzes the dynamics of interracial desire:

> We discover that when a woman lives the fantasy of rape by a Negro, it is in some way the fulfillment of a private dream, of an inner wish. Accomplishing the phenomenon of turning against self, it is the woman who rapes herself. We can find clear proof of this in the fact that it is commonplace for women, during the sexual act, to cry to their partners: "Hurt me!" They are merely expressing this idea: Hurt me as I would hurt me if I were in your place. The fantasy of rape by a Negro is a variation of this emotion: "I wish the Negro would rip me open as I would have ripped a woman open." (138)

In Fanon's view, the white woman thus imagines the Black man as a manifestation of pain that she inflicts on herself. In this case, Blackness becomes an object of the women's "sadomasochistic desire" (Chow 68). While many critics such as Rey Chow and Amber Jamilla Musser have rightly attacked Fanon's discussion of rape, his lack of attention toward the sexuality of black women, and the heteronormative assumptions here regarding a woman's sexuality, Williams was undoubtedly interested in Fanon's examination of the objectification of black male bodies.[12] In an early interview, it is Fanon whom Williams cites to express his frustration with being objectified as a "negro artist."[13] Accordingly, in the novel, as in Fanon, Black bodies function as commodities for white women, as neither of the two Black characters in the text—Gent or the man without a nose—have value beyond their sexual potency; they exist solely as sexual objects.

The Third Temptation mirrors Fanon's depiction of interracial relationships by focusing on the Black male body as an object through which the white women negotiates her sexual trauma. Accordingly, the novel juxtaposes Chloë's monstrous black assailant with her boyfriend, Gent, who

Chloë argues is racial, but not savage; Gent is not dangerous or violent enough. With him, the sexual act becomes a grotesque performance—for, although Chloë's sexual act with Gent depicts explicit racial violence, it produces no pleasure: "It wasn't ever really nice with him—too racial—neither of us was getting the most out of it like; he could only get going by calling me a white swine and trash and that, so I'd say to him Come on me black baboon you wonderful beast give it to me like you know how, like you give your own women and that would make him so he couldn't help walloping me afterwards" (105). Despite the inherent violence in the scene, the relationship is consensual and therefore boring—a stark contrast to the spontaneous encounter with the noseless savage. As Fanon argues, miscegenation is guided by a narrative of self-hatred in which the Black body must function as the manifestation of an unbearable threat and danger; the imagined interracial act thus enacts a feeling of both fear and sexual hysteria. Yet this myth—as Fanon describes in recounting an encounter with a white prostitute who dejectedly remarked that "going to bed with [Black men] was no more remarkable than going to bed with white men"—fails to engender sexual fulfillment, as the stereotype always obviates sexual pleasure (122).[14] The novel, then, both endorses and refutes the myth Fanon describes. Chloë takes pleasure from the noseless man precisely because he is a threat; Gent, however, evokes no such fear, as the violence of their relationship has become routine, formulaic, and largely performative. Just as the prostitute in Fanon's example yearns for a fabrication of a Black body to stimulate and violate her, Chloë and Gent's relationship exists only as a series of impossible, racist stereotypes.

It is worth pausing here to acknowledge that what is significant about Chloë and Gent's relationship is the very fact that racial hatred is, for the first and only time in *The Third Temptation,* unmistakably visible—no longer opaque, but clear. In rendering racism overtly, the scene seemingly violates the textual norms that veil explicit discussions of race and oppression. Thus Williams's text experiments with the degree to which oppressive ideologies and belief systems can be articulated, as the scenes between Chloë and Gent seemingly transgress against the guiding axioms of race that dominate the Wales of the novel: that it must not be discussed, but remain buried below the surface.

This suppression and articulation—particularly concerning the visibility of racial violence and the essentialization of Black bodies—is clearly centered around Chloë's character. Chloë is not just a reporter working for the *Chronicle:* she is a Lobby Lud. In this regard, the novel provides a surreptitious critique of racism inherent in the British concept of the

Lobby Lud, which was started in 1927 by the *Westminster Gazette*. The idea is simple: a newspaper staff member visits a resort or vacation town and, as a publicity stunt, hides in plain sight. The tourist's goal is to find the Lobby Lud and essentially claim them and, in so doing, claim a prize or monetary reward. Accordingly, this is Chloë's role in the novel, which she reveals to Joss soon after they meet in the church. Joss assumes Chloë has entered the church to escape the crowd, but, as she tells him: "A seaside place like this you don't try to escape the crowd, you're strange, they're all looking for me anyway, I'm Chloë. After lunch they'll all be out on the prom looking for me: Chloë the *Chronicle* girl. Looking for me and me knowing all about it" (95). Chloë, who is presumably British, thus blends into the landscape of Caedmon, waiting to be claimed. Yet, historically, the Lobby Lud is always white—this remains the case in the novel, too,—perhaps predictably, given that there are almost no Black characters in Caedmon. In any case, Chloë's ability to hide depends on the establishment of an entirely white space. Given that Williams's visits to Llandudno were predominantly in the summer, he most likely was aware of the most well-known Lobby Lud in Wales, The *Daily Mirror*'s "Chalky White." As Charlotte Williams writes, her initials (C. W.) made her the object of ridicule during the summer of White's visit, as her peers would jokingly claim her as their "Chalky White" Lobby Lud (*Sugar and Slate* 66)—a jab no doubt directed both at her name and brown skin. But Charlotte Williams's narrative perhaps reveals a key truth about the concept: as a seemingly innocuous publicity stunt, the Lobby Lud depends on the degree of privilege granted to white Europeans to confront, and claim, a total stranger without fear of repercussion.

Denis Williams, with his knowledge of Welsh colonialism, was no doubt interested in the racial dynamics of human beings being transformed into financial objects that are central to the Lobby Lud concept. Due to the fact that the Lobby Lud in the novel is British, and to Williams's daughter's own experiences as a mistaken Lobby Lud "object," one can see why the Lobby Lud character in the text instigates a distinct sense of racial violence and racial hysteria. The Lobby Lud is a game of whiteness in which it appears unimaginable for, say, a Black Guyanese man to claim, in this case, the white Lobby Lud woman. Thus, Williams reads the Lobby Lud as an expansion of Welsh colonialism: a British institution in which Europeans claim ownership over Europeans, and in which objectification becomes a lucrative game—a play—for tourists. Williams, then, inverts the image of the Lobby Lud by foregrounding Chloë's need for Blackness. She yearns for the Black body that she must either touch in secret, as is the case with her animalistic lover, or that she cannot connect with beyond a performative sense of hatred. Here, Williams lays bare the racism of the practice, in which the white Lobby Lud seeks the Black body as an object and indeed, can *only* conceive of it as an object. The Lobby Lud becomes an embodiment of colonial practice and, with it, the accompanying views of miscegenation in which Black bodies lay claim to white women.

Williams's inversion of the Lobby Lud, in which white women desperately seek to be found, claimed, and ravaged by hysterical, racist characterizations of savage Black men, returns us once again to William Hughes. In this regard, the Lobby Lud is not the only real-life corollary behind the novel's emphasis on interracial relationships, as it was ultimately a miscegenation scandal that shut down the Congo Institute. In December 1911, the "energetically xenophobic" (Declercq and Walker 219) British publication *John Bull* published an article about the Congo Institute with the scandalous headline "BLACK BAPTIST'S BROWN BABY" (Draper and Lawson-Reay 237). The article was less an attack on Welsh society than a racist diatribe, in keeping with the larger colonialist message of the magazine, which regularly featured articles with titles like "ENGLISH LADIES AND NEGROES" that described how "*black and white may frequently be seen strolling together down the road behind the Institute,*" and how supporters of the Congo House were race traitors who ignored the plight of starving British children (Draper and Lawson-Reay 238; italics in original). To save his reputation, Hughes sued the publication's owner, Horatio Bottomley, for libel in June 1912, but lost the case and was considerably humiliated during the proceedings (239). Following the loss, Bottomley, an unapologetic racist, gloated that "Colwyn Bay is delighted to be rid of the pest Hughes and his niggers . . . a sensuous, barbarous and cunning lot of niggers, some of them of the lowest order of intelligence and morals . . . an ever present menace to the safety of white women" (270; ellipses in original). This statement by Bottomley, who, it is worth noting was a member of British parliament (at least until he was expelled and imprisoned for fraud in 1918), once again brings to mind the ideological colonial conflict between Britain, Wales, and Africa, as Hughes's supposed moralistic racism was dethroned by an even more intolerant form of racism that argued that Black bodies were, and could only ever be, entirely savage.

The novel subtly references the miscegenation scandal, when Chloë expresses an explicit and unyielding desire to produce a Black child. As she reflects on her relationship with Gent, she expresses aching regret that she could not bear his children: "That's why I run away—we was driving each other up the wall and there wasn't no fun in it really except we keep insulting each other. Even though I wanted his children, I really did, I always will I think, I never wanted anybody's children after that, only abortions" (105). While the scene depicts yet another instance of racist fear that white women, once exposed to Black men, will be overcome with sexual longing for them, it also cites and embraces Bottomley's conspiratorial belief that miscegenation poses a threat to white supremacy. In the novel, Chloë tells us that she has aborted any child that was not Black. Given the novel's repeated reference to Hughes, it is likely that Williams had the institute's miscegenation scandal in mind when crafting this scene.

In any case, that the collapse of the Congo Institute occurred not because of a repudiation of colonialist practices, but because of widespread racial hysteria and a public smear campaign, no doubt signals a larger critique of contemporary Welsh society. Indeed, Chloë's need to produce a Black child strongly echoes the *John Bull* scandal that erupted around Hughes's institute, in which Black men corrupt white woman to produce "BROWN BABIES." The dissolution of the institute, frequently intimated in the novel, thus reveals Williams's deep concerns over the history—and future of—interracial relationships in Wales. In citing and resituating the miscegenation scandal in the contemporary landscape of 1960s Wales, Williams implies that the racist ideologies surrounding the collapse of the Congo Institute remain persistent.

In sum, the novel's exploration of historical and biographical trauma is guided by an underlying racial violence that, Williams argues, is an integral aspect of Welsh life. Readers who work to unravel the implications of the text's opaque language will thus find a complex and startling critique of the normalization of racial oppression in contemporary Wales. Hughes, of course, is a real, albeit mostly forgotten, figure that, the text argues, has dominated and influenced Welsh life throughout much of the twentieth century. His legacy is hidden in plain sight, but, in the fictional landscape of *The Third Temptation,* Hughes is not an unremembered symbol of colonialist oppression, but a martyr who is venerated, to whom the entire town is built around as a locus, and to whom all the whites in the novel owe thanks. Strikingly, over fifty years later, this landscape has an eerie contemporary resonance. In 2002, Christopher Draper and John Lawson-Reay published *A Scandal at the Congo House,* which explores the lost history of the Hughes institute—a study sorely needed. Yet Draper and Lawson-Reay's book is hardly objective and views Hughes's work not with impartiality, much less with critique. They argue that the Congo

House represented "the noblest kind of imperialism," and the end of their text resembles an apologist treatise (276). Hughes, they write, "didn't believe Africans were less intelligent or occupied a lower evolutionary plane but he did believe in the ultimate superiority of European civilisation" (276). They conclude, shockingly, that Hughes is a Welsh hero:

> William Hughes achieved a tremendous amount with limited resources, both financial and intellectual. He was brave, imaginative and enlightened but he just wasn't up to the enormous task he set for himself. He allied himself to men far less altruistic and radical than himself. . . . Crushed by a combination of ineptitude and bigotry he remains an inspiration. Hughes' long and close association with Mojola Agbebi and the independent Black African churches is testimony to his integrity, and the enduring influence of his students his abiding legacy. . . . In a final letter addressed from "The African Institute, Colwyn Bay," just before he was shuffled off into penury and obscurity, William Hughes begged of old friends and supporters, and perhaps of us today: "Please do not forget to remember me." (278)

The rediscovery of Hughes, not as a figure of colonial horror, but as a forgotten Welsh hero, paradoxically extends the tragedy of the novel, as Draper and Lawson-Reay venerate Hughes's legacy in almost the same way as many of the novel's characters do. The importance of Williams's novel should be evident, in that it reveals not just that colonial violence is often obfuscated and overwritten, but that it continues to be today. Viewed in this way, the novel is not an apolitical, European tribute to experimental fiction, but an examination of psychological principles and positions that repeatedly threaten to efface Black identity. Williams's novel requires further investigation not only for its radical experimentation but also for its investigation of the role of racial oppression in contemporary Wales and its desperate attempt to articulate the trauma of Caribbean identity.

3 Language as Animosity
Pejorative Speech and National Identity

IN KAMAU Brathwaite's much discussed and often analyzed study of Caribbean poetics, *The History of the Voice,* Brathwaite argues that the word "dialect" is itself a form of oppression. Because dialect is synonymous with a colonial ideology that equates linguistic formality and precision with humanity and worth, Brathwaite thus theorizes the concept of "nation language," an anticolonial, communal vernacular that symbolizes empowerment and resistance rather than inferiority. As Brathwaite argues, nation language functions as a metaphorical machine gun designed to extricate vernacular from its pejorative implications. He contends that

> nation language is the language which is influenced very strongly by the African model, the African aspect of our New World/Caribbean heritage. . . . [It] is an English that is not the standard, imported, educated English, but that of the submerged, surrealist experience and sensibility, which has always been there and which is now increasingly coming to the surface and influencing the perception of contemporary Caribbean people. It is what I call, as I say, *nation language*. I use the term in contrast to *dialect*. The word dialect has been bandied about for a long time, and it carries very pejorative overtones. Dialect is thought of as "bad" English. Dialect is "inferior" English. Dialect is the language when you want to make fun of someone. . . . Nation language, on the other hand, is the submerged area of that dialect that is much more closely allied to the African aspect of experience in the Caribbean. It may be in English, but often it is an English which is like a howl, or a shout, or a machine-gun, or the wind, or a wave. (13)

As the term "nation language" implies, Brathwaite situates linguistic identity and representation as integral to the formation of a national identity. In repudiating colonial discourse that frames verbal and written language as inferior or improper, Brathwaite argues for a linguistic representation that captures the pluralistic uniqueness of Caribbean experience. Thus, nation language, contra dialect, is both a form of affirmation and resistance. Though the term "creole" has largely displaced "nation language" and "dialect" in contemporary Caribbean studies, in theorizing a concept of dialect that severs it from its dehumanizing principles, Brathwaite's idea of nation language remains immensely important in exploring the nuances of language in Caribbean literature.[1]

While Brathwaite's conception of nation language has been helpful in rethinking language as a form of empowerment, throughout the midtwentieth century many Caribbean writers, such as Roger Mais and Eric Walrond, were less optimistic that dialect could be freed from its dehumanizing tendencies. They wrestled with representations of speech and vernacular in their works in ways that expressed skepticism that regional language could function as a productive force. This chapter examines the pejorative implications of creole and vernacular in the Caribbean, in that the employment of vernacular, in the experimental works I discuss, does not represent a multivocal and pluralistic form of empowerment that stands against colonial forces, but rather functions as a solidification of the colonial order. In such works, vernacular is indicative of a fabricated colonial imaginary that both simplifies and obfuscates the nuances and experiences of Caribbean peoples—particularly the poor and impoverished—into an uncomplicated, amorphous mass. In this regard, Brathwaite's theorization of a linguistic poetics that emancipates rather than oppresses bears a thorny relationship to the midcentury experimental Caribbean novel; the works I discuss espouse doubt that vernacular can function as an act of community building or national identity. As I will explore, the writings of Roger Mais and Eric Walrond in particular struggle with imagining a Caribbean vernacular that is disentangled from its pejorative connotations, and their works create linguistic landscapes that thematize the struggle to assert a uniquely Caribbean linguistic identity. Their representation of vernacular thereby functions as a source of immense tension and contradiction, often framing Caribbean speech patterns as spectral, collective, and unintelligible. In these texts, interpreting and understanding the meaning and implications of the impoverished characters' utterances become the primary theme, as the incorporation of vernacular threatens to make the voices of the lower classes inscrutable.

In many ways, such works anticipate the questions raised by Charles Bernstein's cautious rethinking of nation language in "Poetics of the Americas." In the essay, Bernstein expresses skepticism toward what he views as the collectivizing aspects of nation language and theories of communal speech. The crux for Bernstein is that, in attempting to create a new form of collective linguistic identity, Brathwaite does not fully consider the inherent irreconcilable tension between hegemonic forces and the voices of the oppressed. Arguing for a poetic ideology of perpetual rupture that highlights the ever-present tension between subaltern peoples and oppressive institutions—as opposed to the collective empowerment that Brathwaite contends may emerge through nation language—Bernstein proposes a concept of language that he coins "ideolect." Bernstein lays out his critique, noting that,

> for Brathwaite, "nation language" is not a deformation of mastery but the sign of a newly forming collective identity. It moves beyond critique and subversion to a positive expressivity; that is, beyond a bogus universality to what Brathwaite, problematically in my view, understands as a genuine locality. . . . The tension between universality and locality is not simply a deformation or an embryonic phase of group consciousness to be shed at maturity. As against the positive expressivity of nation language I would speak of the negative dialectics of ideolect, where ideolect would mark those poetic sites of contest between the hegemonic and the subaltern. (126)

Though Brathwaite believes that nation language can capture a "genuine" sense of locality by moving toward what might be considered an emergent, communal form of linguistic identity, Bernstein argues that the power and poetic use of dialect lies not in its ability to express communal bonds or resistance, or to reveal true or authentic speech, but in its ability to reveal sites of tension and conflict.[2] As an example, in analyzing John Agard's poem "Listen Mr. Oxford Don," Bernstein asserts that the speaker's use of dialect in the poem does not express a moment of effective rebellion, as Brathwaite suggests, or even "a more authentic representation of speech," but instead opens up an "even more marvelous realization of the yammering gap between speech and writing" (124–25). Thought of in this way, the poem captures less an authentic representation of the speaker's desires or an attempt to undermine the language of the oppressor than a struggle to articulate those very desires. In other words, the poem forces us to think more deeply not only about what can and cannot be expressed but also about the disconnect between speech and the written word, as well as the nature of the linguistic relationship between the oppressor and the oppressed. Simply put, Bernstein's ideology of dialect embraces a poetics of continuous rupture over any sense of communal expression; the communal aspect of ideolect is bound only to its embrace of the radical properties of language, which, Bernstein argues, forever expresses the tension between subaltern expression and hegemonic violence. Bernstein's articulation of ideolect, which theorizes a form of linguistic expression that emphasizes *continuous* rupture and disorientation, is important in analyzing the landscape of mid-twentieth-century anglophone Caribbean literature, in part because the practices of inscrutability I examine in this book are rooted in a sense of productive discomfort that emphasizes acts of perpetual decoding.

Building off of the debate between Brathwaite and Bernstein, the works I discuss in this chapter caution against the embrace of linguistic collectivity and champion instead a view of language that emphasizes its ability to rupture rather than establish or affirm communal, local, or national identities. While both theorists ground their analysis of creole in poetic forms, my focus here on the novel reveals a more sustained engagement with the properties of language that, in the works I discuss, is examined and maintained through the incorporation of experimental narrative devices. My analysis focuses on two novels: Roger Mais's *Brother Man* (1954) and Eric Walrond's *Tropic Death* (1926), texts that express a profound unease with the concept of language as a cultural—or national—unifier. In emphasizing formal and linguistic techniques that render speech and dialogue unintelligible, they convey an overwhelming sense of tension and a deep anxiety about language's role in the formation of a national consciousness. I highlight how in, in Mais's *Brother Man,* the narrative tension between the narrator and the novel's often-inscrutable choral body reveals a critique of monolithic representations of Jamaica's poor. In Walrond's work, I examine not only the novel's formal challenges in terms of its laboring characters' creole but also the way the collection's narrator deploys a racist vernacular as a means of obfuscating the segregationist labor system of the Panama Canal Zone in which *Tropic Death* is set. In short, Mais's and Walrond's work overtly confront the role of vernacular and creole in the Caribbean, examining the ways in which language itself becomes unstable, fragile, and performative. As a result, their writing urges readers to consider the degree to which forms of communal speech may function to obscure—and sometimes enforce—systems of colonial oppression.

Roger Mais and the Voice of The Masses

More so than perhaps any novelist associated with the Windrush generation, the work of Roger Mais has fallen almost entirely out of fashion, in part because his most radical, innovative works remained, until recently, out of print. Born in Jamaica in 1905, Mais is best known for his political writings and his first novel, *The Hills Were Joyful Together* (1953), a yard narrative that, in experimenting with perspective, shares stylistic similarities with C. L. R. James's *Minty Alley* (1936). Mais's writing, it should be noted, was never very well received in Jamaica or the Caribbean. Disappointed with his career, he left Jamaica for London in 1952, where his works were better regarded. After arriving, he quickly published his first two novels. Mais was in Europe just three years, however, before he fell ill and returned to Jamaica, where he abruptly died. A cursory overview of his oeuvre reveals a sense of fiery resentment and scathing anger, often directed at both the colonial order and the Jamaican lower and middle classes, who he felt were too complacent in opposing colonial forces. Indeed, as J. Dillon Brown notes, Mais was often known for being incendiary—so much so that he was greatly disliked by Cedric and Gladys Lindo, editors of *Caribbean Voices*. Nevertheless, his novels found a larger audience in England, and his shocking death led to considerable coverage in the London papers (Brown 134–35).[3] As Brown reminds us, today Mais's work is typically seen through the lens of Caribbean nationalism, and Mais himself is often viewed as "a nationalist author with a predominantly political bent" (135). Yet, with the exception of Brown's work on Mais, as well as that of the work of Faith Smith, there has been almost no significant critical attention directed at Mais's work since the 1980s.[4] This point is no doubt exacerbated by the fact that Mais's two self-published short story collections, *Face and Other Stories* (1942) and *And Most of All Man* (1942) were never reprinted, and, as Daphne Morris has pointed out, Kenneth Ramchand's Longman 1986 collection, *Listen, the Wind and Other Stories,* not only contains a number of grievous errors but is also long out of print.[5] As is the case with many of the other authors discussed in this study, Mais's inventive conceptions of narrative form—combined with his often cutting, acerbic confrontations with colonial indoctrination and complacency—suggest that his work is in dire need of reevaluation.

Typically, Mais's work has been read in terms of its endorsement for a nationalist aesthetic—that is, as part of the larger trend of mid-twentieth-century Caribbean novels designed to enforce a sense of national identity. As Faith Smith contends, Mais's writing, particularly his second novel, *Brother Man,* "can be read as a classic example of the nationalist fiction of the period, with its exploration of working-class life. Such fiction sometimes features a central middle-class character (usually male) both drawn to and repelled by the values of a working-class community in which he finds himself, and the vitality of this community is key to the delineation of the 'authentic' characteristics of an emerging nation" (11). Yet a closer inspection of Mais's work reveals a deeper skepticism toward emerging representations of Caribbean national identity than critics have previously acknowledged. In this chapter, I want to focus on a different, largely unexplored aspect of Mais's aesthetic, concerning his experimental linguistic tendencies that, I contend, function not as an endorsement but as a *repudiation* of nationalism's essentializing tendencies. In experimenting with linguistic representations of vernacular and pejorative creole, Mais's work lodges a scathing critique of the ways in which representations of language can be seen to enforce colonial indoctrination—a critique that has been thoroughly overlooked. I want, then, to argue against Kwame S. N. Dawes's claim that "Mais fails to explore the larger political tensions of colonialism and race in his novel" (31) and, "in *Brother Man*, as in *Black Lightning*, we are never directed to feel that the pathologies of Mais's main characters have been shaped primarily by social degradation" (33).[6] In contrast, I read Mais's experiments with language as a bitter critique of ideologies of nationalism and communal speech that essentialize and obfuscate the multifaceted suffering of the poor by framing them as collectively unintelligible.

It isn't difficult to understand why Mais's work is preoccupied with themes of national identity and essentialism. In the mid-twentieth century, both home and abroad, the appetency to create a new peasant language—or a language of the masses—vied uneasily with the threat of essentialism to which Caribbean peoples were already victim. And while emergent communal and nationalist ideologies served as a potential form of emancipation throughout the middle of the century, they were also met with, especially in Jamaica, a sense of anxious unease that the models that emerged would be restrictive or exclusionary. As Suzanne Scafe writes,

> the late 1930s and '40s in Jamaica saw the development and strengthening of concepts of cultural nationalism and the production of literary and visual cultures that sought to represent the majority African population of the island and indigenous or African defined forms of cultural expression. . . . However, even the most ardent demands for a culture that reflected the lives and experiences of the ordinary people of Jamaica were not without traces of anxiety, fear and feelings of ambivalence as to how that culture might be defined and what would constitute legitimate cultural expression. There was some concern . . . that this surge of nationalist sentiment . . . would be prescriptive and would curb creative freedom. (67)

Mais himself was explicitly concerned with the dangers of prescriptive nationalism. In his 1944 essay "Now We Know"—a work for which he was imprisoned for sedition—he argues that the framers of Jamaica's new constitution failed to imagine a Jamaica untethered to British stereotypes that frame the poor as docile servants. The colonial authority, he writes, hopes that Jamaicans "might rejoice in our poverty and degradation and sickness and ignorance and sores; for it is accounted more blessed to be poor." While the essay functions as a larger critique of colonial rule and complacency, it also seeks to confront and overturn colonial logic that represent the Jamaican lower classes as irredeemably helpless and deficient. In order to repudiate colonial authority, we must, the essay implies, reject nationalism that essentializes and normalizes Jamaican suffering. Mais's essay thus captures deeper concerns about representation, essentialism, and resistance that continued to dominate Caribbean political discourse in the twentieth century.

Such concerns were also explicitly present within Caribbean literary communities. Dangerously monolithic representations of poverty and the masses were troublingly enforced by many middle-class Caribbean writers themselves who, in an attempt to create a literature of the folk, essentialized the lower classes in deeply problematic ways. As the twentieth-century literary canon began to crystallize around George Lamming and the Windrush generation's notion of peasant literature, the concept become a "critical straitjacket" that was difficult to escape (Brown and Rosenberg 4). Literary representations of the lower classes, by writers like Lamming and C. L. R. James, had the unfortunate side effect of exoticizing conditions of poverty, creating sometimes sensational stock images and representations that belied the complexity of poverty in the Caribbean. In creating an imaginary—yet pervasive—image of the lower classes, many Windrush novelists, who had little experience with the people that were at the center of their novels, effectively distorted conditions of poverty through the lens of middle class fantasy. As Lisa Outar argues, a key problem with Lamming's work is its refusal to think beyond its idealization of peasant experience and lower-class emancipation; as a result, it "fails to see the multiple forms of nationalism that were emerging in the region and thus fails to recognize that one such type was not going to be sufficient to encompass the ethnic diversity of the region" (37). Paradoxically, then, in championing the virtue of peasant identity, the lower classes became distorted echoes of tropes that reduced their individual suffering to a troubling collection of stereotypes. The inoculation of the masses that Mais fears in "Now We Know" reemerges here as the encroachment of essentializing rhetoric that comes not simply at the hands of the colonial authority, but in Windrush aesthetics, which also remakes and reframes poverty as a didactic monolith.

Mais's writing expresses a deep unease with simplifying, essentializing rhetoric that frames lower-class Caribbean experience as an amorphous mass of tropes and clichés. Indeed, these themes are prominent in *Brother Man*, a novel concerned with the voices and protests of "the people in the lane"—an impoverished collective of Jamaican peasants who function, at times, as a choral unit. Though seldom read today, the 1954 novel focuses on the birth of early Rastafarian culture in Jamaica in the 1940s and 1950s and may very well be one of the most innovative novels in all of Caribbean literature. It is a novel that systematically—but surreptitiously—overturns and dismantles central tenets of the Caribbean novel and, perhaps most significantly, forces readers to rethink the relationship between text and language. The novel focuses on the life of John Power, a religious healer with ties to the Rastafari movement. Structurally, it is broken into three sections: a chorus, a more traditional narrative-driven story, and a number of illustrations sketched by Mais himself. In terms of plot, however, the events of the narrative are, on the surface, fairly straightforward, in that it depicts a prolonged snapshot of religious intolerance. Brother Man, also known as John Power, is a soft-spoken religious healer who resides with his disciple Minette. Throughout the novel, Brother Man's kindness provides an anchor of hope to the people in the Lane, an impoverished community of Jamaican peasants. The conflict centers around the relationship between Brother Man and the novel's primary antagonist, Papacita, an abusive misogynist and counterfeiter, who grows increasingly jealous of Brother Man because of his closeness to Minette, whom Papacita yearns to seduce. In an effort to pry Minette away, Papacita concocts a successful scheme: he plants counterfeit money in Brother Man's home, and Brother Man's resulting arrest leaves a stain on his reputation that causes people to turn against him. They blame him for a rape and murder he did not commit and, at the end of the novel, violently assault and defecate on him. As the novel concludes, a badly beaten Brother Man and Minette gaze out into an uncertain future, feeling restrained hope and optimism that Mais does not spell out for readers. On the surface, Mais's text appears undoubtedly realist in tone and plot, and it may seem strange to follow an analysis of Williams's rigorous and difficult work with a discussion of Mais. Yet the ingenuity of Mais's experiments with language, representation, and narrative structure are considerably more complex than they initially seem.

What makes the novel remarkable is not its plot, but its examination of abstraction, communal speech, and the essentializing properties of language. Mais's deployment of language in the novel is multifaceted and complex, and the novel establishes at the outset conflictual representations of speech and language in the Caribbean. While the narrator speaks in a mostly refined, formal English, the people he describes speak almost exclusively in creole. Whereas the vernacular of the people reveals a variegated depiction of creole that embraces an array of linguistic flourishes and individual eccentricities, the narrator's speech functions somewhat differently, as it works to evocatively capture the peoples' plight through a formal and almost poetic language. However, it often clashes in tone and style with the voices of the characters it seeks to describe, as more formal English collides with creole speech in a way that exposes a distinct and undeniable economic and linguistic divide between its presumably middle-class omniscient narrator and the impoverished people that it describes. For example, when Girlie goes out dancing at the Rockney Club with her abusive partner, Papacita, she begins to reflect on their relationship and their past, trying to remember what it was like to fall in love. As the narrator explains, Girlie's complicated feelings for Papacita waver uncomfortably between feelings of jealousy and resentment, overt romantic longing, and what the narrator describes as a maternal sense of obligation. As the narrator tells us: "The thought reached down deep inside her with a kind of pang and longing that was instinct and maternal, and brought with it the knowledge of pain. And now, over and above her physical passionate jealous love of him, was this other, this tenderness, this warm maternal yarning that searched out the very springs of her being where it took its issue of life" (78). The juxtaposition of the narrator's more formal poetic language and diction against Girlie's matter-of-fact creole in the novel raises a number of questions: Is this how Girlie would express this sentiment? Are these words an accurate rendering of how she feels? It is unlikely, given that all she can verbalize in the scene itself is the troubling affirmation "You kick me, box me, anyt'ing, I don't care, I love only you in de world" (79). The linguistic chasm here is interesting in its suggestion that there is something its characters cannot say or express that needs someone to translate, to effectively make sense of their thoughts and feelings, as well as other expressions that seemingly cannot be articulated out loud. This sense of tension between the narrator and the characters it describes is made more evident—and perhaps more problematic—by the very fact that complex emotions are seldom rendered in creole in the text, but, rather, translated into more formal language throughout.

While this uncomfortable tension operates below the surface of the text—and is made manifest in the novel's conclusion, which I will discuss later in this chapter—the problem of language grows increasingly more urgent and complicated in the chorus sections, in which Mais more explicitly confronts practices of essentialism. In the novel's five chorus sections that precede each chapter, readers are met with short, lyrical vignettes in which the impoverished masses speak as a collective whole. Unlike in the main narrative, in these sections mass swaths of the Jamaican peasantry share a uniform voice and ideology, speaking one after another, but without any clear indication of individual identity; the voice of the people is typically represented as a communal, but undefined, amalgamation of creole voices:

> —Lawd Ma, people wicked fo' true
> —Me hear say was one bearded man
> —Beard or no beard, man wicked jus' de same. (172)

This seemingly subtle shift in language and representation—from individual to collective speech—marks an important change in both how the narrator represents and reacts to the characters in the novel. If we compare the central characters' speech in the main narrative to the chorus, we find that the creole in the main text often emphasizes individualized experience and a sense of linguistic autonomy that reveals something about the speaker, such as Papacita's catchphrase "riddle-me-riddle" that reflects his larger questioning of the rules and expectations of Jamaican society (77). His speech, as is the case with other characters in the novel, reveals something of his individuality. The result is a tableau of linguistic forms that depict a pluralistic representation of the Jamaican landscape in which the text is set. Yet, in the chorus sections, those individual representations are stripped away. The voices themselves speak but can no longer be tied back to a single source, as the voice and identity of the speaker is seemingly crossed out, replaced with a single dash that precedes their speech.

The effects of the textual disembodiment of the people in the novel—and the severing of body from voice—are subtle but important, as the shift from individual to communal speech engenders a more antagonistic, pejorative relationship between the people and the narrator. Throughout the main narrative, and as seen in the scene with Girlie and Papacita, the narrator simply reports the speech and thoughts of the characters, editorializing at times, while, as we have seen, maintaining a sense of quiet reverence and often respect. In the chorus, however, in which speech and action become collective, the narrator is notably less objective and less sympathetic, and the people, who throughout most of the novel are seen as flawed and struggling but not irredeemable, appear less so in the choruses, as the narrator often frames them as depraved and violent. The representation of the poor in many of the novel's chorus sections is consistently disparaging, and, in the first chorus, the unsettling disconnect between the narrator's speech and the people becomes more overt, as the narrator appears particularly unsettled by the both the people and their communal vernacular—a thick, sometimes hard-to-decipher creole that is more overtly juxtaposed against the narrator's own use of proper English. One of the very first images readers see is a disembodied array not of people, but of "clacking tongues" all speaking in an eerie, collectivized vernacular, musing about how "mis' brody's clubfootbwoy get run... say we is gwine get nodder breeze blow dis yer yet" (7). The vernacular of the people serves as a point of narratorial judgment, as the narrator describes the chorus in almost inhuman terms, emphasizing their sore covered bodies and suggesting that the people themselves are metaphors for moral depravity (9). He notes that "the tongues in the lane click-clack almost continuously, going up and down the full scale of human emotions, human folly, ignorance, suffering, viciousness, magnanimity, weakness, greatness, littleness, insufficiency, frailty, strength" (8). That the full range of human emotion is depicted as an index of predominantly negative characteristics is telling, and it should be noted here that there is an implied economic, social, and cultural divide between the narrator and the people he describes, which he views with resounding disgust. In the main narrative, however, such explicit moralistic critiques are not nearly as common. For example, the narrator seldom comments on the moral depravity of Papacita, who violently beats his girlfriend, Girlie, and certainly deserves rebuke. Rebuke, however, is saved almost exclusively for the people in the chorus. The people are thus repeatedly framed as base, difficult, and almost impossible to rationalize with—and the narrator in these sections is not only more critical, but makes considerably less effort to understand or translate their behaviors or social conditions to the reader.

Through its chorus sections, the novel therefore masterfully depicts how essentializing representations of communal speech breed further distrust and resentment of impoverished populations. It is language—or, more specifically, the vernacular of the people—in the chorus sections that provides the impetus for the narrator's dehumanization of the people in the lane. In this regard, Mais's novel functions as an examination of the dangers of essentialized speech as a tool of marginalization. The poor, in the chorus, unlike in the main text, share the same essential character; they espouse the same collective morals, and their speech and beliefs are reductively similar. The narrator thus views and critiques them as a collective whole. This process of essentialization in the novel—that is, the reductive view of poverty in the chorus which leads the narrator to view the people as *less* human and troublingly alien is enacted and enabled through language. The novel thereby highlights how representations of speech have been frequently used as a method of societal estrangement by framing vernacular as an impoverished monolanguage that imagines poverty as a reductive singularity. In so doing, Mais's work urges us to think more deeply about the societal framing of the poor, especially by the middle classes. The narrator, in depicting the impoverished masses as a spectral yet collective textual chorus, creates a view of poverty that reduces the lower classes to a grotesque amalgamation of cultural and racial stereotypes and strips them of their individuality, ultimately reducing them to an indistinguishable, violent mass severed from the Jamaican landscape in which they reside.

The novel thus highlights the stark danger of essentialized representations of collective poverty and suffering when stripped of individual character. By shifting and altering the tone and nature of the narrative voice and the narrator's relationship to the people in the lane, Mais surreptitiously reveals the ease to which impoverished peoples can become objects of scorn through acts of linguistic framing.[7] This point is supported by the scant criticism on the novel, as Brown has argued that the shifting linguistic patterns in *Brother Man* reveal a larger concern in the novel about "the potential misuses of language" (155). Mais's novel carefully sets up the importance of thinking critically about the nuanced and individual experiences of the poor. If this seems like a simple affirmation, the complexities of the novel's structure repeatedly highlights the challenges of maintaining a more complex representation of economic suffering that escapes essentialized simplification. Throughout the novel, Brother Man insists that suffering is not universal and interchangeable, and that we must be sensitive to one's individual burden and suffering. Jesmina views Brother Man's assertion that "we all can't bear the same burdens... some people have more than they can bear" as her guiding axiom (95). Jesmina reflects on Brother Man's reminder, which affirms a need to be "more patient with and understanding of her sister, in her trouble" (95). Here the text emphasizes the danger of undermining the complexity of individual suffering and cautions readers not to assume that burdens are equal and interchangeable. This point affirms the collective danger of the chorus, in which the people become a horde of singular desire. As the novel warns, Caribbean representations and depictions of the folk or peasant communities must tread carefully to articulate a more complex portrayal of the peoples' varied and individual plights.

Brother Man therefore demonstrates how uncomplicated and simplistic representations of community curtail feelings of empathy for the lower classes in ingenious ways by juxtaposing two competing visions of community: a more complex depiction of communal suffering that focuses more on nuanced and individual plight, and an essentialized vision of community that speaks and thinks as one and shares an ambiguous, collective suffering. Comparing representations of empathy in the novel emphasizes the demarcation between these distinctive visions of community. Midway through the main text, for example, the narrator expresses a concern, felt by both Brother Man and Jesmina, that Cordelia—a single mother afflicted with both physical and mental illness—has become paranoid and secretive. The way the narrator describes Cordelia's plight is matter-of-fact, neutral, in explaining both how she is acting while negotiating the very real repercussions of her behavior. As she struggles with mental illness, Jesmina's behavior is off-putting and frightening. As the narrator describes it, "Cordelia acted 'most like somebody going out of their mind. She went about the house muttering to herself, and that. . . was a bad sign. She was secretive, and had developed a mania for hiding things. Just the oddest things at the oddest places, it was enough to make anyone scared" (91; ellipsis added). The narrator's insistence that Cordelia's behavior is "odd" rather than deviant intimates a sense of concern and empathy for her individual plight, while expressing worry that the narrator can understand both how and why her behavior causes feelings of unease. Her secrecy and paranoia, here, is less a moral failing than a cause for concern. Yet the same trait (i.e., secrecy itself), when the narrator discusses it in the chorus, appears as an utterly grotesque moral failing. It is worth returning to the first chorus to observe the shift in tone that occurs between the novel's central narrative and its chorus, as the narrator in the chorus describes people whose "tongues have not ceased to shuttle to clatter, they still carry their burden of the tale of man's woes. It is their own story that they tell in *secret,* overlaying it with the likeness of slander, licking their own ancient scrofulous sores" (9; emphasis added). Viewed in conjunction with one another, the demarcation between the narrator's tone and style in the chorus and in the main narrative should be clear; in this way, Mais's critique of linguistic essentialism becomes more explicit.[8] In the main narrative, the narrator humanizes Cordelia's suffering when he is able to focus specifically on her individual suffering; its knowledge of her individual circumstances engenders here a more empathetic narrative voice. But, when abstracted from the specificity of one's individual plight, the narrator, in the chorus, views the "secrecy" of the people as a malicious force and effortlessly, and perhaps unthinkingly, dehumanizes them.

The ingenuity of Mais's novel is, then, not a question of plot. Rather, it emerges in the textual tension between the narrator, the people he describes, and the reader, who must work to see through the narrator's troubling veneer by laboring to make sense of the underlying meaning behind the peoples' socioeconomic struggle, which is both ignored and abstracted in the text. In this sense, Mais's critique becomes clear, as the novel reveals how romanticized notions of a uniform peasant identity and language exacerbate and enable forms of colonial oppression. In idealizing a monolithic peasant identity—one rooted in an essentialized vernacular that is simplified to give the masses a singular monolithic language and thought process—their voices are easily stifled, ridiculed, and even dehumanized by the middle-class narrator. This point is tirelessly emphasized in the chorus, as the narrator views the narrative masses' needs and wants as largely inscrutable and pointless; he simply cannot, nor does he try to, understand their plight, noting instead that they wear "the anonymous mask of man" and are "lost beyond the utmost gleam" (60). When viewed through the lens of collective speech, the narrator repeatedly reminds readers that the people he writes of make little sense, that their meaning is lost to him, and that the people of the Lane are decidedly Other. They simply have less value; they are less civilized and less educated. The detachment between the narrator and the people—and his animosity here—is abundantly clear. The narrator, our filter for what we see and hear in the text is a figure who cannot make sense of the gestures and behaviors of the people that he describes, and who views the poor as literal lepers, licking and spreading their disease. The peoples' speech, which, throughout most of the main text, reveals their individual character, in the chorus appears deviant; their worth and morals are reflected by their language, which is too difficult to understand. Through linguistic shifts and an increasing emphasis on communal speech, the chorus sections reveal how suffering can be abstracted through linguistic means.

The novel explicitly rejects ideologies of community rooted in linguistic uniformity, expressing a skepticism about the value of what Brathwaite would later call "nation language," by showing how depictions of the poor that overemphasize vernacular commonalities often essentialize impoverished peoples' suffering and experiences. As shown in the chorus, linguistic essentialization allows the middle and upper classes to more easily Other the poor. Critics, however, have often overlooked the textual, linguistic, and cultural implications of the chorus sections and, in some cases, critiqued their role in the novel. For example, in the introduction to the Heinemann edition of the novel, Brathwaite suggests Mais's use of choral language is often ineffective and stifles the plot; characterization in the novel, he suggests, becomes, like the chorus, "anonymous" (xiii). Yet Brathwaite, in overlooking the cultural implications of this anonymization, does not draw attention to Mais's seething critique of essentializing rhetoric that abstracts the plight of the lower classes, and he largely overlooks the implications of the text's linguistic intervention. Kenneth Ramchand, in turn, asserts that the chorus functions almost as a detached, objective snapshot of the masses that "neither insists upon the specialness of the Jamaican yard-dwellers' situation nor offers indignant 'philosophical' generalisations. Rueful and detached, it abstracts the essential repetitive humanity of what goes on among the urban proletariat" (25).[9] While the influence of Brathwaite's and Ramchand's criticism on Mais—and the period as a whole—cannot be overstated, their readings of *Brother Man*, particularly concerning the nature of the chorus, do not fully capture the significance of the novel's choral structure. That the urban proletariat are sore covered, spectral, and dehumanized in both their speech and description does not reflect a depiction that is unindignant. More recently, critics like Brown have begun to unravel the nuances of the choral language in more depth. In Brown's reading, he contends that "the choruses of brother man . . . reveal Mais's concern to ensure the communal intelligibility of poetic language" (153). For Brown, the novel confronts the challenges of representing the seeming inexpressibility of an unrepresentable gesture and tone that "reveals the novel's apparent anxiety about the controllability of communication" (157). While Brown's acknowledgment that the chorus, and the novel in general, struggles with the threat of intelligibility is astute and compelling, it is clear that more critical work needs to be done on the novel's examination of linguistic essentialism. In this regard, the novel, as I will examine in the next section of this chapter, reveals a significantly more profound confrontation with the dehumanizing principles of colonial rhetoric than previously acknowledged.

Obfuscated Oppression and the Ethnographic Animalization of the Peasant Class

In what follows, I want to examine more deeply the extent to which the novel enacts a critique of the normalization of imperial ideologies of power that animalize the poor through a colonial, ethnographic gaze. While this gaze purports an "objective" articulation of states of poverty, it in fact is designed to naturalize economic inequity and thereby justifies the further perpetuation of systemic disenfranchisement against impoverished colonial subjects. The novel paradoxically affirms the voice of the peasant by giving them excessive commentary on the events of the novel, but it intimates that doing so is a mistake by reminding readers early on that the populace the narrator describes are a decrepit, animalistic horde that lacks morality. As the narrator describes in a chorus section: "Behind the pocked visage and the toothless grin, behind the wrinkled skin gathered and seamed around the lips and under the eyes, behind the façade and haleness and cursing of laughter, slander lurks in ambush to take the weakest and the hindmost, and the tongues clack upon every chance" (8–9). In this sense, it is worth examining the degree to which the narrator frames the impoverished masses as reprehensible, hypocritical brutes whose thoughts are guided by the whim of their own violence—a violence that they naturally and inevitably enact. The last choral scene begins while the people are gathered together, singing a hymn in the street. The scene, which begins with worship, quickly devolves into gossip:

>—Girlie out fo' him! Hm! Papacita better watch him step!
>—Missis, dat somet'ing is one kinda somet'ing yaw!
>—Never see a woman so fret 'pon a man befo'.
>—Mirrie, see yah! de gal look like somebody don' know himself, see her todder de go-long de street, me sorry for her can't tell. (139)

The ethnographic tone frames the masses as Other, emphasizing to readers that the people are corrupt; that they are innately untrustworthy and that the nature of their worship is one of violence and competition. As the narrator describes the scene, he comments that the gossip on display is somehow less violent and spiteful than usual; on this occasion, he notes, "they speak about different things, after a bit the speech turns upon the ordinary topics of gossip, but the voices are a little less sharp, there is less of that vicious underlining both in tone and content" (138). The people's fundamental state of being is thus codified as inherently vicious as the narrator warns readers not to humanize them, reminding us that, if this scene seems to portray harmless gossip, it does not. These people are innately violent, innately vulgar, and to view them as human is a mistake—such moments of civility are temporary anomalies; they become like wild animals that can be momentarily tamed, but never entirely trusted. The linguistic representation of the choral scenes thus invert the classical elements that they parody, in that the chorus in the novel is not a site of enlightenment or knowledge, but a body that acts only through self-interested anger absent a socioeconomic cause.

It should be noted, however, that not every moment of the chorus is equally derisive toward the people, and the narrator's pejorative language is not entirely relegated to the chorus. On a textual level, the hysteria and singular focus of the chorus as a disembodied avatar of suffering spills out, near the novel's conclusion, from the chorus into the main narrative. Toward the end of the text—in the midst of the people's attack on Brother Man—the narrator's descriptions take on a more malicious tone, resembling in many ways the pejorative tone of the chorus. The narrator remarks that "when they had mauled him to the satisfaction of their lust, they voided on him and fouled him. A woman showed them how" (188). Yet on a narrative level, this shift in language, where the people are represented as a collection of base desire, makes sense. After all, Brother Man, who articulates a deeper reverence for individual suffering and perhaps a more complex understanding of the uniqueness of poverty—and who embraces the importance of a more compassionate and complex vision in which to observe the world—is quickly and suddenly struck down by the mob, who associates him with a rape and murder that he did not commit. The stars, which are in their "ascendency" (107) as Brother Man's influence and worldview begins to take hold, burn out "one by one" (152) as he is framed, accused of murder, and then beaten. In this regard, Brown highlights a perceptible change in the tone of the chorus that is associated with Brother Man's fall, arguing that, "in marking the rise and undeserved fall of Brother Man in the lane's esteem, the choruses reveal that the success of Brother Man's rhetoric of hope is exceedingly fragile—quickly and fatally vulnerable to the gossipy whims and self-reinforcing chatter of his neighbors in the lane" (159). It is understandable, then, that the chorus, the textual site in which individuality is stripped from the populace, leaks from its textual and linguistic bounds and pervades the confines of the text's form as Brother Man is struck down. Brother Man's redemptive potential, in his viewpoint of the poor as equal but resoundingly individual in their suffering, is curtailed as the people reject him. Accordingly, the penultimate chorus, which takes place at the time of Brother Man's ascendency and before the attack, is itself not quite so malicious, but even more hopeful in tone.[10]

The seeming "spilling out" of the chorus, paired with the rise and fall of Brother Man, a symbol of hope and community that is quickly stifled in the novel, suggests that Mais was indeed concerned with the potentially societal contaminative effects of essentialization. And while the narrator's representation of Jamaican peasants as immoral, animalized hordes who act without cause is on the surface overt and unyielding, careful readers will note that Mais repeatedly undermines this rhetoric and urges them to see through it. See, for example, a scene at the end of the novel, in which the people, in an act of mob violence, capture and brutalize John Power, who they falsely believe is guilty of rape. The people's rage, notably, is not framed as moral, but primal: they violate Power because it suits them, not because they are morally opposed to the action they falsely presume he has committed. Toward the end of the attack, however, the narrative intimates the presence of a socioeconomic crisis behind their actions. As the text describes, "The crowd rocked and screamed and crowed with laughter. Others suddenly realized that they too wanted to make water . . . and then, as it happens, the game went stale. It suddenly lost its zest [and] the fears and frustrations, which were the constant companions of their thoughts, came home to roost again" (188). The scene ends by acknowledging unspecified fears and frustrations, implying a deeper sense of yearning and pain lurking behind the malice of the people, yet the narrator does not and cannot articulate it, and instead continues to present their actions as driven by base instinct. The narrator's deliberate abstraction of economic suffering depicts a seeming refusal to condemn capitalist and colonial modes of oppression. In this way, the narrator's gaze here functions as a kind of colonial ethnography that always surreptitiously dehumanizes the subject by juxtaposing "appropriate" values and actions against the behavior of the group it seeks to objectively describe. Thus, the narrator's framing of the chorus is less an accurate representation of who the people in the lane are, but rather who he perceives them to be, and the ethnographic component of the narrative reveals more about the narrator's essentialized view of Jamaican peasants than the peasants themselves. But, if we read closely, we can begin to observe what is lost in the narrator's abstractions, as the violence attributed to the masses is not without cause, despite what the narrator would like us to believe. The intimation of socioeconomic oppression bubbles on the surface of the text; it cannot be fully hidden or suppressed. Nevertheless, it is the obfuscation of the historical conditions of oppression that makes Mais's novel and narrator so unsettling. The narrator's repeated efforts to animalize the poor functions as a means to subvert both colonial critique and empathy for the lower classes, and, as such, the reader must actively resist subscribing to the dehumanizing portrait of the masses that the narrator endorses.

Yet far from arguing that Mais's novel urges readers to draw the conclusion that the poor are depraved and undeserving of empathy, I want to suggest instead that his work urges us to think more deeply and reflexively about the linguistic framing of the poor, especially by those who have social and cultural authority. The narrator's dangerous essentialization of Jamaica's poor reveals a space in which readers observe how imperialistic rhetoric undermines the nuances and complexities of the suffering of the impoverished through abstraction. The concept of inscrutability may seem to function differently here than it does in other works discussed in this book, in that inscrutability seemingly takes on potentially dangerous or dehumanizing implications. This is not the case, however. Mais's aim in the novel is not to champion the importance of realism or clarity—or to suggest that a national or communal identity must be entirely scrutable or understandable in its aims—but just the opposite: compellingly, *Brother Man* demonstrates that essentialization strips the impoverished of their complexity, reducing their plight to an ineffectual (and sometimes malicious and animalistic) babble. The peasant chorus does not exist in the novel to reveal the true or authentic voice of the people, but as a warning against how essentialism abstracts us from understanding and processing the needs of those very same people. The difficult vernacular of the chorus, combined with the overwhelming sense of resentment for them on the part of the narrator, thereby ensnares the reader in a contentious space that instigates further consideration of the potentially dangerous implications of uncritical forms of communal speech in the Caribbean that animalize and demean the masses.

The text therefore intimates a bitter critique of colonial indoctrination, suggesting that both the literal and metaphorical transformation of the masses from people to animal is pervasive and common; in turn, we must actively work to see through it. And, while I want to suggest that the seeming absence of political rhetoric in the text is both a deliberate and intentional component of Mais's critique of colonialism and essentialism, it is important to acknowledge that *Brother Man*'s deliberate political ambiguity frustrated early critics of the novel. Braithwaite, for example, laments what he perceives as a lack of political engagement in the novel, arguing that, "by the time he came to write *Brother Man*, Mais appears to have lost that acute sense of political protest that made him write 'Now we know.' Consequently, he never seems to link the condition of his Kingston poor with the persistent poverty of colonial under development, or even with the disillusionment with the historical struggle for independence" (xviii). In Braithwaite's view, the novel is severely lacking in its ethical and political commentary, and, while he praises its similarities to American jazz music, he ultimately concludes that the novel is flawed. Yet closer inspection reveals that the text firmly engages with the politics of colonial oppression, as the animalization of the masses, carried out by the narrator, serves as the physical and ideological colonial embodiment of that which would reduce impoverished peoples to an amorphous mass of inarticulate, sensationalistic desires. In fact, the very notion that the text does not confront the economic and social implications of poverty captures the ease and rapidity with which forms of capitalist oppression are obfuscated in discussions of inequity.

In this regard, Mais's investigation of the myriad of ways that essentializing rhetoric enables further dehumanization of exploited peoples anticipates theories of colonial power's effective methods of subversion, such as those espoused by Achille Mbembe in his seminal essay on colonial politics "Of Commandment." Quite simply, Mbembe argues that the "credo" of colonial power is ensconced in "an image of the colonized that made of native people the prototype of the *animal*" (27). Rethinking Hegel, Mbembe helps us to better understand the degree to which the narrator of Mais's text, in regurgitating simplistic affirmations of peasant identity, interpolates his own superiority by framing the linguistically uniform peasant class as an essentialized, unintelligible animal. As Mbembe reminds us, "The native subjected to power and to the colonial state could in no way be another 'myself.' As an animal, he/she was even totally alien to me. His/her manner of seeing the world, his/her manner of being, was not mine. In him/her, it was impossible to discern any power of transcendence. Encapsulated in himself or herself, he/she was a bundle of drives, but not of *capacities*. In such circumstances, the only possible relationship with him/her was one of violence and domination" (26). Thus the drives of the people are, in the novel (and as Mbembe describes) simply that: drives that indicate an incomplete, undeveloped yearning or sense of emotional development. Isolated from the narrator, who speaks and thinks differently, the people become a body of ethnographic freaks, their speech and desires transcribed to clicking tongues and guttural moans. At the same time, the universal spectral voice that they eschew breeds a kind of familiarity, in that the narrator assumes to know it; indeed, they all speak the same way and share the same drives. In this way, the novel forcefully reminds us that "familiarity and domestication thus became the dominant tropes of servitude" (27).

In so doing, *Brother Man* reflects the extent to which the masses are supplicated through domestication by seemingly literalizing the colonial rhetoric that Mbembe theorizes: here the people in the lane behave like the animals that colonial ideology inscribes them as, acting only through base need, achieving simple pleasures of immediate gratification, such as rage, violence, and self-interested acts of dominance. As Mbembe writes,

> To *command* an animal (the slave or the colonized) was to play the game of attempting to get him/her out of the encirclement while being fully aware that the circle was never thereby reduced, since grooming and domestication occurred almost always in the animals own distinctive drives. In other words, it was to play this game while conscious that, although the animal (the colonized) could belong to the familiar world, have needs (hunger, thirst, copulation), it could never truly accede to the *sphere of human possibility*. For by reason of the sort of life the colonized lived, he/she belonged to those forms of living whose distinctive feature was to remain forever enclosed in the virtual and the contingent. (28)

Taken this way, the narrator can be seen to inscribe and interpolate the rhetoric of the colonizer—a perhaps surprising point, given that he is himself also a victim of colonization. Significantly, the narrator's violent rhetoric mirrors that of Mais's critique of imperial power in his diatribe against the British Empire, "Now We Know," in which Mais argues that British authority maintains colonial order through its scabs, yes-men, and betrayers of one's own people. In an ingenious move, the narrator of the novel himself becomes the figure Mais warns us against: the figure who turns against their own people. The narrator thus serves as a figure to further isolate and estrange the reader from the humanity of the impoverished characters of whom he writes. *Brother Man* can, then, be seen to emphasize a thoroughly exclusionary sense of national identity, in which the presumably middle-class narrator repudiates the lower classes by inscribing the very rhetoric that oppresses him as a weapon against the lower classes. The impoverished suffer because of their own failings and faults, and we should feel no guilt, as the masses cannot approach that which Mbembe theorizes as "the *sphere of human possibility*" (28; emphasis in original). In sum, the novel works to surreptitiously make visible to readers the severing of communal bonds between the lower and middle classes, as the narrator's internalization of colonial, animalizing rhetoric effectively disarms any and all discussion of socioeconomic strife, and instead focuses only on painting the impoverished in broad, unfavorable strokes in a way that blames them for their own suffering and, in so doing, exculpates the colonial authority from responsibility.

Impossible Nationalism and Failure of Resistance

Throughout his work—and especially in *Brother Man*—Mais repeatedly expresses anger toward class divisions that pit Caribbean peoples against each other. Such divisions, he argues, obviate the emergence of a national consciousness. Mais's examination and critique of what he perceives as Jamaica's failure to create a sustainable national consciousness appears in the novel in two key ways: first, in the sense of distrust and resentment between middle- and lower-class Jamaicans, evidenced by the narrator's vitriol at the lower classes; and, second, in the lower class's own resentment and violence toward alternative modes of expression and emancipation.[11] The peoples' attack on John Power and Rastafarianism is indicative of this latter point. *Brother Man* thus echoes the anger over complacency that Mais previously voiced in "Now We Know," in depicting a lower class that has been rendered ineffectual and placid, and a middle class that, far from using their degree of social and economic advantage to champion the suffering of the masses, simply demonizes and dismisses them. This sense of anger and disenchantment over Jamaica's failure to create an anticolonial national identity emerged once again in Mais's 1950 essay "Why I Love, and Leave, Jamaica," in which he writes, "There is in this country, alas, a moated tower of mediocrity, close and unassailable, and it holds such sway. It has acquired such a body of mediocre opinion about it that it is useless to try to make a dent in its smugness and its exclusiveness and its indifference to anything that does not come entirely within its limited scope and compass of influence. It is in a sense like a large sow with farrow who whimsically suckles one meanwhile it turns and devours another" (4). Mais's disgust here is crystallized in the novel, where the people in the lane direct their rage not at their oppressor, whom the novel cleverly obfuscates, but at each other, directing their violence at Power, whose religion and appearance frames him as Other. At the same time, the narrator delights in animalizing the masses, feeling no concern or empathy for them, and adopts an essentialized view of poverty that allows him to unashamedly denigrate the masses as brutes. In the text, the potential emergence of a productive national consciousness is entirely obliterated, as the image of national unity or kindness that John Power tries to adopt is not simply rejected, but proven to be impossible. The novel, through its linguistic and narrative strategies, therefore seeks to reveal the myriad of ways in which colonial indoctrination sabotages the emergence of a national consciousness.

Brother Man, in linking apathy and inaction with a kind of deliberate ignorance, affirms Mais's most serious, sustained condemnation of the essentializing properties of national identity. In framing the people in the lane as a uniform choral mass, the story captures the hopelessness of the present moment in spectral but explicit terms, as, by the end, there exists no form of viable resistance, only disengaged, apolitical masses who have been stripped of their will to fight. Much like in Patterson's *An Absence of Ruins,* the novel suggests that contemporary theories of national identity and communal speech have become both stale and ineffectual and must be rethought. In this way, the questions raised in the novel bring to mind Mark Goble's rethinking of obsolescence in *A New Vocabulary for Global Modernism.* While Goble's essay turns to contemporary artistic interpretations and exhibitions of outmodality as an indication of the continued perpetuation of modernist practice in the contemporary world, he argues that any rethinking of a theory of obsolescence must begin with an acknowledgement of how it "has regularly functioned as an archeology of mythic correspondences and reanimations of dead pasts that point to futures that look a lot like the ruins of a present we are trying to escape" (147). In other words, the rethinking and recycling of outmoded forms of expression that Goble devises might be applied equally to both Caribbean language and form; as Mais argues, the championing of a universalized peasant identity is not only ineffective in breeding emancipation but also, ultimately, detrimental. The novel suggests that such an ideology of national consciousness is, by the time the novel was written, already out of date, as the romanticization of poverty that excises individual suffering in favor of universal values further instills colonial values and ideology. The essentialization of the peasant class that dominates literary and cultural representations throughout the mid-twentieth century—and to which the narrator himself adheres—is rendered obsolete in the novel, collapsing into a self-interested violence that has somehow been severed from its socioeconomic colonial roots.

The novel's hybridized vernacular reflects a bitter animosity and resentment toward outmoded and essentialized ideologies of national identity that, argues Mais, effectively stifle future forms of emancipation. Yet Mais, in the novel's conclusion, intimates, but does not articulate, a potential alternative vision of national community. Explicitly, the community we see throughout the novel—the snapshot of the masses locked in a state of perpetual unrest—is one of only violence and faux unity. By the end of the novel, however, Mais briefly offers competing visions of community, one in which Brother Man and his disciple Minette, following the violent attack of the chorus, become isolated and extracted from the community in which they reside. Power survives the attack, but his rebirth is ambiguous, and the novel does not conclude with reconciliation but with a vague articulation by both Brother Man and Minette that they have seen something. What this "something" is, however, remains decidedly ambiguous, and the novel's ending is unsettling in that Mais does not offer an overt critique of the violence that ends the novel, nor is the attack represented as a transformative force in the life of Brother Man and Minette. Instead, the attack appears, in a sense, inscrutable—though no one in the novel, the narrator included, tries to understand or analyze it.

That the attack and its aftermath cannot be verbally articulated is hardly surprising, given the struggle with articulation that appears throughout the novel. Relatively early on, Brother Man laments that what he and the people need, above all, is clarity and vision—that is, something that can be understood. As he sees it, "what a man needed above all was a clear vision. Sometimes what a man *wanted* to see stood in the way. A man must go inside himself and search himself earnestly, and after that he should stand and wait" (56). On the next page, he reiterates the point: "What a man needed above all was a clear vision" (57). Yet, despite this hope, when Brother Man tries to describe his religious awakening—a moment when he sees a "vision in the hills" and is "commanded by God"—he cannot put it into words. Even when he tries to write out his experience, he cannot. While the text potentially implies that Brother Man understands what he saw, Mais prevents readers from seeing it. As the scene unfolds, Brother Man writes: "I could see the Quarry at Rockfort where the prison gangs work, in the distance, it was like the handkerchief spread out in the sun to dry. Then everything went hazy to black, and in my vision I see. . . ." (112; ellipsis in original). As Brown notes, the novel "casts grave doubt on the efficacy of its own verbal medium, almost literally gesturing to a more plentitudinous meaning beyond the mere reach of language" (161). Brown argues that the book struggles "to articulate the precise nature of how its hero . . . looks" but also his speech and intonation (156). The "anxious impression" of the book's difficulty negotiating speech and description, he affirms, "calls attention to the novel's descriptive incapacity" and intimates an "enigmatic fluency, beyond the reach of words" (156). Just as the communal and collective vernacular of the chorus fails to reveal the complexity of their individual suffering, Brother Man cannot articulate what it is exactly that drives a human being to be a kinder, more loving supporter of their fellow man. This struggle of articulation pervades the novel.

Accordingly, the final scene of *Brother Man* ends without commentary or analysis, and readers are left to reconcile the choral masses' collective act of violence. But if we consider the narrator as a source of tension in the novel—as a figure that, unlike Brother Man, is decidedly confident of its ability to see and perceive the overall "meaning" of the people—then the ending makes more sense. It is thus significant that Brother Man and Minette's observation that they "see" something is something that the narrator, a symbol of colonial oppression, cannot understand or perceive; he does not have access to their "vision." Nevertheless, both Brother Man and Minette see it. Resistance happens—and, indeed, is only possible—in the margins and spaces that authority cannot perceive or witness. The narrator himself is unable to consider the revolutionary possibility of the Rastafarians in objective terms and falls victim to the same resentment that he assumes guides the people. His vision of community exists only in terms of an essentialized colonial imaginary. The reader, then, is left with no answer; the final moment of the text reveals a moment of profound inscrutability. This is the ingenuity of Mais's novel, in that it points to a solution and potential unification that is possible, yet is obscured by socially inscripted feelings of resentment and distrust. In this way, we might consider Brother Man's name, John Power, in a different way. Seemingly, Brother Man lacks a desire for power and, at the same time, is powerless to stop the violent attack at the end of the novel. Rather, his power lies in his ability see something beyond the confines of social authority. In losing his authority—for the people lose faith in him—he finds something else, something outside of a social order that relies on leaders or prophets. This solution is not simply ambiguous: it speculates about the presence of an alternative vision of nationalistic revolutionary praxis. This solution, Mais argues, is visible only outside the gaze and influence of the colonial order.

Language as Inscrutability and the Case of Eric Walrond

Mais's skepticism toward linguistic collectivity—and the examination of problematic vernacular that occurs in his work—may be used as a starting point to propagate further rethinkings of other seminal Caribbean texts. The work of Eric Walrond, particularly concerning its experimentation with intelligibility and vernacular, is notable in this regard. Unlike the majority of authors discussed in this book, Walrond's work requires little introduction. Born in Guyana in 1898, Walrond lived in Colon, Panama, in the Canal Zone, until 1918; he moved to Brooklyn in 1929 and shortly thereafter migrated to France and London. Following his move to Europe, he largely disappeared as he struggled with mental illness: he admitted himself into the Roundway Psychiatric Hospital in 1952 (Davis 6). Depressingly, Walrond, who considered himself a failure, died in poverty; he produced only one significant work, the 1926 collection *Tropic Death* (1). Until recently, Walrond was seen as a minor player in the Harlem Renaissance and he was best known for two stories that appeared in Alain Locke's *The New Negro* anthology (1925). Critical attention toward his work, however, has exploded in recent years, most explicitly with the reissue of *Tropic Death*, which was published by Liveright in 2013. The collection depicts a rare, bleak portrait of Afro-Caribbean life inside the Panama Canal Zone in the early twentieth century. Undoubtedly, the collection is a resoundingly depressing read, as every story ends in death and tragedy. Despite its bleakness, the reissue was surprisingly well received, garnering national media coverage on National Public Radio, among other organizations. Significant criticism also bracketed the rerelease of *Tropic Death*, including James Davis's biography, *Eric Walrond: A Life in the Harlem Renaissance and the Transatlantic Caribbean* (2015), Louis J. Parascandola and Carl A. Wade's *In Search of Asylum: The Later Writings of Eric Walrond* (2011), and *Eric Walrond: A Critical Heritage* (2013). Walrond's rediscovery—like that of Jean Rhys—has raised difficult issues of classification, in part because he was a thoroughly transnational writer, but it is worth noting that recent critical work tends to classify him as an African American writer, rather than a Caribbean one. In any case, his recovery as a forgotten writer of the Harlem Renaissance has made his work widely available in African American collections in universities across the United States.[12]

What is most interesting with respect to the rediscovery of *Tropic Death* is no doubt the question of its difficulty. The collection's newfound availability has been met with the unavoidable acknowledgment that it is "challenging"—or, worse, simply too difficult to make sense of. Reviews that followed the rerelease praised the book, but still lamented its formal challenges, noting in particular the opacity of its language. Oscar Villon's review for National Public Radio, for example, declared *Tropic Death* an uncomfortable, "tough" text. "The regional dialects reproduced on the page," he wrote, "are at times so hard to decipher that they must be read aloud to make sense of them." Similarly, Alexander Nazaryan's *Daily News* review disparagingly affirmed that "there is no use pretending, today, that Walrond is the equal of, say, his contemporary Zora Neale Hurston. His fondness for dialect was too great, his prose a little too humid." As Nazaryan's review helps to make clear, modern reviewers felt that *Tropic Death*'s use of creole, and its narrative structure—steeped in symbolism and a vocabulary that obscures rather than elucidates—made Walrond's text a sometimes inscrutable read. In short, what is striking about these reviews is the degree to which Walrond's experimentalism vies uncomfortably with recent attempts to resituate him within the canon—a point nowhere more evident than in the many reviews that express genuine excitement about Walrond's work that gets quickly, and inevitably, curtailed by readerly frustration.

As Imani D. Owens has convincingly argued, critiques of the novel's difficulty have larger implications for how readers process and understand Caribbean experience. One of the main reasons *Tropic Death* was labeled difficult was in part because audiences were both unfamiliar with and unable to understand the nuances of Caribbean experience it depicted. As Owens states, "By suggesting that *Tropic Death*'s stylistic innovations came at the expense of content, Walrond's contemporaries hint at something more: his failure as a translator and interpreter. In other words, the book's presumed shortcoming lay not merely in its lack of clarity but more precisely in its 'failure' to provide a document of Caribbean folk life that could be translated into existing paradigms. *Tropic Death*'s reception exposes ongoing difficulties with contextualizing experimental prose in black writing" (109). As I have argued throughout this book, inscrutability as a Caribbean aesthetic requires considerable decoding and effort to be made sense of—yet, as Owens's work suggests, critics and readers have often read the inherent difficulty of texts such as Walrond's as a fault rather than a deliberate choice. Some critics have gone so far as to label its vision of the Caribbean as simply incoherent, while others have expressed regret that it renders the Caribbean opaque.[13] Such questions regarding the difficulty of its form perhaps explains why the novel, until recently, was absent in discussions of both Caribbean aesthetics and larger discussions of antiimperialist literature. In this regard, Davis's biography of Walrond traces the reception of *Tropic Death,* noting that, while the novel was written for a North American audience, its experiments with language "refused to make the Caribbean easily accessible" (155).[14] Because reviewers and audiences lacked direct experience or knowledge with the Caribbean—and with the Canal Zone in which most of the novel is set—Walrond's narrative provoked considerable frustration. As Michelle A. Stephens argues, West Indian men in the 1920s and 1930s were "unrecognizable," particularly to

American consumers. As Stephens points out, African American identity was the only familiar or acceptable representation of Black identity (58). Walrond's work thus fragments and shatters conceptions of Blackness in the United States that is then "reframed within different geo-historical accounts" (64). In other words, the contentious debate concerning the novel's difficult experimentation reveals a struggle to imagine, or even reconcile, a depiction of Caribbean suffering and experience in the early and mid-twentieth century, and, as recent reviews reveal, this struggle remains ongoing today.

Yet, with the exception of Owens, critics have been hesitant to deeply explore Walrond's radically experimental incorporation of language and its implications for a Caribbean aesthetic. Walrond's work is guided not only by its explicit, unyielding use of vernacular but also by its perpetuation of racist language and tropes, which frequently intrude upon the collection's narratives. Therefore, I want to further examine the textual tension between *Tropic Death*'s unyielding use of vernacular—which, critics have argued, risks making the text unintelligible—and the clear articulation of racist sentiments also prevalent in the novel. As I will show, in negotiating the relationship between representations of impoverished Caribbean speech and widely perpetuated expressions of racist discourse, Walrond's work reveals an image of migrant Caribbean life in the Canal Zone and across the region that is rendered inscrutable through linguistic obfuscation. Whereas Mais's work implies that the solidification of essentializing representations of impoverished West Indian peoples' language serves as an obstacle to future forms of emancipation, Walrond's linguistic experiments in *Tropic Death* contend that imperial rhetoric actively embraces and distorts vernacular language both to obscure and distract from acts of colonial atrocity carried out throughout the Caribbean and Canal Zone.

Dehumanizing Vernacular and the Language of Distraction

On the surface, the overall function of vernacular in Walrond's work is similar in scope to that of Mais's novel, in that the lower and laboring classes are framed, explicitly and endlessly, in terms of a difficult-to-understand creole. Like in *Brother Man,* there is a significant degree of narrative tension between the narrator and the people he describes, and, as in Mais's novel, the narrator's speech is not narrated in creole, and the Caribbean laborers speak only in vernacular. The narrator's speech, language, and diction thus mark him as from a decidedly different class than the people he describes, and, predictably, he is seldom sympathetic to the suffering of the poor. On the one hand, Walrond's usage of creole can be seen to support my contention that experimental Caribbean artists often incorporated difficult vernaculars as a means of critiquing how linguistic essentialism dehumanizes the lower and working classes. Indeed, Owens contends that the novel's difficult language forces us to resist reductive interpretations of peasant experience: "*Tropic Death*'s moments of illegibility also pose useful challenges to long entrenched methods of writing and reading the 'folk.' . . . [The novel] resists the notion of a simple folk who yield easily to a voyeuristic gaze—their language immediately decipherable, their bodies and cultural productions readily available to the modern reader. Instead, the text's alternate geographies of Blackness require a different kind of interpretive labor" (98). Echoing Glissant, in Owens's view the difficult language of the text compels us to acknowledge the complexity of poverty and oppression by forcing us to decipher and make sense of it: understanding and confronting forms of oppression requires work and effort, and Walrond's text demands serious intellectual labor if it is to be understood. In much the same way, Davis argues that Walrond's text demonstrates a "thorough skepticism toward monolithic notions of race" (8). Taken together, Davis and Owens help us contextualize the extent to which Walrond's collection seeks to critique essentialized and monolithic framings of language, race, and identity. *Tropic Death* suggests that reductive theories of language and identity not only serve as obstacles to future emancipation but also threaten the emergence of linguistic polyphony in the Caribbean.[15] The novel, like *Brother Man,* thereby urges readers to see through the dangers of essentializing rhetoric.

Although *Tropic Death*'s exploration of language and abstraction shares much in common with Mais's *Brother Man,* Walrond's use of racist vernacular as an aesthetic device repeatedly unsettles the reading experience by normalizing the reader's relationship to overtly racist language—and *Tropic Death* is a considerably more jarring read than Mais's text. Its complex depiction of language is one in which peasant speech smashes against the narrator's racist vernacular, which degrades Afro-Caribbean peoples by, strikingly and repeatedly, using racist slang. Walrond's text depicts what we might call "competing dialects"—that is, while it presents the speech of its characters in a vernacular that is difficult to understand, it juxtaposes this vernacular against the presumably white narrator's more scrutable speech that is, essentially, vernacularized hate speech. Early on in "Drought," for example, readers reach a passage in which the word "tot" is used and then immediately defined. "Tot," we are told, is the "zigaboo word for tin cup" (21). On the face of it, such a textual motif is not unusual, as, indeed, similar interruptive and translational narrative strategies are employed in other Caribbean texts by writers like Victor Stafford Reid and Denis Williams. Yet the narrator's remarks in *Tropic Death* are especially unsettling, for they reveal a narrative voice whose goal is not simply to tell the story, but to perpetuate—and normalize—racist rhetoric and language. This is not to say that Walrond's text is unsympathetic to the suffering laborers that the narrator repeatedly demeans, but, rather, that the collection's deployment of language, particularly through its narrative voice, serves as a larger examination of the way colonial agents, and those with cultural and economic authority, perpetuate forms of verbal oppression as a means of devaluing the strife of the people they exploit.

In this regard, it is worth highlighting the nature and degree to which the narrator employs racist vernacular. Throughout the collection, the tone and hatred of the narrator's language often overflows with anger. "The White Snake," for instance, begins by describing a landscape where the inhabitants exist only by their racial classifications: we see "Negro peasant lodgings" that are "vile, backward crescent reeking in brats and fiendish lusts. *Cocabe* among its inkish-rice growers extended to gorillas sentenced to the dungeons of Surinam, Portuguese settlers who'd gone black, Chinks pauperized in the Georgetown fire of '05 and Calcutta coolies mixing *rotie* at dusk to the chorus of crickets and *crapeaux* moaning in the black watery gut" (130). The racist vernacular in this passage is unyielding and explicit as well as thoroughly unapologetic, and it appears throughout all of the stories in *Tropic Death*. As Mittelholzer would explore years later in *Morning at the Office,* racial hierarchy dominates the scenery and effaces any sense of humanity. The characters described at the outset of "The White Snake" exist merely in terms of their racial and social identity; they are without individuality and, as is often evident, resemble bacteria more than human beings. The land itself, "the black watery gut," signifies only pollution, as the narrator pairs blackness with digestive fauna and fecal matter. Black bodies are described not just as savages, but hysterical representations of sickness and infection. The narrator observes how "fetid black snorers rolled restively, clawed, dug at bugs or itching veins rising bluely on bare, languid bodies, as if to say: *don't worry. It's nothing. Nothing but some Hindu coolie, after the evening's erotic debauch, to the roll of goat drums, outside, on the low lamahau earth, severing the head of some jewel-laden, thirteen-year old mate, the third on a string of murdered conquests*" (130; italics in original). The image of suffering Black laborers is framed as a snapshot of disgust and racist imagination, and the snorers' dreams inexplicably present yet another racist portrayal, this time of Hindu workers, whom the narrator also views as savages. Moments later, the narrator continues the racist tirade, labeling the workers "cane trash" and "peons" (131). From the start of the collection, it becomes apparent that the narrator has his own language for dehumanizing the peasants it describes—language deployed continuously throughout the text.

Throughout *Tropic Death*, the narrator's racist vernacular smashes uncomfortably against the vernacular of the laborers who are the text's focus. It is significant, however, that the narrator's racism is often engendered by the speech of the characters he describes, which he cannot seem to truly make sense of and which he always associates with corruption and deviance. In describing a conversation between two characters, Coggins and Beryl, the narrator suggests that their voices and everyday speech are so unpleasant that it disturbs and awakens a nearly dead, nearly deaf dog, noting how their conversations had the side effect of "inciting Rattah ["the half dead dog"] to indolent curiosity" (25; brackets added). Throughout the collection, creole is seen as both uneducated and threatening to civil society. Characters like Beryl and Coggins, who speak only in creole (evident in phrases like, "Sho', gal eatin' mal all de hatahnoon") are never viewed as entirely human (25). Yet the orality on display here is not only unpleasant to the half-dead dog but also has the curious effect of driving the narrator into a rage. Moments after relaying the above conversation, the narrator unleashes another racist diatribe, in which he derogatorily labels the impoverished character he describes as a "peon": "Praying to the lord to send rain, black peons gathered on the rumps for breadfruit or cherry trees in abject supplication" (25). The text depicts, from its outset, a landscape in which the language of its characters engenders a visceral, racist response on the part of its narrator, who insists that their language is indicative of their inferiority.

I want to suggest here, however, that the narrator's emphasis on creole and racist vernacular, which is used as a means of Othering and devaluing the characters it describes, is employed as a means of distraction. In what follows, I contend that Walrond incorporates these elements to reveal the extent to which pejorative and racist language obscures economic and racial suffering—particularly in terms of exploitative labor. In a text about voice and in a chapter on orality, it bears repeating that the narrator as an authorial figure is the arbiter of dehumanization in the text: his language always speaks loudest, and, thus, he directs and encourages the reader to view the characters he describes as broken, savage Others, repeatedly translating their speech through the lens of racist hysteria: calling them ignorant, referring to them as "cane trash," and using racist terminology to ridicule their speech. However, Walrond was deeply invested in examining the relationship between hate speech and labor; indeed, much of *Tropic Death*'s use of racist speech was inspired by Walrond's real-life experiences. As Davis notes, Walrond believed racism "derived from colonial relations," noting that he was called "chombo" while working in Panama, a racial slur (8). Further, Davis argues that "the differences in ethnicity, religion, language, class, and culture that were conventionally subsumed under the designations 'Negro' or 'Coloured' fuel much of his work" (8). Representations of labor in Walrond's work always breed articulations of racist language, and, should we see beyond the narrator's desperate attempt to dehumanize the novel's laboring poor, we can begin to observe the presence of a damning critique of colonial exploitation both at the Canal Zone and throughout the Caribbean. I want to insist, then, that *Tropic Death*'s central theme is not about engendering readerly shock or discomfort over the narrator's callous use of racist speech, but about how the narrator's racial framing of language obscures the horror of the exploitive labor that the impoverished Caribbean masses in the text are interminably forced to perform and endure.[16]

In this respect, a return to "Drought" is illustrative. The story opens with an image of toil, only to immediately undermine the exhaustion and suffering of the laborers by labeling them "sun-crazed blacks" (22). As the paragraph continues, the scene becomes increasingly abstract, as the landscape and people are described in increasingly vague terms. The quarry itself becomes a "dry waterless gut" and a "sun stuffed void" (22). In stories like "Drought," the narrator defamiliarizes the Barbadian landscape in which the text is set by obfuscating the corporeality of the inhabitants' bodies and their labor, as well as the very geography in which each story's protagonists live and work. In this way, the landscape and the characters text are never static; rather, they are broken down and made increasingly obscure and are frequently impossible to pinpoint and discern. Coggins Rum appears as a "black, animate dot" before he is properly named, walking on an "adhesive marl" that, for readers, lacks signification. But, for the characters in the text, the "marl" (or "mal," as the workers often call it) is everywhere and overpowering—an unbearable fact of life that we cannot know (22). In no uncertain terms, the language the narrator uses to describe work at the quarry is always tentative and ambiguous or, worse, left unexplained. The story's narration thus intimates the whims and beliefs of an imperial order that associates the trauma of exploitative labor as something that exists only in unnatural, unfamiliar spaces, and the people that carry out such work appear not as fully fleshed-out characters, but merely in impressionistic or uncertain terms. The people and places in which such suffering resides are resoundingly strange and difficult to perceive or witness—and not, to be sure, something that the reader can or should relate to or understand.

We might be tempted to focus on the narrator's dehumanizing language and his exhausting attempt to demarcate racial boundaries between himself and the characters he describes. However, we would miss seeing what the narrator, curiously, does not translate for his audience—something that is decidedly important, and that the story focuses on only tangentially: the meaning and role of the white marl. The white marl, an obscure substance that blankets the landscape of the story, is in fact an industrial byproduct of the quarry and a chemical hazard of the labor the impoverished people perform, but it is never identified as such. It simply exists and is left unclear. While the reader is free to interpret it as dialect or a euphemism, this misses the very real implications of the physical repercussion of the laborer's effect on the land. The work at the quarry, in the midst of a drought, has thoroughly poisoned the landscape where the workers reside. The marl dust emerges and functions as a toxic byproduct of peasant labor that quite literally marks and infects both the land and body with its physical presence: it adheres to skin and lungs and covers all that it touches in its dusty white film. We see bodies described as "a restless crossing of scaly, marl-white legs in the corner"(29). Furthermore, the marl invades the lungs of the laborers in ways they cannot see or perceive. As Coggins eats a hot meal, we learn about "the dust which had gathered in his throat at the quarry so far down into his stomach that he was unaware of its presence" (30). And, at the end of the story, after Coggins's daughter ingests copious amounts of it, she suddenly, and tragically, dies. Language, here, buries atrocity. Left unexplained, the meaning of the marl must be actively deciphered if it is to be fully understood; otherwise, the violence inherent in the story remains incomplete. Here, language functions as an obstacle to understanding, as the signifier "marl" floats uneasily through the text; it is never described in any depth, and the reader must struggle to translate it as it appears in the text—for, unlike the "zigaboo" cup, in which an everyday object takes on racist nomenclature, the marl remains untranslated and enigmatic.

The text's racist vernacular, in which the narrator often intrudes upon the narrative to remind us of the starving masses' inhumanity by hurling racist slurs, functions as a strategy for Walrond to induce readerly discomfort. After all, taken at face value, the narrator of "Drought" embraces the idea that readers should be wary of empathizing with the Black laborers it describes. By seeking to normalize such racist speech, the story demands a careful and astute reader who will work to see through the mechanisms via which racist language may be seen to obscure systems of oppression. Readers are more inclined to take note of, and respond to, the story's explicit instances of racist speech, while the calamitous effects of the marl dust, a product of imperial exploitation, remain abstracted and mostly hidden from view. The ingenuity of Walrond's critique of colonialism and imperial domination—in revealing the extent to which the colonizer tirelessly reframes atrocity by denying the humanity of those who suffer—thereby rests on narrative strategies of defamiliarization to obscure the horrific cost of exploitative labor. The text relishes in what Viktor Shklovsky refers to as "textual estrangement," in which a text "lead[s] us to a knowledge of a thing through the organ of sight instead of recognition" (6). "By 'estranging' objects and complicating form," Shklovsky writes, "the device of art marks perception long and 'laborious'" (6). Shklovsky's famous example, of a passage in Tolstoy in which readers witness the whipping of a horse, frames the scene as a moment of continuous unease and discomfort by making the horse—an animal that readers should be familiar with—seem alien and difficult to understand. In much the same way, the marl dust in "Drought" forces us to perceive the physical effects of imperial labor on the body implicitly and surreptitiously. For, in abstracting the marl as an ambiguous avatar of destruction, the text captures the means by which colonial violence resists easy explanation. The marl thus functions as a symbol of abstracted labor that ultimately signals inarticulatable suffering that, despite the narrator's or imperial authority's best efforts, can never be fully hidden.

In further examining the narrator's attempts to obscure the trauma of the quarry workers' labor, we can begin to observe the myriad of ways in which *Tropic Death*'s linguistic strategy distracts from and subverts larger issues of economic suffering. Most explicitly, the narrator deliberately fails to examine the colonial labor system in Barbados and the nature of the marl dust and, perhaps more importantly, fails to acknowledge the very fact that the people working in the quarry are literally starving to death. Starvation becomes less important than providing an ethnographic tour of the Caribbean, as the narrator highlights the nature of the cuisine that the quarry workers are able to afford. The narrator, for example, pauses to describe the "cookoo" meal that buckra Johnny, a white English worker, is eating as "corn meal, okras and butter stewed" (22).[17] It is telling that the narrator's attention to the composition of the food and its description vies uncomfortably with the fact that the characters in the story struggle to find and eat any food at all. Thus, the textual locus swirls around the impoverished inhabitants as Other: they appear as unsympathetic curiosities, not suffering human beings. Should the reader read carefully, they will observe, no doubt, that the narrator's foray into the nuances of cultural cuisine effaces the plight of their starvation. Notably, many of the textual interruptions circulate around objects that emphasize the imperial gaze of the tourist, such as moments that describe the tin cup or the cookoo. But none take seriously the workers' articulation of their plight; none of the primary characters' speech is ever translated. A scene in which a character expresses frustration that they are, in the outskirts of the quarry, perpetually caked in an irremovable marl dust—"Bajan gal don wash'ar skin / Til de rain come down"—is dismissed by the narrator as "Grumblings" (22). In this way, Walrond's incorporation of a decidedly racist, colonialist vocabulary thereby captures the ease through which imperial rhetoric obscures the suffering of the people that it interminably exploits.

Hierarchies of Language and Labor in the Canal Zone

The novel's incorporation of interruptive, racist "translations" serve as a means to regurgitate an imperialistic rhetoric of dehumanization and demonstrates the oppressor's ability to manipulate and reframe exploitation in terms of moral degradation. Yet the narrator's repeated use of dehumanizing language is complicated by the novel's historical setting; in this way, the implications of Walrond's experiments with language go beyond a critique of colonial oppression, in that his work provides a rare and direct confrontation with the politics of labor in the Canal Zone, where Walrond worked and lived for time, serving as a reporter for the *Panama Star Herald* from 1916 to 1918. Walrond's connection to Panama runs deep; he has stated, "I am spiritually a native of Panama. I owe the sincerest kind of allegiance to it" (*Winds Can Wake Up the Dead* 332), and his second book, *The Big Ditch,* about the building of the canal and the politics surrounding it, was never finished or published. Essential to Walrond's aesthetic is his confrontation with Caribbean identity and the racial politics of the Canal Zone, and his works represent entrenched systems of oppression and depictions of overt discrimination aimed against the West Indian labor force. Although critics have paid considerable attention to Walrond's connection to the Canal Zone, none have fully considered the relationship between his experiments with language and narration in terms of its relationship to the Panamanian labor system. In other words, we might reconsider the ways in which the textual vocabulary abstracts the labor and suffering of its protagonists as a means to confront the ethics of the Jim Crow labor system of the Canal Zone. This is not to stay that the novel's experiments with language can or should be reduced to a metaphor for capitalistic exploitation—rather, that Walrond's examination of the Canal Zone renders it as a site of racial violence that is difficult to process or understand. Throughout *Tropic Death*, Walrond's experiments with vernacular therefore serve as a means to elucidate how language was used to enforce the hierarchical division of labor in the Canal Zone.

In constructing the canal—which was built and completed between 1904 and 1944, after the United States took control of the project from France—the influx of Caribbean labor to the isthmus resulted in the discrimination of West Indian laborers, most explicitly through a racist policy of color classification that designated Black and minority workers as inferior. The United States incorporated Jim Crow labor laws in the Canal Zone through the implementation of a hierarchical system that grouped workers under "gold" and "silver" status; in fact, however, the vast differences in language, skin color, and culture created a far more robust system of discrimination. The labor system superficially classified workers based not on race, but on categories of work—though it is clear that categories were explicitly dominated by racial distinctions and ethnicity. *Tropic Death* depicts the implementation of US racial policy transnationally, as segregationist legislation is imported and applied as a means to successfully transform the geographical space of the canal into a space entirely dictated by racial hierarchy. The labor system, argues J. A. Zumoff, was effective not only in keeping Caribbean and migrant laborers at the bottom of the economic ladder but also in suppressing uprisings and protests. As Zumoff observes, "The Canal's racial system kept sectors of the workforce at each others' throats, preventing unified labor struggle and blunting the development of a inclusive proletariat in Panama. 'Gold' workers' privileges reflected the Jim Crow–style racism of the U.S. government and lowered overall labor costs while keeping a powerful army of 'Silver' labor in reserve as a battering ram against 'Gold' workers. Yet, West Indian workers appeared privileged to Panamanians who were excluded from Canal jobs, and immigrant workers feared being replaced by Hispanic Panamanians" (435). As Zumoff highlights, the Canal became a site of transnational exploitation in which racial violence proliferated, not just against Caribbean migrants, but between Americans, Panamanians, and

Caribbean workers. Even labor unions endorsed this system: "In the Canal Zone, AFL unions became strong advocates of segregation (and hence higher pay for white unionists) and excluding West Indians and Panamanians from 'Gold' positions. . . . Most vulnerable, however, were the West Indian workers" (436). Education, too, was segregated, and it was not until 1946 that nonwhite students were allowed to receive twelve grades of schooling.

The text's experimental form—and its experiments with vernacular—reflects the stratification of the Canal Zone labor system by framing the characters' humanity in terms of their labor value and, in so doing, cites and critiques the economics of the zone's dehumanizing labor practices. *Tropic Death* places a distinct emphasis on differentiated classes of existence and social acceptability by explicitly confronting the social conditions that devalued West Indians in terms of both race and labor. The Othering potential of language was integral to this process. In this vein, the beginning of "The Wharf Rats"—a narrative set in the Canal Zone—begins by depicting a particularly vulgar representation of its Black characters as "the dusky peons of those coral isles in the Caribbean," the "inky ones," and the "pickaninnies" (66). Depictions of white fear abound, as the narrator emphasizes his fear of "obea," and imagines the workers of the canal hunched "over smoking pots, on black, death-black nights legends of the bloodiest were recited til they became the essence of a sort of Negro Koran" (68). The Negros, the narrator argues, are "enslaved" to obeah and view the white inhabitants as dogs (68). Such depictions, of course, belie the very fact that the story is about the labor system in the Canal Zone, and the tension between the silver and gold workers, and the boys who dive for coins cynically tossed at them off boats by white tourists. The ingenuity of the story emerges in the extent to which it actively dismisses the critique of segregation and labor exploitation that it raises and replaces and reframes the conversation to make the exploited workers its villains by describing them in pejorative, racist language. The character Jean Baptise, for example, speaks with the "petulant *patois* of the unlettered French black" and possesses a "Barbadian bias" (68). Repeatedly, the silver workers and their families are framed as base and immoral. In the story, Walrond, by pairing worker status with racist language and verbal humiliation, intimates the complexities of racial exploitation in the Canal Zone while simultaneously encouraging the reader to ignore it. This performative gesture demonstrates the ease with which discussions of social inequity are often easily disarmed by exhortations of hysterical racist stereotypes.

It is easy to read the ending of the story—the jarring moment in which a boy (who we recall, is a "black peon") is torn apart by a shark that emerges from the "Deathpool" as he dives for coins tossed off a cruise ship—as an image of tragedy and horror, but it is essential not to overlook the racial framing of the story that asks the reader to feel remorse only after dehumanizing the subject that is meant to evoke sympathy. This complicated interplay of racism and sympathy functions in such a way as to erase the earlier articulation of apartheid in the Canal Zone, as the boy's tragic death appears so abrupt and shocking that we may be inclined to forget the narrator's earlier statements about race and labor. Yet Walrond here reminds us that deaths are not equal and interchangeable. In a story that insists on readerly sympathy only after it strips the possibility of it away, we can observe, in its narrative, the racial means through which life is made to have less societal value. The boy's death, we must recall, is a tragedy steeped in racist language: he is a "rat," vermin. The story thus asks: Does vermin deserve our grief? On the one hand, the boy's dehumanized status is theoretically stripped away at the end of the story, as we are made to feel his humanity and mourn his tragic death; however, the narrator's racist gaze occludes the possibility for an unmitigated mourning, as the subject, who was firmly entrenched in that gaze, can never be fully extricated from it.

"The Wharf Rats" reflects the perverseness of racist rhetoric in the Canal Zone while demonstrating how Afro-Caribbeans were made to inhabit a space in which they were perpetually reminded they were not fully human. The story's subtle receptive experiment, which depicts explicit racism only to superficially strip it away, warns us that the effects of racist discourse can never be truly erased, as characters inside the Canal Zone cannot exist outside of a system that interminably classifies them as Other, both by labor status and race. The story thus suggests that the boys exist merely in terms of what Homi Bhabha refers to as a "differentiating order of otherness." In *The Location of Culture,* Bhabha examines a process of hybridity that reveals not simply the subject ascribing to that which they are perceived to be, but a complex interplay of ascribed identity and a self-transformation engendered by oppressive ideological and societal forces. As Bhabha writes,

> The question of self-identification is never the affirmation of a pre-given identity, never a *self*-fulfilling prophecy—it is always the production of an image of identity and the transformation of the subject in assuming that image. The demand of identification—that is, to be *for* and Other—entails the representation

of the subject in the differentiating order of otherness. Identification . . . is always the return of an image of identify that bears the mark of splitting in the Other place from which it comes. For Fanon, like Lacan, the primary moments of such a repetition of the self lie in the desire of the look and the limits of language. The "atmosphere of certain uncertainty" that surrounds the body certifies its existence and threatens its dismemberment. (45)

As "The Wharf Rats" shows, the boys in the story are caught between the narrator's image of them and their own marginalized status within the Canal Zone—a point made all the more complicated because though they are not canal workers per se, the stratification of labor that associates Caribbean identity with inferior "silver" labor adheres to them despite their existence outside of the confines of the labor system itself. That is, the politics of the labor system—evident in the story through the very fact that impoverished Black teenagers perform for a white audience—is one that the boys are no doubt aware of and advertently (and perhaps inadvertently) enforce. By this, I mean that the act of diving becomes both an expression of self-identity (they are talented swimmers who possess admirable skill) as well as a reinforcement of the racial and socioeconomic divide (they are performing menial tasks for the white upper class). Their labor is less valuable than the labor and leisure of the white Canal Zone inhabitants, a point that they both recognize and exploit, and, as such, they paradoxically both enforce and repudiate hierarchies of race and labor by acknowledging the divide and seeking to economically exploit it. The interplay of self-identity in the story, like the one Bhabha highlights, is of both affirmation and denial, with the boys struggling to reconcile white racial dehumanization and labor exploitation while trying to gain advantage from it. What remains, however, is only the rigid presence of overwhelming hierarchies.

These hierarchies are further reinforced by the framing of the Caribbean characters in the Canal Zone's speech. In "The Yellow One," which takes place at sea, the narrator situates the Caribbean characters in vernacular, whereas exiles and immigrants from European nations speak without any encumbrance to the reader. In this sense, the narrator's prejudice emerges surreptitiously, but often. The story begins, for instance, with explicit creole that marks the Caribbean speaker's language as an enigma: "Im did got de fastiness fi' try fi' jump ahead o' me again, but mahn if yo' t'ink yo' gwine duh me outa a meal yo' is a dam pitty liar!" (51). Moments later, however, a conversation between a young mother and a man with "Latin blood bubbl[ing] in his veins" (52) converse in perfect English. As the scene plays out, the woman tells the Latin man, "Oh, many thanks . . . and do be careful, I've got this baby bottle in there and I wouldn't like to break it" (52; ellipsis added). On the surface, such a scene appears banal and mostly innocuous. Yet the clarity of this dialogue, juxtaposed against the earlier speech, is jarring—all the more so because it appears, reportedly, in Spanish, as the narrator remarks: "All of this in Spanish, a tongue spontaneously springing up between them" (52). It is significant here that the translated interpretation of Spanish appears absent any slang or inflection. Whereas much of the ship is referred to in derogatory slang—such as when we read of "the traditional deprivations of Hindu Coolies or Polish immigrants" who are "sunless" and "joyless"—Spain, and the woman's Spanish heritage, is given a kind of cultural capital and respect not accorded to other classes and races (55). In this way, the narrator associates Spanish identity with a sense of superiority and attraction, describing the woman in terms of "the mellow *Spanish* beauty of her" (55). The language becomes a force of derision, a point made more explicit by the fact that speech is seldom reported pejoratively for Europeans and colonizers.

The bitter critique of exploitation in the Canal Zone is perhaps most evident in "Panama Gold," a story that negotiates the trauma and social unrest that emerges for Caribbean workers returning from the canal. The story, set in Barbados, focuses on the relationship between Ella, an impoverished Barbadian woman, and Poyah, who has recently returned from Panama and opened up a store. While working on the canal, Poyah loses his foot in an accident and demands justice, arguing that, as a British subject in transnational space, he is not subject to the discriminatory practices of the American legal system that would deny him economic compensation. He threatens to "sick de British bulldog on all yo' Omericans!" (42). Significantly, however, the accident places Poyah in an indefinable space; as both a victim of imperialism and a colonial subject of another imperial nation, he struggles to find a means to resist. Here, Poyah imagines himself to possess the agency and authority of the nation that exploits him as a methodology of power, insisting, "Let dem understand quickly enough dat I wuz a Englishman and not a bleddy American nigger! A' Englishman—big distinction in dat, Bruing! An' dat dey couldn't do as dey bleddy well please wit' a subject o' de King!" (44). Yet while Poyah claims he received five hundred pounds of compensation, the narrative he tells shows that his claim for compensation is met with overt skepticism by the American authorities. As he affirms, "Heah I wuz losin' my foot fo' dem wit' wit dere bleddy canal an' dey come tellin' me dey wuzn't to blame. . . . And wuzzahmo' dey say dat why I didn't ketch holt o' de cowkatcher an' fling meself out de way!" (44; ellipsis added). In other words, the canal authorities blame the accident not on unsafe labor practices, but on his ignorance. While it seems that Poyah does in fact receive some kind of compensation—he owns a store, after all—it is unlikely, given his very few belongings, that his narrative about the amount of his payout is accurate. Poyah's story seems less a truthful telling of revenge against the colonizer and more a fantasy that his colonial status gives him a power that simply does not exist. In other words, the accident leads him to believe that he possesses a sense of national and colonial superiority without actually possessing it.

The story, therefore, depicts the coercion of colonial subjects into naturalizing their subservience to imperial power. Though it was seemingly impossible for Poyah to make a living in Barbados under the British Crown—and though he traveled to the Canal Zone, presumably, to provide for himself in ways that he could not under British rule—he nevertheless is quick to defend the Crown that symbolizes his own oppression, as he interpolates himself as a loyal colonial subject. He also reveals that, after he was injured, he threatened to blow up the canal and imagines that his threat has the support of the British authority. In an act that both submits to colonial authority and protests against colonial exploitation, he shouts, "Hell wit' de Canal! We wuz gwine blow up de dam cut down de wireless station an' breck up de gubment house!" and, in this way, he oscillates between the role of antagonist and victim (43–44). Significantly, the scant details the narrative provides of Poyah's accident suggest that it—and the ensuing conflict that follows—functioned not as an effective attack on the exploitative labor system in the Canal Zone, but as an understated endorsement of colonial rule, as Poyah's version of the story is one in which he earns both his revenge and compensation only as a result of the hypothetical intervention of Britain, which, in the story, functions as his protector.

Yet as is a pervasive theme throughout the collection, Walrond emphasizes how language enforces sentiments of colonial subservience throughout the Canal Zone and Caribbean. Accordingly, careful readers of "Panama Gold" will notice that the story's narration, and the narrator's tone and speech, shifts considerably as the story progresses. Moments after Poyah confronts his own marginalized status, the tone of the narration becomes more disparaging as it begins to focus more on marginalization and racial difference. Poyah, who lacked a concrete description in the narrative, is described as "one of those black men whose faces present an onion-like sheen, and upon whose brown and flabby jaws fester bright pimples stand out with a plaguing glitter" (46). It is only after critiquing American exploitation—and, perhaps more importantly—threatening sabotage and resistance, that Poyah transforms into a monstrous specimen. He becomes "one of those black men" whose jaws rot and fester, flailing like a decaying insect; his most remarkable feature is his acne, marking him as the avatar of ugliness and disgust. His framing now changed, he quickly moves from a victim of imperialistic exploitation to an embodiment of depravity. Ella, the story's protagonist, also receives a new description after her first interaction with Poyah. Under the narrator's racist ethnographic gaze, she becomes "a typical West Indian peasant," almost alien and Other; she is "free, loose, firm. Zim zam, zim zam" (49). It is telling that the narrator further essentializes Caribbean peoples only after Poyah brings to mind the danger of the canal's exploitative labor system. Thus Poyah's resistance risks becoming contagious, and the narrator reminds us that all Caribbean peoples are, essentially, the same: a collection of uncivilized stereotypes undeserving of empathy and, moreover, a threat to the order and livelihood of colonial rule. As throughout Walrond's collection, language here is the primary force used to estrange the Caribbean Other.

Taken together, Mais's and Walrond's work offers a complex analysis of the myriad of ways in which vernacular in the Caribbean is often deployed as a form of Othering and social and cultural estrangement. Their works express a pronounced concern that representations of communal speech may perpetuate essentialism. Both contend that uncritical forms of vernacular risk further solidifying mechanisms of societal violence that deny agency to marginalized populations and work to occlude the formation of a productive sense of national identity. By experimenting with the intelligibility and inscrutability of such language in their work, Walrond and Mais thus push readers to weigh the degree to which vernacular can be used to abstract us from the reality and nuances of colonial oppression.

4 "The Menace from the Bush"
Abstraction and Indigenous Violence in the Work of Wilson Harris and Denis Williams

IN A key moment in Wilson Harris's 1963 novel, *The Secret Ladder,* the protagonist, Russell Fenwick, a government surveyor, experiences a moment of crisis when, writing to his mother, he is forced to acknowledge that he does not know his past. His ancestry, his genealogy, and his very origins remain an unsolvable mystery that is, at times, all consuming. Yet this crisis of origin in *The Secret Ladder*—indeed, the crisis of origin that dominates much of Harris's writing—shares a consistent theme: it almost always revolves around questions of indigeneity. For Harris, the fading echoes of Guyana's subverted and fractured indigenous populations reverberate throughout all of his novels—continuously fading, but nevertheless present. Though Fenwick cannot know for certain his ancestry, he finds himself "wrestling with" an "indigenous skeleton in the cupboard" that leaves him unsettled and paralyzed (383). This overbearing sense of genealogical uncertainty, in which Fenwick believes he has indigenous origins, but cannot verify them—both because of the eradication of indigenous Guyanese peoples and the absence of a recorded history—brings about a sense of permanent unease in which his ancestry becomes entirely speculative. The past, in the novel, is a series of hypothetical potentials that are always subject to negation. Though Fenwick claims he is "not ashamed" of "the unique vagaries and fictions of the ancestral past," he struggles to cope with them and perpetually constructs and erases his genealogy—and with it, his identity (383).

Accordingly, this chapter examines the extent to which the dehumanization of indigenous bodies emerges as a force of both narrative rupture and textual destabilization in the work of Wilson Harris and Denis Williams. Born in Guyana in the early 1920s, both Williams and Harris became increasingly experimental in their writing as their careers progressed, and, significantly, both remained invested in the historicization of forgotten, eradicated, and displaced Amerindian populations in Guyana. As such, the exploration of subverted, decimated Amerindian peoples in their work manifests itself as an epistemological and ontological crisis in which identity is always in flux. Foregrounding the means through which Harris and Williams experiment with narrative forms to rethink representations of indigenous struggle, this chapter argues that the inherent difficulty and disorientating nature of their works offer powerful insights into the role of indigenous identity in Guyana and the Caribbean.

It must be noted, however, that, unlike the vast majority of writers discussed in this book, there is simply a dizzying amount of writing on Harris's work. The foundational criticism of Hena Maes-Jelinek, Sandra Drake, and Michael Gilkes has long analyzed its ingenuity and also advocated for the often underappreciated importance of Harris's contributions to literature as a whole.[1] In *The Labyrinth of Universality: Wilson Harris's Visionary Art of Fiction,* for example, Maes-Jelinek argues that "few writers have analysed with such devastating honesty and imaginative freedom the nature of the world in which we live and the mechanisms by which we react to it, or probed with his visionary insight the complex causes underlying the crisis of civilization in a conflictual and violent twentieth century" (xvii). Critical emphasis on Harris has continuously sought to both highlight and negotiate his contributions to Caribbean identity and global literature as a whole, and resources like the Wilson Harris Bibliography have worked to index writing by both Harris and his critics, providing a vital resource for scholars.[2] Nevertheless, despite the work of critics like Maes-Jelinek and Gilkes, as Jean–Pierre notes, "Wilson Harris has not yet reached the audience that he deserves, considering his genius and originality" (67). Thus, while critics have long championed Harris's work, the general public has by and large ignored his work.

It is not difficult to understand why. What links Harris's and Williams's work is the experimental difficulty of their prose.[3] On a formal level, what is common to both is an explicit poetics of abstraction, and it is this question of difficulty that has largely guided the critical conversation about their fiction. As such, the inscrutability of both writers' works has sometimes frustrated both critics and general readers. Derek Walcott went so far as to label Harris's *Eye of the Scarecrow* as "unreadable," fearing Harris was "in danger of disappearing in a self-created fog of obscurity" (quoted in Collier xxxv). Walcott's view—the belief that Harris's works are, at best, challenging, and, at worst, self-indulgent—in some ways persists today.[4] After Harris died in 2018, his *New York Times* obituary tellingly included a requisite YouTube link to a video called "How to

Read Wilson Harris" that depicts critics arguing over the difficulty and accessibility of his work.[5] The implication of both the obituary and the video is that readers should approach Harris's work tentatively, for it is all but certain they will not understand what they read. Of course, the cautious, hesitant representation of Harris's work in the obituary seems odd, given Harris's prolific output and critical approval—especially since he was knighted in 2010. Yet, as the obituary intimates, Harris's novels have largely fallen out of fashion, as lingering questions of difficulty and abstraction have threatened his contemporary relevance. Nevertheless, while there remains critical interest in Harris's work today, the same cannot be said for Williams's. Strangely, though Williams—especially due to his archeological work—is a figure of national significance and prestige in Guyana, there remain only two articles on his later fiction.[6] Simply put, Harris's and William's reputations as difficult, experimental writers have obfuscated the many ways in which their works provide deep insights into theories of indigeneity, as the relationship between formal experimentation and the oppression of Amerindian populations in works such as *The Sperm of God* and *The Secret Ladder* has been mostly ignored and unacknowledged. At a historical moment that has finally given credence to the formal academic study of indigeneity (and the emergence of indigenous studies programs)—their fiction, which struggles to reconcile indigenous identity through formal abstraction, are in need of incisive reexamination.

As I argue in this chapter, in the work of Harris and Williams, inscrutability is inextricably bound to the history and culture of bodies long subverted and suppressed. Moreover, their work contends that we should be skeptical of our ability to process or understand indigenous history and culture through a contemporary lens, and that to do so risks further disempowering and dehumanizing indigenous identity. Accordingly, I suggest that formal abstraction serves as a means of critical reflexivity, a dialectical tension that constantly negotiates between contemporizing indigenous identity into a digestible modern narrative and insisting that it remain inscrutable and inaccessible. Essential to the means through which both writers confront readers' ability to know and understand indigeneity is a fundamental emphasis on destabilizing identity—that is, both Harris and Williams force readers to challenge their own vision and perception of the signifier "native" by showing that indigenous experience and legacy reverberates across time and space, and that these reverberations are essential to negotiating the complexities of Guyanese identity. Destabilization, in this way, is paradoxically seen to be a powerful and potentially recuperative means to challenge static and reductive narratives of indigeneity, as well as indigenous experience and trauma—and, what's more, destabilization coerces the reader to feel a sense of loss, confusion, and frustration that seeks to parallel and, in some ways, replicate experiences of Guyanese ancestral trauma and disorientation. The experimental structure of both writers' work thereby forces readers to adopt new methods of understanding indigeneity in Guyana by effectively unsettling, and undermining, conventional reading practices that demand new ways of seeing. As such, this chapter rethinks representations of Harris's and Williams's confrontational aesthetic and shows the way their work establishes a new critical methodology for fictionalizing and negotiating indigenous trauma and struggle.

Catalysis and the Trauma of Origin

The eradication of indigenous peoples in Wilson Harris's works compel readers to confront the legacy of colonial violence against Amerindians in Guyana in particularly unsettling ways, challenging them to question the veracity of what they see and believe. In no uncertain terms, Harris's fiction depicts gruesome, traumatic acts of violence directed at indigenous and creole populations. But, for readers, the nature of indigenous representation in his work is difficult to ascertain and process, as indigenous peoples are filtered through a lens of spectral abstraction, haunting the landscape and seemingly existing outside of the confines of linear time and space. The suffering of indigenous bodies is present, but remote, as indigenous characters in novels such as *Palace of the Peacock* are framed through a lens of obfuscation. The Arawak woman in the novel appears as a wrinkled "statue" that does not speak and cannot be understood (62), her language and movements appear unintelligible to the crew, and she appears to exist outside of time, trapped at the end of "a long timeless journey" (62). To read Harris's novels is to encounter the simple, but undeniable reality: that the nature of indigenous experience and representation is misunderstood, obfuscated, distorted, or forgotten. The textual representation of Arawak identity, therefore, reminds us of the irreconcilable disconnect between modern Guyana and its historical origins. The violence she has experienced lingers below the surface of the text, inarticulable but present, reminding us that the story we are reading is not hers—and that her place in the narrative is simply to remind us of an atrocity that we can never fully understand.

Throughout Harris's oeuvre, the disconnect between contemporary Guyanese peoples and their indigenous and ancestral heritage has destructive emotional and psychological consequences. Frequently, these consequences are so dire that they threaten the very foundation of the fictional landscape, leading readers to question the textual reality of what they see and read. For Cristo in *The Whole Armour* confronting the lingering presence of the Caribs engenders a profound epistemological and ontological crisis that leaves him paralyzed. Alone in the bush, he comes into contact with an impossible, unreal corporeal representation of massacred Caribs. He doubts what he sees, but wonders if "they were too real to be . . . ghosts?" (337; ellipsis added). He confesses that all historical recollection and knowledge is "hopeless," asking, "What is and what is not? One can only repeat what happens to oneself" (337). In the novel, to face the eradication of the Caribs engenders an erosion of the past and present, generating an endlessly circulated articulation of brutality that is ever present, but disconnected from the present moment. For Cristo, after the encounter, time ceases to progress linearly in the novel. As the scene demonstrates, the reverberations of indigenous violence enact a process of endless self-questioning and doubt that, in this case, leaves Cristo unable to perceive who, where, and when he is.[7]

It is this struggle to reconcile one's severed connection to an indigenous and ancestral past that is the central conflict of Harris's work, and it is the epistemological and ontological crises that result from this trauma that Harris confronts, in nearly all of his work, through an experimental rupture of narrative form. This specter of indigenous and ancestral trauma, argues Harris, permeates all facets of Guyanese reality, eroding distinctions between past, present, and future. It is this nuanced, decentered representation of colonial violence that is essential to understanding the role of indigenous representation in his work, as his novels insist that the repercussions of violence against indigenous peoples is a perpetual nightmare that contemporary Guyana must not, and cannot, forget. Far from simply depicting the eradication of indigenous populations as historical acts of violence relegated to the past, the echoes of such colonial atrocities instead cascade across time and space. These atrocities are frequently impossible to reconcile, to the extent that it destabilizes one's grasp on reality. In Harris's novels, identities merge, characters die and then die again, and scenes and events repeat, as the characters struggle to come to terms with the trauma of their fractured origins.

A key claim of this chapter is that Harris's work seeks to generate feelings of ancestral disconnect and alienation by replicating, for readers, experiences of frustration and confusion felt by modern Guyanese people. Through a method of formal experimentation, Harris's early work attempts to capture how questions of genealogy and heritage lead to pronounced and unyielding epistemological trauma—a process that Denis Williams has labeled "catalysis." For Williams, catalysis is a psychological crisis that dominates and afflicts the people of both Guyana and the Caribbean. As he explains in *Image and Idea in the Arts of Guyana,* catalysis is an experience of internal torment that results from the severing of one's ancestral heritage. In theorizing the concept, Williams seeks to explore the extent to which the colonial subject can ever recuperate a sense of psychological well-being in the shadow of colonial atrocity. It is longing and shame that forms the basis of Williams's theory of catalysis—a state of generative, perpetual, existential unease engendered by the colonial project that is unique to Guyanese identity. Catalysis is thus a means to more deeply understand—and in some ways reconcile—the inherent paralysis associated with the trauma of being unable to trace one's origin or ancestry. In sum, Williams contends that modern Guyana must free itself from its reliance on Western conceptions of ancestral heritage, which shackle Guyanese people to a sense of permanent inferiority and unease. Williams argues for a rejection of the concept of "the racial ancestor" (101) and encourages instead a rethinking and resituation of the effects of miscegenation in Guyanese society. The concept of catalysis therefore attempts to remediate the Caribbean subject's inherent disconnect from their own history and genealogy that emerges as a byproduct of colonial atrocity.

Catalysis is a state of being that, while potentially recuperative, locks the subject in an act of perpetual reflection. Like Fenwick's endless wrestling with an "indigenous skeleton" in *The Secret Ladder,* catalysis demands that the subject reckon with one's relationship to their ancestry and indigenous forbearers. On the one hand, experiences of catalysis signal a positive force. In rejecting Western ideologies that privilege the currency of ancestry and origin as a marker of value or self-worth, Williams petitions for the embrace of a redefined, reflexive conception of miscegenation that speaks to a "new world" interpretation of Guyanese identity. This redefinition, counter to simplistic conceptions of "melting pots," is one of positive reflexivity that acknowledges the inevitability of an identity, engendered by colonial violence and acts of genocide, that is never fixed and ever changing. As he contends: "The model of New World society is therefore not one of a melting pot, but that of a crucible in which catalysts of varying degrees of potency operate" (103). Such catalysts foster a dialectical relationship of social division and creative energy that, argues Williams, is a "willing-mutilation of the soul and therefore an aspect of self-annihilation" (103). In this regard, Williams repeatedly reminds us that there is immense trauma in negotiating one's ancestry: for "New World" peoples, there is never a static origin, only a perpetual present in which identity is in permanent flux. Williams imagines Guyanese society locked in an endless form of becoming and constant metamorphosis that always negotiates its severed ancestral origin, a society that exists "as a complex plurality in continual process of achieving a complex singularity—a singularity always open to change" (136).

Yet this process of remaking and critical reimagining enacts both new forms of consciousness and new forms of aesthetic expression, and, Williams argues, "these problems of blood and ancestry, being central to the Guyanese social structure, might be expected to be reflected, in direct or in sublimated form, in much Guyanese creative writing to come" (115). The fundamental confrontation of severed origin and history that emerges through centuries of enslavement, indentured servitude, and the gradual and persistent effacement of Amerindian peoples and cultures serves as a constant reminder not just of loss, but of interminable remaking. Like Fenwick in *The Secret Ladder*, Williams insists that the torn threads of one's past can never be rectified, and, what's more, such reliance on Western forms of ancestry—that is, essentially, the notion that one is incomplete without an origin—relegate the Caribbean to a state of permanent inferiority. Thus, Williams reformulates a theory of Caribbean identity in the interstices of the trauma of lost origins and the rejection of ancestry itself. This productive tension, he writes, has profound implications:

> This lack of witness, this lack of the indwelling of a common ancestor, this lack of any charter whatsoever for a destiny seems to me to establish an entirely unique basis for such a view of man, for the conduct of affairs, and for the realisations of culture; for the human in such a continually changing present, the human as himself a function of the process of catalysis establishes the possibility of a new relationship—individual to individual, individual to society; the possibility of a truly human experiment (if the word might be permitted to describe a shift of consciousness itself rather than a mere shifting of the products of experience); an experiment in human consciousness if not in human responsibility. (114)

Williams's theory of catalysis mirrors the later work of Homi Bhabha, as here he postulates the myriad of ways that cultural hybridity and creolization both destroy and create new modes of perception and, in so doing, lock the subject into a moment of crisis that can be employed for intellectual, psychological, and aesthetic aims.[8] However, his essay, while foreshadowing Bhabha's concept of hybridity, differs, in that its primary concern is the question of origin. In contrast to Bhabha, Williams foregrounds a focus on ancestry that situates the absence of indigenous Guyanese history as both a central crisis and a potential aesthetic emancipation.

For Williams, Harris's novels represent the experience of catalysis par excellence. Indeed, Harris's work imprisons its characters in a liminal space of constant reflection, depicting an interminable process of revision and self-questioning that leads to a perpetual sense of contradiction and confusion. As we see in *The Secret Ladder,* Fenwick laments the effacement and erasure of his potentially indigenous ancestry and yearns for a more stable identity. At the same time, he actively resists any sense of fixity or assuredness. Paradoxically, to affirm an identity in Harris's work is to erase it. In a key scene, Fenwick writes about his past in a letter to his mother, but he repeatedly crosses out what he writes. In an act of both confusion and malice, he makes "thick marks across lines he hated the instant he had written them. Not simply crossing them out. For then it was possible still to decipher what was underneath. But annihilating them" (385). Fenwick exists in a cycle of affirmation and erasure, annihilating what he writes, but doomed to write it and erase it again and again. His attempt to destroy his history manifests itself as it does in most of Harris's fictions: in an almost total breakdown of identity and individuality. As Ashcroft, Griffiths, and Tiffin write in *The Empire Writes Back,* the catalytic subject "is constantly struggling to free itself from a past which stressed ancestry, and which valued the 'pure' over its threatening opposite, the 'composite'" (35–36). The catalytic or "composite" subject must process and effectively share a collective trauma that acknowledges their buried and irredeemable history as an undeniable fact. Fenwick's identity—like Harris's other characters'—fluctuates wildly throughout the text, and, as we will see, in a Harris novel subjective positions routinely collapse. As Williams shows, Harris's novels capture the subject in a moment of prolonged catalysis, as characters are entangled in an exhausting process of continuous remaking, self-doubt, and alteration that annihilates their origin and history.

The catalytic nature of Harris's work produces what I call an "unsettled reading." In other words, the formal abstraction that dominates these novels—in which characters become other characters, dreams become reality, and time and space collapse—attempts to reflect the psychological effects of catalysis by creating new reading practices that perpetually disorient and trouble readers. In Harris's novels, acts of displacement and colonial violence reverberate endlessly and are frequently impossible to represent in logical or scrutable terms. Harris's experimental structure works to untether itself from unproductive representations of Guyanese trauma and ancestral confusion by attempting to capture the experiences of catalytic suffering in literary form, in which contradiction and uncertainty dominate practices of reading. Consequently, Harris's work suggests that narratives of colonization and indigenous erasure must be confronted and effectively unsettled: that the linear or conventional novel cannot properly represent the psychological and physical effects of colonial domination. More overtly, however, my usage of the term "unsettlement" of course signals the physicality of actual displacement, and the near eradication and continued oppression of indigenous populations throughout Guyanese history. In Harris's work, dislocation becomes both a thematic principle and a performative gesture that obliges readers to question what they see, know, and believe to be true. The receptive implications of Harris's effort to destabilize what readers know—or, more importantly, what readers think they know—about indigenous experience continuously asks audiences to rethink their perceptions as they traverse the text. As Boehmer has argued, experiences of textual dislocation may engage readers to rethink their own relationship to the way they identify with the events the narrative describes, and the way they understand them. This experience is often less a radical rupture than a persistent unraveling of the linguistic properties of the text. As Boehmer writes, "Postcolonial *writing* is not always explosive, shattering, or shocking. . . . Its impact also manifests in more mediated forms, through the investigative, exploratory work of language, through how the reader's imagination is engaged, their identification solidified. Such work includes reflections on that chiasmic break into the now *and also* . . . to investigate ways of continuing, to provide a fuller understanding of the painful losses as well as the eventual gains of such acts" (73). What is compelling about Boehmer's theory of postcolonial reading here is that it emphasizes the productive force of temporal and linguistic disorientation as a means to better grasp experiences of horror and displacement. In creating narratives that engage readers in such ways, Harris's novels urge reflection on experiences of Caribbean aporia in a way that is both immediate and urgent, reminding readers that their knowledge of the landscapes and characters the text describes are always illusory and incomplete.

An unsettled reading thus acknowledges that efforts to reconcile indigenous experience within an understanding of contemporary Guyana always results in an erosion of past and present. Readers therefore confront an endlessly circulated articulation of confusion and historical uncertainty that is ever present, but disconnected, to the present moment. In eliminating the clarity—indeed, in severing it from its historical specificity—the catalytic crisis of Harris's texts permeate all facets of Guyanese reality, eroding distinctions between people, places, and time in general. By way of example, as the central characters in *Palace of the Peacock* wrestle with understanding the significance of the Arawak woman whom they abduct, the very landscape itself collapses, as the narrator, who is no longer sure if he is dreaming, suddenly tells us: "The map of the savannahs was a dream. The names Brazil and Guyana were colonial conventions I had known from childhood. I clung to them now as to a curious necessary stone and footing, even in my dream, the ground I knew I must not relinquish" (24). Geography, and one's sense of place and understanding of its inhabitants, becomes here memories warped by colonial imprint. The narrator's sudden moment of disorientation quite literally interrupts the story itself, as neither the narrator nor the reader can determine their place in the narrative—or even what is happening. Unequivocally, the concept of unsettlement does not apply only to the physicality of violence toward indigenous bodies, but also to the act of reading itself. Catalysis in Harris's work is, therefore, not simply a thematic principle: it generates and enables acts of textual disorientation that destabilize and disorient the reading process in ways the seek to replicate and reproduce what, for Williams, is the central epistemological crisis of Caribbean experience.

Moments of catalytic crisis are rife in Harris's work and must be reconciled by both characters and readers. No characters stand on stable ground, and they are frequently tossed between multiple realities, timelines, and ontological planes that disorient our ability to understand them. The narrator of *Palace of the Peacock,* for example, cannot accurately trace his history because he, caught in an endless slumber that collapses dream and reality, simply does not know who or where he is. *Palace* opens with narrator awakening from a dream that is not a dream, and that he is not—ever—fully awake from. He says: "I dreamt I awoke with one dead eye seeing and one living closed eye. I put my dreaming feet on the ground in a room that oppressed me as though I stood in an operating theatre, or maternity ward, or I felt suddenly, the glaring cell of a prisoner who had been sentenced to die. . . . I had felt the wind rocking me with the oldest uncertainty and desire in the world, the desire to govern or be governed, rule or be ruled forever" (19). The narrator is both asleep and awake, dead and alive, existing in a space that he cannot define—here, an operating room, or maternity ward, or prison. Each location denotes a different condition and requires a new ontology: a patient waiting for an operation, a mother giving birth to a child, or a convicted criminal waiting for execution. By the end of the novel, we can no longer distinguish the narrator from other key characters, as he merges into the oppressive Donne, among others, in an endless, horrifying process of rebirth and becoming. In much the same way, Van Brock at the end of *The Secret Ladder* reads his grandmother's stories and meets with a collapse of time, space, and individuality, as he ponders his Dutch, African, and indigenous ancestry. The three figures merge into one another, as he notes: "Sometimes they were all one undivided column and person, sometimes they were two, sometimes they were three, a trinity so singular and real it vanished into obscurity. It was impossible to tell where it stood" (452). Such a process—in which stories, persons, and columns blend into an indistinguishable sameness—sever the characters from their identity, stripping them of their past and memories, leaving them in a state of interminable confusion and uncertainty. Van Brock yearns for an escape, clinging to his last ancestor, but hating her all the same, thinking that "he wanted her to die and melt into the ground with all the rest" (52).

The catalytic subject locked in a moment of self-doubt, erasure, and crisis manifests itself explicitly in one of Harris's most employed tropes: what he calls "the fulfillment of character" (Bundy 140). As Harris describes it in "Tradition and the West Indian Novel," the notion of a static, uniform, cohesive identity is a European tradition, a privilege not garnered to those dominated by imperial and colonial rule. A character with a fixed or stable identity does not reflect Caribbean experience. In this essay and elsewhere, Harris insists that a Caribbean aesthetic must not rely on Western forms but initiate a more explicit sense of dialectical tension that shatters "the historical mould" of capitalist and imperialist ideologies of self-sufficiency. Harris thus seeks to employ a concept of character that eschews fixity and embraces his view that "what . . . is remarkable about the West Indian in depth is a sense of subtle links, the series of subtle and nebulous links which are latent within him, the latent ground of old and new personalities" (135). His works of fiction, which therefore seek to "visualize a *fulfillment* of character," exist in stark contrast to what he calls "consolidation." As he writes, "The consolidation of character is. . . the preoccupation of most novelists who work in the twentieth century within the framework of the nineteenth-century novel. . . . And this is not surprising after all since the rise of the novel in its conventional and historical mould coincides in Europe with states of society which were involved in consolidating their class and other vested interests. As a result 'character' in the novel rests more or less on the self-sufficient individual—on elements of 'persuasion'. . . rather than 'dialogue' or 'dialectic'" (135). Whereas consolidation signals only regressive stagnancy, fulfillment champions flux and potential. Undeniably, Harris's idea of fulfillment shares much in common with the concept of catalysis. In contrast to the European novel, a text that embraces the fulfillment of character does not display a sense of comfortable self-sufficiency, but rather a decided lack of self-assurance; the reader is not permitted to ally herself with what she reads. One cannot relate or connect with any character in Harris's work, for any and every one of them is entrenched in a metamorphic process of obliteration and transformation in which the reader is forced to adopt a sense of uneasy distance and uncertainty. This sense of productive unease, when the comfort of a readerly alliance is denied, is unique in that unlike, for example, the experimental aesthetic of the French Nouveau Roman (from which both Harris's and Williams's work no doubt take stylistic influence), its goal is not predominantly aesthetic, but discursive. In remaking novelistic conceptions of character through catalytic fulfillment, the reader must confront, through frustration, confusion, and disorientation, the visages of postcolonial identity through horrifying, interminable fracture. In other words, social realism is sacrificed in the vortex of endless becoming, disenfranchisement that is, for Harris, the catalytic reality of Caribbean identity.

Resentment and the Poetics of Indigenous Replacement

As I have been arguing, Harris's work incorporates both abstraction and a collapse of subjectivity to confront the extent to which the horror of severed ancestry emerges as a result of colonial atrocity. This trauma of origin, as Williams argues, results in a perpetual state of catalysis—a moment of crisis that, while paralyzing, may engender a new interpretation of Guyanese identity—that emerges in Harris's works not only as a thematic tendency but also in the experience of reading itself. In terms of narrative representation, like Williams, who theorizes catalysis as a potentially redemptive processes, Harris suggests that the indecision, confusion, and disenchantment that catalysis produces is potentially recuperative and may lead to new forms of understanding. In "The Fabric of Imagination," for example, Harris embraces the importance of experiences and texts that challenge temporal and ideological stagnancy to shatter and reimagine new possibilities of diversity. As he writes, "It is the translation of apparently absolute ordeal into infinite poles extending backwards in time, forwards into infinity, that offers a progress, so to speak, into genuine diversity-in-universality. Such progress, I am implying, breaks the mould of habit, breaks a mould of reading that bypasses the enormity and the subtlety of *re-visionary potential* within imageries in texts of being" (180). As Harris's fiction shows, however, enacting the mold-breaking and revisionary potential of catalysis is an enormously difficult and often traumatic process. The representation of catalysis in Harris's work is depicted less as a clear recuperative strategy than a struggle with aporia and loss—a struggle that not every character successfully negotiates. As I see it, while Harris's early novels typically depict catalysis as an exhausting but necessary process of self-discovery, they also show how an inability to productively negotiate the complexity of catalytic experience can and often does have dire consequences. In so doing, Harris points toward a way forward while cautiously reminding us of the challenges of negotiating fracture and ancestral disconnect. Recuperation, in this way, is an immense challenge and not a simple forgone conclusion that can be carried out without labor or profound self-reflection.

Throughout *The Guyana Quartet,* a refusal to engage or embrace catalytic identity as a state of being, or a yearning for the simplicity of what Harris calls "consolidation," often results in the formation of a destructive and imperialist worldview that locks the subject in indecision and resentment and, as I will show, enforces the further perpetuation of indigenous disenfranchisement. Compellingly, Harris's work shows how the crisis of identity that catalysis represents—a crisis that can foster productive self-reflection—sometimes fails and, in failing, instead induces a pronounced sense of displaced anger and resentment toward already marginalized peoples. If, as Williams argues, catalysis is a state of being brought forth by the colonial project, then the inability of catalysis to bring about a sense of self-empowerment is itself often sabotaged by the ideology that brought it into being, as Harris's work forcibly reminds us that, when stripped of their ancestry, the history-less subject is often drawn toward colonial values that emphasize power and domination as a means of self-fulfillment. If not negotiated carefully, such severing of ancestry, as seen in Harris's works, can produce immense societal resentment directed, primarily, at indigenous bodies who become scapegoats for civil, social, and racial unrest in Guyana.

This idea plays out frequently in Harris's novels. His work, perhaps more so than that of any other Caribbean writer, depicts masses of suffering indigenous populations, who, in almost all of his novels, are met with unspeakable resentment and violence carried out not only by colonizers and imperialists but also by contemporary Guyanese peoples. Throughout Harris's work, the animosity directed at indigenous populations—carried out by multiple characters with shifting identities—exposes a collective process of historical trauma in which contemporary Caribbean peoples have been alienated from their historical ancestry, while framing native peoples as obstacles to the foundation of a more just (or even an independent) society. In other words, in what follows I will examine how Harris's experimental use of abstraction serves as a means to highlight intercultural tensions between creole and Amerindian populations and demonstrate how these tensions further marginalize oppressed indigenous peoples from participating in Guyanese society.

A brief overview of *The Guyana Quartet* introduces us to characters who express overbearing animus toward indigenous populations on the part of protagonists who are, in most cases, poor creole laborers. In *The Secret Ladder,* indigenous peoples exist solely as the "menace from the bush": a dark and menacing force that the crew views with horror (357). It is telling, however, that, though *The Guyana Quartet* was written and is set prior to independence, in the text there exists little animosity toward the British on the part of its central characters. Donne, in *Palace of the Peacock* is, to be sure, a thorough brute: a testament to violence, greed, and selfishness. He is also, of course, enmeshed in catalytic crisis; he bears no true, stable identity of his own. At various points in the novel, he merges into the narrator, becomes the Dreamer, becomes his own brother and, as is the case for almost all of Harris's characters, lacks a fixed history. Yet Donne responds to his catalytic state of being only with resentment. Significantly, his anger is directed not at the colonizer or the legacy of imperialism that obliterated his ancestors, but almost exclusively at those that he blames for his misfortune: the Arawaks, whom he derisively labels "buck folk." In fact, his tyranny is rooted in perpetuating a model of colonial oppression, as he embraces theories of cultural superiority to justify extreme acts of violence. Adopting the language of colonization, he argues that ancestry and indigenous heritage is irrelevant to land ownership: "Who would believe that these devils have title to the savannahs and to the region? A stupid legacy—aboriginal business and all that nonsense: but there it is. I've managed so far to make a place for myself—spread myself amply as it were. . . . After all I've earned a right here as well. I'm as native as they are, ain't I? A little better educated maybe whatever in hell that means" (51). Here, Donne affirms the indigenous Arawaks as uncivilized savages who, set apart from the modern world, falsely claim land rights over what he views as an unworthy, pointless legacy. His assertion that "I'm as native as they are" paradoxically affirms the value of indigenous history while also rejecting it, as here Donne dismisses the culture and value of the Arawaks as bankrupt, but nevertheless values—and steals—the cultural capital of the signifier "native." That is, Donne's catalytic creole identity, which is itself ambiguous and uncertain, is imagined here as native; indeed, Donne contends that he, not the Arawaks, is the true and deserving inheritor of Guyanese history. Instead of negotiating how catalytic ancestral trauma may engender a better understanding of the self, Donne seeks to consolidate his identity and repudiates any connection to Guyana's splinted history. Resentment breeds replacement—and, as characters grow increasingly frustrated over their catalytic uncertainty, they increasingly direct their ire at indigenous peoples. Again, paradoxically, they begin not simply to deny the value and humanity of Amerindian people and histories, but to imagine themselves as the legitimate bearers of native and indigenous status, often wrestling away the signifier of "native" or "indigenous" and ascribing it to themselves.

It is this relationship between resentment and replacement that I want to analyze further. In this sense, Harris's early work confronts the social and cultural processes that undermine and devalue indigenous experience in compelling and disturbing ways that push readers to reevaluate their own perceptions of indigenous representation. Such is the case in Harris's 1962 novel, *The Whole Armour*. For, while Donne's animosity toward indigenous people could perhaps be attributed to his violent nature, the process of indigenous replacement that he evokes becomes considerably more complicated in *The Whole Armour*, in which it becomes increasingly difficult for readers to discern if what they are seeing and reading is an authentic representation of indigenous experience or history, or a pale recreation of it. In the text, Harris's experimentation with character takes on a new urgency as historical recreations, specters, and hallucinations blur the line between history and fiction. In a key scene, the Catholic Mission hosts a river carnival that stages a "re-creation" of a battle between the Arawaks and the Caribs from Pomeroon to Moruca, in which contemporary actors step into the role of indigenous peoples. The implications here, in which local nonindigenous people effectively inhabit the role of indigenous tribesmen, literalize Donne's claim that contemporary people have earned the right to call themselves "natives." Moreover, the carnival troublingly functions as a faux celebration of ancestral heritage by embracing an image of Amerindian experience that does not revere their culture or achievements, but rather fetishizes them as warring savages (337). Putting on a costume and posing as indigenous tribes trying to eliminate each other is, perhaps, the height of grotesque fantasy and delusion in Harris's work, especially given the fact that these characters exist alongside the very real presence of actual, suffering indigenous people that are present throughout *The*

Guyana Quartet. There are more dangerous implications lurking in this scene and throughout the narrative of *The Whole Armour*: Cristo insists that what he saw was real, not a mock battle. He affirms: "The Arawaks I saw belonged to two or three centuries ago. As far back as that, I would swear" (337). Cristo's insistence that those he saw were "too real" to be "pretenders" evokes a common theme in the text, in which the indigenous peoples we see in the narrative are always rendered potentially suspect (337). Every potential moment of indigenous encounter is a moment of epistemological uncertainty in which a potential indigenous specter—or a living indigenous Carib or Arawak—may be a nonindigenous actor. If Donne, in *Palace of the Peacock*, demands that his struggles have earned him native status, *The Whole Armour* suggests something considerably bleaker, in that the landscape is of a world in which indigeneity has been entirely displaced and replaced: anyone and everyone can wear the label of "indigenous." Indigenousness becomes both a costume and a charade that all characters can potentially take on, and, in this way, the novel becomes one of Harris's most profound and disorienting confrontations of indigenous displacement and cultural resentment.

The Whole Armour's framing of indigenous identity further complicates the experience of readerly unsettlement that dominates Harris's work. The novel's indigenous obfuscation has considerable implications for readers, as the events of the narrative cast doubt that we can truly evaluate whether or not an indigenous person or setting is "authentic," as every indigenous element of the text is suspect and readers are thus made to doubt—or even view with skepticism—the presence of indigenous characters and testimonies in the text. Because Harris's prose relishes in blurring the boundaries between individual identities, we can never determine with certainty if a specter is truly a specter, or if a temporal shift has transported a major character to a plane in which they are actually interacting with an indigenous ancestor, or even if the character in question is not an indigenous person, but, rather, an actor playing one. The text thus demands extra attention from readers, who must be doubly perceptive if they are to unravel the novel's complex representation of indigenous identity.

In any case, themes and feelings of skepticism dominate the narrative of *The Whole Armour*. Not only do the Catholic missionaries confusingly embody the role of indigenous peoples, but their actions and presence also literalize Donne's claim in *Palace of the Peacock* that he is "just as native as they are" by portraying native status that can be simply tried on for amusement. In distorting the temporal boundaries that demarcate contemporary and indigenous experience in a way that engenders readerly skepticism, readers themselves become distrustful of indigenous bodies in the text. And essentially the trap the novel sets up is in goading readers to question and look for an "authentic indigenous" representation—as if indigenous experience can be reduced to a cohesive narrative that can be simply reenacted. Thus the sense of displacement in the novel breeds dubiousness and enacts a performative gesture that urges readers, like the characters, to doubt the presence and history of indigenous bodies, as nonindigenous creoles continuously play the part of Amerindian characters.

In some respects, it makes sense that *The Whole Armour* conflates and disorients the relationship between indigenous and nonindigenous "actors," and that this scene is framed in terms of a "performance." Essential to Harris's work is the concept of "infinite rehearsal": a phrase for which Harris named his 1987 novel. As Maes-Jelinek explains, "All Harris's fictions are in a sense a continuously renewed dialogue between the living and the dead or the eclipsed, whether people(s), cultures or civilisations. In order to understand this, one must keep in mind that Harris perceives existence as an endless interweaving between life and death; that death never means to him total or final annihilation but a living absence . . . that the realm of the dead is also that of the sacred and of the subterranean tradition" (61). Scholars have long focused on how repetition, spectrality, and temporal disorientation in Harris's novels allow us to rethink the stagnancy of historical representations of the past in new and productive ways. Harris frequently employs the metaphor of "infinitely rehearsed" theatrical performances—and sometimes carnivals—that are interminably practiced but never finalized (and always undergoing edits and revision) as if to remind us that our understanding of the past and present is always unfinished and incomplete.[9] The past, or what we assume we know of the past, is continuously restaged and performed in an effort to coerce readers to rethink and reimagine their own knowledge of historical trajectories of oppression and disenfranchisement. This notion of rehearsal or "re-visionary potential," as Harris explains in "The Fabric of the Imagination," is ultimately a means of confronting "images that need to be consulted in new lights as they bear backwards and forwards upon their partial substance within a theatre of unfathomable wholeness" (180). In other words, by restaging and rethinking historical events and images, Harris urges "us to find new, flexible balances between the past and the future"(183). We may thus learn to "cope with the consequences of our own deeds in the past and the present" (183). Taken this way, the recreation scene in *The Whole Armour* functions as a recuperative means of negotiating trajectories of imperial violence through a radical destabilization of the past and present.[10] As Gilkes has pointed out, despite the fact that *The Infinite Rehearsal* was not released until 1987, the concept that bears its title is foundational and present in almost all of Harris's early work.[11] It is explicitly present, too, in *The Whole Armour*.

With such a definition, the displacement of indigenous bodies by non-indigenous peoples in *The Whole Armour*—and its troubling implications—becomes more clear. Indeed, in an interview with Alan Riach and Mark Williams, Harris argues that indigenous experience cannot be fully extricated from the European forms of oppression that entangle them, and that to represent native or indigenous experience means both unearthing and confronting entrenched vestiges of colonial ideology that obscure and distort our knowledge of indigenous identity. In this way, Harris's work wrestles with the extent to which imperialist tropes and echoes affect the past, present, and future. These tropes and echoes, he contends, must be properly negotiated if we are to engender the imagination of a more progressive, catalytic worldview. "When you go to the so-called Third World," Harris says, "the archetypes, if I may use that word... which they call 'native' archetypes, are all overlaid by European skeletons and archetypes as well. You will never activate them unless you activate the so-called European skeletons as well" (60). This presence of European skeletons lingers throughout *The Guyana Quartet,* as expressions and sentiments of imperialist ideology haunt the text and often occlude the emergence of a progressive, catalytic identity. The interminable search for meaning that dominates *The Guyana Quartet* repeatedly collapses into indigenous resentment and a displaced anger that is almost always directed, in Harris's texts, at native populations. It is in this experience of replication and reinscription that Harris's works force readers to ask deeper questions about experiences of oppression. Yet, in so doing, the remanifestation of acts of colonial violence in new forms and contexts in many ways lays bare processes of disenfranchisement that persist today. Seen this way, Harris's project opens up new methods of understanding trauma and violence by rethinking how systems of inequity are perpetuated.

More recent critics, however, have questioned the efficacy of Harris's deployment of revisioning and restaging, especially in terms of its implications for indigenous identity. Aparna Halpé, for example, in her essay "The Ideology of Archetype: Mythical Strategies in Wilson Harris's Jonestown," examines the problematics of indigenous representation in Harris's more contemporary novel *Jonestown* and urges critics to more seriously consider the relationship between the reader and the historical circumstances Harris's texts often confront and revise. As Halpé notes, "Harris's reading public is not the local or indigenous subject, but the literate consumers who are 'always already' outside the contextual immediacy and historical bias of the events at Jonestown. It is thus important to question what Harris accomplishes for the global reader by invoking [a] Christian quest myth, when the text does not create a space for the collectivized local or indigenous subjects to participate in the narrative. Does this narrative bring us any closer to a more conscious reading of the events of Jonestown?" (207–8). In short, Halpé reminds us that readers are already presumably detached from the historical and cultural experiences of crisis that texts like *Jonestown* describe, and she questions Harris's attempt to "produce a text that brings about the effect of transubstantiating traumatic memory" (208). What is particularly important about Halpé's critique is that it suggests Harris has not fully thought through the practices of reception his novels seek to produce. In interstitching symbols of indigenous history and mythology with imperialism to create a new historical and temporal tableau, Harris's texts inadvertently end up privileging "universal archetypal currency" that its characters "can never hold" (212). In other words, in merging European and indigenous forms, as Harris does throughout his work, novels like *Jonestown* reveal the "difficulty" of "narrating localized traumatic histories" (212). We might ask: Does Harris's emphasis on restaging and revisioning help readers to understand the nature of historical trauma and colonial violence—or does it potentially abstract indigenous experience further?

My goal, however, in acknowledging critical work on Harris's exploration of time and space, is not to argue for or against the recuperative value of the concept of infinite rehearsal, but to consider the readerly implications of how the novel forces readers to confront the reality of indigenous displacement. While the problems inherent in the concept of the infinite rehearsal are complex and have long been debated, what I find remarkable (and in many ways more important) about texts like *The Whole Armour* is the way they ensnare readers into inadvertently embracing sentiments of indigenous skepticism in an effort—and this is the key point—to encourage critical reflection that ultimately sees through those very same schemas of misrepresentation and misunderstanding. In other words, the inventiveness of the text is evident not just in the fact that it performatively coerces the reader to replicate processes through which contemporary Guyanese people devalue and question the presence of indigenous bodies, but in how it seeks to promulgate a deeper understanding of colonial mechanisms that foster intercultural resentment between creole and indigenous peoples by revealing the social and colonial processes that enable them. In this case, readers witness how the missionaries' colonial product, under the guises of "cultural appreciation," breeds a distrust of indigenous people that spreads across Guyana like a plague. At the same time, the text acknowledges that it is extraordinarily difficult to overturn, and in some cases even perceive, the societal apparatuses that enable and exacerbate such forms of intercultural tension. Harris's novel is, then, in many ways, an analysis of both cultural and readerly perception, in that it obfuscates the presence of indigenous bodies but also provides a model for how to better perceive larger societal processes of indigenous erasure. As such, readers must confront indigenous characters in the text cautiously and, as a result, begin to recognize the fact that their perception of indigenous peoples is most likely distorted, incorrect, or misplaced.

The implications for reading, knowing, and understanding indigeneity in the Caribbean here are vast. What is compelling about the degree of skepticism and readerly distrust Harris's early work generates is that it replicates systems of distrust that permeated Guyana at the time the text was written and that continue to permeate it today. In negotiating the novel's disorienting structure of displacement, replacement, and obfuscation, readers encounter the rhetoric and social maneuvers at play that produces animosity between indigenous and creole populations. The practices of decoding central to this book take on a new meaning here, as unraveling the difficulty of the texts' narrative line does not simply uncover a deeper understanding of the story or even of the nature of colonial oppression, but instead the underlying social mechanisms of resentment that permeate modern Guyana—mechanisms that operate tirelessly and relentlessly, regardless if the characters in the text (and perhaps some readers) fail to fully observe or grasp them.

The questions the novel raises share significant (and, I think, largely unexplored) contemporary parallels with the way recent critics in Caribbean studies have theorized practices of indigenous erasure. Indeed, the textual and readerly challenges *The Whole Armour* enacts anticipate a number of contemporary analyses of indigenous displacement in the Caribbean—in particular that of the work of Melanie J. Newtown and Shona Jackson. In "Returns to a Native Land: Indigeneity and Decolonization in the Anglophone Caribbean," Newton examines the marginalization of indigenous peoples in the Caribbean and the extent to which the categorization of "indigenous" or "aboriginal" is often ascribed to—and in some ways overwritten by—nonindigenous people. Newton traces the process through which diasporic peoples "have indigenized in the Caribbean and replaced the region's first aboriginal peoples," investigating how Afro-Caribbean identity's inheritance of indigenous status further threatens the already socially and culturally tenuous position of Amerindians in the Caribbean (108).[12] In addition, Newton's essay convincingly outlines how seminal Caribbean writers and theorists sometimes dismiss—or are in some cases openly hostile toward—the contributions of indigenous Caribbean populations, citing George Lamming's inattention to aboriginal peoples, as well as Kamau Brathwaite's considerably more overt devaluing of the contributions of Amerindians in *Contradictory Omens: Cultural Diversity and Integration*. In this regard, Newton highlights Brathwaite's claim that indigenous bodies did not contribute to the "development" of Guyanese culture (113). As Brathwaite contends, Afro-Caribbean peasants became the new bearers of indigenous culture, possessing "the potential of a real Alter-native Tradition since they have successfully replaced the Amerindians as the folk or 'little tradition' of the society" (113). We can see why Newton highlights this passage, as Brathwaite's troubling dismissal of Amerindian culture situates the status of indigenous bodies teetering between a process of replacement and erasure (113). Newton draws two conclusions in her essay: that the "Caribbean has no retrievable precolonial or aboriginal culture," and that, "when *native* is invoked, the referent is typically the Caribbean's irresolvable relationship to the African continent" (112). The Caribbean thus becomes, as Newton sees it, "a metaphor for a modernity without aboriginality" (112).

In many ways, Newton's observation about indigenous (dis)inheritance is made manifest in Harris's work, in which the status of indigenous identity is, especially in *The Guyana Quartet*, seldom fixed and, more troublingly, routinely stripped away from the Arawaks, Caribs, and other indigenous peoples. Newton's attention to sociocultural processes that enforce what she calls "aboriginal absence" (112) in the Caribbean, of course, echo Donne's statement in *Palace of the Peacock* that *he*, and not the Arawaks and Caribs, have earned the right to call themselves true natives. The novel depicts a Guyana in which "native" is a status that disenfranchised peoples must fight for and that can be wrestled away with violence or force. This process also explicitly plays out in *The Whole Armour*, in which the missionaries' carnival throws the very existence of indigenous people into question. For Newton, such intercultural violence between indigenous peoples and descendants of the slave trade is a necessary and predictable methodology of colonial power. As she writes, "I view the resilience of this aboriginal extinction narrative as a legacy of the racial taxonomies created by European colonial regimes in the Americas. Europeans competed viciously for power in the Western Hemisphere, but they all agreed that unity between enslaved Africans and aboriginal Americans should be prevented at all costs" (121). The erasure of and retrofitting of indigenous identity in the Caribbean, as we see in *Palace of the Peacock* and *The Whole Armour,* instills a distinct, overbearing sense of intercultural resentment without, it must be noted, any lingering animosity toward the colonizer. In this case, the very fact that it is the missionaries, whose goal is to efface and replace native religions with the religion of the colonizer, that enable societal skepticism and enact further erasure of indigenous peoples is both significant and insidious, as the carnival, which superficially seeks to "honor" indigenous experience, not only frames both the Arawaks and Caribs as savage, but also further demonstrates how colonial practice continues to threaten the legacy of indigenous peoples in Guyana. The missionaries' "re-creation" bears enormous influence on the act of reading itself, as the reader is unable to effectively detangle the presence of a true Carib from a missionary, colonial imposter. In other words, colonial practices are not simply discussed, but entrenched to the extent that indigenous identity always exists in a way that signals its own erasure by the presence of the colonizer. We can therefore observe that the disinheritance of indigenous bodies in the text—evident in the creation of a landscape in which readers and the novel's creole characters are made to become dubious of indigeneity—depicts a compelling example of Newton's claim that colonial authority is both reliant on and enforced by cultural tensions that pit disenfranchised creoles and indigenous peoples against one another.

In a similar vein, Shona Jackson, in *Creole Indigeneity: Between Myth and Nation in the Caribbean,* examines the inherent conflict between what she calls settler creoles and indigenous populations in Guyana. In the text, Jackson problematizes the relationship between indigenous and creole identity by arguing that the categorization of creole as indigenous often further displaces and isolates indigenous peoples from modes of social, cultural, and economic belonging. As Jackson writes, "The introduction of new natives, or the extent to which Creoles are able to imagine themselves as natives both politically and culturally, rests upon the management of this radical difference through discursive repetition of native extinction" (25). In this way, Jackson theorizes an antagonistic relationship between creole and indigenous identity, suggesting that Black identity in the Caribbean often depends on the disavowal and continued irrelevance of indigenous experience.[13]

As Jackson and Newton help us to observe, *The Whole Armour*'s use of formal contradiction and narrative instability foregrounds processes of indigenous replacement where readers are made to see latent sociocultural processes that disavow the structural and societal importance of indigenous peoples and cultures, culminating in the stripping away of indigenous status by nonindigenous creoles. What begins to emerge, then, is an understated but always present resentment between disenfranchised creole and indigenous peoples, as indigenous ways of life become detrimental to emancipation and the emergence of a more modern, contemporary society. The experience of catalysis here becomes not one of remaking or renewal, but of eradication: all of the major characters aim not to discover connections to ancestral peoples, but to further eliminate them, as the normalization of skepticism toward indigenous experience makes it less valuable. Thus, indigenous experience is no longer integral to establishing an ancestral and cultural legacy, but an obstacle that stands in the way of progress.

This collective denial of indigenous humanity washes over *The Whole Armour*. For Cristo—unlike his father figure, Abraham, whom he is accused of killing—argues at one point that there is nothing sacred about his ancestry or the region's indigenous heritage. As he muses, "The derelict premises Abraham ruled had no true geographic location Cristo felt, a region of absurd displacement and primitive boredom, the ground of dreams, long dead ghosts and still-living sailors, ancient masters and mariners and new slaves, approaching the poor uncharted Guyana coast and beckoning the aboriginal mummy for whom all trespass beyond" (249). Cristo sees nothing of value in his absent origin; rather, he disparages it, without critical reflection or productive analysis. There exists only resentment and disrespect toward suppressed cultural histories. Worse, in the scene in which Cristo confronts the Arawaks and Caribs in Jigsaw Bay—who we recall may or may not be hallucinations or Catholic actors—he expresses shock and outrage when the Caribs, whom he labels "a degenerate profile and crew," welcome him into their fold. As he describes:

> They were Caribs, I knew. God knows where they were coming from. Their skins were dyed, I tell you. Almost naked. Tattooed. They wore a yellowish muddy dye as if they had been rolling on the ground. Parrot feathers—bright macaw too—framed their heads. Some, no head-dress at all. They had spears, long pointed flying spears. Some, no weapon at all. Moody and savage as the devil looks when he's in love. I swore they'd do me in. Couldn't understand where in God's name they'd come from. *And then I realized they took me for one of themselves.* Would you believe it? (340; ellipsis in original)

Cristo's response is one of utter shock and confusion as, here, he plays the role of the colonizer in a native encounter, viewing the Caribs as entirely savage. His horror is thus not only aimed at the mud-caked Caribs trampling through the bush but also at the very fact that they do not view him as an outsider. Cristo is insistent, however, that their seeming acceptance of him—that he fits within the tribe—is itself a mistake. And just moments after telling the story, he once again aches to relive the experience, to "see himself in an alien body, uncaring and unsentimental as an animal could be" (342). As the scene makes clear, the excitement of becoming indigenous is less a feeling of ancestral fulfillment than a lurid fantasy of becoming a savage (342). As if to echo Jackson's affirmation that Black creole identity is inevitably at odds with indigenous experience, Cristo ultimately repudiates the indigenous associations that are intimated by the Caribs, insisting that "I'm a black man, I said at last, coming to myself a little, from Africa. I'm no confounded Carib. I should be safe across the sea" (341).

For Cristo, no commiseration with or understanding of the indigenous peoples, whom he both yearns for and rejects, emerges, or is indeed possible. All that remains is confusion, in which Cristo never reconciles his misplaced hatred, nor do the Caribs ever truly accept him. The encounter, Cristo notes later, leaves him "all mixed up in my head . . . on all sides like a grotesque tumbled pack of cards" (343). He is now a fractured subject, unable to reconcile his own hatred with the fact that he wants to become what he irrationally hates. As he slips in and out of history, the experience of the rapid shuffle and the reordering of time and space breaks him. As Harris's work shows, negotiating the trauma of Guyanese history means not simply activating and reconfiguring submerged and veiled vestiges of a buried and often forgotten past, but unearthing the "European skeletons" that are seemingly bound to every facet of recorded Guyanese indigenous history. The novel thus exposes the challenges of catalysis: in emphasizing Cristo's confrontation with his shattered history, Harris exposes the degree to which Guyanese people are coerced into adopting imperial discourse. *The Whole Armour,* and much of *The Guyana Quartet,* confronts practices of indigenous erasure in increasingly complex ways, capturing how resentment breeds skepticism that fosters further acts of indigenous displacement in a way that not only reveals the tension between indigenous and creole populations, but also draws the reader into social and cultural practices of indigenous disenfranchisement. In this way, the text's representation of indigenous experience offers a fascinating psychological analysis of the nuances of Amerindian resentment in Guyana and, in so doing, anticipates contemporary analyses of how we might better reconcile indigenous displacement today.

Reading Aporia and the Forms of Amerindian Representation

As I have argued, the conflation and erasure of indigenous and creole identity that culminates in *The Whole Armour* addresses the trauma of Amerindian absence and aporia in Guyana. Yet it bears repeating that, as their careers evolved, both Harris and Williams continued to rethink the relationship between indigenous identity and aesthetic forms. In their later works, both writers created radically innovative texts that, far from simply critiquing thematic and ideological disenfranchisement, argued that indigenous representation cannot and should not be represented through Western forms and representations. As such, both Harris and Williams experimented with narrative techniques to reinvent how we might frame indigenous experience in more productive, ethical ways. Accordingly, while the first half of this chapter focused on erasure, this section negotiates the extent to which nonindigenous writers can—or should—attempt to speak on behalf of eradicated indigenous peoples by examining the formal challenges that arise when attempting to reinvent narrative representations of indigenous experience.

In 1970, Harris published *The Sleepers of Roraima*, an imaginative retelling of Amerindian fables and myths. Curiously, the early stories of *Sleepers* represent Harris at his most readable and most accessible; they abandon many of the difficult narrative elements common to his work. The text catches Harris in the midst of rethinking how to best represent indigeneity in his writing. *Sleepers* is, thus, unique in his oeuvre: its aim is considerably more didactic, its goal being to shine a light on the mythologies and culture of Guyana's indigenous population and therefore provide a counternarrative to the reductive representations of Amerindian peoples regurgitated by colonial authorities. As Mark A. McWatt argues in the introduction to Peepal Tree's recent reissue, "What Harris may be seen to be doing is questioning how the Amerindian legacy might offer some vision of human community that surpasses the prisons of race and ethnicity that have trapped Guyana in division and underdevelopment for 60 years" (9). To that end, the text raises difficult questions concerning reception and cultural appropriation. After all, how do we negotiate the potential that imaginative, speculative retellings may distort, misunderstand, or evacuate the nuances of the original myth? How might larger questions of form and style complicate Harris's goal? Or, in other words, in writing and releasing a collection of fables of a forgotten people, to what extent does abstraction or inscrutability potentially alienate a reading public that might otherwise be receptive to reading the stories of marginalized populations?

As I want to argue, *The Sleepers of Roraima* is a rare misstep in Harris's representation of indigeneity. In eschewing the formal innovation common to his other works, the text simplifies the problematics of historical fracture, making Amerindians familiar, English, and, knowable. The novel inadvertently reveals how imaginative retellings of indigenous mythology frequently contemporize the culture in question in a way that universalizes their experiences. Thus, the fables, in an effort to connect with the reader, embrace simplicity over that of complex representation. Contemporary Christian motifs and symbols abound, and the collection establishes a comparative focus that is unable to imagine the Amerindians outside of the present moment. Whereas works like *The Secret Ladder* convincingly problematize the degree to which creolization affects processes of cultural memory, the fables mostly suppress this tension. Though "Couvade" begins with a disclaimer that "the Caribs have virtually disappeared as a people though their name is attached to the islands of the Caribbean sea and the remnants of their mythology can be traced deep into the South American continent.... This story is an invention based on one of their little-known myths"—troublingly, Harris's attempt to make the myth relatable to a modern audience obscures the cultural specificity of the people he seeks to describe (37). The Caribs become swallowed up by their contemporaneity, as their language and religious practices are made to seem resoundingly modern. Just as in Vera Bell's *Ogog*, the Caribs speak perfect English and, oddly, share contemporary notions of time and aging. In an early scene, Couvade asks about his history: "Tell me, grandfather . . . I'm old enough to be told. After all I am ten years now" (39). Yet his eyes grow "defiant, since he knew there was no record of the day he was born, the month or year, except by word of mouth" (39). Contextually, the scene makes little sense, as Couvade would be unlikely to use his age—which he knows is not recorded—as a bargaining chip, nor would he be frustrated by cultural norms that simply do not exist. In other words, his protest here implies that he possesses another cultural model that he values and can perceive: a practice of more explicit time keeping. The scene, then, reminds the reader that the Caribs keep time differently—one of the text's many intimations of contemporary comparison that render the Caribs cloyingly contemporary in a manner that potentially further distorts and diminishes their already absent presence.

More troublingly, Harris's attempts to contemporize—and, in many ways, universalize—Amerindian mythology was based upon scant historical evidence. In fact, some aspects of Carib ritual, as described in *Sleepers,* are simply incorrect. In his essay "Walter Roth, Wilson Harris, and a Caribbean/Postcolonial Theory of Modernism," which traces Harris's connection to the writing of British ethnographer Walter Roth, who wrote substantially on indigenous people in British Guyana, Russell McDougall points out that Harris, as a purveyor of what he calls "decolonizing fiction," used Roth as a model for how to think through indigenous experience, but did not yet have access to Roth's writing while writing his Amerindian novels. As such, Harris's imaginative retellings are, at times, fundamentally misplaced, particularly in terms of the representation of original sin, as well as other cultural practices. As McDougall writes,

> The concept of original sin is specific to Western cultures (as Levi-Strauss has shown in his study *Totemism*); and without that the attendant concepts of transcendentalism and redemption, so crucial to our own sense of felicitous being, are not possible. . . . But Harris could not know that. It was not until 1970, when he became writer-in-residence at the University of Toronto, and after that in the United States, that he had the opportunity to seek out some of Roth's own essays, full-length and in their original form. By that time, Harris had already published *The Sleepers of Roraima,* a trilogy of stories much inspired by the technology of the bone-flute, the sufferings of couvade, and the cannibal consumption of the Bush Baby. (572)[14]

As McDougall explains, Harris's thinking on indigeneity continuously evolved over his career—a point that is evident in his 1972 essay "The Native Phenomenon."[15] But it is clear that Harris's understanding of the practice of couvade in *The Sleepers of Roraima*—a birth ritual between father, mother, and child that reveals an entirely "different conception of child-life from the European" in which "the newborn Carib child was essentially inseparable from both parents"—was largely uniformed and misplaced (571). In trying to humanize a dehumanized indigenous people, the novel ultimately abstracts them further, remaking ritual and Carib experience through the lens of Western ideologies.

It is telling, however, that, between 1970 and 1971, and the publication of his second volume of Amerindian fables, *The Age of the Rainmakers,* Harris's approach to representing indigeneity significantly changes. Whereas "Couvade" is decisively easier to process and understand than Harris's other works, *Age* resembles more of his typical style: difficult, elusive, and impressionistic. Unlike *The Sleepers of Roraima, Age* insists that eradicated history cannot be digested or definitively made sense of once removed from its historical context; what remains is always speculative and uncertain. The most significant indicator of this shift in approach can be seen in the text's prefaces. What is perhaps most fascinating about *Age*'s fables is not the fables themselves, but the instructive paratexts that precede them. As in the earlier collection, Harris provides a brief italicized introduction before each fable that provides an overview for reading and understanding the ensuing story. In *Sleepers,* each story is prefaced with a mostly clear articulation of some historical context for the fable and how Harris is, in fact, reimagining it. In *Age,* however, the instructions themselves do not clarify, but are more scattered, theoretical, and imprecise. Seldom clear or scrutable, they indicate a struggle to articulate not only the author's intended aims, but how the reader should interpret them. In the preface to the first story, "The Age of Kaie," for example, Harris cannot explain what the story means, nor how we should read it. Instead, he provides an articulation of what he intended to achieve in writing the story, telling readers that he has "attempted in this story to interpret the rainmaking fabric of the Macusis as a conception of opposites which has largely been obliterated by histories of conquest . . . The broken fabric of the Macusi legend conceals its true scale . . . and may never have possessed from the very beginning, an exclusive sum of visual characteristic . . . I have attempted in this fable—through an accumulation of particulars bordering upon self-revelation/ self-deception" (107). In this preface, Harris appears cautious not to speak as boldly on behalf of the histories and experiences of indigenous peoples as he did in *Sleepers,* acknowledging that the emphasis on visual characteristics in the story may not, in fact, be a component of the original fable, and the shifting descriptions suggest that Harris himself is not entirely certain if he should call "The Age of Kaie" a story or a fable. Harris appears almost apologetic here, as if the confident style of "Couvade" was itself a mistake: tentative phrases like "attempt," "try," "may be read," and "may enhance our understanding" permeate the introduction. The preface to the text captures Harris in an unusual moment in which he is wrestling with the clarity and precision of his own writing and expression and, more importantly, the proper style and approach through which to represent indigenous experience.

In many ways, these prefaces show Harris rethinking the confident clarity that dominates his first collection of fables while also rethinking his relationship with the reader. *Age*'s paratexts are perhaps the only instances in Harris's oeuvre in which he seems contrite about the text's difficulty. Nevertheless, despite its tentative language, Harris's preface urges the reader to invest time in understanding his approach; in this sense, the paratexts in some ways anticipate Glissant's theory of opacity, of the belief that working through the difficulty of the text will produce a deeper understanding of the representation of indigenous experience that the text seeks to confront. He argues, "'The Age of Kaie' may be read as a story in its own right but it gains in focus, I believe, when considered as part of the entire context of *The Age of Rainmakers*. For it is related to consciousness incorporating compensatory roles of the evaporation as well as the precipitation of the spirits of the tribe" (107–8). Tellingly, however, Harris does not expound on what he means by "evaporation" or "precipitation," and, while he highlights a key theme for readers, he is also deliberately elusive, leaving readers to decode the larger meaning of the rain metaphor that guides the text. We are told, further, that an understanding of all these stories, if read and evaluated, may be necessary if the reader is to garner meaning from "Arawak Horizon," the most difficult story in the volume. Harris urges readers to pay attention to the themes he establishes in the story: "Each successive story in this volume looks back to 'The Age of Kaie' in some particular way that may enhance a certain train of associations and 'Arawak Horizon,' the last story, serves to condense an overlap between the absence and presence of gods in history through ironical furnitures or economic omens" (108). Understanding, in this case, is a collaborative process between author and reader: the reader may not understand the text, but they should and must try, and the author has provided clues to aid the reader in grasping the text's meaning. Yet the failure of the reader to understand—which is almost a foregone conclusion, given Harris's acknowledgment in the opening "note" that the story is itself an "attempt" at something that may not succeed—brings about a sense of readerly frustration that is exacerbated, not lessened, by the preface. Whether or not the text was too difficult, or if text's frustrating prose risked alienating the audience from the important question of indigenous representation, remained on Harris's mind as he composed the text. As J. J. Healy's archival work on Harris has shown, Harris spent considerable time revising and reworking the nature of the paratexts in the fables, and he pondered how much information he should provide to aid the reader's comprehension of each fable's key themes.[16]

"The Age of Kaie" is, thus, a fascinating read: told that they must make proper sense of it if they are to grasp the meaning of the collection's final story, readers suffer an added pressure to decode the representation of indigenous trauma contained in the story while recognizing the very fact that Harris himself has previously acknowledged that he is uncertain whether or not the fable has succeeded in meeting its intended aims. A brief early passage in "The Age of Kaie" demonstrates a significantly different approach to storytelling than that which was seen in "Couvade," as, here, the experiences of central characters are mired in obfuscation and uncertainty. The landscape itself seems spectral and surreal, as past, present, and future weave together in uncertain and unsettling ways:

> The rain began to fall but on second thoughts [Paterson] said to Kaie—"Not rain—blood." Then he remembered: the torn waterfall of creation pounded on the rocks like mute cannon of an archaic legend sometimes blew its echo or spray (they seemed indistinguishable) far across the land—paint of the sun raining a mythical aspect of landscape which sometimes rose into the wounded guardian at the gate. It was here on this very ground that government troops had appeared and fired with eccentric guns—machines of space—at a parcel of rebellious primitives, Paterson's Indians. Paterson saw them as a parcel—his poor guerilla bands of time—because as they fled a large sheet of paper wrapped around him, half-vapour, half-cloud, split down the middle and they tumbled out of his side. Tumbled out of his paper into the epitaph of space. (110)

The intersection of Paterson, the contemporary Macusi freedom fighter, and Kaie, the mythological figure, engender a typical Harrisian collapse of time and space, in which the ancestral body of myth and legend cascade into the present as the bullets of the government troops explode from their chamber. Yet the language Harris uses to describe the scene, one enveloped in dust and paper, requires considerable effort to unpack, and, as Healy confirms, Harris wrestled with how much context the reader might need, but ultimately omitted a longer, more explanatory note (93). Healy's assertion that Harris's unpublished note wasn't "anything other than a courtesy of clarification" (93), however, is misplaced in the sense that the note exposes a deep conflict with how to situate the myth itself: by conflating it into a conflict between past and present and imperial violence, Harris wondered and worried that its central motifs might be lost. In this regard, it is interesting that Harris did not provide more factual information on the Macusi in contemporary Guyana—of which, of course, considerably more was available—as if to intimate that the history and experiences the fable attempts to represent should elude confident narrativization. This could suggest that Harris was uneasy with espousing mastery over a tradition and culture that was not his. Here, then, the story and its paratexts enact the experience of negotiating an acceptable style or method for representing indigenous experience from the perspective of a nonindigenous voice.

It follows that questions raised by the paratexts and "The Age of Kaie" bring us to "Arawak Horizon," one of Harris's least accessible stories, and the very work for which Harris warns us, at the start of *Age*, that we may not understand. As we will see, in many ways, "Arawak Horizon" continues the project started by Denis Williams in *The Sperm of God*, in which the act of decoding suppressed histories always leads to an epistemological crisis. The difficulty of "Arawak Horizon" has led many critics to simply ignore it. As Mark A. McWatt writes, the story has long "baffled many with its radical impenetrability of form and meaning" (20).[17] In contrast to "Couvade" (and, in some respects, the rest of the fables in *Age*) the story eschews all readability by turning to an invented Arawak mathematics that seeks to explore the nature of time and space. The story, rife with numbers, glyphs, and alien symbols, wrestles with the inscrutability of indigenous peoples' culture, knowledge, and beliefs as its narrator struggles to interpret shreds of Arawak science. Indeed, the legibility of indigenous experience—and, with it, the idea that these fables could and should be retold in a contemporary context as a means of perpetuating the experiences of indigenous peoples for new generations—is entirely erased in "Arawak Horizon." The history of the Arawaks' beliefs and scientific and mathematical advances, the story suggests, can never be made clear. In an early scene, the narrator strains to conjure the physical presence of the Arawaks by seeking to decode vestiges and fragments of their obscure numerology. He explains: "My creation of the room of the Arawak sun therefore possessed a stark almost undreamt-of simplicity- a round head and a stem (O symbol and I symbol) that metamorphosed itself into objects in the room as if these were bound up. . . . The key now turned into the skeleton of memory and became a table, a new item of furniture (O plus line symbol) which revealed and unlocked itself" (159). The symbols, drawn on the page, cannot be properly replicated here, but there is nothing simple about this manifestation, as the narrator confronts lost symbols and numbers and desperately tries to make sense of them and finds that doing so only results in the genesis of more impenetrable symbols. What emerges is a labyrinth of codes that speak to, but do not divulge, the complexity of a culture long forgotten, reminding us that our only method of interpretation is decidedly contemporary and cannot, therefore, begin to unravel the ciphers of ancient cultures. In this way, "Arawak Horizon," is probing and largely impenetrable, as it negotiates a dialectic of knowledge and its inverse—that is, to write of the Arawaks is to always confront what we do not, and may never, know.

To that end, the story's notion of penetration—represented by the search for knowledge and sense—is embodied by the zero or O glyph that begins the story, which bores through history, time, and space leaving, ultimately, only a hole where meaning should be. Thus the struggle to interpret the codes and lost science of an ancient people leads to speculation that results only in aporia and impenetrability. Lost in this vacuum is the very efficacy of language, time, and meaning itself: everything becomes speculative as every moment and possibility collapses into itself. If, then, both novels hail the imaginative transformation of the myths of indigenous peoples through a contemporary lens, the final story confronts an obstacle that cannot effectively be translated and acts only as an attempt of "salvaging an extinct species our ancestors pursued" (159). The philosophical analysis of Arawak numerology becomes private, insular, and inarticulable, as the volume ends with a brick wall—a reminder of all that the reader cannot know, that always escapes them. This absence of meaning is further reinforced by the story's introduction, in which Harris tells readers he seeks to "release" what he calls "vestiges" of Arawak legend as "part and parcel of the mind of history—the fertilization of compassion—the fertilization of imagination—whose original unity can only be paradoxically fulfilled now through aspects of ruin or frailty within the material of consciousness" (155). By the end of *Age*, Harris has entirely abandoned his emphasis on clarity and didacticism, embracing abstraction as the preferable means to represent indigenous experience.

Age, then, is less a collection of Amerindian fables than a metatext that reveals the author's struggle to make sense and articulate a representation of indigenous populations. What's significant about the interplay between the primary text and the prefaces that frame the fables is that meaning making becomes an uncertain and tentative collaborative process, in which the author, in trying to represent scant myths and historical details, acknowledges that his efforts to express the story to readers should be met with caution—that they should not be taken as authoritative statements, but, rather, interpretations. These interpretations, he suggests, may not function as he intends, and the reader is asked to weigh authorial intentionality against their own perceptions. In other words, the fables represent Harris's most overt attempt to articulate a theory of readership in which the act of reading itself becomes a form of collaborative decoding. *The Age of Rainmakers* thus steps back from the newfound emphasis on clarity that appears in *The Sleepers of Roraima* and posits indigenous Guyanese identity as a site of readerly engagement that is important and compelling, but impossible to fully discern or articulate. The prefaces in

Age seemingly seek to curtail frustration—by suggesting to the reader what the author intends—but also paradoxically engender it, as they remind readers that the explanation the author has provided will fail to provide clear answers. While Harris has a sense that the stories he is trying to tell can illuminate the social role of indigenous people in Guyana, the interplay between preface and text reveals that he is considerably less assured that his approach to representing indigenous history and culture is ultimately productive.

These concerns are not unwarranted, and, in this respect, Harris's emphasis on inscrutability as a means to confront indigenous experience demands further examination. In many ways, his encouragement of a readerly praxis that emphasizes abstraction and uncertainty is rooted in a reading of indigenous experience that foregrounds extinction and absence. The Caribs, he tells readers, "have vanished in the twentieth century save for a remnant here and there" (155). Earlier, he notes in the text that they have "virtually disappeared" (37).[18] Harris repeatedly emphasizes that it is absence, and the uncertainty of historical detail, that fosters a generative space in which imagination and creativity may serve as a means to rethink indigenous experience. Yet, often, the emphasis on historical erasure and absence obfuscates the nature of the "vestiges" of Amerindian experience that the text seeks to describe. In this regard, the text leaves concrete Amerindian images and figures obscure, as if to suggest that their presence no longer exists in corporeal reality. What is often made clear, in contrast, is the violence that extinguishes the lives of indigenous peoples. At the conclusion of "The Age of Kaie," for example, the narrative is punctuated by a moment of clarity, when government troops fire on the Macusi as a soldier hears "the muted thunder of the waterfall punctuated by desultory firing" (120). While the officer's act of violence itself is visible and explicit—an act, it should be noted, that results in the further decimation of the Macusi tribe—the historical details surrounding the attack are left obscure. In the story's preface, we are told that a central character is the historical figure Paterson ("the half-caste twentieth-century revolutionary, becomes—in this fable—an intimate extension of ancestor Kaie in a long line of guerilla camouflage—stone flower of the conquistador") but the introduction gives the reader no further detail of when Paterson lived or why he is important, nor does it specify the conflict Harris is referencing in the story (107). At the same time, neither Harris nor the story provides context for what the spirit referenced in the story, Makonaima, signifies, or even who Kaie is or was. In this sense, the distortion of time and space in the story, and its elusive and obfuscated imagery, further obscures the mythology of the Macusi and, in so doing, perhaps inadvertently widens the disconnect between Macusi history and its importance and relevance to contemporary Guyana.

Speaking to this point, in "The Dual Absence of Extinction and Marginality," Maximilian C. Forte argues that discourses and theories of indigenous extinction often devalue the contemporary presence of indigenous peoples and undermine the very fact that indigenous peoples in Guyana and the Caribbean are not and have not been "wiped out." Indeed, as Forte argues, "theses of extinction have been a hallmark of island Caribbean historiography" (3). Forte contends that these theses obscure the fact that Amerindians are by no means extinct throughout the Caribbean, and that scholars often cling to notions of erasure and effacement, ignoring the very real presence of indigenous peoples, cultures, and traditions that persist today, as well as the problems that they face. Forte's point, in essence, is that scholars tend to use violence against indigenous peoples as a means to make an anticolonial argument, but that "indigenous peoples of the Caribbean have, far from vanishing, become more visible than ever. The only way one can 'miss' seeing them is by choosing not to look" (3). As such, Forte's collection, *Indigenous Resurgence in the Contemporary Caribbean: Amerindian Survival and Revival,* foregrounds the work of indigenous scholars to reveal a larger picture of contemporary indigenous experience and culture in a way that counters myths of extinction.

Forte's argument, therefore, reminds us that, in confronting acts of colonial violence, we must not undermine the lived experiences of living indigenous peoples, nor should we attempt to speak on their behalf. The volume confronts the often ignored presence of Caribbean indigenous experience as it exists today and warns of the dangers of framing Amerindian experience in terms of obliteration or destruction. In this regard, Forte emphasizes as a counterargument to "extinction" or "erasure" the notion of what he calls indigenous "resurgence." He notes that "challenges to notions of disappearance, efforts to resist political and economic marginalization, the formation of new regional organizations, and the recent growth in the committed body of scholarship focused on these issues, collectively, produce resurgence. In all cases, contemporary indigenous peoples of the Caribbean refuse to be measured by the relics of their past or to be treated condescendingly as mute testimonials to a disappearing history, or a history of disappearance" (3).

Forte's point—that critics and writers tend to mythologize indigenous identity through the lens of extinction while largely ignoring the continuing presence of those people themselves—becomes more problematic when we consider the idea that Harris frequently represents indigenous experience as lost, shattered, and inaccessible. And, while it is commendable that the fables caution readers that mastery over indigenous experience is both impossible and misplaced, the framing of, for example, Arawak mythology as an almost mystical profound art to be decoded vies uneasily with the fact that Arawak and indigenous peoples were *not* invisible or impossible to understand in Guyana at the time when the fables were written. Thus, in creating a text that privileges decoding and uncertainty as a means of engaging the reader to think through the nuances of indigenous experience without better contextualizing the contemporary experiences of Amerindians in Guyana, Harris inadvertently perpetuates myths of obliteration that imagine indigenous people as relics of history.

It is worth noting that McWatt's brilliant introduction to the collected fables argues that while Harris's text seemingly ignores the contemporary relevance of indigenous peoples, the work nevertheless implies a contemporary historical relevance without stating it. As McWatt contends, "Harris's work is never as politically disengaged as it might appear" (8). While it is true that Harris's work is more politically engaged than critics often acknowledge, the repeated emphasis on erasure is strange, given that Harris is believed to have written the fables in the 1960s—a period when indigenous rights and testimony were visible political and cultural points of discussion. The passage of the Amerindian Act in 1951, election reforms that granted universal adult suffrage in 1953, and the election of Stephen Campbell—an Arawak politician and the first Amerindian member of parliament—in 1957 suggests that the presence of indigenous peoples in Guyanese society was far from invisible or inscrutable (Bulkan 370).[19] As Andrew Sanders points out, the formation of the Amerindian Association of Guyana in 1963 was also significant in that "their aim was to organize as many Amerindians as possible into a group which could pressure the Government to examine Amerindian problems. Full membership was restricted to Amerindians, with associate membership open to non-Amerindians married to Amerindians or interested in Amerindian affairs. . . . Its ultimate goal was integration of Amerindians into an independent Guyana, with the same rights and opportunities as other citizens" (86–87). In addition to the formation of the Amerindian Association, Harris was no doubt aware of the Rupununi Uprising of 1968. The uprising, which centered on a border dispute between cattle ranches and the Venezuelan government, drew many Amerindians into the conflict, as many indigenous peoples were employed by the ranchers, and led to larger conversations about violence against indigenous peoples and their political role in Guyana's future. Such examples are far from representative of the larger discussion of indigenous peoples' role in Guyana both prior to and postindependence. Yet the fables frame the Arawaks and other indigenous peoples through this very same extinction myth that Forte cautions against: in this way, a reader entirely unfamiliar with Guyanese history no doubt assumes that the people of "Arawak Horizon" are distant and lost, when in fact their descendants are elected politicians, and their societal role is in no way imperceptible. By asserting this, I want to be clear that the representation of Amerindian identity in Guyana was and is in no way equitable; indeed, disenfranchisement remains pervasive today. My point is that the fables themselves frame indigenous experiences not simply as something to be indefinitely decoded, but as lost and enigmatic, and that, in so doing, they bear an uneasy relationship between past and present, often relegating Amerindian history to an unknowable mythology. This is not to argue that Harris's work is dangerous or irresponsible, but to suggest that, in his text, the political, social, and cultural presence of indigenous peoples in modern Guyana vies uncomfortably with readerly efforts to imagine lost indigenous history. This assertion thus brings to the forefront an important point: that an aesthetics of inscrutability in regard to indigenous people must better consider how an emphasis on absence and abstraction further veils the visibility and resurgence of contemporary Amerindian experience and cultures. Harris's work, in this way, opens the space for these conversations.

No Proper Sound, No Beginning or End

As I have argued, indigenous representation becomes increasingly problematic when filtered through the lens of assumed historical knowledge. In *The Sleepers of Roraima,* Harris imagines a universe set against the backdrop of a perceived reality that, as McDougall observes, is, at best, far removed from actuality and, at worst, is itself a colonial construction that distorts the nuances of the culture it seeks to represent. Harris's *Age of the Rainmakers* eschews realism in favor of speculation and frames Arawak culture as a philosophically and mathematically advanced civilization that cannot be properly understood via Western systems of knowledge. Consequently, the story risks advancing the narrative that indigenous experience and history has been obliterated and is thus forever alien and abstract—a narrative that, as Maximilian Forte's work reminds us, often ignores the presence and voices of actual Amerindians throughout Guyana. Such questions and impasses bring us to the late fiction of Denis Williams. Williams's later career confronted similar questions of indigenous representation and accessibility, and his last, unfinished novel, *The Sperm of God,* carefully negotiates the cultural implications of indigenous abstraction.

Indeed, the examination of indigenous culture and representation became the focal point of Williams's later work. Interestingly, while Harris would turn to the work of Walter Roth and other ethnographers and anthropologists to frame the representation of indigenous bodies in his writing, Williams would conduct this work himself. It bears repeating that, today, Williams is much more well known for his archaeological work than his fiction, and his final book, *Prehistoric Guiana,* published posthumously by Ian Randle in 2004, is a vast, complex study of Amerindian populations in Guyana. Williams's struggle with indigenous representation, however, began long before he abandoned literature for archeology, as *The Sperm of God* makes radical interventions into how we represent and perceive forgotten and fractured indigenous communities and cultures. In this regard, Williams's most innovative work is the one that he could not finish. *The Sperm of God* was to be his third novel. He wrote and published just two fragments—three chapters in *Transition* in 1967, and a longer, much different extract in *New Writing in the Caribbean* in 1972. Even more so than his earlier work, *The Sperm of God* resists the boundaries of literary form. Composed of visual and phonetic descriptions of sound, geometric diagrams, and dense descriptions of characters and landscapes, the reader is frequently left with a combined sense of loss, confusion, and frustration, as the textual landscape becomes an impenetrable myriad of interdisciplinary devices. More importantly, however, for Williams, the novel's experimental form serves as a way to reveal the complexities and lost echoes of precolonial, indigenous Guyana.

It should be noted, however, that the two published sections of the novel are, in fact, radically different, and that examining them in conjunction with one another reveals much about how Williams views experimentation and interdisciplinarity in terms of Caribbean aesthetics. The first extract, completed in 1966, shows Williams grappling with high modernist forms and centers on African art and expression, while the second focuses on an expedition in Guyana and explodes the former's sense of formal experimentation: it resembles less a novel than an experimental blueprint rife with diagrams, charts, and images of sound. My interest lies primarily with the 1972 text, which, I want to argue, makes a radical intervention into methods of Amerindian representation in Caribbean literature. While the 1967 material deserves future study, its form and content is similar to *The Third Temptation,* albeit with a distinctly more Beckettian flair (Williams was reading Samuel Beckett at the time).[20] This earlier extract, set mostly in Uganda and Kenya, vies uncomfortably between troubling misogyny and a sobering representation of racial objectification, as the narrator is reduced to (and indeed becomes) "a self respecting penis," with Williams further exploring the themes of miscegenation that are foundational to *The Third Temptation* (9). The 1972 extract, however, is considerably more complicated, and it is worth pausing here to acknowledge that, in a book about inscrutability, frustration, and difficulty, Williams's 1972 text is explicitly and undeniably opaque. Even when viewed alongside the work of notoriously challenging writers like Harris, Williams's writing is both more experimental and more difficult to process. As such, a concise plot summary is impossible. Set in Guyana, the text begins in media res in the middle of a paragraph and in the middle of a sentence: "mark now quick, four dead, in a bush or scrubland wilderness. Pitch, black, imagine. Me, Carmichael, Sharp—and the four, limewhite, on the move. *Lame and the halt look to themselves, right?* Three quick—me, Carmichael, Sharp; four dead—Rafferty, Cuffy, Whistler, Short" (301). The general premise of the extract focuses on a seven-member crew in the midst of an expedition to the deepest regions of a Guyanese jungle. Despite the fact that many of the members have died, they persist with their ambiguous excursion, which is always described in vague language. Throughout the expedition, the intimidating and spectral presence of the indigenous Akawaio, whom the crew views as a horrifying threat, permeates the narrative landscape and threatens to obviate their progress. Eschewing traditional elements of plot and characterization, *The Sperm of God* instead attempts to capture the landscape of the Caribbean through the use of geometry, geography, and sound, as the novel's experiments aim to replicate the auditory and topographic landscape of the Guyanese jungle in which the narrative is set. Incorporating increasingly abstract geometrical diagrams that function as an instruction manual for which the reader to read and hear the sounds of the text, Williams creates a perpetual sense of frustration and estrangement that lingers in the narrative, in which the reader can never fully experience or capture the sound—and culture—of what they read.

William's goal in writing *The Sperm of God* was not modest. It was, as he put it, this: to create the "first true Caribbean novel." Thus far, no critics except Andrew Lindsay, in his essay "Preparing the Palate: The Artist in Words," have paid *The Sperm of God* any serious critical attention. In sum, Williams argues that the future of the Caribbean novel can no longer adhere to standard novelistic forms, but must embrace an aesthetic that ruptures expectations of literary form. Accordingly, we can trace the intersections of Williams's later archeological investigations into precolonial Guyana—to which he would devote the later portion of his career—and his literary experimentalism. In particular, the novel's use of sound functions as an examination of the way colonial power has subverted the perpetual wail of Guyana's indigenous population. While there is a tendency to dissociate Williams's archeological and ethnographic work from his fiction, *The Sperm of God* insists that the "true" modern Caribbean novel must be multifaceted and decidedly interdisciplinary, as the printed word cannot properly represent the nuances of Caribbean experience. The text therefore anticipates Brathwaite's later creation of Sycorax video style, which experiments with computer graphics and typeface in a way that pushes the boundaries of literary form. Like Brathwaite's video style, Williams creates a Caribbean artifact that is not easily reproducible and, in many ways, becomes difficult to cite or even discuss. *The Sperm of God* thus unfolds on the page through a style that tries to mirror the process of interpreting the scrawled glyphs on a cliff wall left by Guyana's ancestral people. Drawings, interpretations, sounds, and language seek to create a text that must be constantly deciphered and that requires continuous acts of code switching.

Repeatedly, Williams's text insists that there exists no (written or oral) language, sound, or methodology that currently exists for capturing the experiences and nuances of Guyana, its people, and its landscape. I want to draw attention in particular to the fact that the unfinished novel's central characters—a mixed-race crew not unlike those in *The Guyana Quartet*—are effectively cut off from the geography they inhabit: mainly, the jungle and "undeveloped" land home to indigenous peoples. It is thus worth examining the novel's experiments with form and sound in more depth, as they always convey a sense of detachment and confusion on the part of its characters, especially in terms of their relationship to the novel's setting. Accordingly, at the beginning of the 1972 extract, readers meet with an immediate obstacle: a rudimentary geometrical diagram that purportedly attempts to describe the intricate aural progression of the Guyanese jungle in which the novel is set. Yet this turn to geometry emerges only in lieu of a series of failures, as the narrator attempts, in four instances, to describe the sound he hears. These attempts experiment with syntax to varying degrees. The first attempt employs syntactical experimentation to capture the inhuman sounds of the jungle:

es-s-s-s-s-s-s-s-s-s-s-s-s-s-s-s-s-s ! . . . . . .
- - - - - - - - - - - - - - - - - - - (301)

When this method proves ineffective in capturing the intended sound, the narrator tries again to formulate the experience of the narrative by replacing letters and lines with approximations of sound:

whzz whzz whzz whzz whzz whzz whzz
   zwh zwh zwh zwh zwh zwh zwh . . . . etcetera (301)

Soon after, the "pulsing rhythm" is replaced with a numerical progression that reduces its "rhythm" to "1-2-1 or 2-1-2 according to the way in which the stresses are considered to fall," until ending in a brief attempted articulation of what the narrator calls the "sps" or "pscs" sound of the crickets (301).

While these attempts to articulate sound incorporate syntactical experimentation to capture auditory processes, they always fail to capture the sound that they mean to represent. Further, in the text's opening, it is clear that the narrator is struggling to represent what he hears. Thus, the ensuing diagram tries to capture how the sounds mirror "illusory depth" using "well-known geometrical figures, but in a musical way, of course" (302). The diagram, however, reveals nothing; it does not clarify, in any way, what Skipper—the character that draws the diagram—attempts to describe, and anyone with any mathematical knowledge could no doubt create a more convincing articulation of the relationship between mathematics and sound (302).

We learn that the superficially careful mock scientific analysis of sound is "readily scratched in the sand with the big toe, a microlith, a thorn, a twig" as Skipper repeatedly shows how critical models of capturing the physical sensations of experiencing Guyana are doomed to failure, for the rudimentary models the text creates are always hesitant and uncertain (302). In a scene that follows the drawing of the diagram, the narrator stumbles in articulating what he means, suggesting that the word "rhyme" instead of "rhythm" might lead to a clearer explanation (303). The attempt to diagram the sounds provides little in the way of clarity, as both Skipper and the narrator lack a vocabulary for talking critically about the sounds that they hear: the diagram, drawn in the sand, should be understood in a musical way, but neither can articulate exactly how.

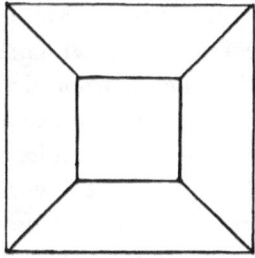 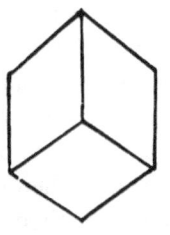

Two geometric shapes from Denis Williams's *The Sperm of God*

The sounds they struggle to describe, in other words, always escape them and can never be accurately represented or understood.

The textual implications here are vast. As the text progresses, the diagrams and articulations of sound grow more and more convoluted. Incorporating increasingly abstract geometrical diagrams that function as an instruction manual for the reader to read and hear the sounds of the text, Williams creates a lingering sense of frustration and estrangement in the narrative, in which the reader cannot make sense of the sounds (and culture) of what she or he reads. As Andrew Lindsay remarks in "Preparing the Palette: The Artist in Words," Williams is in no way interested in making "concessions to the reader" (138). Readers enter into a thoroughly alien textual space in which an endless struggle of signification produces only disorientation, as they are forced to effectively try out the methods of understanding Skipper and the narrator provide, unsure if the textual clues they receive will lead to enlightenment or confusion. What is most interesting is the text's repeated difficulty negotiating an understanding of the Guyanese landscape where it is set, and where the crew is always isolated from the world they inhabit. The present, past, and future thus spiral out of control, with Skipper experiencing "the end of the ultimate banging or whimpering blasted end" only to continue his story and, moments after his supposed end, boasting about the "brutal advantage" he has over the crew, as he struggles to exercise power in a world where he has none (309). Skipper's permanent inadequacy—that is, his existence in a world in which he never can convincingly articulate what he sees and hears, but nevertheless relishes his power over those who have less than he does—implies a Guyana steeped in a perpetual sense of dread and unease, where the impossible potentiality of reconciling the past or future engenders a sense of hopelessness and frustration that results in emotional and physical violence.

Yet the struggle to enact power in a world in which it is constantly denied appears most explicitly in terms of the textual representation of

Amerindians. Early on, readers meet with the presence of the Akawaio, a real tribe who reside in the upper Mazaruni region, where Williams settled when he returned to Guyana (Lindsay 131). The incorporation of the Akawaio in the text, and their emergence in a fictional landscape in which the geography and people of Guyana are largely inscrutable, is made all the more interesting when we consider the archeological work Williams was conducting at the time. Appointed director of art soon after his return to Guyana, Williams's goal in Guyana was the "transformation of a multi-racial colony of dispossessed immigrants into a dynamic modern state" that required a rebuilding of Guyana's "national self-image" (E. Williams 112). Indeed, Williams had a hand in establishing Guyanese sites of historical significance, such as Fort Kyk-over-al, Fort Nassau, and Aishalton, as symbols of national importance, and his own archeological work led to the discovery of petroglyphs that are believed to be dated from 3000 to 5000 BCE. Lindsay notes that "Williams was captivated by the jungle, and his investigations into petroglyphs brought him to realize that in this remote hinterland there was an authentic cultural heritage that dated back at least even millennia, pre-dating colonialism, slavery, and ethnic division" (131).

Williams's archaeological work sought to provide a counternarrative to colonial dominance, in the presence of the unseen, unheard, and thoroughly forgotten history of indigenous and precolonial peoples whose image has been obliterated by the colonizer, and that none of the characters in *The Sperm of God* can perceive rationally. Thus, the novel reveals the extent to which indigenous bodies, when effaced from recorded history, are Othered and dehumanized. Like the Amerindian voices in Harris's work, the Akawaio's language in *The Sperm of God* is indiscernible, but, at the same time, it functions as a source of terror for those who struggle to hear it. To that end, the discussion of the Akawaio takes a predictable turn, when the crew perceives them, explicitly, as man-eating cannibals. Skipper notes, "**We've never seen them, these Akawaio, properly speaking. I mean, shadows only, nor heard twig crack under their foot. Suppose I tell you: Their blow darts in the hour rot flesh from bone man or beast flight light as light as feather**" (303; bolded in original). In the story, the "sounds of savages" forms a language that is imbricated in the very fabric of Guyana, but is now Other and imperceptible and seemingly unable to be processed or understood.

It bears emphasizing here that Williams is not suggesting that the language of the Akawaio is itself impossible to interpret—his later archaeological and historical work seeks very much to make Amerindian voices legible and audible—but that the characters of the text, like many contemporary Guyanese people, cannot and choose not to make the necessary effort required to make sense of it. Similar to "Arawak Horizon," *The Sperm of God* does not textually suppress the voices of indigenous peoples, but, rather, represents them as a grammatical and syntactical void that cannot be processed. Early on in the text, the directive "Now listen" is followed by a sound that exists only as an aural and grammatical abstraction:

? ? ? ? ? ? ? ? ? ? ? ? ? ? ? . . .

That is the sound of days as they hear it, days on end:
? ? ? ? ? ? ? ? ? ? ? ? ? ? ? . . . (303; ellipses in original)

These sounds—many of which are too alien and too remote to be represented as anything other than a series of question marks—are, in fact, the "chants of the red people . . . chants raised to the spirits of their dead—their dead, not our dead" (303). What's significant here is that the syntax of the passage, unlike other sounds in the text, can simply not be replicated in verbal form: it is unutterable and unintelligible. Whereas, even in the earlier sections of the text, the narrative captures what it perceives to be the "ING ING ING" of the jungle, in this instance the articulation is impossible to express and cannot be deciphered. In framing their language in this way, the Akawaio become remote and unclear and less than human. The text thereby raises interesting issues of accessibility: the explorers of the text cannot and will not understand the history that they devalue, and so the reader is denied the opportunity to do so. In other words, Williams's novel demonstrates how easily fundamental ignorance and misunderstanding of indigenous peoples may spread, as our vision of the tribe is filtered through hate and disgust. We see only what Skipper and the narrator see. It should be noted, however, that this phenomenon is not unusual in Williams's oeuvre: as discussed in chapter 2, *The Third Temptation* is told from the vantage point of the white Europeans, and, though a colonial monument to the Welsh missionary William Hughes punctures the landscape of that novel, readers are never given access to the interiority of the novel's only two Black characters. *In the Sperm of God,* problems of access function similarly, as inarticulable, "improper sound" functions to performatively estrange the readers from the history and voices of indigenous peoples who are, in the text, entirely inscrutable.

As the text proceeds, the representation of the Akawaio's language begins to shift, appearing not simply as a grammatical void, but as a grotesque, frightening abomination. Their bodies, and not their mouths, start to speak; even the sound of their limbs—which can only be described as "churaak aaak-ak churaak aak-ak churaak aak-ak shshsh aah" (304)—is a source of horror. The scene ends with a guttural, capitalized "YHRUUUUUUUUUUGH" that, we are told, manifests a curious, alien "sound released by the mind long after the ear has heard" (304). These sounds, of bodily, and not verbal origin, are met with the "impervious silence of white men," who are trapped in fright (304). It is not, then, simply the inscrutable speech of the indigenous body that engenders a sense of terror, but the body itself, which is, here, reduced to a terrifying signifier of fear. The Akawaio's limbs and joints propagate an inhuman sound that, for the first time, *can* be described, as a threat: a kind of fabricated monstrosity, suggesting that the Akawaio rule the bush with a decree of savage, profound terror. In the presence of a speech and language that cannot be linguistically rendered or understood but only represented on the page as a question mark, the body becomes the primary means through which the crew can demonize indigenous peoples. In so doing, Williams traces the process in which the crew fails, at least initially, to fully dehumanize the Akawaio; their speech, their very language, exists outside the realm of understanding and thus functions as a syntactical and grammatical impossibility that frames them as a vague, but frightening, threat. Yet it is the sound of their bodies that fully allows the crew to transform them into monstrous subjects, reading their physical presence as threatening in a way that their language cannot. Consequently, the body is made to speak in lieu of a language that cannot be understood. The Akawaio's savageness is inscribed into their physical presence, as the momentary aporia of their speech is quickly overwritten and replaced with another characteristic that ensures their inhumanity.

Yet the inevitable dehumanization of the Akawaio is complicated by an abrupt critique of the gaze that dehumanizes them, as the process that reduces the tribe to aporia, then savageness, is laid bare by briefly shifting to the vantage point of the tribe itself in which whiteness becomes a threat. The text provides a snapshot of "the fear of these red people for white men and whiteness being ancient in their lore that human life through the races proceeds from virginal back through brown, red, yellow, etc. to white, senility impotence extinction" (305). For the Akawaio, whiteness symbolizes a form of inhuman extinction: a corruptive force at the bottom of a racial hierarchy that collapses into aging, decrepitude, and death. For Williams, this abrupt shift in positionality is signified in the dialectical tension between two key images, "INVERSION" and "VACUUM." While the terms are used most explicitly in relation to Shortie—a character who is dead and experiences a process of transfiguration—in the passage just described the narrative perspective is suddenly inverted, and the label of "savage" emerges as a signifier of white European rather than indigenous identity. In the eyes of the Akawaio, it is whiteness that is ancient, eternal, brutal, uncivilized, and overwhelming; it is whiteness that effaces and, most importantly, distorts. In this equation, the Akawaio exist not as inarticulate brutes, but as valiant soldiers locked in an eternal struggle with a malicious force that pre-dates them.

As previously discussed, the association of Black and indigenous bodies with violence and fear is a common trope in Williams's later fiction. Deeply engrossed in the work of Fanon, Williams punctuates his novels with racist stereotypes of Black men; indeed, he once wrote that all of his future work must confront themes of racist stereotypes and miscegenation to achieve "autonomy and authority" (E. Williams, *Art of Denis Williams* 104). In the heart of Guyana, the explorers gaze upon the land with the "eye of a savage" (307), and, at times, the descriptions of the sounds of Guyana devolve entirely into stereotype, depicting images of boomerangs, wild animals, and untamed brutality: "Dead and blind blood boomer . . . aaa. . . . aaaaang URRRRR UUUGRGWH!! Vehement pursuit, each, instinct apart, bears" (307). Elsewhere in the narrative, an indistinct humming is described as a sound like "an everlasting orgasm in the rape of a white by black, black by white" (quoted in Lindsay 130). Here, culture and language is heard, perpetually and interminably, as resoundingly savage, with whiteness dominating the text, framing Black and indigenous bodies as resoundingly Other.

Yet *The Sperm of God*'s representation of suffering and disenfranchisement clashes with momentary fragments of hope and emancipation, producing a dialectical tension that embraces the inescapability of oppression while imagining its end. In brief moments, the text represents whiteness as a concept that is slowly losing its power. At the start of the first chapter of the 1967 text, for example, the narrator remarks that whiteness is "fading" along with the post-European breed (9). The assertion that whiteness is nearing its end—perhaps the boldest assertion in the text—points toward a moment of hope for newly independent Guyana. However, the novel's structure and theorizations of a time and space void of linearity threaten any potentiality of an emerging emancipation. As Lindsay astutely points out, the novel's major characters are all variations of historical figures that bear some resemblance to Guyanese history (132). They are concurrently alive and dead, present and not present, and it is never certain what and how a dead character exists in the world separately from a living one. Like the sound of the jungle, their description and identity is always elusive. The crew, strangely, is composed of an array of oppressors and liberators. Cuffy is based on a historical figure that led the Berbice slave uprising in 1763, while the name "Carmichael" echoes two colonial governors who governed from 1812 to 1838 (Lindsay 132). The disenfranchised crew member Porter first meets Wheelwright in a "workshop on the coconut coast" as well as "two thousand months and years later" at a sawmill (315). The novel's characters are living, breathing figures who exist in contemporary Guyana, but are also long dead historical relics, living on only, as the narrator remarks, "in the ruin of . . . our scholarship, our tourist board" (315). Thus, there can be no progress; whiteness cannot "end" because the very concept of time in the novel forbids distinctions between past, present, and future, as historical atrocities are simply remade and historical figures reborn in new contexts.

Toward the end of the novel, Williams introduces his final narrative device: a geometric numbered wheel, which repeatedly undermines any potentiality of progress or social advancement and serves as a constant reminder that every thought and action remains under duress, as characters constantly search for and, tragically, fail to find a way out. The wheel, crafted by Wheelwright (who is also referred to at various points in the text as "Short," "Shortie," and "Cartwright") embodies the text's emphasis on perpetual cycles of disenfranchisement, suggesting that events and actions will happen over and over again. The diagram of the wheel appears suddenly in the narrative, just moments after readers are granted access to Wheelwright's workshop, a dust-covered enclave (310). As Wheelwright languishes in his shop, he ponders his dying craft and views the wheel as metaphor for oppression that seems both exhausting and repetitive, noting that there is "nothing in the end but foundering trade to show for craft passed rule of thumb hand to mouth down the generations" (310). He concludes that "the times and age, some say, ends impossible of meeting save to bind a man in problematical blind knots" (310). As expected, however, the wheel as a narrative device is not a simple metaphor, but an abstract equation that must be made sense of. Following its appearance, the narrator works to decipher it. The wheel represents an intersection of sound, geometry, and geography, consisting of sixteen spokes that are numbered clockwise (1, 3, 2 4) and created with balance and rhythm in mind, most explicitly to capture the sound of traversing through the jungle. "The degrees of inversion of its rhythm created by the vagaries of simple joinery and the dynamics of centrifugal

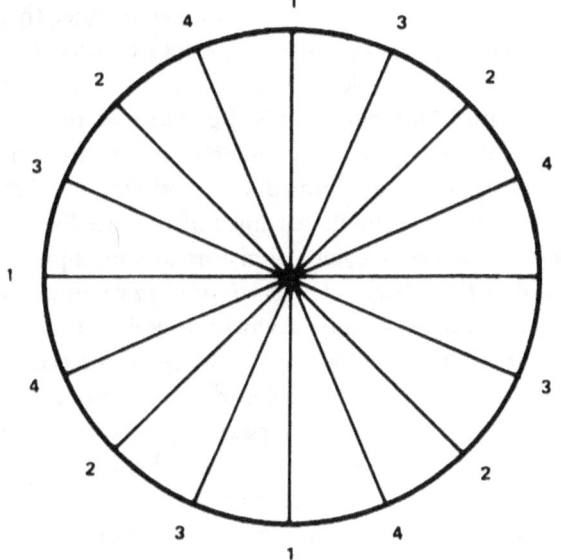

Numbered wheel drawing from Denis Williams's *The Sperm of God*

motion, balance, stress, etc" thus appear as "? Hoppity-skip hoppity skip Hoppity-skip hoppity skip, etcetera or pity skip hop pity skip hop pity skip hop pity skip hop etctera" (312).

Yet in the midst of an explication of what the wheel could or may mean, Cuffy, "a brute from the Antilles," enters Wheelwright's shop and begins to thrash him (311). A scene of almost comic violence ensues, as Cuffy and Wheelwright unleash a flurry of kicks to each other's solar plexuses and scrotums. While Wheelwright ponders the circular nature of repetition and economic stagnancy in Guyana, the wheel means nothing to Cuffy. As the narrator asks: "What does a pity skip hop or unsuspecting jump matter, in the balance, to Cuffy?" (312). The significance of the wheel is therefore partially articulated, but then immediately undermined, as Wheelwright's theory of the wheel is quickly rejected and replaced with an act of violence. Moments later, the "pity-skip hop" represented by the wheel becomes all the more absurd, as the wheel's repetitive clop is used not to represent the repetitive nature of historical acts of oppression, but the sound of an enormous, flatulent Cuffy, who emits "crescents of shit" in a relentless and repetitive manner that mirrors the sound of the wheel (313). In this way, the text captures a profound sense of struggle and failure: the narrator's explanation of the historical significance of the wheel that begins the scene is both hesitant and incomplete, unable to capture, (at least not exactly) the significance of the way the wheel and its movement reverberates across Guyanese time and space. At the same time, this struggle of articulation is itself displaced by a separate act of violence—and then, later, a moment of comic scatology—that ultimately throws a wrench in the difficult articulation of what the wheel can or may mean.

It is telling, however, that, despite this comic undercutting of the seriousness of the meaning of the wheel, Williams quickly emphasizes that we should not be so quick to dismiss the importance of the intellectual labor required to unpack the nuances of cycles of historical and imperial violence. After the dismissal of the wheel, *The Sperm of God* reminds us of what is at stake in this attempt to imagine a world in which one can escape from systems of oppression by following the image of the wheel with a snapshot of indigenous suffering. If the violence that interrupts the narrator's examination of Wheelwright's wheel appears mostly comic, the violence that follows it is decidedly not. Bookended by scatological images that close the novel—at the end of the novel, after the Cuffy scene, Porter, too, quite literally shits his pants—lies a damning critique of the repetitive nature of violence directed at indigenous populations. Immediately following Cuffy's excremental exploits, the narrative pivots to a scene of repetitive exploitation in which indigenous "mudhead inhabitants" are coerced into supporting an ever-changing but persistently oppressive cycle of governmental oppression. As the narrator describes:

> This city or town or town or camp built on the effluvia of many a river—Orinoco, Essequibo, Demerara—is a vast common floodplain or depression or prison suitable, in season, between flood and flood that is, to the hasty culture and sugarcane and rice which its mudhead inhabitants sow and reap like lightning cat-thieves from the cod. Floodtime they fish, naturally, their homes awash. Othertimes buy and sell, give and take, court small trade, support the government of the day, sometimes days on end mindless, some times two or three, sometimes one, any and every government, each certain in a sense of its support it being the one and the same government, each certain, inevitably, first one government, and then the other government, and then the next government, turn by turn each government distinguished by a name. (314)

On the one hand, the tone of the passage, which reduces the indigenous populations to a slur and compares them to thieving animals, is firmly rooted in a portrayal of indigenous identity that mirrors the racist representations seen earlier in the text. No empathy or sorrow is shown for the indigenous peoples whose homes are "awash" in the floodwaters. On the other hand, the passage captures the grotesque repetition of governmental oppression aimed at indigenous populations. Laid bare in the novel's diverse set of historical characters that encompass both colonial authorities and anticolonial revolutionaries apparently working together is the fact that, for indigenous populations, the result of all systems of government is the same. Buried in the shit is thus the constant reminder that indigenous suffering and cycles of historical violence are all too often made trivial and comic. Despite the novel's exploration of distraction and its troubling examination of the social processes that obfuscate acts of violence, the implications of the wheel and the narrative's attempt to make sense of it cannot be fully erased or obscured. Though the meaning of the wheel remains elusive, and readers and characters cannot fully understand its abstract mathematical and geographic implications, what ultimately emerges alongside its unveiling is a startling glimpse of the sickeningly interminable despair of indigenous populations in Guyana. The text explicitly reminds readers that acts of emancipation lead only to new forms of oppression, as the same atrocities are repeated again and again. Comic obscurity, Williams suggests, can never fully bury the historical reverberations of indigenous violence.

We can see that Williams, like Harris, is tracing a familiar trajectory here, albeit through a much more overtly experimental lens. In these works, the confrontation between contemporary and indigenous Guyana is always both an ontological and epistemological crisis, in which the severing of origins engenders a struggle to represent forms of knowledge and self-expression. These novels repeatedly unsettle readers and demand the acknowledgment that linearity and clarity and origins are a product of colonial entrenchment. They argue that the Caribbean novel must serve as a site of rupture and destabilization that always bears traces of the trauma of indigenous suffering. There is no logical or linear means to examine such suffering, nor, more troublingly, to capture the overwhelming, perpetual horror of genocide and displacement. Taken together, Harris and Williams negotiate a new methodology of confronting indigenous violence by framing it through problems of inscrutability and spectrality that destabilize the reader's ability to process the story they have just read. At the same time, their works suggest a deeper confrontation of historical processes of genocide and displacement by insisting that atrocity is ever present and, in so doing, suggest that we must find new strategies of understanding the complex interplay of trauma that emerges as a result of colonial violence.

5 Rhysian Disgust and the Politics of Complacency

IN HIS seminal and widely debated essay "The Occasion for Speaking," George Lamming, after exploring the relationship between exile and literary production, turns his animosity toward "a colonial middle-class educated . . . for the specific purpose of sneering at anything which grew or was made on native soul" (40). Lamming's explicit disgust for those who are too complacent to resist colonial rule lays the foundation for what he would call "peasant literature": narratives of poverty focusing on marginalized Caribbean populations that reveal the economic and social repercussions of colonialism. Lamming's argument, like that of the *Beacon* group before him, is rooted in a visceral anger not aimed at the British crown, but, rather, at the colonized Caribbean middle class. In other words, Lamming's overwhelming revulsion is directed not at the complacency of the uneducated starving masses, but at the educated. The essay thus serves as an acerbic takedown of the refusal of the Caribbean middle class to challenge colonial forms of oppression. Indeed, the middle classes' complacent acceptance of colonialism—and its endorsement of British art and culture—leads Lamming to conclude, bitterly, that "the West Indies is, perhaps, the only modern community in the world where the desire to be free, the ambition to make their own laws and regulate life according to their own impulses, is dormant" (35).

Such avowed resentment toward the middle class, especially throughout the 1930s and 1940s, was common in the Caribbean. Years before Lamming wrote his essay, the *Beacon* group argued that colonial injustice must be brought to light through literary and political engagement that eschews colonial tendencies, noting that the middle classes have historically been uninterested and unwilling to engage in serious ideological or political critique. In this sense, the *Beacon* group's attack on the middle class was in no way limited to their notoriously disastrous short story contest. Considerable energy was also directed at literary clubs, whom the group spent considerable energy antagonizing, viewing them as bourgeois, indulgent expressions of colonial mimicry. After their initial exposé of the clubs, they spent additional time and energy mocking their defenders, in an effort to humiliate their middle-class supporters.[1] The group's invective, however, was intended not only as a critique but also as an urgent call to Caribbean middle-class artists and intellectuals to extricate themselves from an overreliance on colonial aesthetics and beliefs.

Rather than recycle the discussion of Lamming and the *Beacon* group discussed earlier, this chapter aims to take seriously the aesthetic implications of a rhetoric of disgust designed to confront the very nature of middle-class complacency. It is this very point that brings us to the unlikely focus of this chapter: Jean Rhys. On the surface, Rhys bears almost nothing in common with Lamming or the *Beacon* group; nevertheless, their work shares similar goals. My aim is not to make the relatively easy connection between Rhys's own rootless migration and Windrush displacement—which has been made perhaps most explicitly by Sasha Jensen's oft-quoted assertion that in *Good Morning, Midnight* she has "no pride, no name, no face, no country" (172).[2] Instead, I intend to take seriously the fundamental resistance in Rhys's work against middle-class politics that actively deny the agency, humanity, and freedom of marginalized peoples. Indeed, this form of resistance emerges as a point of force in theorizations of early and mid-twentieth-century Caribbean literature, the point in which Rhys herself was writing, and manifests in her early works as well. This is not to suggest that Rhys herself was in any way invested in active social protest for Caribbean independence, or that she engaged with any Caribbean writers of the period. Yet Rhys's work also confronts the complacency of the middle class, especially its denial of the value of impoverished and disenfranchised peoples. In working to establish these connections, we can thus resituate Rhys, via her resentment of middle-class politics, in terms of a wider Caribbean aesthetic of antagonism and social protest.

Jean Rhys's place within Caribbean studies has, of course, been much discussed.[3] In terms of her relationship to modernism, postcolonial studies, postmodernism, and feminist theory, among other fields, critics have tirelessly debated where and how to categorize her writing, particularly in terms of the stylistic and thematic shift between that of her early and later works.[4] While the bulk of Rhys criticism focuses on her 1966 novel *Wide Sargasso Sea,* two relatively recent collections—most notably Mary Wilson and Kerry L. Johnson's collection *Rhys Matters: New Critical*

Perspectives (2013) and Erica L. Johnson and Patricia Moran's *Jean Rhys: Twenty-First-Century Approaches* (2015)—attempt to reinvigorate the conversation by pivoting away from questions of classification and focusing instead on how Rhys's work contributes to fields such as ecocriticism, religion, topography, and materialism. In addition, recent works such as Mary Lou Emery's "On the Veranda: Jean Rhys's Material Modernism" have made convincing new linkages that highlight Rhys's investment in Caribbean politics and resistance movements. To that end, Emery contends that *Wide Sargasso Sea*, in particular, incorporates the historical motif of the veranda to "open to view obscured areas of the Caribbean past and connect distant, conflicting worlds" (60). In tracing connections between Rhys's work and the Haitian Revolution, Emery suggests that the veranda's, "cultural environment with its reminders of the revolutionary past of the Caribbean—its betrayals and shifts in power and the resurgence of Afro-Caribbean spiritual practices—along with the revelations of history's silences and all the ambivalence and anxiety these revelations tapped into . . . becomes a portal word, opening to this deeper, complex and largely unrecorded past" (73). Such work is foundational in tracing unexplored pathways and linkages between Rhys and Caribbean resistance movements. Yet while Emery's work provides a remarkably ingenious rethinking of *Wide Sargasso Sea*'s political engagement, considerably fewer studies have considered the numerous ways in which Rhys's early work can establish similar trajectories of Caribbean resistance.

Accordingly, this chapter seeks to reconsider Jean Rhys's early, experimental narrative strategies in terms of a wider Caribbean aesthetic. Centered on articulations of disgust and frustration, my argument suggests that the explicit interminable reality of social inefficacy and disenfranchisement in Rhys's novels reveals a theory of reflexive resistance that demands acknowledgment—and, perhaps, accountability—on the part of those who do not necessarily engender, but, rather, accept, social and cultural stratification as a social norm. Rhys's work implicates the reader in complacency and, through innovative narrative devices, forces them to engage their own views of oppression through mechanisms of narratorial disgust. In other words, Rhys's antagonistic narrative strategy frequently frames the reader as an avatar of disgust in which the protagonist evinces anger and resentment over the implied reader's dismissal of their plight. At the same time, Rhys's narratives urge readers to be similarly repulsed by forms of social oppression. This push and pull, which compels readers to reject processes of alienation while accusing them of supporting these injustices, results in a tense reading experience that raises larger questions of inequity. Specifically (and, perhaps, controversially) I want to suggest that this essential component of Rhys's work—that is, the struggle and failure to assert productive resistance against not only oppressive institutions but also the middle and lower classes that enable them—allows us to resituate Rhys within a wider Caribbean aesthetic, particularly in terms of George Lamming and the *Beacon* group. Thus, this chapter focuses on how Rhys's works experiment with perspective and narrative structure to induce disgust in an effort to startle the reader into rethinking both their own and society's complacency within systems of oppression.

In experimenting with perspective and inventive narrative strategies, Rhys's early work seeks to render visible inscrutable and often invisible mechanisms of oppression by forcing the reader into an uncomfortable space of disgust, shame, and guilt that implicates them in larger practices of disenfranchisement that would not, I want to argue, be otherwise perceptible. This process thereby works to make both present and legible the nuances of middle-class oppression. As Boehmer writes, narrative strategies, particularly those of juxtaposition, "oddities, and incommensurabilities . . . can work to jolt the reader, pushing them back in shock or dismay or (at times) wonder, encouraging them to imagine or infer what til now has been silenced or suppressed." (41). More explicitly, Rhys's early work confronts the very fact that the suffering of the poor—and marginalized peoples in general—is often obscured by middle-class rhetoric that frames them as Other. If we read carefully, we can observe how Rhys's early work employs performative narrative strategies that draw the reader into the events of the story in an effort to force readers to more deeply consider their own participation within systems of oppression. By aiming to induce an emotive response on the part of the reader, Rhys's writing works to expose underlying mechanisms of oppression that are typically veiled. While almost all of Rhys's work depicts the disavowal, and sometimes outright dismissal, of suffering, considerably less critical attention has been given to the compelling implication raised by her experiments with narrative form: the very idea that oppression often remains opaque until it is experienced or felt. As such, I show in this chapter how Rhys's early work aims to elicit sentiments of readerly disgust that make the inscrutable more immediate.

Disgust and Readerly Complacency

While my focus in this chapter is on the receptive implications of the way Rhys's work negotiates and enacts feelings of readerly disgust and frustration, it is important to note that these emotions appear as a prominent narrative theme throughout her early corpus. Rhys's depiction of disgust reveals a complex interplay of suppressed rage and a yearning for resistance and social change, as her protagonists present narratives that serve as ardent, bitter rejections of their own social rejection. Her protagonists, in other words, are represented as locked in a state of perpetual rage against those who deny them agency. A careful observation of Rhys's oeuvre uncovers a desperate struggle by marginalized groups to both understand and challenge the ideological and physical aggression directed at them. As such, disgust on the part of Rhys's disenfranchised protagonists functions in her work as a form of psychological violence. Largely intellectual, it frequently clashes with hypothetical, hoped-for resistance against oppressive peoples or institutions that is not actually possible.

A cursory overview of Rhys's work discloses a yearning for physical harm to the oppressor—for example, in *Good Morning, Midnight,* when Sasha, resentful over repeated harassment and judgment of her appearance, stares at her oppressor and thinks: "One day, quite suddenly, when you're not expecting it, I'll take a hammer from the fold of my dark cloak and crack your little skull like an egg-shell. Crack it will go, the egg-shell; out they will stream, the blood, the brains. One day, one day. . . ." (52). The scene ends without any form of direct action or confrontation, but instead employs emotions of disgust as a form of psychological empowerment. In much the same way, Sasha, moments after she is unjustly fired by her boss, Mr. Blank, imagines unleashing unrelenting invective at him that both exposes the cruelty of his character and ridicules his failing business: "Let's say that you have this mystical right to cut my legs off. But the right to ridicule me afterwards because I am a cripple—no, that I think you haven't got. And that's the right you hold most dearly, isn't it? You must be able to despise the people you exploit. But I wish you a lot of trouble, Mr. Blank, and just to start off with, your damned shop's going bust! Alleluia!" (29). Sasha's bitter retort, in which she spits, "That's the right you haven't got," appears in the text as a hypothetical act of resistance that exists in the absence of physical retaliation, as Sasha has not the means nor the strength to properly oppose Blank's tyranny. Sasha's imagined monologue, while not able to enact social or physical change, is nevertheless important in that it challenges the values of the oppressor and frames them as indecent. In the scene, it is Blank himself and the ideology he represents that becomes the repugnant object. Disgust, then, functions here as a form of internal violence against the oppressor in a world in which the very potentially of verbal and physical resistance has been entirely suppressed. Rhys's work, especially *Voyage in the Dark* and *Good Morning, Midnight,* depict landscapes in which the female protagonists, in not adhering to socially acceptable positions, suffer at the hands of patriarchal institutions that deny them agency and are ultimately unable to critique or confront the forces that disenfranchise and dehumanize them. Instead, they are guided by their disgust, endlessly yearning and searching for a means to protest against those that oppress them. In so doing, they remake and reframe the disgust directed at them as a form of internal resistance.

Although much has been written on Rhys's protagonists' struggle to rebel against their oppressors, critics have paid less attention to the myriad of ways in which her novels unmask the very fact that it is often the lower and middle classes that perpetuate and enable forms of social, cultural, and economic oppression. In particular, Rhysian disgust is aimed not simply at the social order or the institutions that deny the agency of marginalized peoples, but at those who are complacent regarding (and sometimes complicit in) sustaining systemic forms of oppression. While Mr. Blank is undeniably wealthy, Sasha's manager, Salvatini, and her coworkers are not; however, they do not question the inequity and cruelty they witness, nor do they take issue with Blank's actions. Indeed, Rhys's oeuvre frequently depict lower- and middle-class characters who refuse to challenge forms of oppression, even though those very same characters often themselves acknowledge the pervasiveness of societal inequity. For example, in *After Leaving Mr. Mackenzie*, Julia's lover, Mr. Horsfield, understands that the world is unfair, but argues nonetheless that one should not challenge its inherent cruelty. Rather, Horsfield pushes Julia to adopt an ideology that accepts suffering and subservience are a natural part of existence and insists that to acknowledge otherwise is "embarrassing and annoying" (45). The state of the world simply cannot be changed; thus there is no need to talk about, or challenge, forms of oppression. Rhys's novels, then, do not simply aim disgust at those who possess immense social or economic capital, but at the middle and lower classes as well. This observation mirrors Lamming's critique of apathy in that a refusal to action—that is, a refusal to openly resist oppression—is the primary obstacle to intellectual and physical emancipation.

However, in this chapter, I am less interested in the Rhysian protagonist's struggle to resist than in examining textual processes that coerce the reader into rethinking their own complacency. The disgust that Rhys's protagonists express toward their oppressors is not simply a thematic tendency, nor is it directed solely at the figures in the text, but at the reader themselves, whom Rhys frequently frames as unsympathetic. Rhys frequently anticipates a reader who is in no way empathetic and must be effectively jostled out of their own indifference to suffering. In that sense, the use of the second person, combined with narrative techniques that repeatedly situate the reader within systems of oppression, operate as a means to prompt readerly self-reflexive critique. In framing the reader (or the reader's beliefs) as inherently disgusting, Rhys suggests that everyday people, not simply the wealthy, share responsibility for social inequity. In this way, Rhys's protagonists weaponize the societal disgust they face as a form of psychological resistance that redeploys deep-seated feelings of social resentment against those who sustain forms of oppression: the individuals who remain complacent. The receptive implications Rhys experiments with through perspective shifts raise an important question: Will a frustrated reader—that is, one who is implicated within systems of oppression and subject to narratorial disgust, or who themselves is made to feel disgusting or embarrassed—begin to better understand the nuances and experiences of oppression?

In no uncertain terms, in "Hunger" Rhys aims her revulsion directly at readers, implying that they themselves are the oppressor, thereby forcing them to evaluate their own feelings of guilt and shame. The story's central narrative device is one of startling confrontation: having described the process of starvation, by the end of the story the protagonist insists that her suffering is a form of amusement for the reader. The detailed experience of hunger ends with an affirmation: "I have never gone without food for longer than five days, so I cannot amuse you any longer" (42). In the story, Rhys's narrative shifts frequently between first and second person, as the second person "you" that intrudes on the narration signals both a larger societal critique and an attack on the reader's presumed resentment. In this sense, the narrator's explanation of starvation is less a story than a defense, as she anticipates readerly animosity. "I tell you it is *not* my fault," she asserts. "It happened suddenly, and I have been ill. I had no times to make plans. *Can* you not see that one needs money to fight? Even with a hundred francs clear one could make plans" (40). As the story progresses, this theme of the impossibility of commiseration repeatedly interrupts the narrative, as if to remind the reader: you will not understand. You will judge me. You will punish me. The narrator seemingly predicts the imagined critique, theorizing the ways in which the reader will blame her for her own condition, a point made evident in an early scene in which she angrily erupts: "Sell my clothes. . . . You cannot get any money for women's clothes in Paris. . . . Oh God! leave me alone. I don't care what you think; I don't" (41; ellipses added). Yet the tension between the statement that the narrator doesn't care what "you" think is belied by the very fact that she tells the story anyway. Simply put, the story, the narrator knows, cannot and will not result in any degree of understanding or acceptance, only resentment and blame. Nevertheless, the story is told, thereby fulfilling and reinforcing the narrator's marginal status: she will tell the story, you will not listen, you will judge her, but, still, she must tell it. Suffering is never given the possibility of kindness, but, rather, becomes predictable.

The final line of the story—that the narrator's suffering functions as a form of amusement—is therefore immensely important: it directly confronts the reader and, perhaps, is intended to jostle them out of their own complacency and cruelty, turning the reader's own disgust back on them. It is thus the narrator, the disenfranchised woman, who has the last word: it is you, reader, who are disgusting. You are the one who is callous, who is cruel. As Veronica Marie Gregg argues in *Jean Rhys's Historical Imagination: Reading and Writing the Creole,* the story, "implicates the reader by calling attention to the assumptions that shape a reading of the text. The implied reader is someone who will not understand, who mocks her suffering and the expression of that suffering, someone whose system of values is opposed to that of the narrator" (145). While it is of course impossible to determine readerly response, the story works most effectively in its attempt to bait the reader: to coerce them into blaming the starving woman for her own plight. In such a reading, the final sentence functions as a potential moment of epiphany, in which the reader is made to face their own animosity through feelings of guilt.

The narrative mechanisms that aim disgust at the reader, I want to suggest here, are designed to bring to light larger issues of inequity that are often dismissed as natural and inevitable. Unrelentingly, the story exposes social processes in which impoverished women are codified as repellent and immoral subjects, and, what's more, how their suffering is often disregarded. Interrupting her narrative to mock the reader's presumed judgment, the narrator spits, "What does it matter, anyway? Women are always ridiculous when they struggle. . . . Primitive beings, most women" (41; ellipsis added). Adopting the language of her oppressor, the narrator discloses that her starvation is perceived as a question of gender inferiority, highlighting the grotesque misogyny that would presume a woman's suffering to be trite or "ridiculous." Equally troubling, the woman's condition is framed as socially and morally deviant. While starvation becomes a question of morals, it is not, the narrator indicates, the worst transgression. "But I have clung and made huge efforts to pull myself up," she relates. "Three times I have . . . acquired resources. Means? Has she *means?* She has means. I have been a mannequin. I have been . . . no: not what you think . . ." (41; ellipses in original). Physical suffering is framed here as immoral, in that the impoverished subject's plight is suspected to be the result of a series of improper decisions. Although the act of starvation is itself rendered taboo, it is nevertheless implied to be preferable to the act of prostitution. Thus, the invisible interlocutor—who here functions as the implied reader—argues that the woman is responsible for her own plight, and, though she can no doubt make a decision to appease her hunger, to do so would be deemed immoral by the social order. While at the same time acknowledging the reader's moralistic assumption, the narrator makes clear that she has not crossed that threshold; she is expected to uphold codes and conventions even though, theoretically, she opposes them. The scene demonstrates a pervasive societal and readerly sense of distrust and resentment toward women while recognizing that literal starvation is viewed as more justifiable than improper sex. Morals and cultural conventions overwrite survival, as the scene captures a kind of bourgeois horror in which the imagined reader would rather see the protagonist die than offend their sensibilities. Rhys's confrontational narrative aesthetic brings such issues to light in a way that suggests the potential of antagonistic engagement to reveal a mechanism of oppression not otherwise visible or understood.

Nevertheless, the elision of narrative details—in which the narrator implies, but does not fully reveal, the nature of the critique made against her—suggests, significantly, that we can never fully know the extent of cruelty and suffering she experiences. As Cathy Caruth has argued, trauma "resists simple comprehension" (6). Readers, through Rhys's performative shifts in perspective, must thus acknowledge that "the most direct seeing of a violent event may occur as an absolute inability to know it" (91–92). We know that the narrator has been told to sell her clothes; we know she has been told her suffering is her own fault. Explicit and undeniable gaps in the narrative nevertheless remain. By leaving our knowledge of these conservations incomplete, readers have to fill in the gaps and imagine what has been said and thereby, in turn, imagine what they would say and how they would respond. In this regard, "Hunger" is unusual in Rhys's oeuvre, in that it marks the rare occurrence in which the story denies the oppressive social force both a clear and present voice and a physical presence; instead, it engages in an act of readerly transference in which the reader is made to inhabit the role of the antagonist. However, if the physical absence of the oppressor is unusual in Rhys's work, the nature of the critiques made against the protagonist are not. Should we look closer, the implied view of the narrator's tormentor that women are primitive beasts mirrors real conversations in Rhys's other works. In fact, such a sentiment appears almost verbatim in *Quartet*—written and published around the same time as "Hunger"—in a scene in which Stephan viciously taunts Mayra, whom he labels "incoherent" and entirely responsible for her own plight, solely because she is a woman. Stephan verbally batters Mayra, screaming, "How can I help you? What fools women are! It isn't only that they're beasts and traitors, but they're above all such fools. Of course, that's how they get caught. Unhappy! Of course you're unhappy" (182). Yet resentment in "Hunger" lacks both a name and a face. In a text about wasting away, the clarity and precision of censure becomes itself a skeleton: the critique leveled against the protagonist is void of wholeness. The absent oppressor is thus stripped of his body and becomes only a hypothetical entity that, here, is ascribed to the reader, who becomes the hypothetical "you."[5] In this way, the obfuscated resentment that pervades the story is vague enough to become almost universal. The elision of key details therefore allows Rhys's use of the second person to draw the reader into a larger social critique that suggests that the invective hurled at marginalized peoples by characters such as Stephan, Mr. James, and Salvatini is not unique, but generic: to turn away from suffering is so commonplace that doing so has become banal. Thus, while we cannot fully process or understand the exact nature of the narrator's suffering, readers are not only made to feel responsible, but coerced to rethink the pervasiveness of social resentment directed at marginalized populations.

I want to reemphasize here that the mechanisms of disgust in Rhys's work are firmly rooted in class politics and thus frequently indicate an effort on the part of the protagonists to overturn—and, in some ways, redeploy and redirect—the opprobrium aimed at women and the poor by the middle and upper classes. In this way, Rhys's work helps us to think more deeply about concepts of complacency, particularly in terms of the normalization via disinterest of states and systems of oppression. It bears repeating that, while critics sometimes isolate Rhys from the Caribbean literary boom of the 1930s and onward, theorizing Rhysian disgust in terms of a wider struggle of emancipatory aesthetics allows us to recontextualize Rhys as a forbear of a burgeoning Caribbean schema of class antagonism.[6] To be sure, in the Caribbean, it is the middle classes who refuse to hear the desperate cry of the "colonial wail" that pervades the region (Lamming 34). For Lamming, the perpetuation of inequity depends on the educated middle classes, who have a social and economic capital unavailable to the impoverished lower classes, but nevertheless make no effort to challenge forms of colonial oppression. As he laments: "We have had to live with a large and self-delighted middle class, who have never understood their function. One cannot accuse an illiterate man of avoiding books, but one wonders what is to be done with people who regard education as something *to have* and not *to use*" (42). Lamming's scathing critique of the middle class's refusal to act when, as he argues, they have the power to enact a sense of social change urges readers to confront those who remain apathetic in the face of injustice. Like Lamming, Rhys's experiences in Europe made her similarly resentful and distrustful of the middle class. Rhys's "lack of money as well as her West Indian accent kept her out of the middle class," and we can attribute this status as well to nearly all of her protagonists (Savory 24). Concerning Rhys's own class status, Sue Thomas notes, "On arrival in England Rhys's colonial cultural difference cannot be assimilated to a middle-class English feminine norm and this consigns her to a limbo, a place of the socially cast aside or outside, a place of abandonment" (91). Her sense of isolation is overt in her novels. The central figures of Rhys's narratives, impoverished and excluded, are judged by the middle class as deviant failures. There exists, then, an endless outpouring of disgust on the part of the protagonists at those who would enable their suffering and deny them alms. In Rhys's work, this embrace of disgust is redeployed as a means of critique against those that would remain complacent regarding systemic injustice. This redeployment of disgust guides her early work and, further, allows us to more firmly situate her writing within a critical discourse of class resentment and confrontation that is so important to Caribbean modes of resistance.

What makes Rhys's work different is its emotive intent and receptive antagonism, which works not simply to narrate but, rather, to cajole the reader into responding with frustration or dismay. In this regard, "Discourse of a Lady Standing a Dinner to a Down-and-Out-Friend" is perhaps Rhys's bleakest work and most bitter critique. The story's narrative conceit is fairly simple, in that the "lady's" superficial advice to her "down and out friend" is juxtaposed against her true feelings, which are represented in the text as parenthetical asides. The story offers a view of an inscrutable conversation in which meaning is always incomplete. It completely eliminates the voice of the impoverished woman on which it focuses and instead provides one side of a dinner discussion in which the "down and out friend" is repeatedly humiliated but disallowed to speak. "Discourse" is a work of pronounced disgust, as the lady continuously expresses revulsion for her friend's poverty, sadness, and depression. What's more, the woman's callousness is framed as an act of generosity—not hatred or resentment, but constructive criticism. Whereas "Hunger" is narrated from the perspective of the starving woman, "Discourse" effaces that perspective entirely. Indeed, she is given no voice and no dialogue, and her perspective exists only through her "friend's" interpretation of the conversation, which occurs in parenthesis. The story is an exercise in cruelty and resentment, as the narrator's benevolence is an utter farce: her compassion is a pose, and the commiseration she expresses is lip service rather than genuine emotion. Far from capturing the trauma and suffering of the impoverished protagonist, as is common in Rhys's novels, in "Discourse" the protagonist's perspective has been entirely obfuscated, her voice thoroughly suppressed, as she is denied an existence beyond that which is ascribed to her by her "friend" who oppresses her. The narrative mechanisms at play depict the silencing of the suffering woman by an individual who purports good intention and insists, moreover, that the lecture she provides and the cruelty she expresses is in the oppressed woman's best interest.

"Discourse" is, therefore, one of Rhys's most powerful critiques of complacency, as the narrative goads the reader to feel disgust with those that view the poor as Other. Moreover, it encourages readers to critique hypocrisy by forcing them into a hopeless position in which they are made to feel the callous cruelty of the speaker. The story inverts the central premise of "Hunger" by framing the reader as the oppressed rather than the oppressor, by making them feel the helplessness and frustration of the protagonist, who simply cannot resist. For the narrator, the suffering woman's appearance belies her condition, and she is unable to reconcile internal agony and physical starvation with her friend's seemingly normal physique, noting that "(it is all very well, but she has not forgotten to rouge her lips)," and "(A woman supposed to be starving ought not to go about in silk stockings and quite expensive shoes)" (43). Yet the narrator's insistence that "one cannot judge by *appearances*" (43) no doubt encapsulates the sense of self-delusion that guides many of the characters in Rhys's work. In fact, everything depends on appearance: of being kind, of showing compassion, of offering help, of not appearing callous, and, most explicitly, of not showing or expressing resentment or animosity. The narrator's offer of assistance to her friend is in no way genuine, as she seeks only the appearance of being kind, when in reality she believes that "it is dreadful to try to help poor people," because they "will not help themselves" (44). Her friend's plight "is her own fault" (45). As in "Hunger," for the narrator of "Discourse" the woman's plight is not due to entrenched forms of capitalist exploitation or oppression, but to her own choices and behavior.

The logic of cruelty displayed in "Discourse" bears an eerie resemblance to contemporary critiques of societal disenfranchisement and economic inequity that scapegoat poverty as a personal failing. Yet, in terms of the story itself, what is most significant is not simply the discourse of cruelty wrapped in the veneer of generosity, but the narrative tension between resistance and submission, in which the starving woman hopelessly struggles to assert herself against the overt rhetoric of inhumanity on display. We know, early on, that she is angry and resentful, particularly over the narrator chastising her for wearing clothes that hide her condition, telling her, "You cannot buy special clothes to starve in" (43). But we cannot truly *see* or witness her protests in the text—we know only that they exist, evidenced by the narrator's acknowledgment that her friend "is not pleased" with her statement (43). Thus the starving woman's presumed moment of outcry is marked merely though its absent presence. Over and over in the text, a protest suddenly emerges, but is quickly lost in the narrative ether. In much the same way, the narrator's assertion that "she knows someone at Neuilly who wants a mother's help" is met with the simple remark that "she does not like that," while recognition of her unhappiness is met with tears and an outburst that we are not privileged to see (43). The woman's trauma—indeed, her very struggle—is not only not taken seriously but is also suppressed by the narrator's dismissal of her pain. Textual gaps and aporias thus always swallow suffering and grief. Even the narrator's surprising, blunt assertion that "I hate myself" is uttered in parenthesis: it appears on the page but is and cannot be spoken, because self-loathing and disgust, the story reminds us, must always and forever be suffered internally. The interplay of what is said and what cannot be said smashes together uncomfortably here, and, while the sentiment of despair from the middle-class friend is, if not verbally articulated, at least given expression, the impoverished starving woman's protest is omitted altogether. There is simply no one to hear her plea. Rather, it is swallowed and regurgitated, made present only through the judgment and narrative consciousness of her social betters, who deny her suffering.

The story's experiments with narrative perspective captures the impossible struggle to resist, articulate, and overthrow oppressive ideologies and, more generally, the extent to which disenfranchised and minority voices are always evacuated and remade by the oppressor. Indeed, the narrator's aforementioned assertion that she "hates herself" engenders a potential sense of readerly empathy for the unfeeling friend: the individual who carries out the social pose, who acts cruelly and regrets it, who gains our sympathy at the expense of the individual they abuse. Frequently, in Rhys's work, the powerful (or more powerful) insist that they are oppressed—that they are slighted, that it is someone else's fault. To read "Discourse" is to meet with an overwhelming sense of frustration in which the oppressor not only refuses to empathize with the oppressed but also insists that they suffer *more*. It is this representation of middle-class complacency and cruelty that is, perhaps, Rhys's most damning critique of inequity.

In both stories, Rhys's work negotiates the bodily reverberations of disgust and the interplay and implications of being framed as disgusting while, at the same time, implicating the reader in larger processes of social rejection and disenfranchisement. It is this tension, this push and pull, that Sara Ahmed argues is inextricable from an ethics and ideology of disgust. As Ahmed contends,

> Disgust does not end with the proximity of such contact. The body recoils from the object; it pulls away with an intense movement that registers in the pit of the stomach. The movement is the work of disgust; it is what disgust does. Disgust brings the body perilously close to an object only then to pull them away from the object in the registering of the proximity as an offense. . . . That distancing requires proximity is crucial to the intercorporeality of the disgust encounter. The double movement (towards, away) is forgotten, however, as the body pulls back: it is as if the object moved towards the body, rather than the body having got close enough to the object. Hence the proximity of the "disgusting object" may feel like an offence to bodily space, as if the object's invasion of that space was a necessary consequence of what seems disgusting about the object itself. Pulling back, bodies that are disgusted are also bodies that feel a certain rage, a rage that the object has got close enough to sicken, and to be taken over or taken in. To be disgusted is after all *to be affected by what one has rejected*. (86; emphasis in original)

The rhetoric of disgust Ahmed describes here is a state of unstable, perpetual anxiety, and we can trace this double movement in Rhys, as her corpus negotiates the trauma in which one is ascribed the status of "disgusting" in an effort to express the extent to which those with social capital dehumanize marginalized populations while goading the reader into replicating that very process. This interplay of longing and rejection dominates Rhys's textual landscapes and compels readers to consider more deeply the potentiality of resistance against oppressive power structures, while confronting the instantiated and veiled social processes that make lower- and middle-class peoples complicit in practices of disenfranchisement. Thus, the complex, convoluted ethics of Rhys's protagonists'

Racist Complacency and the Framing of Afro-Caribbean Identity in *Voyage in the Dark*

disgust coerces readers into feeling a sense of shame and guilt over the narrator or protagonist's vitriol and, in so doing, unapologetically urges audiences to consider the implications of their own cruelty.[7]

The rhetoric of disgust—and narrative mechanisms that force the reader to confront their own resentment of marginalized groups—appear throughout Rhys's work. Yet these mechanisms become more complicated in her 1934 novel, *Voyage in the Dark*. Of all of Rhys's early fiction, *Voyage* has received the most attention, especially in Caribbean and postcolonial criticism. Sections of the novel are set in the Caribbean, and the protagonist, Anna Morgan, is a white creole émigré, not unlike Rhys herself, who struggles to adjust to the cruelty of life in London. However, in the novel readers confront a protagonist that, far from simply being a victim of middle-class cruelty, overlooks and is thoroughly ignorant of her own privilege. Anna Morgan both imagines herself and yearns to be Black, but, in so doing, almost entirely ignores the politics of race in the Caribbean and seems generally uninterested in thinking deeply about the horrors of racism and inequality. Whereas "Hunger" initiates a sense of guilt on the part of readers for their inability to understand the nature and reality of oppression, *Voyage* presents us with a protagonist that is herself guilty of the same complacency that Rhys's works typically critique. Throughout the novel, Anna's resentment of her stepmother—who is both proudly English and unabashedly racist—is always juxtaposed against her own ignorance, in which she trivializes and misunderstands the suffering of Black bodies at both her family's estate and in the Caribbean as a whole. Indeed, Anna is desperately afraid of, "getting like [her stepmother] Hester," but continuously Others and exoticizes the Black characters in the text (72). What emerges in the novel is a repeated theme in which overt racism is decried only to be replaced by a more subtle, but no less harmful, racism espoused by the narrative's main character.

The novel's racial politics have received considerable critical attention, and, as Kristin Czarnecki observes in "Jean Rhys's Postmodern Narrative Authority: Selina's Patois in 'Let Them Call It Jazz,'" the troubling representation of Black identity in works like *Voyage* have led some scholars to question Rhys's opposition to forms of racial oppression. As Czarnecki points out: "Scholars continue to deliberate over cultural and linguistic authenticity and appropriation in Rhys's works. Perhaps

Rhys participates in racial masquerading: gazing from the outside into Dominica's black community, insisting throughout her life that she felt more black than white, and referring to 'us' blacks in *Smile Please: An Unfinished Autobiography*. . . . She certainly appears to essentialize black Dominicans" (31–32). Yet if Czarnecki's critique of Rhys's racial politics appears damning, her essay (citing Helen Carr) quickly pivots to remind us of Rhys's long history of resistance against racism and inequality. In any case, as Czarnecki helps to show, Rhys's relationship to Dominica and her analysis of race remains a key point of tension in evaluating her work.[8] Building off the critical debates about racist ideology in Rhys's corpus, I want to suggest here that any analysis of the role of middle-class complacency in *Voyage*—as well as its strategies of readerly engagement and manifestation of veiled forms of oppression—must begin with a confrontation of the novel's depiction of race and dehumanization. Investigating the novel's inventive, performative narrative devices can serve, as I will show, as a means to rethink the novel's oft-discussed questions of race.

As I argued earlier in this chapter, the ingenuity of works like "Hunger" and "Discourse of a Lady Standing Dinner to a Down-and-Out Friend" effectively goad the reader to experience sensations of disgust, shame, and guilt in an effort to encourage them to rethink the often invisible cruelty and complacency directed at oppressed populations. The function of disgust in *Voyage* is significantly different and more complex: on the one hand, readers are urged once again to see through the vitriol that the middle class espouses toward women and marginalized figures and to rightly empathize with Anna's suffering. On the other hand, the novel's sometimes barbaric framing of race works to strip away that readerly empathy, framing Anna as a woman entirely ignorant of the history of violence and oppression in the Caribbean, as she essentializes and romanticizes Blackness without any sense of critical reflection. As such, I want to argue that Rhys's tense, antagonistic relationship with the reader is not simply a thematic principle, but a central crisis of her novel. Further, I want to suggest that *Voyage* in particular is frequently misread in terms of its negotiation of racial politics in the Caribbean, and that, in fact, the novel is a work of immense tension that urges the reader to see beyond the racist vantage point of its protagonist to examine how marginalized peoples remain complacent and therefore enable further systems of oppression. Centered around a protagonist who, as an impoverished, white creole émigré, suffers enormously, but also evinces a profound racial ignorance, the novel negotiates a dialectical tension between empathy and disgust, forcing readers to acknowledge the abuse Anna suffers while carefully intimating a critique of her privilege and callousness, especially concerning issues of race. *Voyage*, unlike the earlier, more explicit confrontations with perspective in "Hunger" and "Discourse" that direct their ire at the reader, thus employs different mechanisms to engage and frustrate the reader, in that Rhys's protagonist, obtuse and unable to see beyond her own privilege, repeatedly critiques practices of oppression but nevertheless overtly perpetuates them. The reader, in this way, is asked to see what Anna cannot—that is, the novel works to expose entrenched practices of oppression that are seldom observed or articulated.

The novel employs racist language to foster an emotional response that seeks to make visible latent and normalized oppression, especially forms of oppression espoused and carried out by already marginalized populations. Accordingly, unlike the majority of Rhys's works, *Voyage* begins with a jarring moment of explicit racism on the part of the protagonist that firmly establishes the novel's negotiation of readerly disgust. The text begins by capturing the protagonist's overwhelming loneliness and isolation, painting a bleak portrait of Anna's life in England. Wandering through the cold, alien streets of London, Anna imagines herself safe from the hostile British landscape by conjuring an image of her life back in the Caribbean. Yet the fantasy she imagines is punctured by a sense of colonialist nostalgia and searing racism. The Caribbean she fantasizes is one in which her race situates her as a symbol—perhaps unwittingly—of superiority. The fantasy she imagines begins: "Market Street smelt of the wind, but the narrow street smelt of niggers and wood-smoke and salt fishcakes fried in lard" (8). In the passage, the ephemeral smell of smoke and fried fish conflicts uncomfortably with Anna's racism as Anna, repeatedly, sees and asserts race as window-dressing: not a crisis of oppression and dehumanization, but an ornamental scenic detail that bolsters her romanticized memory of her homeland. Moreover, while images of overt racism are displayed throughout Rhys's corpus, the scene marks the only time we see a Rhysian protagonist use a racial slur—one used most frequently in the text by Anna's overtly racist stepmother, Hester, whom Anna thoroughly resents. Nevertheless, Anna casually uses the slur here. While she opens the text isolated, impoverished, and disenfranchised, still she nonchalantly dehumanizes black bodies throughout the text and, more generally, is unable to commiserate with the plight of the colonial subjects of Dominica. As is the case with *Wide Sargasso Sea*, *Voyage* thus obliges readers to navigate Anna's suffering against the backdrop of a real, ever-present callousness toward issues of race and cultural appropriation of which she is entirely ignorant.[9] As such, the novel is one of perpetual frustration, as Anna's racism threatens to obviate readerly empathy and encourages the reader to pass judgment in such a way that mirrors the actions and beliefs of Anna's oppressor. My point here is not simply that Anna's romanticization of the Caribbean curiously aligns with a British worldview that she finds repulsive, but that the text depicts a labyrinthine array of cultural assumptions and misunderstandings that suggest that its central theme may very well be the readerly act of negotiating an empathetic response toward Anna's suffering in the face of her unyielding, pervasive racial ignorance. The text is therefore performative in that its confrontational relationship with its audience asks readers to reckon with the question of how they should and can respond to systems of oppression that pit marginalized peoples against one another.

Rhys's novels always bear an uneasy relationship with their readers, who may (and often do) judge or reject altogether the protagonist's suffering. In this regard, *Voyage* further problematizes notions of readerly empathy by metafictively suggesting that the reader and protagonist share similar views, thereby encouraging readers to evaluate their own perspectives of race and marginalization. By way of example, the novel opens by effectively "translating" Afro-Caribbean culture for the presumably ignorant reader but, in so doing, exacerbates racial stereotypes. Its opening narrative technique is reminiscent of Reid's *The Leopard* in that the incorporation of an immediate moment of cultural translation explains for the reader the connection between blackness and the Caribbean. Anna notes, "When the black women sell fishcakes on the savannah they carry them in trays on their heads. They call out, 'Salt fishcakes all sweet an' charmin', all sweet an charmin'" (8). Anna's narration aims to educate the reader, who is presumably unfamiliar with the culture she describes: it is designed to clarify the meaning of the scene, while capturing a snapshot of life in the Caribbean. Instead, it others the women as exotic and linguistic curiosities. Worse, it depicts them in the midst of strange but decidedly pleasant and stress-free labor. Blackness here is simple, easy, and happy. These people, the text implies, are not like you. It is telling, then, that Anna, as an émigré and outsider, perceives herself perpetually isolated from English society, but nevertheless imagines that she speaks to an audience that is decidedly English. Englishness, which, in Hester, represents only sadness and resentment, is here embraced in all its familiarity, as Anna demarcates clear boundaries between white and Black identity—boundaries that are rooted in racist stereotypes. Such moments of what we might call "cultural translation" effectively normalize Anna's deeply racist views of Caribbean culture while tacitly suggesting that readers share Anna's views and are equally ignorant of the people of which she speaks. Yet careful readers note that Anna's unthinking usage of the slur, which occurs on the same page as the passage just discussed, suggests that she is not a reliable or objective "translator" of Caribbean experience. In this regard, the novel's narrative strategy—which quickly undermines Anna's reliability by revealing that her knowledge of the Caribbean is both prejudiced and deeply problematic—suggests that we should be skeptical of Anna's assumptions about her audience. Rhys's text not only asks us who has the authority to speak to other cultures but also suggests that readers should remain wary of essentializing tendencies that ensnare everyday people into adopting oppressive ideological positions. In so doing, the novel works to excavate veiled processes of oppression by bringing them into the foreground through its receptive strategy.

It should be acknowledged that, in many ways, my theory of readerly engagement—that the novel's narrative strategy urges the reader to evaluate and reconcile Anna's sense of unthinking complacency within larger schemas of racial violence and inequity—is shaped by recent work on the novel that privileges the textual importance of suspicion, bewilderment, and concealment. Recently, scholarship has begun to focus more on the ways in which Rhys's novels develop an uneasy relationship with the reader. Of particular note is J. Dillon Brown's "Textual Entanglement: Jean Rhys's Critical Discourse," in which Brown argues that *Voyage in the Dark* and *Wide Sargasso Sea* encourage readers not to simply question the presentation of knowledge depicted in the texts, but to consider the larger implications of how knowledge is made, articulated, and disseminated. As Brown writes, both novels display a "shared thematic and formal interest in exploring the structuring effects of cultural, verbal, and written production. Both *Voyage in the Dark* and *Wide Sargasso Sea* focus intensely on books and textual representation and display a distinct self-consciousness about writing and interpretation. Ultimately, both suggest the pragmatic necessity of a careful and consistent hermeneutic of suspicion when approaching any system of signs, whether in life or on the page" (569). Emphasizing the textual importance of suspicion, Brown argues further that "Rhys strives to lay bare the insidiously naturalizing effects of the semiotic discourses surrounding her characters" (570). In terms of my argument, the kind of suspicious reading that Brown suggests may well be implicit in the readerly act of unraveling the narrator's racist complacency as well as in the fact that Anna herself suggests that the reader shares her views: a point that the careful reader should no doubt be suspicious of. Similarly to Brown, Andrzej Gąsiorek in "(The Knocking) Has Never Stopped: Jean Rhys's (Post)colonial Modernism" contends that *Voyage in the Dark* "locks" the reader in a "bewildered perspective" (166). For Gąsiorek, Anna's first-person perspective forces the reader to confront degrees of textual uncertainty (167). The act of reading becomes a textual process of decoding that "conceals, or elides, a relationship of power" (170).

In building off of Brown's and Gąsiorek's arguments that the novel should be confronted with a sense of suspicion, and that readers must actively seek to unveil the mechanisms of power revealed in the text, we can better examine how the narrative's repeated eruptions of racism urge a greater reflection on the mechanisms of class resentment, especially in terms of the novel's representation of labor. *Voyage* complicates conceptions of power and privilege by providing her protagonist—who is thoroughly broken by the violent, misogynistic world she inhabits—with a sense of racial privilege of which she is utterly unaware. Anna's relationship to Dominica's countryside always marks her privileged relationship to the landscape, in which the fields and stables are not a symbol of labor, but, rather, of play. Dominica is thus remembered most for its scenery and wistful memories: "The mangotree was so big that all the garden was in its shadow and the ground under it always looked dark and damp. The stable-yard was by the side of the garden, white-paved and hot, smelling of horses and manure" (42). And though she recalls a church service in which the message is, bleakly, "The poor do this and the rich do that . . . and nothing can change it. For ever and ever turning and nothing, nothing can change it," Anna still inhabits the countryside as a spectator; her memory of the Caribbean is not one of longing or suffering, but of a utopia that is largely severed from questions of injustice, labor, and racism (43). Unlike the protagonist of other Rhys novels, Anna possesses power, but it is a power she is entirely ignorant of. In Dominica, Anna's whiteness means that she possesses authority and social capital not available to the Black characters she describes—a point, I want to emphasize here, that is incredibly important, given representations of labor in Rhys's oeuvre. Rhys, perhaps more so than any modernist writer, is concerned with the economics of labor. All her protagonists frequently struggle to "get money" and link economics with social power. Indeed, the aforementioned Mr. Blank scene in *Good Morning, Midnight,* in which Blank humiliates Sasha, is made possible solely by his economic and cultural status. Money and status permit and govern all opportunities and are almost always wielded to gain advantage over one's social inferiors. In *Voyage,* Rhys creates a protagonist who suffers enormously but is not, as she assumes, at the bottom of the social and economic ladder. Nevertheless, Anna replicates acts of systemic oppression by devaluing the suffering of Black bodies by ignoring and romanticizing their labor.

Indeed, Anna enacts a continuous and explicit romanticism of labor that is not her own, especially that which is carried out by Black characters and servants, a point made all the more odd given that Anna is, in fact, superficially attentive to the horrifying effects of labor on the body, noting: "People are much cheaper than things. . . . Some dogs are more expensive than people, aren't they?" (46; ellipsis added). Yet Anna's memory of her family's servants curiously ignores the toil and physicality of the backbreaking labor they carry out and, at the same time, valorizes their labor and essentializes them through the lens of racist tropes that imagine Black bodies as happy and jovial, imagining Blackness as a kind of utopic state. As she states, "I wanted to be black, I always wanted to be black. . . . Being black is warm and gay, being white is cold and sad." (31) Yet Anna bears no understanding of the grief and trauma of servitude, reading Francine, her family's servant, and the other Caribbean characters as content or joyous. She ignores the toll servitude takes on the body and paradoxically inscribes the memory of the servants' labor as an act of imaginative emancipation, in which their image of suffering becomes a momentary escape from her own. Equally troubling, Anna cannot fathom that her memories of her family's happy servants—and, more importantly, the relationships that she has with them—are dictated by a forced submission that demands nicety. Francine's kindness, after all, is monetary: she is a caretaker and a servant. She changes Anna's bandage and kills a monstrous cockroach because she has to, but Anna reads these acts as unassuming kindness, not servitude (31). Similarly, the toil of the servant Joseph is firmly fixed in Anna's memory; she remembers him spit-shining a shoe as a kind of virtuous, skilled labor. Anna recalls him "cleaning the shoes with blacking and spit. Spit—mix—rub; spit—mix—rub. Joseph had heaps of spittle and when he spurted a jet into the tin of blacking he never missed" (41). Later she remembers "the sweat rolling down Joseph's face when he helped me to mount and tear in my habit-skirt" (151). What is significant about these scenes is that Joseph exists to Anna solely in terms of his utility. In other words, her memories are only and always of his servitude: the time he spit-shined a boot and the time he helped her get on her horse. Though she recalls the sweat dripping down Joseph's face, she never feels guilt or remorse for the labor he is forced to perform.

As should be clear, the novel pushes readers to think more critically about racial and economic oppression in the Caribbean by highlighting the extent to which the nuances of these issues are often elided and obfuscated. Given the pervasive critique of capitalism and exploitation in Rhys's canon, Anna's inability to critique systemic racial oppression in the Caribbean is a key point of tension in the text, where readers are made to face a protagonist that is herself, as a white creole woman, profiled and marginalized, but nevertheless harbors dangerous racial fantasies that ultimately enforce harmful, romantic stereotypes about race and oppression in the Caribbean. What is telling in these scenes is the extent to which labor, toil, and suffering is reframed to formulate an idealized representation of a pastoral, utopic Caribbean free of exploitation and violence. While Anna struggles to feed herself and scrounges for every dime she earns, she is unable to think critically or seriously about oppression and servitude, as she thoroughly ignores the racial and economic implications of Joseph's labor. I want to be clear that my goal is not to undermine the discrimination Anna suffers as a white creole in cosmopolitan London; indeed, many critics have significantly explored this theme.[10] Rather, I want to argue that Rhys suggests the kind of racist vitriol to which Anna sometimes unknowingly subscribes should be acknowledged as similarly disgusting. The novel asks readers to confront with anger, disappointment, and frustration the refutation of Black suffering and to consider the ways in which histories of oppression are trivialized. To be certain, Anna further perpetuates myths that exacerbate the suffering of Caribbean peoples, ascribing to a grotesque simplification of the legacy of colonial violence that her family has helped to sustain.

Such a reading—that focuses on textual devices that produce an uncomfortable sense of tension between reader and protagonist, especially concerning issues of race and labor—thereby demonstrates that Rhys's narrative strategy is more deeply invested in analyzing the fundamental problems of colonialism than is often acknowledged. Indeed, as Gąsiorek reminds us, Rhys's work "is concerned with the ways in which colonial ideology sought to maintain its authority by refusing to budge from a hierarchical conception of race that denied black people social and cultural equality long after emancipation" (167). In a similar vein, Mary Lou Emery argues in "The Poetics of Labor in Jean Rhys's Global Modernism" that the horrific essentialization of Black bodies in *Voyage* is not a textual oversight but a scathing critique of colonial oppression by which the reader is intended to be rightly repulsed. Accordingly, Emery attempts to rethink "ongoing debates about racial identifications—that is, how we should judge Rhys or her characters if they seem to conflate the position of an Afro-Caribbean woman with that of a Euro-Creole woman" by focusing on the social codes and conventions that influence Anna's views and opinions (192). Emery contends that such textual moments reveal the inherent racism of "material production" and thus work to expose racist forms of colonial oppression. As she continues, "The careful qualification that an oppressed white creole woman is not the same as an enslaved black woman is important. However, we can read these scenes, not as moments of racial identification or as assertions of some real or fantasized social identity, but as recognition of a contradictory and unstable subjectivity produced through discrepant colonial systems of labor brought in relation to one another" (193). Taken this way, Anna's inability to reconcile the nature of her own oppression with the suffering of Black bodies in the Caribbean is a byproduct of a pervasive colonial rhetoric that distorts the relationship between bodies and labor by framing labor as an inextricable and natural state of being for Black servants.[11] In naturalizing the relationship between Blackness and labor, Anna disassociates the plight of Black servants from their own toil and thereby yearns for an identity in which labor is not punishing and overwhelming, but rather pleasant and enjoyable. Her yearning to be Black, therefore, is built upon inscribed colonial perceptions of the relationship between Blackness and labor. Given her colonial view of labor in the text, Anna is ultimately unable to observe or understand the nuances of capitalistic acts of violence in the Caribbean. The novel provides us with a protagonist who obfuscates the presence of colonial economic oppression in the Caribbean and in the process shines a light on the manner through which marginalized peoples often inadvertently embolden forms of racial disenfranchisement. *Voyage* is a work that bitterly critiques the effacement of colonial oppression, and to that end, the larger ignorance and tendency to devalue labor. We can and should, then, not assume that Anna's ignorance of her own privilege is an oversight or a curiosity in the novel: rather, it is its primary theme and, to be certain, one of Rhys's most biting attacks on the nature of oppression.

Therefore, the theory of reading that is the focus of this chapter—that is, one in which Rhys's readers are made to experience and negotiate emotive responses of disgust and frustration—helps us to reconcile two seemingly contradictory positions in Rhys's work: the at times overt condemnation of middle-class complacency and the competing disavowal of racial empathy and a privileging of white creole disenfranchisement that often comes at the expense of the suffering of people of color. Far from viewing these positions as irreconcilable, the novel urges readers to respond with frustration and, what's more, to think through the practices of colonial indoctrination that exacerbate resentment between marginalized peoples in ways that are often contradictory and seemingly irrational. As Boehmer has shown, for the reader, narrative devices that experiment with perspective and juxtaposition "often [spark] a stepping back . . . yet that also demands the reader or critic's creative input and involvement, intensifying the continual, often dilatory, and wayward transactions that take place between the reader and the text" (43). Viewed this way, we might read *Voyage*'s wrestling with seemingly contradictory positions as a method of engagement that thereby "intensif[ies]" the reader's response to the text. This emotive intensification works to enhance the reader's investment in and understanding of the larger practices of disenfranchisement and dehumanization that the text seeks to expose.

Narrative Disavowal and the Practices of Rupture

As I have been arguing, *Voyage of the Dark* urges readers to confront racist ideologies by revealing the extent to which marginalized populations inscribe racist beliefs. By instigating feelings of disgust and frustration directed at Anna's often contradictory behavior, the novel exhorts us not to dismiss the plight of marginalized peoples, but to think more deeply about the pervasiveness with which racist ideologies take root in impoverished and disenfranchised populations. Rhys thereby challenges readers to negotiate sentiments of empathy and scorn in our response to Anna's suffering and to not refrain from confronting heinous ideologies that permeate lower- and middle-class communities. Yet, if we look more closely, we can observe the occasional presence of an intrusive narrative voice that undermines the reliability of Anna's first-person viewpoint. Indeed, a close reading of the novel reveals a number of textual intrusions designed to sabotage the realism and believability of Anna's narration; in so doing, the novel's narrative voice carefully complicates the novel's representation of race, in that the narrative begins to depict competing viewpoints and representations of race and oppression by suggesting that Anna's viewpoints are both unstable and unsustainable. Negotiating the text's depiction of race thus becomes all the more difficult and disorienting as lapses in narrative coherence challenge readers to question the veracity of Anna's worldview.

Though the narrative is told in the first person, throughout the text readers are met, in several instances, with a new narrative voice that, in many ways, resembles Anna's but is more formal, erudite, and detached. In these scenes, Anna articulates facts, figures, and information that she simply would not know, leaving aspects of the text an interruptive experience, and forcing readers to wonder who, exactly, is narrating. To take one example, in an early scene, in the midst of a performance, the geographical coordinates of Dominica suddenly emerge, rupturing the logic of the passage. Readers meet with the following description: "Lying between 15 10' and 15 40'N. and 61 14' and 61 30'W. 'A goodly island and something highland, but all overgrown with woods,' that book said. And all crumpled into hills and mountains as you would crumple a piece of paper in your hand—rounded green hills and sharply-cut mountains" (17). Geographical coordinates (which would later be central to the aesthetic tendency of Denis Williams) function here as a means to disrupt the process of reading, as Anna's typical emotive narration is replaced with a formal tone that resembles that of an encyclopedia entry. It is clear that the language of the passage and the presentation of the coordinates is not Anna's, and the scene depicts the appearance of a new, more formalized narrative perspective. The intrusive second voice that descends upon the narrative further complicates the novel's representation of life in the Caribbean. While its description of the island seems at first glance painfully sterile, the objective recitation of the coordinates quickly collapses into imperial rhetoric, and it concludes by comparing the island's landscape to a piece of crumpled trash that is both unnatural and unkempt. The scene is significant in that it highlights the interplay of warped colonialist imaginations of Caribbean space by juxtaposing Anna's racist imagination with an official record that is also glaringly dismissive and equally racist, in which the Caribbean appears as an untamed, underdeveloped wilderness in disarray fit only for the trash heap of history. The scene, in which Anna's racism is momentarily displaced by an intrusionary imperialist rhetoric, is a jarring moment that suggests the presence of a deeper, surreptitious ideology of racism lurking behind the narrative veneer. Thus, Anna's racism is effectively swallowed up—and her words literally replaced—by the intrusion of a new voice of oppression. Through this narrative intrusion, Rhys situates Anna's racism against a more formalized imperialist rhetoric that demeans and distorts representations of Caribbean life and people.

Critics have devoted significant attention to these interruptive scenes, especially in terms of their implications for Rhys's confrontation with colonial ideology.[12] As Gąsiorek notes, such moments have a profound effect on how we understand colonial violence in Rhys's work. As he writes, these scenes reflect "on the ideological authority of textbooks and encyclopedias, as well as considering richly symbolic material artifacts like commemorative inscriptions in churches and on gravestones. . . . Because Rhys deploys first-person narrators . . . there is no external commentary on these textual moments. They are dropped into the novella like bombs that will eventually explode, shattering the façade of colonial respectability" (175). Encyclopedic definitions smash against Anna's utopic fantasy of the Caribbean and represent it instead as a series of abstracted geographic details, disorienting the plot and raising pivotal questions about the nature of how we frame colonial discourse. In much the same way, J. Dillon Brown argues that these scenes reveal "the novel's suspicion of the effects of discourse" and further suggests that the demarcation of the "final clause, indicating Anna's distance from the words, implies some doubt about the accuracy of such an account" (571). In Brown's words, such interruptive moments highlight "the colonial archive's rhetoric of power" (571). On the one hand, we might be quick to conclude that these moments throw the entirety of the narrative into uncertainty in a way that further alienates the reader from identifying with Anna's narration, in that they remind us that the language Anna uses is, in a sense, not her own. In this case, the intrusive emergence of a second voice insists that we not ignore the pervasiveness of colonial ideology, which increasingly functions in the novel in a myriad of forms and contexts.

Yet this is a chapter about the engaging potential of readerly disgust and its ability to raise new insights about practices of complacency, and, if we further evaluate textual moments of interruption, we can in fact observe that there is, despite a difference in tone, little ideological difference between the encyclopedia's more "formal" framing of the Caribbean and Anna's glaring racial ignorance. Frustration abounds—for though the new voice suggests a different perspective, it ultimately endorses a very similar worldview and endorsement of oppression. In other words, I want to argue here that the interruptive scenes are not so much used to demarcate and distinguish Anna's viewpoint from imperialist practice as to enforce her position and participation within that very practice. In a key scene midway through the novel, Anna tries to remember the lyrics to a song, but, in doing so, oddly begins to articulate a robotic overview of indigenous struggle in the Caribbean that appears to be imperialist. The voice that intrudes is once again decidedly not hers, and the passage represents a chasm that ruptures the novel's first-person narration. In the scene, Anna begins by reciting the lyrics to a song that she promptly forgets:

> "And drift, drift
>   Legions away from despair."

It can't be "legions." "Oceans," perhaps. "Oceans away from despair." But it's the sea, I thought. The Caribbean Sea. "The Caribs indigenous to this island were a warlike tribe and their resistance to white domination, though spasmodic, was fierce. As lately as the beginning of nineteenth century they raided on of the neighboring islands, under British rule, and overpowered the garrison and kidnapped the governor, his wife and three children. They are now practically exterminated. The few hundreds that are left do not intermarry with the negroes. Their reservation, at the northern end of the island, is known as the Carib Quarter." They had, or used to have, a king Mopo, his name was. Here's to Mopo, King of the Caribs! But they are now practically exterminated. "Oceans away from despair . . ." (105)

This scene is incredibly important in that it represents an explicit rupture in the logic of the plot. What's also interesting here is that the narrative intrusion, in which Anna somehow recites the entirety of a passage about the history of the Caribs, breaks off to suggest that Anna is not simply reading from a book or encyclopedia, but rather knows more about Caribbean history than the text reveals. This juxtaposition, between a character who cannot perceive the Black servants of her estate as anything but playthings, is oblivious to the nuances of racial oppression, and yet is able cite a detailed articulation of indigenous extermination, makes little narrative sense. However, though this passage hints that Anna supports Mopo's act of resistance by her assertion "Here's to Mopo, King of the Caribs!," it is worth noting that Anna has expressed no real empathy for indigenous people throughout the novel, and her citation of Mopo, in that she celebrates him without attempting to understand or empathize with him, is in line with her fetishization of Black bodies throughout the text. Mopo, and indigenous bodies in general, appear here mostly unintelligible, as a momentary aside within the larger schema of the plot. In other words, Anna's acknowledgment of indigenous eradication in no way leads her to think more deeply about her former servants or the economics of labor in the Caribbean, nor does it alter her behavior or views. In sum, while the tone and style of these passages is different from Anna's narration throughout the novel—in fetishizing Black identity in the Caribbean she denies her former servants' agency but romanticizes the nature of their struggle, while the textbook passages often depict a more detached perspective, casually and coldly remarking on the extermination of indigenous peoples—it is telling that such interruptions do not challenge, but rather reinforce, Anna's complacency and refusal to think more deeply about her own views on race and oppression.

The implication that both forms of racism are seemingly interchangeable, and that Anna quite literally speaks the language of her perceived oppressor, suggests that Rhys, far from simply undermining the perspective of Black characters in the text, works painfully to show how pervasively their voices are erased, and how marginalized peoples are made to redeploy the language of their oppressors. As Rhys shows us here, Anna's racism is, in fact, inextricable from the colonial ideology that she believes her stepmother, Hester, and, to a lesser extent, England, represents. In this way, the novel exposes the pervasiveness with which languages of disenfranchisement are inscribed across social classes. In so doing, it reminds us that Anna's voice and views are, to some degree, not her own, in that she has internalized a larger belief system of which she herself is largely unaware. Textual moments of interruption indicate to readers that overarching ideologies of racism and the larger schema of oppression and violence toward Black bodies that envelops Europe are largely interchangeable and are universally deployed. There is, in other words, little difference between Anna's disavowal of the trauma of labor exploitation in the Caribbean and the casual dismissal of the eradication of the Caribs that is articulated by the intrusive voice. Such encyclopedic scenes therefore dismantle the consistency of Anna's narration through interruption and align it with imperialist ideology, thus encouraging readers to trace as well as reject and find fault with the regurgitation of racist rhetoric that she espouses throughout the novel.

In sum, the novel's employment of narrative intrusion and rupture forces readers to negotiate a sense of empathy for Anna—a character who, to be sure, suffers enormously and is often herself a victim of grotesque social and cultural violence—against her racist, ignorant interpretation of the Caribbean. Readers must therefore confront the extent to which a sympathetic protagonist espouses violent and dangerous rhetoric that, troublingly, she unthinkingly adopts as what she perceives to be a progressive position. The mechanics of disgust in the novel function to further alienate the reader; the audience, as in all of Rhys's novels, may judge her decisions, her sex life, and her drinking, as as well as her unrelenting racism. The ingenuity of the novel depicts two counternarratives, one in which the reader is forced to watch as its female protagonist is tortured by those that inhabit the sadistic, thoroughly patriarchal landscape of 1930s Europe while forcing the reader to face the very fact that Anna herself has contributed and continues to contribute to the suffering of the long-exploited Black populace in the Caribbean. The novel both urges us to think beyond her perspective and encourages a sense of readerly commiseration. In this way, *Voyage*'s narrative reveals a complex negotiation of the politics of empathy and disgust and, in so doing, compels readers to think more deeply about their own complacency about issues of racial injustice.

Caribbean Engagements

Rhys's early works anticipate the central crises espoused by George Lamming and the *Beacon* group by directly challenging readers to confront social complacency and to rethink their own positions. Accordingly, the goal of this chapter was to situate the work of Jean Rhys within a larger schema of Caribbean writing that opposes complacency toward forms of oppression through sentiments of disgust. I have worked to highlight performative narrative mechanisms that draw out readerly emotions of disgust as a means to better reflect on the nature of oppression. Given that this is a book on inscrutability, my point is that the methods of readerly engagement Rhys's works produce allow us to witness and better process the myriad of ways in which lower- and middle-class populations are coerced into perpetuating the further disenfranchisement of marginalized populations. In rethinking *Voyage of the Dark* as well as Rhys's other works in terms of a more overt relationship to Caribbean politics and culture, we can observe that her writing contributes to the larger conservation about inaction and apathy that pervaded mid-twentieth-century Caribbean literature.

In parallel with this conversation, Rhys's writing thus exposes the rhetoric used by the middle (and sometimes lower) classes that Other and repudiate the suffering of marginalized and oppressed people. Rhys's novels both build off of and allow us to reconsider George Lamming's assertion in *The Pleasures of Exile* that the Caribbean is trapped in a "state of complacency" and that "the higher up" one "moves in the social scale, the more crippled his mind and impulses become by resultant complacency" (36). In works such as *Voyage*, complacency is *not* restricted to the middle and upper classes, and *Voyage* demands that readers reckon with the protagonist's racism and dangerously ignorant views of Afro-Caribbean peoples while thinking more deeply about the colonial politics that foster resentment between marginalized groups. Such a reading of Rhys's corpus allows us to firmly establish the ways in which her writing reveals a distinct anticolonialist confrontation with cultural and social mechanisms that seek to naturalize oppression in the Caribbean. In experimenting with narrative techniques that produce sensations of readerly disgust, Rhys surreptitiously reveals a number of ways in which Caribbean peoples' suffering is normalized and dismissed and, in doing so, urges readers not to lose sight of the ways in which oppressed peoples are abstracted from their labor and stripped of their basic human rights.

Coda
Inscrutable Pasts, Inscrutable Futures

THIS BOOK has sought to demonstrate how the struggle to articulate Caribbean experience in literary form that emerged in the mid-twentieth century reveals not simply a uniquely Caribbean stylistics of difficulty, but an emergent theory and practice of reading—one that seeks to capture the sense of aporia and loss that is inextricable from Caribbean life. In emphasizing the performative implications of inscrutability, I have worked to show how readerly experiences of frustration, particularly in terms of what is produced when confronting midcentury Caribbean texts perceived as "difficult," can be rethought as productive confrontations with the mechanisms of colonial oppression. The experiences of struggle such texts induce enrapture the reader in a state of disorientation and performative discomfort that aim to draw them into—or, at the very least, more deeply consider—historical trajectories of Caribbean oppression. In analyzing this process, *Difficult Reading* has showed how such a theory of reading can shine light on previously ignored texts, while allowing us to reconsider the narrative strategies of canonical writers like Wilson Harris and Jean Rhys in new ways.

As I have emphasized, the receptive and readerly strategies of both forgotten and canonical writers in the Caribbean have often gone unnoticed or, more troublingly, been misread or perceived as ahistorical or isolated from larger traditions of Caribbean writing. In each chapter, I have worked to open up new spaces of debate and investigation in the field by demonstrating how such experimental works provide new methodologies for reconciling colonial violence and Caribbean experience. In this way, *Difficult Reading,* embraces Alison Donnell's affirmation that critics of Caribbean literature should seek to "fray the edges" of the discipline rather than "neaten the seams" in an effort to "keep returning to what remains unknown and seemingly unknowable, as well as to what has been disavowed" (408). The crux, for Donnell, is to "generate a richer and more comprehensive, although always unfinished, account of the past and the present" (409). Fraying such edges, as it were, depends not simply on opening a space to discuss ignored or forgotten writers—a noncontroversial claim, I'd hope, for we need only consider the lack of attention paid to writers like Vera Bell and Lindsay Barrett in twentieth-century Caribbean studies to acknowledge the simple fact that large holes remain in critical pictures of the field—but also by rethinking both the formal and thematic demands that the Caribbean novel often places on readers.

In unearthing and rethinking texts perceived as inscrutable, we can expand on the narrative implications of difficulty in a way that eschews assertions that such texts are "too hard" or can and should only be read and studied by academics. As this book has hoped to show, the endeavor to make meaning of the inscrutable—and the experiences of frustration, longing, and exasperation that come with reading inscrutable texts—perhaps engenders what the *Beacon* group imagined all along: a unique form of Caribbean writing and reading that embraces the struggle to make sense of imperial legacies while acknowledging that those legacies cannot often be easily articulated. In the works I have discussed, confronting these legacies is in many ways an experience of profound unease and disorientation—an experience that becomes, in the inscrutable text, the reader's burden.

It is this emphasis on reading practices that I want to reiterate here, as the central premise of this book is that an aesthetics of inscrutability can open up new ways of understanding Caribbean-ness through acts of reading that helps to resituate—and, hopefully, reshape—the purview of twentieth-century Caribbean literature. Building off of Elaine Boehmer's theory of postcolonial reception, which does not repudiate the immersive strategies of formal experimentation but instead shows how "the putting together of strongly contrasting and divergent images, states of being, or orders of reality, is something that solicits the particularly close and focused involvement of the reader" (42), *Difficult Reading* has highlighted how linguistic and experimental strategies that emphasize a struggle and a failure to make sense of language, the Caribbean, and experiences of disenfranchisement work to produce experiences of readerly frustration and disorientation that prompt deeper reflection on the nature of Caribbean oppression. In this way, the works I have examined in this book are solely a starting point.

Indeed, increased critical attention toward the receptive and performative implications of mid-twentieth-century experimental Caribbean literature is sorely needed. In this regard, it is also worth noting that inscrutable elements of more canonical Caribbean writers' works have, in some cases, been met with critical silence, leaving incomplete portraits of those writers' careers and the innovative and experimental methods of engagement that their works contain. At the same time, work remains to be done on understudied novels that challenge the reader to think through the nuances of oppression in inventive and frustrating ways. It is my hope that this book will be an impetus for readers to turn an eye toward forgotten writers like Barrett, Bell, and Reid, among others, as well as provide a means to rethink the inventive receptive and immersive techniques of writers like Roger Mais and Jean Rhys.[1]

I want to suggest, however, that an aesthetics of inscrutability can be used not only to rethink practices of Caribbean reading and reception but also to negotiate longstanding impasses within the field of Caribbean criticism itself: the tension between looking forward, as it were, and looking backward. As Donnell contends in *Caribbean Literature in Transition, 1970–2020,* the increasing popularity of contemporary Caribbean writing has in some ways distracted from the very fact that there remains a need to both rediscover and reconsider Caribbean writing from the nineteenth and twentieth century. As she notes,

> Somewhat ironically, while the future success of Caribbean writers and writing looks bright, the future of Caribbean literary studies may arguably be diminished by the increased mainstream profiling and commercial credibility of its feted contemporary and predominantly diasporic writers. The celebrated presence of contemporary Caribbean writing within the global literary scene may mask the still pressing need to address significant gaps in its literary histories that continue to obscure a more complete and pluralized understanding of the field. The forceful profiling of the successful few that characterizes literary publishing in the twenty-first century can too easily create a narrow literary lens in any field, but Caribbean literary studies is arguably more vulnerable to this constrained perspective on account of the partiality of existing accounts of its literary history. (406)

Here, Donnell articulates a no doubt inadvertently antagonistic relationship between contemporary and what may be referred to as pre-twenty-first-century Caribbean texts and, in so doing, urges critics to continue to look backward to rethink Caribbean canonicity and gaps in the field as they embrace and celebrate contemporary Caribbean writing. It is important to Donnell to see "connections across the freshly extended period" while emphasizing "distinctive forms and tropes that have emerged in isolation and yet hold interest in their connectedness" (410).

While I want to stress the fact that the aesthetics of inscrutability I outline in this book is a product that emerges from a unique cultural and historical moment instigated by the indignant frustration espoused by the *Beacon* group—a frustration that grew into a considerably more pronounced aesthetic tendency throughout the mid-twentieth century—recent works that privilege formal innovation and difficulty to consider their own intelligibility, particularly those by writers such as Anthony Joseph and Marlon James, in many ways cast a backward glance toward the experimental novels I consider in this book. In so doing, they suggest an evolving relationship between Caribbean aesthetics and inscrutability. In this sense, the proliferation of recent Caribbean experimental writing suggests that an aesthetics of inscrutability need not be relegated to the past and may indeed serve as a means to not simply reevaluate the Caribbean canon, but as a means to confront and better negotiate a Caribbean literary future.

To both read and situate twenty-first-century Caribbean novels within a larger Caribbean tradition of inscrutability and frustration can help to elucidate the complex narrative strategies of contemporary texts in new ways, especially when questions of difficulty continue to prove problematic. See, for example, Anthony Joseph's 2019 novel, *The Frequency of Magic*. In many ways, Joseph's work follows the tradition of Williams's experiments in *The Sperm of God*. Joseph, an accomplished musician, emphasizes the lyrical properties of composition and creates a novel that is tightly wound and structured, but that at every moment threatens to burst free from its narrative seams. Following a model of Oulipian experimentation, the novel—or, rather, each chapter of the novel—is rooted in a unifying narrative device: all one hundred chapters of the novel are exactly one thousand words; thus, the novel's form forces readers to consider how formal and generic constraint breed new narrative possibilities. Yet its form is not the only challenge that the novel provides. Densely written and sometimes hard to decipher, *The Frequency of Magic* centers on a metafictional struggle in which, as the story opens, the protagonist Raphael the butcher is entrenched in the midst of writing a novel that he has been working on for forty-one years and that he cannot finish. The plot of *The Frequency of Magic* is about Raphael's struggle to write the novel. Some chapters are excerpts from Raphael's unfinished book, while others focus on his life and his difficulty completing the book. The excerpts from his novel, however, are particularly difficult for readers to negotiate. Over forty-one years, the narrative of Raphael's novel and its characters become fragmented; plot lines spiral off into unforeseen or contradictory directions, while the characters' histories start to unravel, as

Raphael forgets or loses track of what he has previously written. Instead of revising or editing his work-in-progress novel to make it cohere, however, Raphael continues adding characters, subplots, and narrative threads. As it happens, Raphael's characters, who are in many ways contradictory sketches without coherent histories or consistent backstories, rebel. Together, they metafictively search for a larger meaning and significance that their maker cannot give them. Throughout the novel, they team up, conspire, and often resent the narratives that they have been given, all while Raphael continues writing and adding to their stories. The reader is thus left to make sense of a narrative landscape that both its fictional author and characters cannot understand.

In this way, meaning and understanding in the novel is repeatedly severed: the strands never entirely come together, and the reader, like the characters, must work—and come to terms with—the very idea that the narrative's larger meaning always eludes their grasp. The novel, therefore, challenges and frustrates readers in a manner that is mirrored and replicated in the experiences of the characters in Raphael's novel themselves and thereby investigates what happens to writing and fictive creation when meaning cannot be properly understood or expressed. Raphael's language always escapes him, even though he is the "author" of the text, and he struggles to write and make sense of the world. *The Frequency of Magic*, in short, asks how we make sense of a disconnected world, and readers are asked to negotiate interminable aporias. Raphael's novel becomes something powerful because it refuses to cohere, yet nevertheless offers moving and evocative snapshots of Caribbean life and suffering. Readers and characters must work to connect disparate narrative threads, and in many ways the novel demands a new way of reading, in that it seemingly goads readers to make connections that can simply not be made. In this sense, Joseph asks that his readers take a novel approach to reading *The Frequency of Magic:* they need not read linearly, he argues, but rather start where they see fit. For Joseph, "disrupting the linearity of the text" serves as a "political impetus" to embrace multitudes of reading that reflect experiences of simultaneity (Joseph).[2] He suggests that experimental forms of writing and reading reflect Caribbean experience in a way that conventional forms cannot. While, on the surface, the text may resemble earlier experiments with form like Julio Cortázar's *Rayuela*, Joseph has Caribbean experience firmly in mind, reminding readers that the goal of the text is to, in many ways, break free of Eurocentric traditions and imagine a Caribbean literary space that "dash[es] 'way Hemingway and Henry James, and praise Earl Lovelace instead" (85).

Compellingly, *The Frequency of Magic* provides a self-reflexive analysis of the anxieties that inscrutability produces. In one chapter, a villainous character called the Bandit bests his heroic adversary, Luke, and, to his surprise, finds pages written by the author—that is, Raphael the butcher—in his archenemy's back pocket. Both Luke and the Bandit are characters in Raphael's larger story, but, significantly, when the Bandit finds excerpts from this story, he cannot read or understand them. As the scene plays out, the Bandit struggles to read the pages, but he cannot make sense of what they say. His inability to comprehend drives him to despair: "Sudden images tear at the bandit's brain, the image of the butcher's writing hand, the desk facing east, the daggers of verbs and conjunctions, the impasto process of Raphael's prose. He study the page he found in Luke's pocket, but he could not decipher the old man's hand. . . . He could not know how he himself would come to be written, or whether and how he would die" (19; ellipsis added). For the Bandit, the fact that he cannot discern or process the text that he holds in his hand instills in him a pronounced sense of horror. Locked in a moment of panic, he searches tirelessly to find meaning in the inscrutable text. The absence of clarity is, for the Bandit, an utterly disenchanting experience. Inscrutability, here, is read as deviant, as the Bandit notes, "There are beasts that live in the holes of the desert, like gaps in language, like holes in the plot, beasts with smoke for eyes" (18). In this moment, the struggle to understand merges into the landscape of the narrative itself, as the generic Western scene that he and Luke are forced to interminably play out becomes smoking "holes in the desert" that make no sense. Nevertheless, the Bandit's greater fear is not just that he cannot understand the story or his part in it *but the very idea that someone else can.* The Bandit fears that his rival, Luke, *can* understand the story; that Luke knows what happens, and that the story is inscrutable *only* to himself.

Yet the Bandit in fact misunderstands the author's goal as, indeed, aporia and absence, *The Frequency of Magic* suggests, generates potential moments of profound creativity. As Raphael the author later affirms, the gaps in his writing serve as a form of creative empowerment. He writes that "he knew that words should be allowed to land where they would, and not be subsumed by fixed meaning, that poetry created meaning in the gaps of language" (122). Joseph's novel, in other words, depicts a world in which its very characters are frustrated by an interminable, deliberately impossible attempt to make sense of their own narratives. In this case, the characters become fictive readers who share the literal reader's frustrations as they struggle to discern the plot—but, as Joseph's work argues, it is the gaps in meaning and experience that reveal more about Caribbean experience than the Bandit's desire for clarity and linearity.[3] As Glissant reminds us, "Because the Caribbean notion of time was fixed in the void of an imposed nonhistory, the writer must contribute to reconstituting its tormented chronology: that is, to reveal the creative energy of a dialectic reestablished between nature and culture in the Caribbean" (65). In this way, Joseph's work negotiates a tormented chronology that cannot simply be reordered, but must instead be confronted again and again. To do so, the novel suggests, is both an act of profound frustration and disorientation, but ultimately one that rejects the constraints of a fixed meaning.

In many ways, the lack of critical attention given to *The Frequency of Magic* implies a continued hesitancy to think through the readerly implications of difficult forms. At the same time, the novel emphasizes the importance—and, in many ways, contemporary relevance—of the aesthetics of inscrutability outlined in this book. By situating contemporary works like Joseph's in a historical trajectory of works that emphasize readerly frustration as a means to negotiate Caribbean aporia and trauma, we can perhaps begin to establish new connections between contemporary Caribbean literature and its literary forbears. An embrace of the potentiality of frustration as a form of Caribbean reading and engagement may not only serve, then, as a way to chart new methods of analysis for rethinking midcentury formal experimentation in the Caribbean, but also as an avenue to rethink the relationship between a Caribbean literary past and Caribbean literary present.

Joseph's work, in embracing acts of narrative impasse that become metafictional experiences of crisis, returns us to the central moment of artistic and aesthetic impasse where I began this book: the inextricable relationship between frustration and artistic production, and the very idea that the Caribbean novel is locked in an endeavor to enunciate what cannot be readily expressed. As such, this book has sought to posit the potential of inscrutability, and the resulting frustration it engenders, as a means of reading that embraces Caribbean experience of trauma and fracture. My aim was to demonstrate how we might reevaluate pejorative connotations of inscrutability by thinking through the unique problems of reception that such texts offer and demand from their readers. As each chapter of this book has shown, the struggle to articulate colonial trauma and Caribbean experience—or, rather, the failure to do so in linear or scrutable terms—embraces readerly frustration as a way to confront often-inexpressible practices of colonial violence. In examining the implications of the reader's frustration and struggle to understand, I have worked to show how the narrative strategies of writers such as Denis Williams, Vera Bell, and Lindsay Barrett offer new ways of seeing and processing indigeneity, linguistic impasse, and moments of violence that challenge the nature of how such experiences of crisis can be represented in literary form. In the process, I have sought to present the landscape of mid-twentieth-century Caribbean fiction as a site of powerful and profound creativity that experiments with form and narration to reverberate legacies of colonial trauma in increasingly unsettling and inventive ways.

Notes

Introduction

1. This dated and in many ways restrictive view of Caribbean literature has been largely undone by recent critical work, including that of Brown and Rosenberg's *Beyond Windrush* and Donnell's *Twentieth-Century Caribbean Literature*. Archival work conducted by Donnell, as well as a renewed focus on largely ignored writers like Andrew Salkey, has been particularly important in rethinking the anglophone Caribbean canon. The notion that the *Beacon* represents the starting point of Caribbean literature has also been undercut by the publication of forgotten nineteenth-century novels that situate Caribbean literature in considerably broader historical terms (Rosenberg 13).

2. In *Nationalism and the Formation of Caribbean Literature,* Rosenberg details the conservative politics of Gomes and Mendes. As she puts it, "The unrevolutionary nature of the Beacon's politics challenges the nationalist and teleological history of West Indian literature because they demonstrate that literature and political action did not progress hand in hand toward anticolonial nationalism in Trinidad. The Beacon may have had a relatively revolutionary aesthetics, but the political agenda of Gomes and Mendes, who dominated the journal, was decidedly less anticolonial than much of the black middle class and Indo-Trinidadian political establishment" (157). The conflicting ideologies and politics of the writers and editors associated with the *Beacon* thus reveals a snapshot of the magazine that is considerably more conflicted and contradictory in its aims than is often acknowledged.

3. For more on these contradictions, see Reinhard's *Trinidad Awakening*.

4. The infamous short story contest was not, it should be noted, the only impetus for the editors' rage. In 1933, a year after the short story editorial, the group published another attack on the literary scene—this time aimed at literary clubs—in which they argued that "the very atmosphere" of the clubs "reeks of an unctuousness, a stupid formality and hypocrisy, from which any man or woman of true artistic sensibilities would flee in disgust" (2). The group's scathing critique of the clubs was in keeping with their critique of the short story contest: mainly,

they were critical that the aesthetic the clubs embraced was rooted in British cultural traditions. As they write, "It is important, moreover, that we break away as far as possible from the English tradition. . . . To label a childish tampering with the classics paving the way towards a West Indian literature is to be not only amusing but down-right dishonest" (11, no. 12 [June 1933]: 3). As made evident by the repudiation of the clubs and short story submissions, the *Beacon*'s editorial articles express not just a sense of disenchantment with the colonial authority, as it were, but an even more pronounced frustration with the artists and writers in their audience who were failing to create anticolonial art.

5. For more on rethinking the role of the midcentury in Caribbean studies, see Felski's "Writing at the End of Empire"; and Emery's "Questioning Modernism."

6. See Perry's *London Is the Place for Me,* pp. 44–47.

7. For more on the federation, see Duke's *Building a Nation.*

8. In *Conscripts of Modernity,* Scott explores what he calls the temporality of the problem-space, a term that "is meant first of all to demarcate a discursive context, a context of language. But it is more than a cognitively intelligible arrangement of concepts, ideas, images, meanings, and so on—though it certainly is this. It is a context of argument and, therefore, one of intervention . . . an ensemble of questions and answers around which a horizon of identifiable stakes (conceptual as well as ideological-political stakes) hangs. That is to say, what defines this discursive context are not only the particular problems that get posed as problems . . . but the particular questions that seem worth asking and the kinds of answers that seem worth having" (4). Scott's desire to ask new questions through which to evaluate both Caribbean and postcolonial literature is important in that it suggests critics should force themselves to consistently reevaluate and question the approaches through which they examine historical artifacts in lieu of contemporary events.

9. Contra to romance, Scott argues for a reemphasis on tragedy that has "significant implications for how we think the connections among past, present, and future" in that it "questions . . . the view of human history as moving teleologically and transparently toward a determinate end, or as governed by a sovereign and omnisciently rational agent" (12). Scott continues: "Tragedy sets before us the image of a man or woman obliged to act in a world in which values are unstable and ambiguous. And consequently, for tragedy the relation between past, present, and future is never a Romantic one in which history rides a triumphant and seamlessly progressive rhythm, but a broken series of paradoxes and reversals in which human action is ever open to unaccountable contingencies—and luck" (13). Most important here is Scott's view of tragedy as a kind of breakage and reversal—or a breakdown of linear progression. Of course, given Scott's project—which seeks to rethink how we view concepts of anticolonial resistance after those forms of resistance fail to subvert systems of capitalist and imperial oppression—his critique of the problem of anticolonial romance makes sense. He thus foregrounds the idea

that the questions we ask today about postcolonial literature and resistance need to shift to acknowledge what he calls the tragic times of the present (210).

10. See also Benwell, James, and Robinson, *Postcolonial Audiences*.

11. As Hall writes, "The degrees of 'understanding' and 'misunderstanding' in the communicative exchange—depend on the degrees of symmetry/asymmetry (relations of equivalence) established between the positions of the 'personifications,' encoder-producer and decoder-receiver. . . . What are called 'distortions' or 'misunderstandings' arise precisely from the lack of equivalence between the two sides in the communicative exchange. Once again, this defines the 'relative autonomy,' but 'determinateness,' of the entry and exit of the message in its discursive moments" (510).

12. As Barthes explains in *S/Z,* in the readerly text the reader is rendered inactive and stagnant. He writes that in such a text, "[the] reader is thereby plunged into a kind of idleness . . . instead of gaining access to the magic of the signification, to the pleasure of writing, he is left no more than the poor freedom either to accept or reject the text: reading is nothing more than a *referendum*. Opposite the writerly text, then, its countervalue, its negative, reactive value: what can be read, but not written: the *readerly*. We call any readerly text a classic text" (4).

13. For more on the distinctions between realist and opaque texts, see Glissant. For example, in *Caribbean Discourse,* using the example of *Roots,* Glissant argues that a realist work "can go directly toward its objective, which in this situation is to clarify, at least to simplify *in order to be better understood*. This no doubt explains the impact of *Roots* by Alex Haley, whose aim was to bring to light an obliterated historical continuum" (107–8). While Glissant does not deny the success of *Roots,* he nevertheless is skeptical of the degree to which it—and narratives like it—embrace simplification to the extent that they often undermine the complexity of the historical event they seek to narrate. Glissant is particularly critical of the novel's "calm picture of the journey by slave ship" and its simplistic, idealistic ending (108).

14. Building off the work of Craps in *Postcolonial Witnessing,* in "Decolonizing Trauma Theory" Visser argues that if contemporary trauma theory is to shed its Eurocentric focus, it must unshackle itself from an overreliance on psychoanalysis and "its emphasis on melancholia and stasis" (20). In turn, Visser contends that trauma studies can take on a more recuperative focus, noting that "in postcolonial studies today, trauma is recognized as a very complex phenomenon. It is not only understood as acute, individual, and event-based, but also as collective and chronic; trauma can weaken individuals and communities, but it can also lead to a stronger sense of identity and a renewed social cohesion" (20).

15. Brown's study differs from other interpretations of Caribbean modernism in that it situates Caribbean writing abroad as more engaged within local and national literary communities than often acknowledged. He contends that, "far from writing in splendid, anticolonial isolation," such authors and texts "were necessarily enmeshed in the local politics of British literary production" (9). Taking

a page from Bourdieu, Brown's text reveals how such authors "were obliged to negotiate an ostensibly colonial publishing structure in order to tender their own anticolonial message—in a form recognizable within that very structure" (9).

16. Perhaps Pollard's most important contribution is in his rethinking of Caribbean modernism in terms of discrepant cosmopolitanism. He argues that "an understanding of modernism as discrepant and cosmopolitan better recognizes the subtle duality of this synergy and divergence" (19).

17. Brathwaite's essay does not focus solely on frustration. He argues that the contemporary Caribbean novel should be divided into three categories, each of which confronts the reality of Caribbean life in different ways. He suggests, in turn, that there are those novels created to "accept the situation"—works such as Lovelace's 1965 novel, *While Gods Were Falling,* and Wynter's 1962 novel, *The Hills of Hebron.* These works, he contends, negotiate a sense of consolation while also reluctantly accepting the current situation. He also investigates works, such as those by writers like Wilson Harris, that divert from a reliance on acceptance or frustration and attempt instead to create an alternative tradition (8).

18. See both versions of Brathwaite's "West Indian Prose Fiction in the Sixties" in *Critical Survey* (1967) and *Caribbean Quarterly* (1970).

19. In examining fictions of "moral degeneracy," Rosenberg analyzes the extent to which the *Beacon* group's fictions attempt to invert the social order by framing those who held economic and cultural power as fundamentally immoral. As she writes, "The *Beacon* group sought in short to turn Trinidad's moral order on its head, making the nonmarrying working class the image of the national identity while highlighting the moral degeneracy of the ostensibly respectable upper classes" (124).

20. This point brings to mind Benítez-Rojo's contention in *The Repeating Island* that Caribbean literature functions as a site of turbulence, in which the reader must negotiate two distinctly unique forms of reading, one rooted in an epistemology that functions as an attempt to think beyond and outside the confines of Caribbean space, and another that seemingly cannot escape that space. "The Caribbean text," Benítez-Rojo writes, "is excessive, dense, uncanny, asymmetrical, entropic, hermetic, all this because, in the fashion of a zoo or bestiary, it opens its doors to two great orders of reading: one of a secondary type, epistemological, profane, diurnal, and linked to the West—the world outside—where the text uncoils itself and quivers like a fantastic beast to be the object of knowledge and desire; another, the principal order, teleological, ritual, nocturnal, referring the Caribbean itself, where the text unfolds its bisexual sphinxlike monstrosity toward the void of its impossible origin, and dreams that it incorporates this, or is incorporated by it" (23). Ultimately, in articulating these competing methodologies of reading, Benítez-Rojo postulates a decentered vision of reading and understanding in the Caribbean.

The Repeating Island, however, has long proved controversial. Torres-Saillant, for example, accuses Benítez-Rojo of looking at the Caribbean through "borrowed eyes" for citing too much critical theory and embracing what Torres derisively calls the "postmodern perspective" (41) and argues instead that we must accept that the Caribbean is "an area that has produced its own metadiscourse with which to speak about its own cultural artifacts" (42). More recently, Niblett's critique of Benítez-Rojo in his book *The Caribbean Novel since 1945* is that it ignores the larger sociopolitical implications of fracture and chaos, so much so that, "social conflict is evacuated, so that those polyrhythmic cultural practices now appear inherently emancipatory" (7). Niblett concludes that Benítez-Rojo does not provide a "consideration of the social formation that might materialize this potential: creolization or polyrhythmic interaction of cultures is reduced to an 'aesthetic experience.'" (17).

1. The Politics of Interruption

1. A similar strategy is evident throughout Reid's corpus, particularly in his 1949 novel *New Day,* which creates a fictional version of the 1865 Morant Bay rebellion, and which Reid later revised into an educational text aimed at children, the novel *Sixty-five* (1968). The common theme in these works is that of informed, calculated physical resistance. Reid's works of fiction contend that political emancipation and social change emerges through physical conflict and struggle, and they therefore embrace a model of resistance and direct action fostered by historical knowledge and precedent.

2. Reid's approach to historical realism—especially in terms of Africa—is significantly different than that of many of his contemporaries. Unlike Brathwaite or Williams, who went to Africa in an effort to experience and negotiate their ancestral connections more overtly, the Africa of *The Leopard* is purely imaginative. Though *The Leopard* is set in Kenya, and Reid claims to have thoroughly researched the landscape and people of which he writes, he nevertheless argued that direct and personal experience was not necessary to write the novel. In addition, in the absence of the author's direct experience, Reid contended that Caribbean audiences might connect to the novel's African focus by acknowledging what he perceived as glaring geographical similarities between Africa and the Caribbean, and the many parallels that exist between the landscapes of both regions. Indeed, Reid describes the novel's hybrid focus in a strange and fascinating 1987 interview in *The Journal of West Indian Literature,* in which he argued that he created his vision of Africa in the novel by merging it into the landscape of Gordon Town, Jamaica, where he lived while writing the novel. As he put it, "Now here I am in Jamaica, how many thousand miles away from Africa, never been there, and to write about the Africans! . . . I decided to steep myself in African lore, in African experiences . . . and since I was then living in Gordon Town right across from a huge mountain, I decided that this could do very well for Africa and so it turned out that I would sit at this window and watch this almost-jungle across the river from us because we lived right on the bank of the river in a big old house. And I would sit there and watch this place and get to know the countryside properly

and since I knew that the book would have to deal a good deal with rain, I would spend literally hours watching the rain fall on the side of the mountain, see how it leaked down through the trees, see how it talked to the roof, how it splashed in the puddles of the river and so on, and imagine that I'm Kenya (which was fairly easy because there was hardly any difference, except that Kenya is a bit higher than Gordon Town)" (6). Reid's presumably tongue-and-cheek assertion "that there was hardly any difference" between Kenya and Gordon Town no doubt undermines *The Leopard*'s status as a historical novel, but it also foregrounds the textual relationship between history and the imaginary. At the same time, it immediately calls into question the veracity and accuracy of the novel's African landscape. The interview reminds us that what Reid is doing in the novel is less an accurate rendering than an attempt to process and understand Africa through a Caribbean lens.

3. Brathwaite, too, is skeptical of what he perceives as superficial forms of African cultural connection in the Caribbean novel. He is particularly critical of what he calls "rhetorical" representations of Africa. As he explains, in such literature "the writer uses Africa as mask, signal, or *nomen*. He doesn't know very much about Africa necessarily, although he reflects a deep desire to make connection. But he is only saying the word 'Africa' or invoking a dream of the Congo, Senegal, Niger, the Zulu, Nile, or Zambesi. He is not necessarily celebrating or activating the African presence" (80–81).

4. Most critics have not provided any critical analysis of the use of Kikuyu in the text. Craig, in *The White Spaces of Kenyan Settler Writing*, argues that the novel's use of African language is ineffective: "Reid's novel is written in his characteristic over-lyricized style that makes the entry into a Kikuyu mind seem almost religious, if not exactly convincing. . . No real attempt is made to translate ideas via the Kikuyu language" (48). For Craig, the novel fails to capture the concepts and culture of the Kikuyu people it tries to represent.

5. Donnell, "Gender, Genre, and Lost Caribbean Voices," 85–86.

6. As Fanon writes in *The Wretched of the Earth*, "The colonialist bourgeoisie had hammered into the native's mind the idea of a society of individuals where each person shuts himself up in his own subjectivity, and whose only wealth is individual thought. Now the native who has the opportunity to return to the people during the struggle for freedom will discover the falseness of this theory. The very forms of organization of the struggle will suggest to him a different vocabulary. Brother, sister, friend—these are words outlawed by the colonialist bourgeoisie, because for them my brother is my purse, my friend is part of my scheme for getting on" (47).

7. Studies of metafiction and the postcolonial are, of course, not relegated to the Caribbean. See, for example, Mwangi's *Africa Writes Back to Self*.

8. See D'haen, "History, (Counter-)Postmodernism, and Postcolonialism" (205–16).

9. It should be noted that metafiction is not the same is historiographic metafiction. Hutcheon posits a distinction between the two, arguing that "historiographic

metafiction, in deliberate contrast to what I would call such late modernist radical metafiction, attempts to demarginalize the literary through confrontation with the historical, and it does so both thematically and formally" (108).

10. Hearne's invective of Patterson is among the most bitter, cutting critiques seen in Caribbean criticism and, interestingly, mirrors the kind of overt, public attack that the *Beacon* group frequently embraced. Indeed, in "The Novel as Sociology as Bore," Hearne's review of Patterson's third and last novel, *Die the Long Day* (a historical novel set in eighteenth-century Jamaica), Hearne writes, "As far as fiction is concerned, Dr. Patterson is an intruder. He moves about it with considerable intelligence, but so encumbered by extraneous equipment that we wait for him to break surface with a certain measure" (78). For Hearne, it is the "extraneous equipment" in Patterson's novels that he finds fault with—that is, he feels that the emphasis on sociology and interiority in Patterson's novel makes them unrealistic and unbelievable. "Dr. Patterson's fiction," he continues, "beginning with *Children of Sisyphus* through *An Absence of Ruins* and now, we must devoutly hope, ending with *Die The Long Day* is 'Barbie doll' fiction. It is slick, it is exact and it is corrupt. There is no life in it because Dr. Patterson cannot believe the reader needs only the North Star from the novelist to sail himself into a world of life" (79). Hearne's assessment, which is, on the one hand, seemingly moralistic in nature (in that it argues that Patterson's style is not simply problematic, but "corrupt") is also decidedly misogynist; Hearne's metaphor focusing on the sexualization of Barbie dolls is gleefully sexist, as he notes that the dolls "are obscene not because they come with little plastic breasts, penises and vaginal lips, but because they leave nothing for the child's imagination to fashion in the shape of tits, cunt and cock" (79). Thus, while Hearne is quick to assert that Patterson's characters are "dead" and "horrible" (81), and that his work offends the true Caribbean novelist's sensibilities, he is similarly quick to embrace the kind of overt misogyny typical of the period. In other words, Hearne's claim that Patterson violates Caribbean artistic tradition fails to acknowledge the deeply problematic views of sex and gender that are instilled in that very tradition.

11. In the essay, Steinmetz suggests that Patterson's work reveals an "alternative understanding of sociology" that "is unique among postcolonial sociologists in being the first fully historical postcolonial sociologist, in exploring the dialectical, reciprocal interplay between fictional and historical-sociological writing, and in placing slavery squarely at the center of his thinking. Above all, Patterson is unique in generating an original framework for the analysis of slavery centered on the category of social death, and an original historical genealogy of the concept and practice freedom itself, also grounded in experiences of slavery" (2).

12. Hearne's work has been mostly critically ignored—in part due to its romanticism, but also because it exists decidedly outside of the predominant focus on Caribbean peasantry that dominated the middle twentieth century. His work, however, has begun to garner critical attention as of late. See Brown and Rosenberg's *Beyond Windrush*.

13. Poynting provides a much more thorough list of intertextual references in his introduction to the novel.

14. See, for example, McDonald's "The Crisis of the Absurd," which remarks that the novel could be read as "a rather self-indulgent fantasy written primarily to work through an author's own problems of identity and direction and could be regarded as the least successful of Patterson's three novels" (86).

15. The novel's focus on Sartre has received some attention, a point that is addressed in David Scott's interview with Patterson, "The Paradox of Freedom." Interestingly, Patterson argues that Sartre's theory of existence guides the novel, but neither he nor Scott acknowledges the seeming mockery of Satrean philosophy in the text. The exchange occurs as follows:

> DS: It's interesting that you put it that way, because in that very brief passage that I just read—"A being deprived of essence, a willing slave of every chance event"—one notices its deliberately paradoxical character. The passage notes the power structure, that he's not merely devoid of essence but deprived of essence. He's both a willing being and an enslaved being. He's caught in a web of paradoxes.
>
> OP: And that, of course, is a very powerful philosophical trope, which is behind that Sartrean dictum that "existence precedes essence." You may be deprived of essence but you still have an existence. It's like a pure existential state, which I was trying to argue and which may well be the basis of a viable way of survival. . . . "Blackman," as the name indicates, is about black people and the black condition. So I found working through existentialism very valuable then, in that you didn't need an essence, you didn't need a tradition, you didn't need the bourgeois sort of anchorage—that, indeed, in the world in which we live, it may well be that you have the possibility of starting from scratch and creating a world for yourself. (168–69)

Patterson does not address the fact that much of Blackman's existential crisis in the novel is largely juvenile and unproductive. While Blackman no doubt rejects his place in the world and tries to start anew, his existential crisis is seldom worthwhile and frequently collapses into parody.

16. See also Baugh's "The West Indian Writer and His Quarrel with History" for an examination of the idea of history as an "intolerable pile" in *The Castle of My Skin* and Lamming's discussion of the "backward glance" in "The West Indian People."

2. To Become So Very Welsh

1. Ramraj echoes a similar sentiment in his introduction to *The Third Temptation,* arguing that the novel is marked by an "avoidance of explicit postcolonial issues" (13).

2. Robbe-Grillet's work attempts to replace individualism with objectivity. As he argues, the novel's emphasis should no longer be on individuals—or characters—but, rather, on the world itself. As he writes in *For a New Novel,* his novels seek to "renounce[e] the omnipotence of the person" (29). For Williams, the Nouveau Roman depicts a model of fiction in which there is no longer a narrative center of control; the center has been dispersed. Williams's citation of the Nouveau Roman as a means to examine identity is understandable, given his fascination with rethinking modernist forms in terms of race and violence. In "The Closeness of Profound Curiosity," James writes, "Both Denis Williams and Wilson Harris were exploring ways by which to dismantle the colonial structures implicit in the Western concept of 'realism,' a form seen as one based on a materialist concept of reality and a rigid, clock bound sense of historical time. Liberation from a colonial or postcolonial mentality involved rejection of such Western aesthetic structures" (79). James suggests that both Williams and Harris employ and distort Western aesthetic forms. In this sense, Robbe-Grillet's experimentation with time and identity was no doubt appealing to Williams, who uses it as a springboard for larger musings on oppression and exploitation in *The Third Temptation.*

3. See the work of Williams's daughter, Charlotte Williams, whose 2002 *Sugar and Slate* examines the relationship between racial oppression and contemporary Wales. See also Jane Aaron and Chris Williams's collection, *Postcolonial Wales;* and Bohata's *Postcolonialism Revisited.* These books consider the role of British oppression in the development of a Welsh identity and are particularly instructive in analyzing attempts by the British to stifle and suppress Welsh language and identity.

4. Williams was often frustrated with the reception of his work. As Evelyn Williams notes in *The Art of Denis Williams,* "Part of the critical acclaim of Williams' work was no doubt due to the novelty of his colonial status. Critical reaction to his 'alien,' 'exotic' or 'foreign' presence in the art scene was ambiguous and sometimes inept. In a *Time* magazine article, Williams was further characterized using the following words in a sequence: 'Negro,' 'threatening,' 'jungle,' 'loin-cloth,' primitive,' and 'savagery.' Even for its era the article had patronizing overtones" (31).

5. It is unclear what interview or interviews Charlotte Williams is referring to here.

6. In fact, upon repeated visits, the myth of the idyllic Welsh countryside became increasingly stained by his racial discomfort, and scenes like the confrontation with the photograph become more and more common. Enveloped by whiteness and dislocated from the site of his newfound aesthetic power, Williams once caught an image of himself in the mirror and, exclaimed, "WHAT KIND OF GHOST IS THIS? WHAT IS A BLACK MAN DOING IN THIS MAUSOLEUM? I CAN'T LIVE WITH THIS FAIRYTALE!" (*Sugar and Slate* 55).

7. Hughes's attempt to associate religion with power is not only suggested by the presence of the statue but also by the very title of the text. The "third temptation," concerning the question of religious power and temptation, is no doubt a reference to Hughes's quest for racial purification. Yet it is also a biblical temptation, in which Satan offers Christ dominion over the Earth. A discussion of this biblical reference emerges following Lho's death: moments after he dies, he ponders the third temptation of Christ and wonders, "But the third: Power? Whence it offered or conferred, who the agent?—a concept different entirely from the other two: a true temptation, profoundly horrifying, a proposition without the conditional. So he clobbered to the inescapable conclusion that power and evil are one—and divine" (46). The implication here is that Lho's death is in part a religious death, though he has expressed no religious sentiments. Given the significance of the statue of Hughes, it is almost impossible to dissociate power from religion in the text, and we can see that theme emerge here once again.

8. See Charlotte Williams's *Sugar and Slate,* which narrates a visit from African nationalist Mojolo Agbebi: "The reverend himself preferred to pray in Welsh and the Africans in Wales gave a spur to the congregations' efforts to sing and pray in their own language and to protect their culture in local chapels. Speaking Welsh was banned in schools in Wales and children caught speaking it were punished, but these Africans attested to the fact that English was not the only valid language" (30). Williams's text spends considerable time examining Hughes's hypocrisy of championing freedom for some but not others.

9. Paraphrasing his speech, Charlotte Williams recalls her father's Welshisms, such as, "What dat damn *rig-a-rig* foin' on down dere? Yuh banging round like a damn *felyfecli*" (53). Reflecting on their speech, she notes that the family spoke "the creolized, syncretic language registers that relate to station stops across Wales. We spoke Llandudno Welsh or was it Llandudno English?" (53).

10. Cambridge argues in "Denis Williams and the New Novel" that the setting and characters displays an anticolonialist sentiment, and that the novel functions, in part, as a critique of British suppression of the Welsh language. While much of Cambridge's argument is based solely on the connection between Williams and Robbe-Grillet, he does suggest that the novel "can be seen as a novel of affinity and solidarity with the subalternized people of Wales and other internal colonies of Europe" (121). Cambridge, however, does not explore this connection in any depth. For more on Welsh linguistic suppression in the mid-twentieth century, see Phillips, "New Beginning or the Beginning of the End?"

11. In terms of Caribbean literature, Williams, along with Lamming, Selvon, and other Caribbean writers living in Europe, have frequently commented on European fears of miscegenation. Williams himself once discussed an incident in London in which a shopkeeper stopped him to remark, "Betcha women don't leave you alone. What is it you chaps got?" (Dance 25). For more on miscegenation in relations to Williams and the Windrush generation, see Dance, "Matriarchs, Doves, and Nymphos."

12. See Chow, "Politics of Admittance"; and Musser, *Sensational Flesh*.

13. The full quotation appears: "Paradoxically, however, as Fanon has so perceptively shown, given the circumstances of the day, Western acceptance on this level was in fact the most unacceptable, indeed probably the most humiliating of choices open to the Colonial artist" (Locher 557).

14. As Fanon describes in the passage in question, "There is something in the mere idea, one young woman confided to me, that makes the heart skip a beat. A prostitute told me that in her early days the mere thought of going to bed with a Negro brought on an orgasm. She went in search of Negroes and never asked them for money. But, she added, 'going to bed with them was no more remarkable than going to bed with white men. It was before I did it that I had the orgasm. I used to think about (imagine) all the things they might do to me: and that was what was so terrific'" (122). Here, it is the racial fantasy of the act, and not the act itself, that gives sexual pleasure.

3. Language as Animosity

1. See Bertacco, "Translation in Caribbean Literature," in which Bertacco notes that "while Brathwaite in the late 1970s saw 'nation language' as opposed to the scribal order, today it has become such a pervasive feature of written texts that this dichotomy does not apply anymore" (21).

2. While he is generally sensitive to the political and cultural context in which Brathwaite conceived his concept of nation language, Bernstein seems unconvinced of nation language's communal and collective implications. As he argues, "Dialect, understood as nation language, has a centripetal force, regrouping often denigrated and dispirited language practices around a common center; ideolect, in contrast, suggests a centrifugal force, moving away from normative practices without necessarily replacing them with a new center of gravity, at least defined by self or group" (*My Way*, 121). Ideolect, therefore, is seen to reject the "centripetal" force of nation language.

3. For an overview of Mais's work, see also James, *Caribbean Literature in English*.

4. Interestingly, "Jazz in the West Indian Novel," Brathwaite's essay on Mais's second novel, is widely anthologized and has become, in some ways, more canonical and widely read than the novel itself. See *Roots*.

5. See Morris, "Reviewed Work: *Listen, The Wind and Other Stories*."

6. I do not mean to discount the importance of Dawes's work on Mais, as Dawes convincingly articulates what is an undoubtedly deeply misogynist framing of gender in the novel. It must be acknowledged that the representation of women in Mais's work is often deeply troubling, and that such misogyny runs deeps in the veins of an overwhelming majority of midcentury Caribbean texts.

7. See the work of Griffith, who wrestles with the role of individuality in the chorus in his book *Deconstruction, Imperialism and the West Indian Novel*. As he argues, "The choric voices in *Brother Man* are not assigned individual identities,

and yet the dialogic interchange suggests individual voices. The alternating statements and responses suggest the presence of individual community members and yet the lack of assigned names linked to the voices implies the absence of the individual" (93). For Griffith, the chorus concurrently signals moments of collectivity and individuality.

8. Brown also argues that the chorus sections and their representation of communal speech appears at odds with the speech patterns of other characters in the novel. Brown juxtaposes Papacita's self-centered, coercive speech, which he points out is described in the novel a "soft, silky voice" and operates as a "decorative distraction from his underlying ill intentions" against the communal speech of the chorus (154).

9. For more on the novel, see Ramchand, *West Indian Novel and Its Background*.

10. Toward the end of the chorus, the people see a shooting star and break into a hopeful hymn as "they lift their voices, all, and sing" (140).

11. See also Smith, "Kingston Calling," which examines Mais's complicated relationship to his own class status.

12. For more on how Walrond's work is seldom perceived in a Caribbean context, see Brown, "Escaping the Tropics."

13. See, for example, Bone, "From Down Home," which argues Walrond's work represents the uneven genesis of a burgeoning cultural tradition. Bone writes that "the quality of the collection is uneven. Certain of the stories contain lumpy autobiographical ingredients inadequately metamorphosed into art. Others, while more successfully distanced, are lacking in coherence and design" (45). Citing Robert Herrick, Bone highlights the lack of unity as an inability to properly represent reality (45). Bone contends that only five of the stories effectively captivate the reader. Bone and Herrick's observations are not uncommon; the experimental nature of the collection is often perceived as a narrative failure.

14. Davis contends further that the texts' language disorients readers. As he states, "Relying heavily on reported speech, [the text] is an extended exercise in code switching, moving deftly between vernaculars and linguistic registers" (155). *Tropic Death*'s experiments, he further suggests, are made more notable when we acknowledge that they pre-date *Banana Bottom*'s and *Minty Alley*'s experiments with language and perspective by seven and ten years (158).

15. Davis argues that Walrond was drawn to the "linguistic polyphony, intercultural contact, political alliances, and emancipatory social movements" that emerged as a result of colonialism (9).

16. According to Davis, Walrond, upon further reflection and presented with the possibility of a reissue of *Tropic Death*, considered removing the slurs from the novel (183). Yet it is almost impossible to imagine the opening of the story without their presence, in that they remind the reader of the racial hatred looming over the geography of the text.

17. It should be acknowledged that while white characters in the text, as seen in this example, are also the occasional victim of stereotypes and pejorative language, the narrator bears them considerably less animosity.

4. "The Menace from the Bush"

1. For a summary of critical approaches to Harris's work, see Poynting, "Half-Dialectical, Half-Metaphysical."

2. See the Wilson Harris Bibliography, http://www.cerep.ulg.ac.be/harris/whprim.html (accessed December 23, 2022).

3. While critics seldom read both Harris and Williams in conjunction with one another, Gilkes's "Introduction" provides a brief discussion of Williams's work in relation to Harris.

4. For an overview of how critics and readers have typically responded to issues of difficulty and reception in Harris's work, see Maes-Jelinek, "Foreword" (9–11); Williams and Riach, "Reading Wilson Harris" (51–60); and Hamlet, "Sustaining the Vision" (201–9).

5. The obituary's headline describes Harris as a "writer of intricate novels" and goes on to say, "His novels were sometimes described as difficult, eschewing conventional plotting in favor of multiple narrators, intermingling viewpoints, jumps in time and a free-form prose that demanded concentration of the reader."

6. See Lindsay, "Preparing the Palette"; and Marley, "To Become So Very Welsh."

7. For an overview of how Harris views calendrical time, see Maes-Jelinek, *Labyrinth of Universality* (xxiv); and Delfino, *Time, History, and Philosophy*.

8. In *Location of Culture,* Bhabha explores the means through which disjunction and discord serve as a central characteristic of postcolonial identity. He ponders: "How are subjects formed 'in-between', or in excess of, the sum of the 'parts' of difference (usually intoned as race/class/gender, etc.)? How do strategies of representation or empowerment come to be formulated in the competing claims of communities where, despite shared histories of deprivation and discrimination, the exchange of values, meanings and priorities may not always be collaborative and dialogical, but may be profoundly antagonistic, conflictual and even incommensurable?" (2). Like Williams, Bhabha's sense of hybridity does not result in a comfortable synthesis, but, rather, feelings of discomfort, duress, and incommensurability.

9. See Maes-Jelinek's edited collection *Wilson Harris,* which features many essays on *The Infinite Conversation* as both a text and a concept. See, in particular, Emery, "Reading 'W. H.'"; and Creighton, " Human Comedy *Carnival*" (192–99), both of which address repetition and rehearsal.

10. For more on the hopeful aspects of Harris's revisionary strategies, see the final chapter of Drake, *Wilson Harris and the Modern Tradition,* "Language and Revolutionary Hope." See also Dubois, "Redemptive Power."

11. As Gilkes argues in his review of *The Infinite Rehearsal*: "That technique of 'rehearsal' is at the root of all his work from *The Palace of the Peacock* (1960) onward, and the overwhelming concern is with avoiding the 'sovereign,' absolute nature of Tradition, or the tyranny of 'hard fact.' His use of Classical myth and allegory, or of the European literary tradition, is part of a process of reinterpreting or 'retrieving' values that have become ossified, their links with other, so-called 'primitive' cultures, lost. In the unlocking of those 'sovereign' traditions, there is a release of potential energy for creative change" (109).

12. This is a claim made, essentially, by both Sylvia Wynter and Kamau Brathwaite, whom Newton is critiquing here.

13. Going further, Jackson contends that Black identity in the Caribbean is built on the effacement of indigenous bodies: "Native displacement and either real or figurative disappearance serves as the necessary or enabling condition of black being in the Caribbean, both epistemological and ontological, and is essential for the constitution of that being through the rise of national consciousness and class consolidation" (*Creole Indigeneity* 28).

14. It is not surprising that McDougall finds fault with Harris's citation of original sin. As I have previously pointed out, critics such as Halpé are skeptical of Harris's employment of mythology and archetype. As Halpé argues, "Harris's negotiations of differing mythic systems within the Caribbean create a radically polysemous sense of narrative, but his universalist approach to archetypal image diminishes the contextual frames that provoke culturally differentiated responses to myth" ("Ideology of Archetype" 202).

15. See Wilson Harris, "Native Phenomenon."

16. In an unpublished manuscript, Harris worries that his introduction to "The Age of Kaie" should be longer and more thorough, but ultimately decides on an abbreviated note. As he writes, "This note—as with other Notes appearing in *The Age of the Rainmakers*—raised certain problems in keeping it as succinct as possible. I wanted to imply that a re-imagination of textures of Macusi and other Amerindian legend brings into play a mythical dialogue with creatures in the air, on the land or in the water that goes deeper in intuitive terms than naturalism or naturalistic premises implies. This intuition (for example take the 'savage' bat of Makonaima) seems closer to what science has to say now about various creatures that baffled naturalists in the nineteenth century who could observe them as apparently eccentric or beautiful or repulsive or diabolic. The flight of the bat, for example, appeared decidedly eccentric and off-putting to naturalists. In vestiges of Macusi legend which survive, an intuition appears to survive which relates creatures to many in an 'ultrasonic ballet' or implicit 'musical gesture'" (Healy, "Wilson Harris at Work" 93).

17. In addition to work by McWatt, Durix's "Crossing the Arawak Horizon," published in 1979, provides a close reading of the text, but is concerned primarily with patterns and symbolization in the story and does not delve into the sociocultural implications of indigenous experience in "Arawak Horizon" in any depth.

18. The word choice here is odd, as it seems to undermine the relationship between indigenous disappearance and colonialism. This point becomes even stranger, given that many of the fables directly confront colonial violence against Amerindians. After all—and as Harris well knows—indigenous peoples did not simply "vanish" of their own accord.

19. It should not, of course, be assumed that Campbell, whose politics were deeply conservative, spoke for all of Arawak culture and history; rather, my point here is that Arawak history and culture continued to be present in Guyanese society. Campbell's victory simply reiterates my assertion that indigenous representation was more visible in contemporary Guyana than Harris's texts suggest.

20. See Adonis, "His Master's Voice."

5. Rhysian Disgust and the Politics of Complancy

1. See, for example, "Literary Clubs," *Beacon* 2, no. 12 (1933), pp. 2–4; "The Literary Club Nuisance," *Beacon* 2, no. 2, pp. 1–2; and "A West Indian Literature," *Beacon* 2, no. 12 (1933), pp. 2–3. See also Hugh Stollmeyer's poem "The Time Has Come," *Beacon* 3, no. 4, (1933), pp. 85–86.

2. Sasha's much-quoted assertion is a central point of analysis in studies of the novel and, more generally, is frequently used as a lens to explore Rhys's ambiguous status in terms of nationality and literary classification. See, for example, Issacharoff, "No Pride, No Name." Similarly, Clukey's "No Country Really Now" builds off of Rhys's statement in her letters that she is "white" but has "no country" as a way to better examine Mayra's exilic isolation in *Quartet*.

3. See Lai, "The Road to Thornfield Hall"; and Ramchand, *West Indian Novel and Its Background,* for early analyses of Caribbean connections in Rhys's work.

4. Seshagiri, for example, reads Rhys's *Voyage in the Dark* as a repudiation of modernist experimentation in her essay "Modernist Ashes, Postcolonial Phoenix." Seshagiri argues that the novel rejects the formal qualities of high modernism to usher in a new postcolonial aesthetic.

5. Elsewhere, I have written on the implications of the second person in *After Leaving Mr. Mackenzie,* arguing that the novel's experiments with perspective and narration offer a damning critique of cosmopolitan tendencies that universalize the trauma and suffering of marginalized groups. See Marley, "Every Day You are a New Person."

6. This is not to discount Rhys's complex and often convoluted relation to race, both in her work and life, and that will be discussed further in this chapter.

7. For more on the relationship between shame and Rhys's work, see Moran, "The Feelings Are Always Mine." It should be noted, however, that Moran's analysis focuses more on the thematic, rather than readerly, implications of shame.

8. For a larger discussion of race in the novel, see Clarke, "Caribbean Modernism."

9. It is difficult to discuss representation in Rhys's work without, of course, acknowledging the important, if contentious, discussion of race and creole identity in *Wide Sargasso Sea* between Spivak and Parry. See Mardorossian, "Shutting up the Subaltern" for a concise summary of the debate, as well as a rethinking of how the novel negotiates racial subjectivity.

10. Seshagiri's work on the novel explicitly explores the trauma of white creole identity. As Seshagiri writes, "Having disavowed the whiteness that signifies political, moral, and intellectual authority in the colonies, Anna cannot move into any of the cultural plots available to English protagonists of imperial fiction. Her Creole identity, coupled with her impossible desire to be black, sets her apart from her peers and predecessors in early twentieth-century novels of Empire" ("Modernist Ashes" 495).

11. In contrast, Brown warns that we should be skeptical of these connections in the novel, arguing that "the novel's anticolonial bona fides appear less persuasive when examined from a perspective sensitive to the concerns of postcolonial criticism" ("Textual Entanglement," 575). Brown is wary that "the novel's tendency to equate Anna's dominated subject position as an immigrant woman in Britain with her previous life in the Caribbean is too quick to elide Anna's membership in the elite, white plantocratic society of her home island" (576) Here, Brown argues that the problematic nature of Anna's obliviousness and ignorance, combined with the novel's troubling representation of race, should warrant pause in thinking of the novel in stark, anticolonialist terms.

12. For more on the implications of these textual interruptions, see Emery, *Jean Rhys at "World's End."*

Coda

1. As Donnell reminds us in *Caribbean Literature in Transition,* questions of canon are inextricable from colonial legacy, and rethinking and remaking the Caribbean canon is an act of utmost importance: "The contestations over who counts as a Caribbean writer, who is worth remembering and who is worth acclaiming have, from the start, been entangled with the thick histories of oppression and resistance that ensued from centuries of enslavement, indenture, the plantation economy and its imperialist capitalist afterlives, including tourism. It took great exertions to imagine and realize Caribbean literatures—against the abjuration of colonialism, the repudiations of racism, and the scars of their creeping legacies and injuries over centuries" (407).

Canonization and exclusion in the Caribbean is also affected by what Donnell calls a "spotlight effect" in which shifting political, cultural, and scholarly trends sometimes leave emerging traditions and writers lurking in the shadows, while overemphasizing others (408). This was, of course, the phenomenon that embraced Windrush as the predominant critical lens through which to read Caribbean literature for much of the twentieth century.

2. See Anthony Joseph, "The Frequency of Magic," Goldsmiths College Department of Art MFA Lectures 2017–18, Series 3.2: Rhythm, YouTube video, 1:09:44, January 15, 2018, https://www.youtube.com/watch?v=lexmeTirrfQ.

3. Joseph's book, it should be noted, is doing something different than other contemporary works like Junot Díaz's *The Wondrous Life of Oscar Wao* and other works that examine themes of intelligibility. In contrast to Joseph, Díaz's Pulitzer Prize–winning novel, through its incorporation of clarifying footnotes, in many ways seeks to dismantle problems of access and translatability by providing an overview of Dominican history to which the reader might not be otherwise privy.

Bibliography

Aaron, Jane. "Slaughter and Salvation: Welsh Missionary Activity and British Imperialism." *A Tolerant Nation? Revisiting Ethnic Diversity in a Devolved Wales,* edited by Charlotte Williams, Neil Evans, and Paul O'Leary, U of Wales P, 2015, pp. 51–68.

Aaron, Jane, and Chris Williams, editors. *Postcolonial Wales.* U of Wales P, 2005.

Adonis, Isabel. "His Master's Voice." *Journal of Caribbean Literatures,* vol. 6, no. 1, 2009, pp. 161–76.

Adorno, Theodor, Walter Benjamin, Ernst Bloch, Bertolt Brecht, and Georg Lukács. *Aesthetics and Politics.* Verso, 2007.

———. *Minima Moralia: Reflections on a Damaged Life.* Translated by E. F. N. Jephcott. Verso, 2005.

Ahmed, Sara. *The Cultural Politics of Emotion.* Edinburgh UP, 2014.

Allsop, Joy. "Brother Man." *Kyk-Over-Al,* vol. 6, no. 20, 1955, pp. 159–60.

Andermahr, Sonya, editor. *Decolonizing Trauma Studies: Trauma and Postcolonialism.* MDPI, 2016.

Apter, Emily. *Against World Literature: On the Politics of Untranslatability.* Verso, 2013.

Ashcroft, Bill, Gareth Griffiths, and Helen Tiffin. *The Empire Writes Back: Theory and Practice in Post-Colonial Literatures.* Routledge, 1989.

Barrett, Lindsay. *Song for Mumu.* Longman, 1967.

Barthes, Roland. *S/Z.* Translated by Richard Miller, Hill & Wang, 1974.

———. *Writing Degree Zero.* Translated by Annette Lavers and Colin Smith, Hill & Wang, 1968.

Baugh, Edward. "The West Indian Writer and His Quarrel with History." *Small Axe,* vol. 16, no. 2, 2012, pp. 60–74.

Begam, Richard, and Michael Valdez Moses, editors. *Modernism, Postcolonialism, and Globalism: Anglophone Literature, 1950 to the Present.* Oxford UP, 2019.

Benítez-Rojo, Antonio. *The Repeating Island: The Caribbean and the Postmodern Perspective.* Translated by James E. Maraniss, Duke UP, 2001.

Bell, Vera. *Ogog*. Vintage, 1971.
Benwell, Bethan, James Procter, and Gemma Robinson, eds. *Postcolonial Audiences: Readers, Viewers and Reception*. Taylor & Francis, 2012.
Bhabha, Homi K. *The Location of Culture*. Routledge, 2004.
Bernabé, Jean, Patrick Chamoiseau, and Raphael Confiant. *Eloge de la Créolité / In Praise of Creoleness*. Gallimard, 1990.
Bernstein, Charles. *My Way: Speeches and Poems*, U of Chicago P, 1997.
Bertacco, Simona. "Translation in Caribbean Literature." *Small Axe*, vol. 24 no. 2, 2020, pp. 17–34.
Birat, Kathie. "Seeking Sam Selvon: Michel Fabre and the Fiction of the Caribbean." *Transatlantica*, vol. 1, 2009, pp. 1–10.
Boehmer, Elleke. *Postcolonial Poetics: 21st-Century Critical Readings*. Palgrave Macmillan, 2018.
Bohata, Kirsti. *Postcolonialism Revisited: Writing Wales in English*. U of Wales P, 2004.
Bone, Richard. "From Down Home: Origins of the Afro-American Short Story." In Parascandola and Wade, pp. 35–54.
Borzaga, Michela. "Trauma in the Postcolony: Towards a new Theoretical Approach." *Trauma, Memory, and Narrative in the Contemporary South African Novel: Essays*, edited by Ewald Mengel and Michela Borzaga, Rodopi, 2012, pp. 65–92.
Brathwaite, Kamau (Edward K). *The African Presence in Caribbean Literature*. American Academy of Arts and Sciences, 1974.
———. *History of the Voice: Development of Nation Language in Anglophone Caribbean Poetry*. New Beacon Books, 1984.
———. "Introduction." *Brother Man*, by Roger Mais, Heinemann, 1974.
———. *Roots*. U of Michigan P, 1993.
———. "West Indian Prose Fiction in the Sixties: A Survey." *Critical Survey*, vol. 3, no. 3, 1967, pp. 169–74.
———. "West Indian Prose Fiction in the Sixties: A Survey." *Caribbean Quarterly*, vol. 16, no. 4, 1970, pp. 5–17.
Breiner, Laurence A. *An Introduction to West Indian Poetry*. Cambridge UP, 1998.
Brown, J. Dillon. "Escaping the Tropics through New York: Eric Walrond and Claude McKay in the American Grain." *Global South*, vol. 7, no. 2, 2013, pp. 37–61.
———. *Migrant Modernism: Postwar London and the West Indian Novel*. U of Virginia P, 2013.
———. "Textual Entanglement: Jean Rhys's Critical Discourse." *Modern Fiction Studies*, vol. 56, no. 3, 2010, pp. 568–91.
Brown, J. Dillon, and Leah Reade Rosenberg, editors. *Beyond Windrush: Rethinking Postwar Anglophone Caribbean Literature*. U of Mississippi P, 2015.
———. "Introduction: Looking beyond Windrush." In Brown and Rosenberg, pp. 3–23.

Bulkan, Janette. "The Struggle for Recognition of the Indigenous Voice: Amerindians in Guyanese Politics." *Round Table,* vol. 102, no. 4, 2013, pp. 367–80.

Cambridge, Vibert C. "Denis Williams and the New Novel: The Status of *The Third Temptation.*" In Williams and Williams, pp. 111–24.

Caruth, Cathy. *Unclaimed Experience: Trauma, Narrative, and History.* Johns Hopkins UP, 1996.

Chetty, Raj. "'Prophet of a Coming New World': Eric Walrond at the Crossroads of Pan-Caribbean, Pan-American, and Pan-African Literary Studies." *Anthurium: A Caribbean Studies Journal,* vol. 11, no. 9, 2014, pp. 1–7.

Chow, Rey. "The Politics of Admittance: Female Sexual Agency, Miscegenation, and the Foundation of Community in Frantz Fanon." *The Rey Chow Reader,* edited by Paul Bowman, Columbia UP, 2010, pp. 56–75.

Clarke, Joseph. "Caribbean Modernism and the Postcolonial Social Contract in *Voyage in the Dark.*" *Journal of Caribbean Literatures,* vol. 3, no. 3, 2003, pp. 1–16.

Clukey, Amy. "No Country Really Now: Modernist Cosmopolitanisms and Jean Rhys's *Quartet.*" *Twentieth-Century Literature,* vol. 56, no. 4, 2010, pp. 437–61.

Collier, Gordon, editor. *Derek Walcott, The Journeyman Years, Volume 1: Culture, Society, Literature.* Rodopi, 2013.

Craig, Terrence L. *The White Spaces of Kenyan Settler Writing: A Polemical Bibliography.* Brill, 2017.

Craps, Stef. *Postcolonial Witnessing: Trauma Out of Bounds.* Palgrave Macmillan, 2013.

Creighton, Al. "The Human Comedy *Carnival* and *The Infinite* Rehearsal." In Maes-Jelinek, pp. 192–99.

"Cultural Clubs." *Beacon,* vol. 11, no. 12, 1933, pp. 2–3.

Cummings, Ronald, and Alison Donnell, editors. *Caribbean Literature in Transition, 1970–2020.* Cambridge UP, 2020.

Czarnecki, Kristin. "'Born in a Hot Place': Kristevan Foreignness in Jean Rhys's *Voyage in the Dark.*" *CEA Critic,* vol. 73, no. 1, 2010, pp. 15–33.

———. "Jean Rhys's Postmodern Narrative Authority: Selina's Patois in 'Let Them Call It Jazz.'" *College Literature,* vol. 35, no. 2, 2008, pp. 20–37.

D'haen, Theo. "History,' (Counter-)Postmodernism, and Postcolonialism." *European Journal of English Studies,* vol. 1, no. 2, 1997, pp. 205–16.

Davis, James. *Eric Walrond: A Life in the Harlem Renaissance and the Transatlantic Caribbean.* Columbia UP, 2015.

Dalleo, Ralph. *Caribbean Literature and the Public Sphere: From the Plantation to the Postcolonial.* U of Virginia P, 2011.

———. "The Public Sphere and Jamaican Anticolonial Politics: *Public Opinion, Focus,* and the Place of the Literary." *Small Axe,* no. 32, vol. 14, 2010, pp. 56–82.

Dalleo, Raphael, and Curdella Forbes, editors. *Caribbean Literature in Transition, 1920–1970.* Cambridge UP, 2020.

Dalley, Hamish. *The Postcolonial Historical Novel Realism, Allegory, and the Representation of Contested Pasts.* Palgrave Macmillan, 2014.

Dance, Daryl Cumber. "Matriarchs, Doves, and Nymphos: Prevalent Images of Black, Indian, and White Women in Caribbean Literature." *Studies in the Literary Imagination,* vol. 26, no. 2, 1993, pp. 21–31.

Dawes, Kwame S. "Violence and Patriarchy: Male Domination in Roger Mais's *Brother Man.*" *ariel: A Review of International English Literature,* vol. 25, no. 3, 1994, pp. 29–49.

Deena, Seodial Frank H. *Situating Caribbean Literature and Criticism in Multicultural and Postcolonial Studies.* Peter Lang, 2008.

Delfino, Gianluca. *Time, History, and Philosophy in the Works of Wilson Harris.* Ibidem Verlag, 2014.

Dell'Amico, Carol. *Colonialism and the Modernist Moment in the Early Novels of Jean Rhys.* Routledge, 2006.

Dubois, Dominique. "The Redemptive Power of Bone's Revisionary Fiction." In Maes-Jelinek and Ledent, pp. 196–204.

Donnell, Alison. "'The African Presence in Caribbean Literature' Revisited: Recovering the Politics of Imagined Co-Belonging, 1930–2005." *Research in African Literatures,* vol. 46, no. 4, 2015, pp. 35–55.

———. "Caribbean Literature and Literary Studies: Past, Present, and Future." In Cummings and Donnell, pp. 405–25.

———. "Gender, Genre, and Lost Caribbean Voices." In Brown and Reade, pp. 79–96.

———. *Twentieth-Century Caribbean Literature: Critical Moments in Anglophone Literary History.* Routledge, 2006.

Donnell, Alison, and Michael A. Bucknor, editors. *The Routledge Companion to Anglophone Caribbean Literature.* Routledge, 2011.

Donnell, Alison, and Sarah Lawson Welsh, editors. *The Routledge Reader in Caribbean Literature.* Routledge, 1997.

Draper, Christopher, and Lawson-Reay, John. *Scandal at the Congo House: Williams Hughes and the African Institute, Colwyn Bay.* Gwasg Carreg Gwalch, 2012.

Drake, Sandra E. *Wilson Harris and the Modern Tradition: A New Architecture of the World.* Greenwood, 1986.

Duke, Eric D. *Building a Nation: Caribbean Federation in the Black Diaspora.* UP of Florida, 2015.

Durix, Jean-Pierre. "Crossing the Arawak Horizon." *Literary Half-Yearly,* vol. 20, 1979, pp. 83–92.

———. "The Legacy of the Imagination: Reading Wilson Harris after Hena Maes-Jelinek." *The Cross-Cultural Legacy: Critical and Creative Writings in Memory of Hena Maes-Jelinek,* edited by Gordon Collier, Brill, 2016, pp. 67–80.

Edwards, Nadi. "Contexts, Criticism, and Quarrels: A Reflection on Edward Baugh's 'The West Indian Writer and His Quarrel with History.'" *Small Axe,* vol. 16, no. 2, 2012, pp. 99–107.
Edwards, Norval (Nadi). "Tradition, the Critic, and Cross-Cultural Poetics: Wilson Harris as Literary Theorist." *Journal of West Indian Literature,* vol. 16, no. 2, 2008, pp. 1–30.
Ellis, David. "'The Produce of More Than One Country': Race, Identity, and Discourse in Post-Windrush Britain." *Journal of Narrative Theory,* vol. 31, no. 2, 2001, pp. 214–32.
Emery, Mary Lou. "Caribbean Modernism: Plantation to Planetary." In Wollaeger, pp. 48–77.
———. *Jean Rhys at "World's End": Novels of Colonial and Sexual Exile.* Texas UP, 1990.
———. *Modernism, the Visual, and Caribbean Literature.* Cambridge UP, 2007.
———. "The Poetics of Labor in Jean Rhys's Global Modernism." *Philological Quarterly,* vol. 90, no. 2, 2011, pp. 173–203.
———. "On the Veranda: Jean Rhys's Material Modernism." In Johnson and Moran, pp. 59–82.
———. "Reading 'W.H.' Draft of an Incomplete Conversation." In Maes-Jelinek, pp. 171–83.
———. "Questioning Modernism: The 1950s–1960s." In Dalleo and Forbes, pp. 37–51.
Fanon, Frantz. *Black Skin, White Masks.* Translated by Charles Lam Markmann, Pluto, 2008.
———. *A Dying Colonialism.* Translated by Haakon Chevalier, Grove, 1965.
———. *The Wretched of the Earth.* Translated by Richard Philcox, Grove, 2004.
Fehskens, Erin M. "The Epic Hero in Wilson Harris's *Palace of the Peacock.*" *Journal of Modern Literature,* vol. 41, no. 4, 2018, pp. 90–106.
Felski, Erin M. "Writing at the End of Empire." In Dalleo and Forbes, pp. 21–36.
Fenwick, Mac. "Fenwick's Vision: Liberal Tyranny in *The Guyana Quartet.*" *ariel: A Review of International English Literature,* vol. 32, no. 2, 2001, pp. 45–66.
Forte, Maximilian C. "Introduction: The Dual Absences of Extinction and Marginality—What Difference Does an Indigenous Presence Make?" *Indigenous Resurgence in the Contemporary Caribbean: Amerindian Survival and Revival,* edited by Maximilian C. Forte, Peter Lang, 2006, pp. 1–18.
Francis, Donette. "Radical Skepticisms: Literatures of the Long Jamaican 1960s." *Small Axe,* vol. 21, no. 3, 2017 pp. 48–62.
———. "'Transcendental Cosmopolitanism:' Orlando Patterson and the Novel Jamaican 1960s." *Journal of Transnational American Studies,* vol. 5, no. 1, 2013.
Frederick, Rhonda D. *"Colón Man a Come": Mythographies of Panamá Canal Migration.* Lexington, 2005.

Fumagalli, Maria Cristina. *Caribbean Perspectives on Modernity: Returning Medusa's Gaze.* U of Virginia P, 2009.

Gamal, Ahmed. "Rewriting Strategies in Tariq Ali's Postcolonial Metafiction." *Postcolonial Text,* vol. 6, no. 4, 2011, pp. 1–19.

Gąsiorek, Andrzej. "'(The Knocking) Has Never Stopped': Jean Rhys's (Post)colonial Modernism." In Begam and Moses, pp. 163–80.

Genzlinger, Neil. "Wilson Harris, Guyanese Writer of Intricate Novels, Dies at 96." *New York Times,* 16 March 2018, www.nytimes.com/2018/03/16/obituaries/wilson-harris-guyanese-writer-of-intricate-novels-dies-at-96.html.

Gikandi, Simon. *Maps of Englishness: Writing Identity in the Culture of Colonialism.* Columbia UP, 1996.

———. *Writing in Limbo: Modernism and Caribbean Literature.* Cornell UP, 1992.

Gilkes, Michael. "Book Review: Wilson Harris, *The Infinite Rehearsal.* Faber & Faber, 1987." *Kunapipi,* vol. 11, no. 3, 1989, pp. 108–11.

Gilkes, Michael, editor. *The Literate Imagination: Essays on the Novels of Wilson Harris.* Macmillan, 1989.

———. *Wilson Harris and the Caribbean Novel.* Longman, 1975.

Glissant, Édouard. *Caribbean Discourse: Selected Essays.* Translated by J. Michael Dash, U Virginia P, 1999.

———. *Poetics of Relation.* Translated by Betsy Wing, U of Michigan P, 2010.

———. *Treatise on the Whole-World.* Translated by Celia Britton, Liverpool UP, 2020.

Griffith, Glyne A. *The BBC and the Development of Anglophone Caribbean Literature, 1943–1958.* Palgrave Macmillan, 2016.

———. *Deconstruction, Imperialism, and the West Indian Novel.* UP of the West Indies, 1995.

Goble, Mark. "Obsolescence." *A New Vocabulary for Global Modernism,* edited by Eric Hayot and Rebecca L. Walkowitz, Columbia UP, 2016, pp. 146–68.

Gonzalez, Maria Cristina. "An Ethics for Postcolonial Ethnography." *Expressions of Ethnography: Novel Approaches to Qualitative Methods,* edited by Robin Patric Clair, State University of New York P, 2003, pp. 77–86.

Gregg, Veronica Marie. *Jean Rhys's Historical Imagination: Reading and Writing the Creole.* U of North Carolina P, 1995.

Gunne, Sorcha. "Mind the Gap: An Interview with Neil Lazarus." *Postcolonial Text,* vol. 6, no. 3, 2012, pp. 1–15.

Hall, Stuart. "Encoding, Decoding." *The Cultural Studies Reader,* edited by Simon During. Routledge, 1993, pp. 507–17.

Halpé, Aparna. "The Ideology of Archetype Mythical Strategies in Wilson Harris's *Jonestown.*" *Interférences Littéraires/Literaire Interferenties,* vol. 17, 2015, pp. 199–212.

Hamlet, Desmond. "Sustaining the Vision." In Maes-Jelinek, *Wilson Harris*, pp. 201–9.

Harris, Wilson. *Ascent to Omai*. Faber, 1970.

———. *The Eye of the Scarecrow*. Peepal Tree, 2011.

———. "The Fabric of the Imagination Author." *Third World Quarterly*, vol. 12, no. 1, 1990, pp. 175–86.

———. *Heartland*. Peepal Tree, 2009.

———. "History, Fable, and Myth in the Guianas." *Beacons of Excellence: The Edgar Mittelholzer Memorial Lectures, Volume 1: 1967–1971*, edited by Andrew O. Lindsay, Caribbean Press, 2014, pp. 153–202.

———. "The Native Phenomenon." *Common Wealth*, edited by Anna Rutherford, Aarhus, 1971, pp. 144–50.

———. *The Guyana Quartet*. Faber & Faber, 1986.

———. *Selected Essays of Wilson Harris: The Unfinished Genesis of the Imagination*, edited by Andrew Bundy, Routledge, 1999.

———. *The Sleepers of Roraima & The Age of the Rainmakers*. Peepal Tree, 2014.

———. *Tumatumari*. Faber, 1968.

Harrison, Sheri-Marie. *Jamaica's Difficult Subjects: Negotiating Sovereignty in Anglophone Caribbean Literature and Criticism*. Ohio State UP, 2014.

Healy, J. J. "Wilson Harris at Work: The Texas Manuscripts with Special Reference to the Mayakovsky Resonance in *Ascent to Omai*." *ariel: A Review of International English Literature*, vol. 15, no. 4, 1984, pp. 89–107.

Hearne, John. "The Novel as Sociology as Bore." *Caribbean Quarterly: A Journal of Caribbean Culture*, vol. 18, no. 4, 1972, pp. 78–81.

Hughes, Rev. W. *Dark Africa and the Way Out, or A Scheme for Civilizing and Evangelizing the Dark Continent*. Negro Universities Press, [1892] 1960.

Hulme, Peter. *Colonial Encounters: Europe and the Native Caribbean, 1492–1797*. Methuen, 1986.

Hutcheon, Linda A. *Poetics of Postmodernism: History, Theory, Fiction*. Routledge, 1988.

Issacharoff, Jess. "'No Pride, No Name, No Face, No Country': Jewishness and National Identity in *Good Morning, Midnight*." In Wilson and Johnson, pp. 111–29.

Jackson, Shona. *Creole Indigeneity: Between Myth and Nation in the Caribbean*. Minnesota UP, 2012.

James, C. L. R. *Minty Alley*. UP of Mississippi, 1997.

James, Louis. *Caribbean Literature in English*. Routledge, 1999.

———. "'The Closeness of Profound Curiosity': The Parallel Visions of Wilson Harris and Denis Williams." In Williams and Williams, pp. 77–88.

Johnson, Erica L., and Patricia Moran, editors. *Jean Rhys: Twenty-First-Century Approaches*. Edinburgh UP, 2015.

Johnson, Joanna. *Topographies of Caribbean Writing, Race, and the British Countryside*. Palgrave Macmillan, 2019.

Johnson, Joyce. "Fiction and the Interpretation of History: The Fiction of Orlando Patterson and Erna Brodber." *World Literature Written in English*, vol. 32, no. 2, 1992, pp. 72–86.

Joseph, Anthony. "The Frequency of Magic," Goldsmiths College Department of Art MFA Lectures, 2017–2018, Series 3.2: Rhythm, https://www.youtube.com/watch?v=lexmeTirrfQ.

———. *The Frequency of Magic*. Peepal Tree, 2019.

Juneja, Renu. *Caribbean Transactions: West Indian Culture in Literature*. Macmillan, 1996.

Konzett, Delia. "Ethnic Modernism in Jean Rhys's *Good Morning, Midnight*." *Journal of Caribbean Literatures*, vol. 3, no. 3, 2003, pp. 63–76.

Lai, Wally Look. "The Road to Thornfield Hall: An Analysis of *Wide Sargasso Sea*." *New Beacon Reviews*, vol. 1, 1968, pp. 38–52.

Lamming, George. *The Castle of My Skin*. U of Michigan P, 1991.

———. *The Emigrants*. U of Michigan P, 1994.

———. *The Pleasures of Exile*. U of Michigan P, 2012.

———. "The West Indian People." *Caribbean Quarterly*, vol. 2, no. 2, 1966, pp. 63–74.

Lazarus, Neil. *The Postcolonial Unconscious*. Cambridge UP, 2011.

Lindsay, Andrew. "Preparing the Palette: The Artist in Words." In Williams and Williams, pp. 125–42.

"Literary Clubs." *Beacon*, vol. 2, no. 12, 1933, pp. 2–4.

"The Literary Club Nuisance." *Beacon*, vol. 2, no. 11, 1933, pp. 1–2.

"Local Fiction." *Beacon*, vol. 1, no. 10, 1932, pp. 1.

Locher, Francis C. "Williams, Denis Joseph Ivan." *Contemporary Authors: A Bibliographical Guide in Current Writers in Fiction, General Nonfiction, Poetry, Journalism, Drama, Motion Pictures, Television, and Other Fields*, vols. 93–96, Gale Research Company, 1980, pp. 557.

MacDonald, Katherine. "Telling Stories, Being Places: Indigenous Ontologies in Guyana." *Diálogo*, vol. 19, no. 1, 2016, pp. 33–46.

Mackey, Nathaniel. "Limbo, Dislocation, Phantom Limb: Wilson Harris and the Caribbean Occasion." *Criticism*, vol. 22, no. 1, 1980, pp. 57–76.

Maes-Jelinek, Hena, editor. *Wilson Harris: The Uncompromising Imagination*. Dangaroo, 1991.

Maes-Jelinek, Hena, and Bénédicte Ledent, editors. *Theatre of the Arts: Wilson Harris and the Caribbean*. Rodoi, 2002.

Maes-Jelinek, Hena. "Foreword." In Maes-Jelinek, *Wilson Harris*, pp. 9–11.

———. "'Immanent Substance': Reflections on the Creative Process in Wilson Harris's *The Infinite Rehearsal*." *C. L. R. James Journal*, vol. 7, no. 1, 1999/2000, pp. 59–77.

———. *The Labyrinth of Universality: Wilson Harris's Visionary Art of Fiction*. Brill, 2006.

———. *Wilson Harris*. Twayne, 1982.

Mais, Roger. *Black Lightning.* Peepal Tree, 2013.
———. *Brother Man.* Heinemann, 1974.
———. *The Hills Were Joyful Together.* Peepal Tree, 2016.
———. *Listen, the Wind and Other Stories.* Longman, 1986.
———. "Now We Know." *Public Opinion,* 11 July 1944.
———. "Why I Love, and Leave, Jamaica," 10 June 1966, Roger Mais Collection, University of the West Indies, Mona Jamaica.
Mardorossian, Carine M. "Shutting up the Subaltern: Silences, Stereotypes, and Double-Entendre in Jean Rhys's *Wide Sargasso Sea.*" *Callaloo,* vol. 22, no. 4, 1999, pp. 1071–90.
Marley, Jason R. "'Every Day You Are a New Person': Narration and Cosmopolitan Universalism in Jean Rhys's *After Leaving Mr. Mackenzie.*" *Criticism,* vol. 59, no. 1, 2017, pp. 1–26.
Martínez-Falquina, Silvia. "Postcolonial Trauma Theory in the Contact Zone: The Strategic Representation of Grief in Edwidge Danticat's *Claire of the Sea Light.*" *Humanities,* vol. 4, no. 4, 2015, pp. 834–60.
Mbembe, Achille. *On the Postcolony.* U California P, 2001.
McDonald, Avis G. "The Crisis of the Absurd in Orlando Patterson's *An Absence of Ruins.*" *Kunapipi: Journal of Postcolonial Writing and Culture,* vol. 8, no. 2, 1986, pp. 85–96.
McDougall, Russell. "Walter Roth, Wilson Harris, and a Caribbean/Postcolonial Theory of Modernism." *University of Toronto Quarterly,* vol. 67 no. 2, 1998, pp. 568–91.
McWatt, Marc A. "The Amerindian Fables of Wilson Harris." *The Sleepers of Roraima and The Age of the Rainmakers,* by Wilson Harris, Peepal Tree, 2014, pp. 35–49.
Mendes, Alfred H. *The Autobiography of Alfred H. Mendes 1897–1991,* edited by Michele Levy, UP of the West Indies, 2002.
Miller, Tyrus. *Late Modernism: Politics, Fiction, and the Arts Between the World Wars.* U of California P, 1999.
Mittleholzer, Edgar. *Latticed Echoes: A Novel in the Leitmotiv Manner.* Secker & Warburg, 1960.
———. *A Morning at the Office.* Peepal Tree, 2010.
———. *My Bones and My Flute: A Ghost Story in the Old-Fashioned Manner.* Peepal Tree, 2015.
Moore, Brian L. *Cultural Power, Resistance, and Pluralism : Colonial Guyana, 1838–1900.* UP of the West Indies, 1995.
Moran, Patricia. "'The Feelings Are Always Mine': Chronic Shame and Humiliated Rage in Jean Rhys's Fiction." In Johnson and Moran, pp. 190–208.
Morris, Daphne. "Reviewed Work: *Listen, The Wind and Other Stories* by Kenneth Ramchand, Roger Mais." *Journal of West Indian Literature,* vol. 1, no. 2, 1987, pp. 79–81.

Murdoch, H. Adlai. "The Discourses of Jean Rhys: Resistance, Ambivalence, and Creole Indeterminacy." In Johnson and Moran, pp. 146–68.

Musser, Amber Jamilla. *Sensational Flesh: Race, Power, and Masochism*. NYU Press, 2014.

Mwangi, Evan. *Africa Writes Back to Self: Metafiction, Gender, Sexuality*. SUNY Press, 2009.

Nazaryan, Alexander. "Lost in the Tropics: The Forgotten Writings of Eric Walrond." *New York Daily News*, March 1, 2013, www.nydailynews.com/blogs/pageviews/lost-tropics-forgotten-writings-eric-walrond-blog-entry-1.1640010.

Newton, Melanie J. "Returns to a Native Land: Indigeneity and Decolonization in the Anglophone Caribbean." *Small Axe*, vol. 17, no. 2, 2013, pp. 108–22.

Niblett, Michael. *The Caribbean Novel since 1945: Cultural Practice, Form, and the Nation-State*. U of Mississippi P, 2012.

O'Callaghan, Evelyn, and Tim Watson, editors. *Caribbean Literature in Transition, 1800–1920*. Cambridge UP, 2020.

Outar, Lisa. "Indianness and Nationalism in the Windrush Era." In Brown and Rosenberg, pp. 27–40.

Owens, Imani D. "'Hard Reading': U.S. Empire and Black Modernist Aesthetics in Eric Walrond's *Tropic Death*." *MELUS: Multi-Ethnic Literature of the U.S.*, vol. 41, no. 4, 2016, pp. 96–115.

Parascandola, Louis J., and Carl A. Wade. *Eric Walrond: The Critical Heritage*. UP of the West Indies, 2012.

Patterson, Orlando. *An Absence of Ruins*. Peepal Tree, 2017.

———. *The Children of Sisyphus*. Peepal Tree, 2011.

———. *Die the Long Day*. William Morrow, 1972.

Perry, Kennetta Hammond. *London Is the Place for Me: Black Britons, Citizenship, and the Politics of Race*. Oxford UP, 2015.

Phillips, Dylan. "A New Beginning or the Beginning of the End? The Welsh Language in Postcolonial Wales." In Aaron and Williams, pp. 100–113.

Pollard, Charles W. *New World Modernisms: T. S. Eliot, Derek Walcott, and Kamau Brathwaite*. U of Virginia P, 2004.

Poynting, Jeremy. "Introduction." *Absence of Ruins*, by Orlando Patterson, Peepal Tree, 2017, pp. 5–28.

———. "Half-Dialectical, Half-Metaphysical: A Discussion of Wilson Harris's novel *The Far Journey of Oudin*." In Gilkes, pp. 103–28.

Puri, Shalini. *The Caribbean Postcolonial: Social Equality, Post-Nationalism, and Cultural Hybridity*. Palgrave Macmillan, 2004.

Raiskin, Judith L. "Jean Rhys: Creole Writing and Strategies of Reading." *ariel: A Review of International English Literature*, vol. 22, no. 4, 1991, pp. 51–67.

Ramazani, Jahan, editor. *The Cambridge Companion to Postcolonial Poetry*. Cambridge, 2017.

Ramchand, Kenneth. "Literature and Society: The Case of Roger Mais." *Caribbean Quarterly*, vol. 15, no. 4, 1969, pp. 23–30.

———. *The West Indian Novel and its Background*. Faber & Faber, 1970.

Ramraj, Victor J. "Denis Williams (1923–)." *Fifty Caribbean Writers: A Bio-Bibliographical Sourcebook*, edited by Daryl Cumber Dance, Greenwood, 1986, pp. 483–92.

Ray Lewis, Krishna. "The Infinite Rehearsal And Pastoral Revision." *Callaloo*, vol. 18, no. 1, 1995, pp. 83–92.

———."Introduction." *The Third Temptation*, by Denis Williams, Peepal Tree, 2010, pp. 5–19.

Reid, Victor Stafford. *The Leopard*. Chatham Book Seller, 1958.

———. *New Day*. Peepal Tree, 2016.

———. "The Writer and His Work: V. S. Reid." *Journal of West Indian Literature*, vol. 2, no. 1, 1987, pp. 4–10.

Riach, Alan and Mark Williams. "Reading Wilson Harris." In Maes-Jelinek, *Wilson Harris*, pp. 51–60.

Rhys, Jean. *After Leaving Mr. Mackenzie*. Carroll & Graff, 1990.

———. *The Collected Short Stories*. Penguin Classics, 2017.

———. *Good Morning, Midnight*. W. W. Norton, 1986.

———. *Quartet*. W. W. Norton, 1997.

———. *Tigers Are Better-Looking*. Penguin, 1982.

———. *Voyage in the Dark*. W. W. Norton, 1982.

———. *Wide Sargasso Sea*. W. W. Norton, 1982.

Robbe-Grillet, Alain. *For a New Novel: Essays on Fiction*. Translated by Richard Howard, Northwestern UP, 1989.

Rosaldo, Renato. "Imperialist Nostalgia." *Representations*, no. 26, Spring 1989, pp. 107–22.

Rosenberg, Leah Reade. *Nationalism and the Formation of Caribbean Literature*. Palgrave Macmillan, 2007.

Royster, Philip M. "The Narrative Line of *Song for Mumu*." *Obsidian*, vol. 8, nos. 2–3, 1982, pp. 57–70.

Sander, Reinhard, editor. *From Trinidad: An Anthology of Early West Indian Writing*. Hodder & Stoughton, 1978.

———. *The Trinidad Awakening: West Indian Literature of the 1930s*. Greenwood, 1988.

Sanders, Andrew. "British Colonial Policy and the Role of Amerindians in the Politics of the Nationalist Period in British Guiana, 1945–68." *Social and Economic Studies*, vol. 36, no. 3, 1987, pp. 77–98.

Savory, Elaine. *The Cambridge Introduction to Jean Rhys*. Cambridge UP, 2009.

———. *Jean Rhys*. Cambridge UP, 1998.

Scafe, Suzanne. "'Gruesome and Yet Fascinating': Hidden, Disgraced, and Disregarded Cultural Forms in Jamaican Short Fiction, 1938–50." *Journal of Caribbean Literatures*, vol. 6, no. 3, 2010, pp. 67–79.

Seshagiri, Urmila. "Modernist Ashes, Postcolonial Phoenix: Jean Rhys and the Evolution of the English Novel in the Twentieth Century." *Modernism/Modernity,* vol. 13, no 3, 2006, pp. 487–505.

Selvon, Samuel. *An Island is a World.* Tsar, 1993.

———. *The Lonely Londoners.* Longman, 2001.

Scott, David. *Conscripts of Modernity: The Tragedy of Colonial Enlightenment.* Duke UP, 2004.

———. "The Paradox of Freedom: An Interview with Orlando Patterson." *Small Axe,* vol. 17, no. 1, 2013, pp. 96–242.

Sheehan, Tom. "Jean Rhys's Caribbean Space-Time." *Journal of Caribbean Literatures,* vol. 4, no. 3, 2007, pp. 141–54.

Shklovsky, Viktor. *The Theory of Prose.* Translated by Benjamin Sher, Dalkey Archive, 1991.

Sindoni, Maria Grazia. "Creole in the Caribbean: How Oral Discourse Creates Cultural Identities." *Journal des Africanistes,* vol. 80, nos. 1–2, 2010, pp. 217–36.

Smith, Faith. "*Brother Man*'s 'Asceticism.'" *Caribbean Quarterly,* vol. 59, no. 2, 2013, pp. 10–24.

———. "Kingston Calling: Mais's Paris, 1954." In Brown and Rosenberg, pp. 361–91.

Steinmetz, George. "Sociology and Sisyphus: Postcolonialism, Anti-Positivism, and Modernist Narrative in Patterson's Oeuvre." *Theory and Society,* vol. 48, 2019, pp. 799–822.

Stephens, Michelle Ann. "'All Look Alike in Habana': Archaeologies of Blackness across Eric Walrond's Archipelago." In Parascandola and Wade, pp. 57–71.

Stollmeyer, Hugh. "The Time Has Come." *Beacon,* vol. 3, no. 4, 1933, pp. 85–86.

Thomas, Deborah A. "Caribbean Studies, Archive Building, and the Problem of Violence." *Small Axe,* vol. 17, no. 2, 2013, pp. 27–41.

Thomas, Sue. "Jean Rhys and Katherine Mansfield Writing the 'Sixth Act.'" In Johnson and Moran, pp. 21–39.

Torres-Saillant, Silvio. *Caribbean Poetics: Toward and Aesthetic of West Indian Literature.* Peepal Tree, 2013.

Villon, Oscar. "'Tropic Death' Presents Life's Horrors In Beautiful Prose." National Public Radio, January 16, 2013, www.npr.org/2013/01/16/169169040/tropic-death-presents-lifes-horrors-in-beautiful-prose.

Visser, Irene. "Decolonizing Trauma Theory: Retrospect and Prospects." *Decolonizing Trauma Studies: Trauma and Postcolonialism,* edited by Sonya Andermahr. MDPI, 2016, pp. 7–23.

Wade, Carl A. "African-American Aesthetics and the Short Fiction of Eric Walrond: *Tropic Death* and the Harlem Renaissance." *CLA Journal,* vol. 42, no. 4, 1999, pp. 403–29.

Wainwright, Leon. "Speaking to Contemporary Art History: Denis Williams and Guyana." In Williams and Williams, pp. 67–75.

Walker, Julian. "Wartime Citations in Ernest Weekley's *An Etymological Dictionary* (1921) and Contemporary Dictionaries." *Languages and the First World War: Representation and Memory*, edited by Christophe Declercq and Walker, Palgrave Macmillan, 2016, pp. 214–36.

Walrond, Eric. *Tropic Death*. Liveright, 2013.

———. *Winds Can Wake Up the Dead: An Eric Walrond Reader*, edited by Louis J. Parascandola, Wayne State UP, 1998.

Ward, Abigail. *Postcolonial Traumas: Memory, Narrative, Resistance*. Palgrave Macmillan, 2015.

Wa Thiong'o, Ngugi. *Decolonising the Mind: The Politics of Language in African Literature*. Heinemann, 1986.

"A West Indian Literature." *Beacon*, vol. 2, no. 12, 1933, pp. 2–3.

Williams, Charlotte, and Evelyn A. Williams, editors. *Denis Williams: A Life in Works*. Rodopi, 2010.

Williams, Charlotte. *Sugar and Slate*. Planet, 2002.

———. "'A Young Man with a Hope': Side Notes in the Novel *Other Leopards*." In Williams and Williams, pp. 89–110.

Williams, Denis. "Image and Idea in the Arts of Guyana." *Beacons of Excellence: The Edgar Mittelholzer Memorial Lectures, Volume 1: 1967–1971*, edited by Andrew O. Lindsay, Caribbean, 2014, pp. 85–152.

———. "Guiana Today." *Kyk-Over-Al*, vol. 2, no. 9, 1949, pp. 131–33.

———. *Other Leopards*. Heineman, 1983.

———. "The Sperm of God: Chapters from a Novel in Progress." *Transition*, no. 28, 1967, pp. 9–13.

———. "The Sperm of God: Extract." *New Writing in the Caribbean*, edited by A. J. Seymour, Guyana Lithographic Company, 1972, pp. 301–16.

———. *The Third Temptation*. Peepal Tree, 2010.

Williams, Evelyn A. *The Art of Denis Williams*. Peepal Tree, 2012.

———. "The Uncanny-Potency of Art." *Denis Williams: A Life in Works*, edited by Charlotte Williams and Evelyn A. Williams, Rodopi, 2009, pp. 1–24.

Wilson, Mary, and Kerry L. Johnson, editors. *Rhys Matters: New Critical Perspectives*. Palgrave Macmillan, 2013.

Wollaeger, Mark, editor, with Matt Eatough. *The Oxford Handbook of Global Modernisms*. Oxford UP, 2012.

Woubshet, Dagmawi, Charles Henry Rowell, Rizvana Bradley, Nathaniel Mackey, Joshua Bennett, Howard Dodson, and Ben Okri. "Performances, Acknowledgments, and Dinner: Closing of the 40th Anniversary Celebration." *Callaloo*, vol. 40, no. 1, 2017, pp. 197–203.

Zumoff, J. A. "Black Caribbean Labor Radicalism in Panama, 1914–1921." *Journal of Social History*, vol. 47, no. 2, 2013, pp. 429–57.

Index

Aaron, Jane, 95, 245n3
Afro-Caribbean identity, 3, 10, 132, 135, 144, 169–72, 185, 200, 215, 220, 226, 241n2; in Williams, 29–30, 33–48, 51, 82–87, 88–89, 91–92, 97
Ahmed, Sara, 211
Agard, John, 109–10
agency, 3, 35, 93
Akawaio, 186, 190–92. *See also* indigeneity
alienation, 13, 18, 34, 89, 154, 162, 174, 177, 200, 223, 225
allegory, 8, 51–52, 250n11
Amerindian Act of 1951, 183
Amerindian Association of Guyana, 183
animalization, 100, 104, 121–26, 128
anticolonial romance, 11, 60, 238n9. *See also* Scott, David
aporia, 5, 9, 15, 39, 48, 52, 62, 157, 161, 173, 180, 192, 210, 229, 233–35
Arawak, 16–17, 152, 158, 162–64, 169–70, 177, 179–80, 183–84, 191, 250n17, 251n19. *See also* indigeneity
Ashcroft, Bill, 156
autonomy, 86, 88, 95, 101, 116, 193, 239n11

Barbados, 140, 146–47
Barrett, Lindsay, 6, 12, 23–29, 31, 230–31, 236; *Song for Mumu*, 23–29
Barthes, Roland, 15–16, 30, 239n12; readerly and writerly texts, 15–17, 30
Baugh, Edward, 77; "The West Indian Writer and His Quarrel with History," 77, 244n16

Beacon Group, 1–6, 35, 226, 230, 232, 240n19, 243n10; aesthetics of, 1–4, 8; audience and resentment, 1–2; and the Caribbean canon, 2, 237n1; and classism, 2–3, 198–99, 201; contradictions in, 2–3, 237n2, 237n4; and critiques of literary clubs, 199, 237n4; short story contest, 198, 237n4
Bell, Vera, 4, 6, 32, 52–66, 80, 230–31, 236; "Ancestor on the Auction Block," 53; *Ogog*, 39, 52–61, 174
belonging, 40, 89, 97, 127, 164, 170
Benitez-Rojo, Antonio, 49, 240n20
Bernabé, Jean, 21. *See also* Créolistes
Bernstein, Charles, 108–10; ideolect, 109–10, 247n2
Bhaba, Homi, 155–56; *The Location of Culture*, 144–45, 249n8
blockage, 29–30. *See also* experimentation; Gikandi, Simon
Boehmer, Elleke, 13–17, 25, 31, 157, 201, 221, 230. *See also* juxtaposition; nonsynchrony
Bohata, Kirsti, 96, 245n3
Bone, Richard, 248n13
Brathwaite, Kamau, 20, 29, 77, 240n17, 241–42nn2–3; on Lindsay Barrett, 23–25; on frustration, 23–24, 60; and indigenous identity, 169; on Roger Mais, 121, 125–26; nation language, 107–10, 120; Sycorax video-style, 30, 187
Brown, J. Dillon, 20, 29, 113, 223, 239n15, 252n11; *Beyond Windrush*, 6, 7, 237n1; on Roger Mais, 111, 118, 121, 123, 130, 248n8; on reception, 22–23, 216, 217

270 *Index*

Cambridge, Vibert C., 87–88, 97, 246n10
Campbell, Stephen, 183, 251n19
canonicity, 4, 6–7, 36, 67, 113, 133, 229, 231–32, 237n1, 247n4, 252n1
capitalism, 27, 35, 74, 124, 126, 142, 159, 203, 207, 209, 219–20, 238n9, 252n1
Carib, 153, 163–64, 171–72, 174–75, 181, 224–25. *See also* indigeneity
Caribbean labor revolts, 8. *See also* resistance
Caribbean Voices, 111
Caruth, Cathy, 17, 206
catalysis, 35, 152, 154–63, 166, 171–72. *See also* Williams, Denis
Chamoiseau, Patrick, 21. *See also* Créolistes
Chow, Rey, 101
Clukey, Amy, 251n2
colonialism. *See* decolonization; difficulty; trauma; violence
community, 108, 111, 114, 119–20, 123, 129–31, 173, 198, 213
Confiant, Raphaël, 21. *See also* Créolistes
Congo institute, 33, 83, 92–95, 98; contemporary interpretations of, 105–6; *John Bull* scandal, 104–5. *See also* Hughes, William
counterarchive, 76–79
Craig, Terrence L., 242n4
creole, 12, 21–22; identity in Jean Rhys, 212–13, 219–21, 252nn9–10; language, 108, 110–17, 133–37, 145; relationship to indigeneity, 35, 152, 162–73, 250n13. *See also* dialect; nation language; vernacular
Créolistes, 21–22, 29. *See also* Bernabé, Jean; Chamoiseau, Patrick; Confiant, Raphaël
Czarnecki, Kristin, 212–13

Dalley, Hamish, 51–52, 54, 59
Davis, James, 132, 135, 138, 248nn14–16
Dawes, Kwame S. N., 112, 247n6
decoding, 9–15, 19, 30, 80, 110, 133, 168, 177, 179–80, 183–84, 217, 239n11. *See also* Hall, Stuart
decolonization, 4, 6, 9, 11, 20, 21, 23, 28, 32, 40, 168, 175, 239
Desani, G.V., 62

dialect, 2, 132–33, 135, 139, 247n2; pejorative implications of, 108–9. *See also* creole; nation language; vernacular
Díaz, Junot, 253n3
difficulty: as an aesthetic, 4–6, 9–36, 66, 83–84, 90, 114, 150, 200–201, 221–26, 229–36; and anticolonialism, 3, 38, 43, 63; audience rejection of, 9, 30, 82, 150–51, 230; and behavior, 21, 177; in Édouard Glissant, 12, 18; and indigenous representation, 152–53, 156–97; and language, 114–25, 131–41, 142–48; and periodization, 6, 9. *See also* experimentation; inscrutability
disgust, 68, 78 117, 128, 137, 148, 191, 198, 237n4; in Jean Rhys, 35–36, 199–215, 219–21, 223, 225–26
Dominica, 213–14, 217, 222
Donnell, Alison, 6–7, 20, 40, 229–31, 237n1, 252n1
Drake, Sandra, 15
Draper, Christopher, 104–6
Durix, Jean-Pierre, 250n17

Emery, Mary Lou 20, 200, 219–20
Eurocentrism, 17, 233, 239n14
exclusion, 112, 127; and Caribbean literary history, 5, 7, 252n1; racial, 89, 97
exile, 6, 7, 145, 198
experimentation, 4–10, 14, 16, 22–26, 30–32, 62, 221, 229–31, 236, 245n2; in Vera Bell, 52, 54–55; in Wilson Harris, 34, 149–53, 156, 160, 162–63, 173; in Anthony Joseph, 232–35; in Roger Mais, 34, 108, 110–12, 114; and modernism, 19–20; in Orlando Patterson, 33, 64–70, 79–90; in Victor Stafford Reid, 32, 38–39, 42; in Jean Rhys, 201, 204, 210, 227, 251nn4–5; in Eric Walrond, 34, 108, 110, 131, 133–35, 141–44, 148, 248nn13–14; in Denis Williams, 33, 34, 81–85, 89–90, 102, 106, 149–52, 185–88, 197. *See also* blockage; difficulty; inscrutability; interruption; juxtaposition; metafiction; nonsynchrony

failure, 1, 3, 23–25, 28, 38, 52, 59–60, 62, 71–72, 79–80, 97, 132, 133, 187–88, 195, 201, 208, 248n13; readerly emotions of, 4, 19, 33, 67, 177, 230, 235;

and resistance movements, 10, 22–23, 31, 39, 60, 72, 75, 80, 128. *See also* frustration; reception
Fanon, Frantz, 59, 65, 101–2, 145, 193, 247nn13–14
First Person Feminine, 53
folk: representation of, 23, 34, 74, 113, 118, 133, 135, 169. *See also* peasant literature; yard fiction
Forte, Maximilian C., 182, 184
Francis, Donette, 60, 73–74
Francophone Caribbean literature, 6
frustration, 4–11, 14–21, 23, 29–32, 229–30, 232, 240n17; in Lindsay Barrett, 23–29; and the *Beacon* group, 3–4, 232, 237n4; in Vera Bell, 60; in Wilson Harris, 152–53, 160, 177, 181; in Anthony Joseph, 234–35; in Roger Mais, 124; in Orlando Patterson, 63, 66–67, 71–72, 75; in Victor Stafford Reid, 39, 49, 60; in Jean Rhys, 200, 201, 208, 209, 211, 215, 219, 220–21, 223; in Eric Walrond, 133, 141, 152; in Denis Williams, 90, 99, 101, 185–86, 189. *See also* failure; reception

Gamal, Ahmed, 63
Gąsiorek, Andrzej, 217, 219, 223
Gikandi, Simon, 20, 29. *See also* blockage
Gilkes, Michael, 150, 166, 250n11
Glissant, Édouard 12, 16, 21, 42, 45, 135, 177, 235, 239n13; *Caribbean Discourse,* 12–13, 18. *See also* opacity
Goble, Mark, 129
Gomes, Albert, 2, 237n1
Gregg, Veronica Marie, 205
Griffith, Glyne, 247n7
Griffiths, Gareth, 156
guilt, 75, 127; in Jean Rhys, 35–36, 201–14. *See also* reception
Gunne, Sorcha, 70–71
Guyana, 10, 16, 34, 87, 88, 132, 149–97. *See also* indigeneity

Hall, Stuart, 15. *See also* decoding
Halpé, Aparna, 166–67, 250n14
Harlem renaissance, 132
Harris, Wilson, 6, 13, 19, 20, 24, 34–35, 81, 149–86, 190, 197, 229, 240n17, 245n2, 249n3, 249n5, 250n14, 250n16, 251nn18–19; *The Age of the Rainmakers,* 16–17, 175–84; *Eye of the Scarecrow,* 150; "The Fabric of Imagination," 160, 165; infinite rehearsal in, 165–67, 250n11; *Palace of the Peacock,* 152, 158–59, 162–64, 169; *The Secret Ladder,* 149, 152, 154–56, 159, 162, 174; *The Sleepers of Roraima,* 173–76, 178–80, 184; "Tradition and the West Indian Novel," 159–60; *The Whole Armour,* 153, 163–73
Harrison, Sheri-Marie, 22, 29
Healy, J. J., 177–78
Hearne, John, 64–65, 243n10, 243n12
historiographic metafiction, 61–63
Hughes, William, 33, 83, 92–100, 104–6, 191, 246nn7–8. *See also* Congo institute
Hurston, Zora Neale, 133
Hutcheon, Linda, 61–63
hybridity, 21, 52, 96, 129, 144, 155

impasse, 8, 11, 19, 29–30, 32, 38, 60, 80, 185, 231, 235–36
independence, 8, 10, 20, 28, 39, 40, 59, 62, 64, 73–74, 123, 162, 183, 184, 193, 199
indigeneity, 10, 16–17, 34–35, 54, 59, 63, 112, 149–97, 223–25, 236, 250n13, 250–51nn17–19. *See also* Akawaio; Arawak; Carib; Guyana; Macusi
inscrutability, 50, 52, 64, 84, 90, 97, 108, 120, 130, 131, 133 134, 150, 179, 183, 190, 192, 197, 208; theory of, 1–36, 41, 57, 61, 110, 125, 133, 148, 151, 174, 181, 184, 186, 201, 226, 229–36. *See also* difficulty; experimentation
interruption, 13, 25, 82, 90, 136, 141, 158, 196, 204–5, 222–23, 225; in Jamaican fiction, 32–33, 37–80. *See also* experimentation

Jackson, Shona, 35, 168, 170–72, 250n13
Jamaica, 10, 22, 23, 24, 28, 32–33, 53, 59–61; and Roger Mais, 110, 118–28; and Orlando Patterson, 64–65, 68, 72–74; and Victor Stafford Reid, 19, 37–40
James, C. L. R., 6, 111, 113
James, Louis, 245n2
James, Marlon, 232
Jameson, Frederic, 22
jazz, 23, 126, 212, 247n4

Johnson, Erica L., 200
Johnson, Kerry L., 199–200
Joseph, Anthony, 232–36
Joyce, James, 262
juxtaposition, 2, 14, 15, 25, 71, 91, 101, 115, 117, 119, 124, 135, 146, 201, 208, 212, 221, 222, 224, 248n8. *See also* Boehmer, Elleke; experimentation

Lamming, George, 7, 22–23, 24, 29, 36, 54, 113, 169, 198–99, 201, 207–8, 226, 246n11; the backward glance, 78; *The Castle of My Skin*, 78; "The Occasion For Speaking," 2, 198; *The Pleasures of Exile*, 65, 78
Lawson-Reay, John, 104–6
Lazarus, Neil, 16
Lewis, Wyndham, 81
Lindsay, Andrew, 187, 189–90, 193–94
linguistic essentialism, 34, 119, 121, 125, 135, 148
Lobby Lud, 102–4
Locke, Alain, 132
Lovelace, Earl, 233, 240n17

Macusi, 176, 178, 181–82, 250n16. *See also* indigeneity
Maes-Jelinek, Hena, 150, 165
Mais, Roger, 6, 24, 34, 65, 108, 110, 134, 148, 231, 247n4, 247n6; *Black Lightning*, 112; *Brother Man*, 34, 110–31, 135; *The Hills Were Joyful Together*, 110; *Listen, the Wind and Other Stories*, 111; "Now We Know," 2, 112–13, 125, 127, 128; "Why I Love, and Leave, Jamaica," 128. *See also* Jamaica
Mardorossian, Carine, 252n9
Mau Mau rebellion, 10, 19, 32, 37–38, 40–51, 60, 62, 242n4. *See also* resistance
Mbembe, Achille, 126–27
McDonald, Avis G., 70–71, 244n14
McDougall, Russell, 175, 184, 250n14
McWatt, Marc A., 173, 179, 183, 250n17
Mendes, Albert, 1–2, 237n2
metafiction, 16, 32–33, 37–39, 42–43, 49, 51–52, 54–66, 69–71, 75, 76, 79–80, 215, 232–35, 242n9. *See also* experimentation
middle-class identity, 2, 36, 39, 66, 73, 111, 113, 115, 118, 120, 127, 128, 198–99; in Jean Rhys, 199–203, 207–8, 210–13, 221, 226, 237n2
mid-twentieth century fiction, 4–9, 11, 13, 19, 20, 29, 31, 32, 36, 39, 61, 63, 108, 110–12, 129, 134, 199, 226, 229–32, 235–36. *See also* Windrush
migration, 20, 23, 73, 85, 100, 132, 134, 142, 145, 146, 190, 199, 252n11
miscegenation, 99–105, 154, 186, 193
misogyny, 82, 114, 186, 205, 217, 243n10, 247n6
misunderstanding, 3, 15, 27, 28, 31, 42, 48–51, 57, 60, 80, 152, 167, 173, 191, 212, 215, 234, 239n11. *See also* reception
Mittelholzer, Edgar, 136
modernism, 19–22, 29, 64, 74, 81, 89, 129, 175, 185, 199–200, 217, 219, 239–40nn15–16, 245n2, 251n4
Moran, Patricia, 200
Morris, Daphne, 111
Musser, Amber Jamilla, 101

national aesthetic, 2, 60, 111
nation language, 30, 107–10, 120, 247n10. *See also* Brathwaite, Kamau; creole; dialect; vernacular
national identity, 4, 8, 31, 34, 39, 54, 60, 61, 93, 240n19, 251n2; and language, 107–10, 112, 125, 127–29, 147–48
nationalism, 8, 9, 74, 94–96, 111–13, 131, 151, 190, 237n2, 246n8
Nazaryan, Alexander, 132–33
Newton, Melanie J., 35, 168–71, 250n12
Niblett, Michael, 240n20
nonsynchrony, 14. *See also* Boehmer, Elleke; experimentation
Nouveau Roman, 33, 81, 83, 160, 245n2. *See also* Robbe-Grillet, Alain

obsolescence, 129
opacity, 12, 13, 17, 19, 21, 23, 31, 42, 132, 177. *See also* Glissant, Édouard
Outar, Lisa, 113
Owens, Imani D., 132–35

Panama canal, 10, 110, 132–34, 138, 141–48. *See also* Walrond, Eric
Parascandola, Louis J., 132
Patterson, Orlando, 32, 243nn10–11; *An Absence of Ruins*, 6, 13, 33, 39, 63–80,

129, 243n10; *The Children of Sisyphus,* 64, 73, 243n10; *Die the Long Day,* 64, 243n10; "The Paradox of Freedom," 73, 79, 244n15; *Slavery and Social Death: A Comparative Study,* 64. *See also* Jamaica
peasant literature, 4, 6, 113, 198. *See also* folk; yard fiction
Pollard, Charles W., 20, 30, 240n16
postmodernism, 62, 70, 199, 212, 241n20
Poynting, Jeremy, 65, 244n13
Public Opinion, 53
Puri, Shalini, 21–22

Ramazani, Jahan, 53
Ramchand, Kenneth, 111, 121
Ramraj, Victor J., 82–83, 92
Rastafarianism, 10, 114, 128, 131
realism, 10, 16, 19, 24, 31, 37, 38, 42, 55, 59, 65, 114, 125, 160, 184, 221, 239n13, 241n2, 243n10, 245n2; allegorical realism, 51–52; anti-realism, 54, 64, 70; social realism, 8
reception, 4–7, 9–10, 13, 15, 22, 25, 29, 31, 34, 36, 133, 144, 229–31, 235, 245n4; and antagonism, 201, 204, 208, 216; and indigenous experience, 157, 167, 173–74; and resistance narratives, 38, 42. *See also* failure; frustration; guilt; misunderstanding
Reid, Victor Stafford (V. S.), 24, 52, 53, 54, 59, 60, 61, 62, 63, 64, 66, 80, 136, 231; *The Jamaicans,* 38; *The Leopard,* 19, 32, 37–51, 57, 69, 215, 241n2, 242n4; *New Day,* 38, 241n1; *Peter of Mount Ephraim,* 38; *Sixty-five,* 38, 241n1. *See also* Jamaica
repetition, 17, 33, 81, 165; historical acts of, 170, 194–97
resistance, 2–5, 8–12, 21, 27, 31, 32, 52, 59, 63, 83, 98, 113, 132, 213, 224, 238n9, 252n1; in Lindsay Barrett, 25–29; and class, 198–99, 201, 202–11; ideological forms of, 64–67, 69, 71, 78, 79–80; and language, 107–10, 129, 140, 146, 148; and missionary work, 95; movements, 19, 23, 32, 37–51, 60, 62, 200, 241n. *See also* Caribbean labor revolts; Mau Mau rebellion
Rhys, Jean, 6, 20, 30, 35, 132, 199–201, 229, 231, 251nn6–7; *After Leaving Mr. Mackenzie,* 203, 251n5; "Discourse of a Lady Standing a Dinner to a Down-and-Out-Friend," 209–12, 213, 214; *Good Morning, Midnight,* 30, 199, 202–3, 217; "Hunger," 35, 204–7, 209, 212, 213, 214; *Quartet,* 207, 251n2; *Voyage in the Dark,* 30, 35, 202, 212–27, 251n4; *Wide Sargasso Sea,* 199–200, 214, 216, 252n9
Riach, Alan, 166
Robbe-Grillet, Alain, 81, 83, 245n2, 246n10. *See also* Nouveau Roman
Rosenberg, Leah, 3, 6, 7, 20, 113, 237n1, 240n19; *Nationalism and the Formation of Caribbean Literature,* 2, 27, 237n2
Rupununi Uprising, 183
Rushdie, Salman, 52, 62

Salkey, Andrew, 237n1
Sartre, Jean Paul, 68–69, 72, 244n15
Savory, Elaine, 208
Scafe, Suzanne, 112
Scott, David, 6, 10–11, 31, 238nn8–9, 244n15. *See also* anticolonial romance
second-person narration, 43–48, 49, 204–7, 251n5
Selvon, Samuel, 7, 24, 29, 246n11
Seshagiri, Urmila, 250n4, 252n10
Shklovsky, Viktor, 140
Smith, Faith, 111
Steinmetz, George, 64, 243n11
Stephens, Michelle A., 133–34
surrealism, 6, 26

Thomas, Deborah, 76–77
Thomas, Sue, 208
Tiffin, Helen, 156
Torres-Saillant, Silvio, 240n20
translation, 28, 37, 43, 46, 48, 57, 115, 117, 133, 136, 138, 139, 141, 146, 160, 180, 215–16, 242n4, 253n3
transnationalism, 38, 40, 43, 132, 142, 146
trauma, 39, 64–65, 68, 76, 83, 84–85, 97, 106, 139, 211, 235, 251n5; and ancestry, 152–57, 161, 163, 166–67, 172–73, 177, 197; colonial, 4–6, 9–13, 15, 16, 29–30, 32–33, 36, 38, 56, 91, 236; domestic, 82, 97; and gender, 209, 210; and labor, 138–40, 146, 218, 225; psychological, 72, 86, 89–90; racial, 88–89, 99, 105, 251n2; sexual, 101; trauma studies, 17–18, 206, 239n14
Trinidad, 1–3, 237n2, 240n19

unsettlement, 70, 117, 124, 130, 134, 136, 149, 152, 178, 236; as a concept of reading, 34–35, 156–58, 164, 197

vernacular, 10, 33–34, 96, 107–48. *See also* creole; dialect; nation language

Villon, Oscar, 132

violence, 38, 68, 74, 76, 82, 110, 122, 124, 126–31, 139, 142, 148, 189, 213, 216, 236; in Lindsay Barrett, 25–29; colonial, 4, 5, 9–18, 25, 32–34, 56–61, 140, 166, 167, 178, 219, 223, 229, 235, 251n18; comic, 195–97; indigenous,152–54, 156, 158, 161, 162, 166, 169, 181–82, 188, 193, 197; and modernist forms, 245n2; psychological, 202; and resistance movements, 40, 42–51; in Wales, 83–106

Visser, Irene, 17, 239n14

Wade, Carl A., 132
Walcott, Derek, 20, 77, 150
Wales, 10, 29, 33, 81–106
Walrond, Eric, 4, 6, 7, 10, 34, 108, 110, 131–38, 141–43; *The Big Ditch*, 141; "Drought," 135–36, 138–41; "Panama Gold," 146–48; "The Wharf Rats," 143–45; "The White Snake," 136–37; "The Yellow One," 145–46. *See also* Panama canal

Walter Rodney riots, 73–75

West Indian Federation, 8, 39–40, 59–60

Williams, Charlotte, 83, 85, 87, 88, 89, 96, 103, 245n3, 245n5, 246nn8–9

Williams, Denis, 4, 6, 12, 31, 34–35, 114, 136, 155–56, 158–61; *Image and Idea in the Arts of Guyana*, 154; indigenous representation, 149–52, 173; *Other Leopards*, 81, 82; *Prehistoric Guiana*, 185; *The Sperm of God*, 35, 179, 185–97; *The Third Temptation*, 29–30, 33, 65–66, 81–106. *See also* catalysis

Williams, Mark, 166

Wilson, Mary, 199–200

Windrush, 6–7, 20, 110, 113, 199, 237n1, 252n1. *See also* mid-twentieth century fiction

Wynter, Sylvia, 240n17, 250n12

yard fiction, 2, 4. *See also* folk; peasant literature

Zumoff, J. A., 142

RECENT BOOKS IN THE SERIES
New World Studies

Rum Histories: Drinking in Atlantic Literature and Culture
Jennifer Poulos Nesbitt

Imperial Educación: Race and Republican Motherhood in the Nineteenth-Century Americas
Thomas Genova

Fellow Travelers: How Road Stories Shaped the Idea of the Americas
John Ochoa

The Quebec Connection: A Poetics of Solidarity in Global Francophone Literatures
Julie-Françoise Tolliver

Comrade Sister: Caribbean Feminist Revisions of the Grenada Revolution
Laurie R. Lambert

Cultural Entanglements: Langston Hughes and the Rise of African and Caribbean Literature
Shane Graham

Water Graves: The Art of the Unritual in the Greater Caribbean
Valérie Loichot

The Sacred Act of Reading: Spirituality, Performance, and Power in Afro-Diasporic Literature
Anne Margaret Castro

Caribbean Jewish Crossings: Literary History and Creative Practice
Sarah Phillips Casteel and Heidi Kaufman, editors

Mapping Hispaniola: Third Space in Dominican and Haitian Literature
Megan Jeanette Myers

Mourning El Dorado: Literature and Extractivism in the Contemporary American Tropics
Charlotte Rogers

Edwidge Danticat: The Haitian Diasporic Imaginary
Nadège T. Clitandre

Idle Talk, Deadly Talk: The Uses of Gossip in Caribbean Literature
Ana Rodríguez Navas

Crossing the Line: Early Creole Novels and Anglophone Caribbean Culture in the Age of Emancipation
Candace Ward

Staging Creolization: Women's Theater and Performance from the French Caribbean
Emily Sahakian

American Imperialism's Undead: The Occupation of Haiti and the Rise of Caribbean Anticolonialism
Raphael Dalleo

A Cultural History of Underdevelopment: Latin America in the U.S. Imagination
John Patrick Leary

The Spectre of Races: Latin American Anthropology and Literature between the Wars
Anke Birkenmaier

Performance and Personhood in Caribbean Literature: From Alexis to the Digital Age
Jeannine Murray-Román

Tropical Apocalypse: Haiti and the Caribbean End Times
Martin Munro

Market Aesthetics: The Purchase of the Past in Caribbean Diasporic Fiction
Elena Machado Sáez

Eric Williams and the Anticolonial Tradition: The Making of a Diasporan Intellectual
Maurice St. Pierre

The Pan American Imagination: Contested Visions of the Hemisphere in Twentieth-Century Literature
Stephen M. Park

Journeys of the Slave Narrative in the Early Americas
Nicole N. Aljoe and Ian Finseth, editors

Locating the Destitute: Space and Identity in Caribbean Fiction
Stanka Radović

Bodies and Bones: Feminist Rehearsal and Imagining Caribbean Belonging
Tanya L. Shields

Sounding the Break: African American and Caribbean Routes of World Literature
Jason Frydman

The Haitian Revolution in the Literary Imagination: Radical Horizons, Conservative Constraints
Philip Kaisary

www.ingramcontent.com/pod-product-compliance
Lightning Source LLC
Chambersburg PA
CBHW021656230426
43668CB00008B/639